PRAISE FOR *CODE OVER COUNTRY*

"Matthew Cole has produced a searing and unvarnished history of a state-sponsored organized crime syndicate that operates globally with impunity bestowed upon it by the United States government. Since 9/11, Navy SEAL Team 6 has been elevated to legendary status in the media, and its members showered with medals and accolades from presidents, especially in the aftermath of the raid that killed Osama bin Laden. Through an evenhanded accounting of the failures and successes of SEAL Team 6, from its Cold War origins to the present, Cole has masterfully documented the bloody, dark underbelly of these 'quiet warriors.' He exposes the sociopaths and murderers who operate on the tip of the spear of the covert US war machine, along with the military and political leaders who have shielded them from accountability. *Code Over Country* is a meticulously crafted corrective aimed at dismantling the dishonest mythology that dominates the public understanding of the most elite fighting force in US history."

—JEREMY SCAHILL, *New York Times*–bestselling author of *Blackwater: The Rise of the World's Most Powerful Mercenary Army* and *Dirty Wars: The World Is a Battlefield*

"Matthew Cole is telling us what we, in America, need to know about some of those men celebrated in movies and media as heroes in SEAL Team 6. The real issue, as Cole makes clear, is the leadership and command structure that shields and protects criminal behavior. This is not a book about heroism, although there is much, but tolerated wrongdoing."

—SEYMOUR M. HERSH, Pulitzer Prize winner and author of *Chain of Command: The Road from 9/11 to Abu Ghraib*

"Matthew Cole's *Code Over Country* is a remarkable achievement. Cole has flanked the hagiography that has for so long protected the image of SEAL Team 6, and has cut deep behind the lines to tell the brutal truth. After reading this book, I realized that there is the Hollywood version of SEAL Team 6, and then there is the truth, laid bare by Matthew Cole."

—JAMES RISEN, Pulitzer Prize winner and author of the forthcoming *The Last Honest Man: How Frank Church Fought the CIA, the Mafia, J. Edgar Hoover, and the National Security State*

CODE OVER COUNTRY

THE TRAGEDY AND CORRUPTION OF SEAL TEAM SIX

Matthew Cole

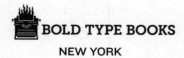

BOLD TYPE BOOKS

NEW YORK

Bold Type Books
116 East 16th Street, 8th Floor, New York, NY 10003
www.boldtypebooks.org
@BoldTypeBooks

Printed in the United States of America

First Edition: February 2022

Published by Bold Type Books, an imprint of Perseus Books, LLC, a subsidiary of Hachette Book Group, Inc. Bold Type Books is a co-publishing venture of the Type Media Center and Perseus Books.

The Hachette Speakers Bureau provides a wide range of authors for speaking events. To find out more, go to www.hachettespeakersbureau.com or call (866) 376-6591.

The publisher is not responsible for websites (or their content) that are not owned by the publisher.

Some material appeared originally, in a different form, in "The Crimes of SEAL Team 6," published by *The Intercept* in 2017. It appears here with permission from *The Intercept*.

Print book interior design by Linda Mark.

Library of Congress Cataloging-in-Publication Data
Names: Cole, Matthew, author.
Title: Code over country : the tragedy and corruption of SEAL Team Six / Matthew Cole.
Other titles: Tragedy and corruption of SEAL Team Six
Description: First edition. | New York : Bold Type Books, [2022] |
   Includes bibliographical references and index.
Identifiers: LCCN 2021034459 | ISBN 9781568589053 (hardcover) |
   ISBN 9781568589046 (ebook)
Subjects: LCSH: United States. Naval Special Warfare Development Group—   History. |
United States. Navy. SEALs—History—21st century. | United States. Navy. SEALs—
Biography. | Military discipline—United States—History—21st century. | Special operations
(Military science)—Moral and ethical aspects. | Iraq War, 2003–2011—Atrocities. | Afghan
War, 2001—Atrocities. | War crimes—United States.
Classification: LCC VG87 .C645 2022 | DDC 359.9/840973—dc23
LC record available at https://lccn.loc.gov/2021034459

ISBNs: 9781568589053 (hardcover), 9781568589046 (ebook)

LSC-C

Printing 1, 2021

FOR JACKSON, JUNE, CLARA, AND LIZZIE

In times of war or uncertainty there is a special breed of warrior ready to answer our Nation's call. Common citizens with uncommon desire to succeed. Forged by adversity, they stand alongside America's finest special operations forces to serve their country, the American people, and protect their way of life. I am that warrior.

My Trident is a symbol of honor and heritage. Bestowed upon me by the heroes that have gone before, it embodies the trust of those I have sworn to protect. By wearing the Trident I accept the responsibility of my chosen profession and way of life. It is a privilege that I must earn every day.

My loyalty to Country and Team is beyond reproach. I humbly serve as a guardian to my fellow Americans always ready to defend those who are unable to defend themselves. I do not advertise the nature of my work, nor seek recognition for my actions. I voluntarily accept the inherent hazards of my profession, placing the welfare and security of others before my own.

I serve with honor on and off the battlefield. The ability to control my emotions and my actions, regardless of circumstance, sets me apart from others. Uncompromising integrity is my standard. My character and honor are steadfast. My word is my bond.

—Excerpt from the US Navy SEAL Ethos

CONTENTS

PROLOGUE   1

PART I **A Special Breed of Warrior:**
Naval Special Warfare [1943–2001]

CHAPTER 1   FROGMEN   15

CHAPTER 2   ENSIGN PENNEY   27

CHAPTER 3   THE BIRTH OF SEAL TEAM 6   39

CHAPTER 4   THE ROGUE WARRIOR   59

CHAPTER 5   THE ETHICAL WARRIOR   77

PART II **Forged by Adversity:**
The Wars [2001–2011]

CHAPTER 6   ROBERTS RIDGE   97

CHAPTER 7   THE WEDDING PARTY   121

CHAPTER 8   SEAL TEAM 6, 2.0   133

CHAPTER 9   THE HATCHET   143

CHAPTER 10   HEAD ON A PLATTER   161

CHAPTER 11   HOSTAGES—BACK TO BASICS   179

PART III **Recognition for My Actions:**
            The Brand [2011–2016]

CHAPTER 12   THE BIG MISH   207

CHAPTER 13   "YOU CAN'T EAT HONOR"   217

CHAPTER 14   THE POLITICS OF BRAVERY   237

PART IV **My Word Is My Bond:**
            Reckoning [2017–2021]

CHAPTER 15   MEDALS OF HONOR   251

CHAPTER 16   OUT OF CONTROL   267

CHAPTER 17   A "REAL TEAM GUY"   281

CHAPTER 18   "YOU WOULD LOVE THEM"   297

             EPILOGUE   309

             Acknowledgments   319
             Notes   323
             Index   335

PROLOGUE

May 24, 2018—The White House

Britt Slabinski entered trailing a step behind President Donald J. Trump as a four-piece brass band made its way through a cheerless "Hail to the Chief." The retired Navy SEAL master chief petty officer strode past a collection of family and colleagues standing in the audience, across the room's parquet floors and wool rugs, to a small podium. The ceremony took place in the East Room. This is where Presidents Dwight Eisenhower and Gerald Ford took their oaths of office and where Abraham Lincoln and John F. Kennedy lay in repose after their assassinations. This place holds a distinct significance for members of the military: it is where the commander in chief presents the highest award for battlefield valor, the Medal of Honor. That was the occasion that brought Master Chief Slabinski to the East Room that day. But as he took his place on the dais, standing between portraits of George Washington and Martha Washington, his expression didn't register whether he was there for a coronation or a funeral.

Slabinski stood off to the side of the president and faced the now seated audience. The forty-eight-year-old was still boyishly handsome with placid blue eyes, the only evidence of his age the slight receding of his brown hair combed to one side. Six feet tall and lean, Slabinski wore a pressed, all-white Navy dress uniform with a stiff tunic collar, closed and adorned with two brass pins indicating his rank as a noncommissioned officer. His left breast displayed twenty-five different military service ribbons, including a Navy Cross; just beneath his collarbone his treasured gold Navy SEAL Trident remained pinned in place, as it had when he passed the group's brutal BUD/S training program twenty-eight years earlier. For the son of a retired Navy "frogman"—the precursor to the SEALs—and a former Eagle Scout from central Massachusetts who enlisted in the Navy after graduating from high school, the White House ceremony must have been awe-inspiring. Yet, as he stood in front of senior Pentagon officials, Navy admirals both active and retired, and several living Medal of Honor recipients, Slabinski appeared humble. He smiled sheepishly as President Trump introduced him and his family, including his son, who sat just across from him in the first row. Slabinski looked every part the American hero.

Slabinski's distinguished career in the SEALs came to an end four years earlier, when he retired as a command master chief, a rank of E-9. He spent much of his career with the Naval Special Warfare Development Group, called DEVGRU and known by everyone as SEAL Team 6, where he'd been a sniper, before rising to become a senior leader. In that time, he completed fifteen combat tours and took home five Bronze Stars with a "V" device for valor, denoting heroism on the battlefield. He was a charismatic leader whose stature at SEAL Team 6 and the broader SEAL community led to his helping write the SEAL ethos that codified the Navy SEAL culture. His email signature read, "Strength and Honor."

"Today we pay tribute to Britt's heroic service," President Trump said, "and proudly present him with our nation's highest military honor. I would go so far and say our nation's highest honor."

The Medal of Honor is, in fact, the highest award for military service. Initially established by the Navy during the Civil War, the award was quickly adopted by the Army to honor the battlefield bravery of enlisted and volunteer soldiers who fought for the Union. Signed into law by President Lincoln, the Medal of Honor could be awarded to officers as well. More than 40 percent of the almost thirty-five hundred awards come from the Civil War, and more than half of the awards since World War II have gone to service members who died on a battlefield. Some view awards with skepticism in the military—as imperfect artifacts of a culture that does not know how to value their labor. But when it comes to the Medal of Honor, most Americans have reached something of a consensus: the recipients are the closest thing our society has to heroes.

President Trump continued his remarks, addressing Slabinski and his surviving teammates, some of whom looked on from the audience.

"You waged a fierce fight against the enemies," the president said. "Through your actions, you demonstrated that there is no love more pure and no courage more great than the love and courage that burns in the hearts of American patriots. We are free because warriors like you are willing to give their sweat, their blood, and if they have to, their lives for our great nation."

Slabinski stood silently in front of a framed Medal of Honor flag, blue with thirteen white stars; the president spoke for him. "Britt wants the country to know that for him the recognition he is about to receive is an honor that falls on the whole team, on every American warrior who fought the forces of terror on that snowy Afghan ridge. Each of them has entered the eternal chronicle of American valor and American bravery.

"Britt, we salute you, we thank you, we thank God for making you a United States SEAL, we love our Navy SEALs."[1]

Slabinski looked out at the audience, his blue eyes frequently coming back to his son just in front of him. A military aide to the president read the citation aloud. It credited Slabinski for "conspicuous gallantry and intrepidity at the risk of his life above and beyond the call of duty" while serving in Afghanistan.

"In the early morning of 4 March 2002," the citation reads, Slabinski led a SEAL Team 6 reconnaissance element "to its assigned area atop a 10,000-foot snow-covered mountain. Their insertion helicopter was suddenly riddled with rocket-propelled grenades and small arms fire from previously undetected enemy positions. The crippled helicopter lurched violently and ejected one teammate onto the mountain before the pilots were forced to crash land in the valley far below."

Slabinski then led his remaining team on a rescue mission for their missing teammate back on top of the mountain. Despite facing more enemy fire as the group exited their helicopter, one teammate jumped off the aircraft, charging uphill toward enemy fire.

Slabinski, known as Slab by his SEAL Team 6 teammates, looked unsteady as the citation retold the events in 2002. His head nodded slightly, and his eyes appeared to water.

"Without regard for his own safety," the citation read, Slabinski charged uphill in thigh-high snow to join one of his teammates. Together, they assaulted and cleared the first of three bunkers. Machine-gun fire from another hardened position poured out from twenty meters away at the two Americans. Slabinski "repeatedly exposed himself to deadly fire" to attack the second bunker as his teammate was struck down by enemy fire. Slabinski and team were too close to the enemy to call in air support, and after three casualties, "the situation became untenable." Slabinski moved his team into a better defensive position and called in air strikes as well as reinforcements. The enemy forced Slabinski and his other wounded teammates down the mountainside with mortar fire. Slabinski led his team down an almost sheer, snow-covered mountainside, where they were finally rescued fourteen hours later.

"By his undaunted courage, bold initiative, leadership, and devotion to duty, Senior Chief Slabinski reflected great credit upon himself and upheld the highest traditions of the United States Naval Service."[2]

After the announcer completed the citation, Trump placed the light-blue silk ribbon around Slabinski's neck, the medal hanging near his Trident.

For Slabinski, the award secured his integrity and honor. For the crowd gathered, it was a solemn, proud moment. For a few men who knew Slabinski well, it was a disgrace.

March 4, 2002—Takur Ghar, Eastern Afghanistan

Slabinski charged off the Chinook's rear ramp first as machine-gun fire crackled all around him. His first steps landed in heavy snow and he quickly fell over. His five teammates, including John Chapman, an Air Force combat controller known as Chappy, followed, fanning out in practiced formations. Enemy fire rattled from three positions above the men, forcing them to scramble for cover. The SEAL Team 6 reconnaissance element had lost the one tactical advantage they valued most: the element of surprise.

The team had tried to land on the 10,200-foot mountaintop three hours earlier to establish an observation post. As their helicopter began to set down, they flew directly into an ambush. A force of foreign al Qaeda fighters had successfully hidden their position before the mission started, and the moment the Chinook entered the kill zone, the fighters opened up. As the helicopter shook and rattled from RPGs and small arms fire, one of the SEALs, Neil Roberts, slipped off the open ramp and tumbled ten feet into the snow. The helicopter continued its descent to two thousand feet beneath the summit where it was forced to make an emergency landing, to wait for rescue by another helicopter and evacuation back to the SEALs' base.

When the rescue helicopter arrived, Slabinski ordered the Chinook pilot to bring his team of six remaining SEALs back up to the top of the mountain, where entrenched fighters would be waiting, in the hope of recovering Roberts. They would have to fight uphill against an enemy force that was mostly hidden, and whose strength was unknown.

The team was, by design, part of the most elite fighting force in the US military. SEAL Team 6 was a small unit of so-called Tier 1 operators trained as a counterterrorism and hostage rescue force. If any group of US servicemen was going to jump out of the back of a helicopter at an altitude of ten thousand feet, at night, in the snow, and fight uphill to recover a teammate, Slabinski and his men were the ones you would want on the job.

Even so, few at the command had seen combat. There had been missions and small deployments, and a few older members remembered the

Black Hawk Down incident in Somalia ten years earlier. The 9/11 attacks had galvanized and motivated the unit to take down Osama bin Laden, al Qaeda, and the Taliban, but few would enter Afghanistan with any experience fighting terrorists and insurgents. The firefight unfolding on the mountaintop that night finally gave them that opportunity.

As Chapman ran uphill to try to establish radio communications with air support, Slabinski picked himself up and followed. The two other teams of two quickly sought cover behind a cropping of small boulders, but they were all downhill and at a severe tactical disadvantage. Automatic-weapons fire cracked through the trees and ricocheted off the boulders. Chapman fired a three-round burst from his M4 into a hidden bunker, suppressing one of the three sources of enemy attack.

Within minutes of exiting the helicopter, Chapman was hit by enemy fire. Slabinski was closest to him when it happened. He could see Chapman through night-vision goggles on the ground, silent and still, but breathing. Slabinski kept firing while trying to direct the other two teams to the nearest enemy bunker. Shortly after Slabinski led a failed assault of the bunker, two more of the SEALs fell wounded, including one whose leg had been nearly severed by gunfire.

With half of his force unable to fight, Slabinski had few choices to continue the assault. The team was effectively pinned down under descending fire. He scanned the mountaintop and looked for the best exit route. To get out of his position, Slabinski would later claim he passed closely over Chapman's body, looked at him, and saw no visual signs of life, and that his only choice to save the rest of his team was to retreat. Slabinski had lost one teammate, and now another in an attempt to save the first. Two others were injured, one critically. The only rational decision was to escape down the mountainside and keep his remaining men alive. Slabinski continued past Chapman without checking his pulse or confirming that his fellow operator had died.

But the day's losses were only beginning. The battle lasted for another fourteen hours. Two other quick reaction forces had landed on the mountaintop as well, calling in air strikes as they made their retreat, and another five US servicemen were killed in action.

By the time Slabinski and his team landed back at the SEAL Team 6 headquarters at Bagram Air Base, outside the Afghan capital of Kabul, several hours later, a fuller picture of what had occurred on the top of Takur Ghar emerged. A drone flying above the mountain captured the unfolding chaos. After the initial failed helicopter assault, Roberts was discovered quickly by an al Qaeda fighter. The video showed the enemy fighter firing a round through Roberts's head; the fighter then taking out a knife, bending down over Roberts's body, and attempting to behead the dead SEAL. The fighter was unable to finish the job; he gave up and dragged the body toward the bunkers. Although there was no way for his teammates to know at the time, Roberts had died more than thirty minutes before the SEALs returned to attempt a rescue.

The video also captured the team's thwarted attempt to take the mountaintop. More than eleven hundred miles away in Masirah, Oman, a group of officers from the Joint Special Operations Command, known as JSOC, watched live, real-time video of Slabinski's firefight from a drone high above Takur Ghar. The drone's video revealed a strange scene after Slabinski's team egressed off the mountaintop. The footage appeared to show a single man maneuvering and firing toward positions held by enemy fighters for almost an hour. For the JSOC commanders far removed from the battlefield, it wasn't quite clear yet who was fighting. There was no communication from the mountaintop to the operations center. Had an internal battle broken out between the al Qaeda fighters? Or could the enemy forces have mistaken their own forces for the Americans? The JSOC officers didn't know, for example, that an Air Force combat controller in Gardez heard John Chapman calling on an emergency radio frequency using a unique call-sign identifier. Nor did the video at the time clearly show the same lone fighter exposing himself, coming out of one of the bunkers to lay down suppressing fire as the first of the rescue helicopters landed nearby.

Only years later, when an Air Force intelligence analyst began reviewing the video footage with technology that didn't exist in 2002, did it become clear who that fighter was. It was Chapman; he had survived. After his team retreated, he regained consciousness and resumed fighting, alone and badly outnumbered, for nearly an hour. Moments after the Army Rangers exited their Chinooks to come save him and Neil Roberts, Chapman was killed. The video memorialized an unthinkable act: SEALs had left a man for dead behind enemy lines.

But Slabinski would never fully accept that. Nor would SEAL Team 6 admit that on a day filled with heroism, tragedy, and sacrifice, the man leading the mission violated one of special operations' most fundamental codes: never leave a man behind. Facing an unwinnable scenario, Slabinski made a decision to preserve the lives of his remaining teammates. But SEAL Team 6 did not fashion its reputation based on tactical retreats. After the events of Takur Ghar, Slabinski and the command had created a template that members of SEAL Team 6 would follow in the decades of fighting to come. When faced with a mistake or transgression that brought dishonor to the team, and thus dishonor to the country, the best path was to disregard the truth and sell a myth of heroism.

The Battle of Roberts Ridge, as it came to be known, had a devastating, though unspoken, effect on SEAL Team 6—akin to a dark family secret. And, like any painful secret, it created its own unique pathologies. The events of that day would set off a cascade of extraordinary violence. Roberts's mutilation and Chapman's abandonment and heroics became two separate features of the psychology within the team. These events haunted America's most elite military unit and set off a culture of rogue violence and cover-ups, a corrupt culture that is still active today.

The legend of SEAL Team 6 grew as the War on Terror expanded beyond Afghanistan to Iraq, Somalia, and Yemen. And with it, the team's rogue culture continued to spread, operating outside the Navy's established mechanisms for command and investigation. A segment of SEAL Team 6 began acting with an air of impunity that disturbed observers within the command. Some senior members of SEAL Team 6 believed the pattern of brutality was not only illegal but rose to the level of war crimes.

"To understand the violence, you have to begin at Roberts Ridge," a SEAL Team 6 operator who deployed several times to Afghanistan told me. "When you see your friend killed, recover his body, and find that the enemy mutilated him? It's a schoolyard mentality. 'You guys want to play with those rules? OK.'" Although this former SEAL acknowledged that war crimes are wrong, he understood how they happen. "You ask me to go living with the pigs, but I can't go live with pigs and then not get dirty."

WHETHER BY INTENT OR NEGLECT, SLABINSKI'S AWARD SERVED TO rewrite SEAL Team 6's troubled post-9/11 history, including the corruption, cover-ups, and crimes, all of which originated at Roberts Ridge, to not just claim honor that had been lost but to insulate the unit from accountability. By putting the Medal of Honor silk ribbon around Slabinski's neck, Trump ignored SEAL Team 6's dark secrets.

"By giving Slab the award, you close the door on our criminal history," a former SEAL Team 6 officer told me. "The cover-up wins. You've closed this ugly part of our command's history, and everyone gets away with it. What everyone learns from this is that cover-ups work. 'Don't say anything bad about your teammates, keep quiet and we'll get through it.' It's disgraceful."

Slabinski's conduct wasn't an aberration at SEAL Team 6; the unit's moral collapse was not his responsibility, even if he contributed to it. He was not an officer, and just one of many SEALs. In fact, in the East Room audience were current and retired SEAL Team 6 admirals who'd enabled this. Together, these senior officers helped build the myth of SEAL Team 6 and the Navy SEALs. Among themselves, these Naval Academy graduates would encourage fellow SEAL officers to "protect the brand." The leadership made a Faustian bargain: they could champion enemy kills and ride their SEALs' successes to promotions and post-retirement wealth in exchange for allowing the enlisted inside the unit to establish their own rules—and a code that sought to protect the command at all costs.

The myth of SEAL Team 6 had secured the unit's place in America's imagination as the unambiguous heroes of the War on Terror—silent, deadly, professional. Still, Slabinski's medal served to whitewash the image of the unit well-known within its ranks, which had been defined by two decades of failed leadership, shameless propaganda, criminal activity, cover-ups, and war crimes. That day the nation's highest military honor served as a coda for the tragedy that became SEAL Team 6 after 9/11. It hid the consequences for the men who served in the unit, men who had experienced an unprecedented amount of war. Indeed, during no previous American conflict had the military faced as much battlefield exposure as the post-9/11 wars in Afghanistan, Iraq, and elsewhere. As first described by journalist Dexter Filkins, these have indeed been Forever Wars. At twenty years and counting, the wars have tallied scores of tactical successes but delivered no strategic victories.

The Navy SEAL Ethos, which Slabinski helped write, states, in part:

"I serve with honor on and off the battlefield. The ability to control my emotions and my actions, regardless of circumstance, sets me apart from others. Uncompromising integrity is my standard. My character and honor are steadfast. My word is my bond."

For many at SEAL Team 6, little of that is true. Their Ethos is indeed noble, but the SEALs were not, in fact, built to live up to it. From the first days of the frogmen and combat swimmers of World War II, the Navy sought men to do a job that was necessary, but which few wanted. What the service never reckoned with is that the qualities that draw men to be SEALs are the same qualities that undermine their effectiveness.

THERE'S AN INHERENT CHALLENGE THAT COMES WITH WRITING A book about the Navy SEALs and, in particular, SEAL Team 6. It isn't that SEALs are unwilling to share stories. In fact, there's an industry built around this. A cursory glance at the military section of your local bookstore will feature any number of bestsellers authored by the quiet professionals of the SEALs. But the stories these select SEALs are willing to share are too often embellished and fabricated for a purpose: to enhance the author's profile and burnish the SEAL myth.

This book serves a different purpose. It focuses on the stories that the SEALs have not been willing to share—at least until now. Many of these stories testify to the bravery and the singular capabilities of these men, but also identify failings—and the consequences that follow from them. That is the project of this book: to investigate the history of the military's most elite—and secretive—fighting force. And to do so without fear or favor. With this in mind, the reader should note two considerations about what follows.

First, much of the reporting in the book will be denied and denounced by the Department of Defense and the US government. This is not because the facts in this book are not true, but because the government is not yet required to acknowledge their truth. Many of the people, places, and events covered in these pages remain classified as Top Secret by the US government. The military has been consistent in responding to the stream of accusations against SEAL Team 6, saying that allegations are either unsubstantiated or there is no record of the events described. Both are dishonest. This book details these crimes—and the cover-ups that followed—to offer substantiation and to create a record that cannot be so glibly denied.

Second, few sources have gone on the record or chosen to be named in these pages. This reflects the reporting environment: the classified world of national security and tribal culture of the very few chosen and trained by the government to conduct clandestine war. There is rigor behind this anonymity. I have conducted hundreds of interviews with dozens of current or former Navy SEALs, most of whom served in SEAL Team 6. I understand their biases and have challenged them when appropriate to ensure the information reflects the closest proximity to an authoritative rendering. Where possible, I have also relied on documents. For the reader's ease, I have placed all attribution details about the sourcing in the endnotes.

Most reporting about covert operations conducted by the United States examines events and facts that the government has gone to great lengths to conceal—and resists mightily any effort by journalists to make public. Journalists must rely, then, on those who are willing to come forward. As the distance in time from the events grows, more people will appear with more facts, and newer details about these events will emerge. All of history is a work in progress. But *Code Over Country* presents the closest public accounting of the events to date. I hope the reporting and history here will lead to more public accountability about the wars this country fights, and the heroes we claim.

PART I

A Special Breed of Warrior: Naval Special Warfare

[1943–2001]

CHAPTER 1

FROGMEN

I N THE EARLY HOURS OF NOVEMBER 20, 1943, MORE THAN FIVE
thousand Marines from the 2nd Marine Division pushed toward the
beach of a palm-tree-covered Central Pacific island at a speed of four
knots in small landing craft, ready to establish a beachhead and bring the
offensive closer to the Japanese mainland.

For more than a hundred years, American military power has been
built on its dominant Navy. The modern Navy grew to reflect America's
geographic reality: two oceans necessitated two stand-alone fleets capable
of fighting at least two wars across the globe simultaneously. By the Second World War, the American Navy was a modern marvel that reflected
military strength, industrial output, and economic dominance. Fleets of
gunships, destroyers, aircraft carriers, and submarines could navigate the
world's oceans to protect shipping lanes, reinforce American military
strength, and project America's rising stature as a global power.

The landing craft, called "alligators," were rudimentary, no more than
a metal rectangle box with caterpillar tracks on either side and a gasoline

motor. Two platoons in the initial Alligator made it over the reef and
through the shoaling waters and onto the beach. Now the bulk of the
force headed in behind them from the line of departure roughly two miles
from shore.

The small vessels made it into the reef, only five hundred yards from
the shore, when they began catching the coral and rocks just beneath the
surface.[1]

The Alligators opened their front gates, and Marines spilled out onto
the reef, trudging through waist-high water, weighed down by their gear.
Entrenched Japanese soldiers opened up. Mortars exploded across the reef
and machine-gun fire cut through the Marines as the line of landing craft
began to stack up at the reef's edge. The boats got stuck in the reef as the
tide effectively stopped their forward movement to land. Behind them,
a row of tank-laden landing craft started dumping the vehicles because
there was no way to turn back. Many sank or became permanently stuck.
The Marines who successfully made it to shore were quickly cut down by
Japanese soldiers in sand-dune bunkers farther inland.

By the time the 2nd Marine Division was done storming Betio Island
in the Tarawa Atoll, almost a third of their five thousand were dead or
wounded. The reef and the beach were littered with American bodies. An
update back to the Marine command reported, "Issue at doubt."

A Marine filming the landing captured the human devastation on the
beach that day. He documented gruesome images of Marines bobbing in
the water, their bodies floating in and out of the surf with each small wave
that crashed on the beach. The images were considered so disturbing that
President Franklin D. Roosevelt had to personally approve their release to
the public. The human toll at Tarawa became the first images of American
dead in the war.

The American forces would eventually clear the Japanese forces from
the tiny atoll in the Gilbert Islands, but the US Navy had learned a brutal
and lethal lesson. The multiple failures at Tarawa crystallized the need
for dedicated reconnaissance and demolition units in future operations.
It wasn't a failure of equipment or personnel, it was of not knowing the
tides.

If the United States were to win the war in the Pacific, the Navy would have to ensure they never found themselves stuck in a coral reef again. Fortunately, the Navy quickly identified their flaw. All the guns, mortars, rockets, and steel were useless if military planners were ignorant of the local tides. Although various Navy elements interviewed local fishermen as well as British sailors who warned of a unique tidal phenomenon called neap tides, the information did not make it to the planners of the amphibious assault. A neap tide happens when, during the lunar cycle, the moon and the sun are ninety degrees from each other from the earth's vantage point. The sun's tidal pull inhibits much of the lunar tide pull, leaving the sea essentially flat. The failure to know the precise tidal schedule led to a mass backup at the shoreline, where entrenched Japanese snipers and mortars killed scores of Marines in the surf. "It became apparent that estimates were not enough," wrote a naval officer, who would help create a new force of naval special operations warriors, about the lessons learned in Tarawa. "Men must go in ahead of the troops to measure the depths exactly, and to search under water for mines and obstructions."[2]

What was needed were unarmed men who could slip off a small boat a mile or two from land, swim to the shoreline, and examine up close the depth of coral and inspect enemy defenses and even the quality of the sand on the beach, all while facing enemy fire if they were spotted. The admiral in command of the amphibious forces during Tarawa requested a new unit of combat swimmers who would help conduct shoreline reconnaissance and guide soldiers and Marines to shore from their line of departure.[3]

As it happened, part of the blueprint for the modern SEALs had already begun a few months before the Tarawa invasion. A group of volunteers from the Seabees, the Navy's construction branch, men from underwater salvage and demolition units, assembled in secret in Fort Pierce, Florida, a military installation on a twenty-five-mile stretch of a barrier island on the Atlantic, for an "indoctrination" training for one of the Navy's new underwater units. Much of what became SEAL Team 6 can be traced to the weeklong training for the Naval Combat Demolition Unit (NCDU). The concept was unique at the time. The volunteers, both

officers and enlisted, would go through water and beach training designed
to bring them to mental and physical exhaustion. The officers had to be
just as competent as the enlisted—even as they held command responsibilities. This ensured that each man who survived training had suffered
equally. They swam, ran, and worked with inflatable boats. They learned
to build explosives and operate both on land and in the water—while
withstanding the impact of blasts and detonations. The week of training
culminated with the men forced into a trench on the Atlantic beach while
explosives were set off nearby for an hour. The goal was to ensure that each
man they would send into enemy water had proved they could handle the
stress. Many couldn't. Between 60 and 75 percent dropped out by the end
of the week.[4]

Still, Hell Week forged a bond for the frogmen, as they would come to
be known. The compact size of the inflatable boat created the template for
SEAL Teams operating as a small unit. Each boat could fit six men—one
officer and five enlisted—plus explosives, and the number has remained
the starting point for a team or squad through the years. For swimming,
each man had a buddy, and so as the recruits progressed through Hell
Week, they did so by forming close ties to a partner and a small team. The
men who graduated were physically fit, tough, and considered impervious
to the concussive forces of explosions. The officer leading the training, Lt.
Cdr. Draper Kauffman, recognized the beginnings of a new class of naval
warriors. The top-secret classification of the new unit combined with the
sheer difficulty of completing training had created a group outside the
Navy's "spit and polish" regulations, one that saw themselves as special
and above. Kauffman and his officers were concerned that elitism would
pervade their ranks. But there was a war to win—and this new unit could
help the Navy do that.[5]

Within six months of Tarawa, Kauffman was transferred from Florida
to a makeshift training camp in Hawaii, where the Navy had a second unit
under development. In Maui, not far from the Navy's Pacific Fleet headquarters at Pearl Harbor, Kauffman and others refined the combat swimming and demolition skills in preparation for the next major amphibious
assault at Saipan. These were named the Underwater Demolition Teams,

or UDTs. During the next month, Kauffman, who was now leading a UDT, used small assaults in the Pacific theater to prepare and hone his unit's skills for Saipan.[6] Where his men at Fort Pierce had trained with bulky suits and oversized helmets to help them dive, in Maui he increased the swim training, while bulky underwater demolition gear was out. The men of the Underwater Demolition Teams would operate wearing swim trunks, sneakers, swim fins, a mask, gloves, a sheathed knife, and water-proofed explosive satchels. As they began operating in the Pacific, they added plexiglass slates along with waterproof lead pencils for underwater surveys.

When it came time for the landing at Saipan in June 1944, the un-derwater reconnaissance and demolition units had evolved into one of the Navy's closely held secrets. They'd expanded in size in an effort to "fleet up" and shipped off to help the 2nd and 4th Marine Divisions land. Kauffman and his team led a successful mission, losing only one man during the operation while scouting underwater, helping the Marines advance onto land with none of the difficulty or death that transpired in Tarawa. For the rest of the war, the UDT was used for every major amphibious landing: at Saipan, Guam, Okinawa, Iwo Jima, and Borneo, among others. Navy swimmers would survey and destroy underwater defenses, measure reefs and the tides, and take sand samples to help determine which US track-wheeled vehicles could move up the beach.

Men trained at Fort Pierce also deployed to Europe, where they took part in the Normandy invasion. The Navy Combat Demolition Unit par-ticipation in the storming of Omaha and Utah Beaches in France didn't go as well.[7] In what would be the worst day in Naval Special Warfare until after 9/11, the NCDU lost thirty-seven men and suffered seventy-one additional casualties at Omaha, a casualty rate of over 50 percent.[8] Eight days later Kauffman would lead a more successful UDT operation in Saipan. The frogmen helped the Navy learn from its mistakes and showed that a small unit of highly trained men could influence the battle as much as an armada of naval warships.

For special warfare, it was the dawn of a new era, that of the "naked swimmer," "naked warrior," "combat swimmer," and frogmen. During the war, the various units would be attached to a ship for the duration of their deployment. Sailors would see these early special operators on the deck camouflaged in blue paint, with black stripes painted in one-foot intervals on their bodies to measure depth underwater.[9] The color contributed to the coining of the name "frogmen" for the UDT during the war, but the men stood out among a ship's crew for their attitude and presence as much as they did for their appearance.[10] One of the first Navy SEALs, Roy Boehm, would later describe the frogmen he saw as "chiseled, hard-muscled young specimens, they carried themselves with a reckless, special air."[11]

During World War II, several secret units of combat swimmers would conduct special underwater missions throughout the Pacific, in Europe, and in North Africa. Some scouted Normandy's landings, helping lead the invasions of Omaha and Utah Beaches for D-day in France. Others used early versions of scuba gear to conduct underwater explosives missions. Still more attached limpet mines to enemy vessels or navigated waterways by disarming enemy mines. The units, all predecessors to the Navy SEALs, included Scouts and Raiders, Naval Combat Demolition Units, and the Underwater Demolition Teams.[12] The units each had an underwater reconnaissance or demolition role but varied in tactics. Eventually, they would all evolve into UDTs, but together they were all part of a capability the Navy would come to call Naval Special Warfare, colloquially known as Navy frogmen.

Less than two months after World War II ended, the Navy let the public in on its new secret unit. An article in the *Saturday Evening Post*, titled "They Hit the Beach in Swim Trunks," described the UDT mission in Saipan. The article would start a long tradition of revealing secret Naval Special Warfare operations to the public, combining facts with an irresistible addition of myth. At the time, the *Saturday Evening Post* was one of the bestselling magazines in the country and helped establish the new unit's brand. Calling the UDT the Navy's "human secret weapon" and describing them as "heathen idols" and "Battling Mermen" who moved in the water "like a porpoise," the article bolstered the image of the combat swimmers who had fought bravely during the war.

The Navy helped produce a Hollywood film demonstrating their new elite unit's unambiguous heroism—in what would become a standard after-action information campaign. As was typical for the time, the film, titled *The Frogmen*, starring Richard Widmark and released in 1951, lacked subtlety. In the opening scene, the men of the UDT introduce themselves to the enlisted sailors on a ship in the Pacific as both special and consequential, the "fearless, red-blooded, death-defying, He-men." Despite the heavy-handed script and depiction of World War II UDT swimmers, the film accurately captured the unit's own mythology of bravery and what distinguished frogmen from the average sailor.

The UDT even adopted a fight song that memorialized this view:

When the Navy gets into a jam
They always call on me
To pack a case of dynamite
And put right out to sea....
Like every honest sailor
I drink my whiskey clear.
I'm a shootin', fightin', dynamitin'
De-mo-li-tion-eer.
Out in front of the Navy
Where you really get the heat
There's a bunch of crazy bastards
Pulling off some crazy feat.[13]

WITHIN THREE YEARS OF WORLD WAR II'S END, THE NAVY DRASTI-cally shrank the UDT from thirty-five hundred men and thirty-four teams to roughly two hundred frogmen assigned to four teams. They would remain split between the Pacific and Atlantic Fleets, one based on Coronado Island, and the other at Little Creek, on an inlet at the Chesapeake Bay's mouth in Virginia Beach, Virginia. In those lean years, a few officers contemplated how to move the naked swimmers into water-based commandos. The SEAL forebears helped develop underwater breathing devices and conducted training in small arms, land warfare, and small units.[14] The intention was to create a commando force that could do more than just lead amphibious landings: they were meant to reach land and secretly search and destroy.

The foresight and training paid off when the UDT expanded for the Korean War in 1950. Although the frogmen were again attached to an amphibious fleet, small teams conducted inland raids on the Korean Peninsula, infiltrating from the sea, using their explosives expertise to conduct sabotage operations. During and after the Korean War, UDT officers also began experimenting with using helicopters to insert and exfiltrate combat swimmers from the shoreline to expand Naval Special Warfare forces' capabilities and uses. But as they had when they began, the Teams remained outside the broader Navy culture. The distinction from the Big Navy and its early corporate culture of strict adherence to rules and regulations freed UDT officers to experiment with and evolve their tactics without being forced into the Navy's doctrine. The frogmen were allowed to improvise, and as they had in World War II, they worked to develop solutions to different combat problems. But the freedom to experiment came with a downside: UDT officers had no chance at real career advancement or promotion. Rising in the Navy still required being the skipper of a ship, commanding a piece of hardware and all the men needed to run it.

By the time John F. Kennedy was sworn in as the thirty-fifth president, that began to change. By 1961, the Cold War was under way and had changed the military's strategic calculus. Mutually assured destruction between the United States and the Soviet Union, the world's two superpowers with nuclear arsenals, reduced the likelihood of the massive multicountry conventional land-and-sea warfare of the two world wars. Instead, the young president, who had served in the Navy as a PT boat commander, looked to unconventional forces to fight communism worldwide. Less than a month after taking office, Kennedy authorized the Pentagon to "examine means of placing more emphasis on the development of counter guerilla forces."[15] The Navy soon sought to "augment present naval capabilities in restricted waters and rivers with particular reference to the conduct and support of paramilitary operations. It is desirable to establish Special Operations Teams as separate components within Underwater Demolition Units One and Two."[16] The Pentagon issued a directive to build a new force, as President Kennedy requested, to the men already working on the Navy's commando capability: Southeast Asia and Cuba.

In May 1961, four months into his presidency and just a month after the disastrous Bay of Pigs invasion of Cuba, President Kennedy delivered a special address to Congress. In it, he declared his intention for the United States to land men on the moon and described a new world conflict that required new kinds of forces. Kennedy announced that the United States had to respond to the reality of the Cold War. Communist countries, he explained, were forgoing large-scale conventional battles. Conflict was now proxy wars throughout the world in the form of "guerillas striking at night, by assassins striking alone—assassins who have taken the lives of thousands of civil officers in the last twelve months in Vietnam alone...."

"I am directing the Secretary of Defense to expand rapidly and substantially, in cooperation with our allies, the orientation of existing forces for the conduct of non-nuclear war, paramilitary operations and sublimited or unconventional wars. In addition, our special forces and unconventional warfare units will be increased and reoriented."[17]

Kennedy's intention to escalate the conflict in Southeast Asia required a new breed of frogman. This unit would be detached from a Navy fleet and operate in small boats and insert into the deltas, marshes, and jungles of Vietnam. Capt. William H. Hamilton Jr., a UDT veteran of the Second World War who had helped advance UDT training and tactics in the intervening years, was assigned the task of creating the new Navy special operations unit. Hamilton and a few other frogmen went about selecting from the Underwater Demolition Teams for the new group. Hamilton would later describe the explicit vision of the type of men who would compose the unit:

> We knew what we wanted for our unit. Swift, deadly, like a shark. Capable of infiltrating or striking from the air by parachute or helicopter, from overland, from the surface of the sea, or from underneath the sea.

They had to be more than killers, all muscle and neck and attack-dog mentality. I wanted—*demanded*—creative men who operated with their brains as well as with their muscles. Men of courage, dedication to duty, sacrifice, personal dexterity, and intelligence. Team and mission must come first. At the same time, they must be individuals, near rogues in fact. Rough men, tough men who could kick ass and operate outside protocol.[18]

Hamilton sent his men to prisons to learn from criminals—thieves in particular—how to break into safes, pick locks, and hot-wire cars. He wanted men who were comfortable as part soldier, part criminal, but who served the government. In the context of a military unit, they were to be engineers to tackle tactical problems on a battlefield.

Less than a year after Kennedy's address, in January 1962, the Navy commissioned a new unit. Two teams would comprise the group, one based at Coronado and the other at Little Creek in Virginia Beach, each alongside existing UDT units. Although Hamilton pulled the first recruits from UDT teams, this new unit developed its own training program, which would feed new members to both groups. The division of teams to each coast harkened back to World War II and the desire to attach the commandos to both the Pacific and Atlantic Fleets, as the Navy had done with Underwater Demolition Teams. Ten officers and fifty enlisted men made up each team, with a basic unit structure of one officer with five men, just as the first small boat training at Fort Pierce had dictated. The Navy identified the unit by the environments operators would be experts at infiltrating—the Sea, Air, and Land—which gave this force its name: the SEALs.

Their insignia was the Trident, also known as the Budweiser, because of its faint resemblance to the Anheuser-Busch logo. It featured an eagle, a trident, and a flintlock pistol, which represented their areas of expertise: the sky, the sea, and land warfare.

Shortly after the Navy commissioned the SEALs, members of SEAL Team 1 were sent to Vietnam to conduct assessments and figure out how they could be used in the growing conflict. Even more than the Pacific theater during World War II, the Vietnam War forged Naval Special Warfare as a unit and a culture. Besides training South Vietnamese forces and conducting deep reconnaissance, the first SEALs engaged in a new Navy warfare. A standard operation might have a SEAL squad driving a small boat up the rivers and estuaries in the Mekong Delta, quietly slipping into the water and swimming or wading to shore to conduct an ambush operation. Their faces painted with green-and-black camouflage, the squad would make its way into mangrove and other jungle, walking through mud, often in bare feet to keep silent, and set up. There, they would sit for hours or even several days, sleeping in shifts, waiting for Vietcong movements, which would lead to an ambush. The SEALs conducted what the military euphemistically called "direct action"—raids where they would kill or capture enemies. SEAL kidnappings and interrogations of Vietcong agents produced intelligence, which the SEALs then used to generate combat operations. The SEALs developed a successful cycle of guerilla and counterinsurgency tactics during the war that would have echoes in the SEALs', and SEAL Team 6's, tactics decades later.

Brutality distinguished the type of violence the unit experienced—both what was inflicted on the SEALs and what the SEALs inflicted on the enemy. Even among their own, they recognized a lust for killing that had developed after several years of fighting in Vietnam. The *New York Times* reported that at one base in the Mekong, the SEALs hung a sign above their bar that read, "People who kill for money are professionals. People who kill for fun are sadists. People who kill for money and fun are Seals."[19] The slogan reflected the macabre machismo of the era before the fall of Saigon—and before the humbling of US military power. It was also an unintentional premonition of the developing SEAL culture. But at the time, it showed something else: these men were exactly what Capt. Hamilton and Naval Special Warfare wanted.

The regular Navy was less enthusiastic about these small groups of assassins who were entirely separate from the fleet. SEAL Capt. Ted Grabowsky described to an author how the service viewed the SEALs during the war: "We had no status, no standing in the regular navy. Some part of the navy saw us as some sort of quasi-criminal element, not a respected profession, that should only be used in desperate circumstances. And when you were through using it, you would stop forever. Like it was some sort of immoral activity."[20]

The SEALs were good at tracking and killing in Vietnam. The SEALs, when compared to the non-special operations elements, were disciplined and effective fighters. Their abilities to track, ambush, gather intelligence, and kill led to their involvement with the Central Intelligence Agency. The CIA oversaw the project PHOENIX, which targeted what they believed was a shadow Vietcong government infrastructure throughout allied South Vietnam. The Phoenix Program became little more than a highly classified US government assassination program, and SEALs frequently served as the assassins. The SEALs were assigned to lead what were called provincial reconnaissance units, or PRUs, composed of irregular Vietnamese forces to gather intelligence and hunt the enemy hidden within a civilian population. For these SEALs in particular, the war was up close and visceral. They carried silenced weapons and collected knife kills—the idea being that they could sneak into a target at night, kill, and leave without alerting any unintended party that they were there. Although the war allowed the new unit to demonstrate their operation skills and lethal capability, they made no discernable impact on the conflict. They were simply too small, fighting in an unwinnable war. The SEALs' success in Vietnam also revealed their limitations: violence for the sake of violence would not win the war. They could be effective and lethal, and they had proved themselves tactically. But, as one RAND military analyst who spent a few days observing the SEALs in Vietnam later said, "SEALs were a tactic in search of a strategy."[21]

CHAPTER 2

ENSIGN PENNEY

Late April 1979

Naval Amphibious Base Little Creek, where the frogmen had completed their training since World War II, sits on an inlet at the Chesapeake Bay's mouth in Virginia Beach, Virginia. Just to its east is the southern tip of land where the Chesapeake meets the Atlantic and where, in 1607, the English settlers who established Jamestown first touched the North American shore. For many years, this would be home to SEALs training on the East Coast.

On an uneventful day in the spring of 1979, Ralph Stanley Penney reported for duty to begin his first assignment in the Teams. Penney arrived almost a month early, eager to join Underwater Demolition Team 21. He had left Coronado, California, having just graduated from SEAL training, and driven across the country, stopping in Georgia to visit his sister before arriving in Virginia Beach. As an ensign, Penney, then twenty-three years old, was the picture of an ambitious young man dedicated to serving his country.

Penney showed up to UDT-21 prepared to demonstrate his bravery, and he had big shoes to fill. As a child, Penney revered his father, a highly decorated Air Force fighter pilot who flew over two hundred combat missions in the Vietnam War in the notoriously vulnerable F-105—an aircraft that suffered nearly 40 percent losses during the conflict.[1] The younger Penney had never wavered on his goal to follow his father's career in the cockpit. Bright, determined, and patriotic, Penney won a commission to the Air Force Academy in 1974 and quickly set about making his mark. He was well liked and easy to get along with, according to his classmates. Penney was small, not much taller than five feet six inches, and slight but very fit. He carried with him a "small man's syndrome," one of his classmates recalled, often trying to prove himself in physical challenges. Boxing gave him an arena in which to test himself, and he was better than most in his weight class. Unfortunately, despite an excellent academic record, the younger Penney failed to qualify as a pilot. Poor eyesight, which required thick corrective lenses, dashed Penney's dream. Some of Penney's academy classmates saw his decision to join the Navy as the extension of his determination to prove his toughness and worth. "He had a chip on his shoulder because he couldn't be a pilot," one of his classmates recalled. By the time Penney graduated in 1978, he had already enrolled in the Basic Underwater Demolition/SEALs training program, also known as BUD/S. Rebecca Penney, Stanley's younger sister, would later say that her brother decided that if he couldn't be a pilot, he would choose the single most challenging unit in the military, the Navy SEALs.

Penney's decision to enroll in BUD/S didn't sit well with his parents, especially his father, Col. Ralph Stanley Penney Sr., known as Stan and Stanley's namesake. Stanley Jr. grew up in a strict Baptist home with no alcohol and addressed his mother and father as ma'am and sir. When Stanley informed his father that he wanted to go to BUD/S after graduating from the academy, Col. Penney tried to forbid him. This wasn't simply a matter of branch-of-service rivalries. The elder Penney had developed a dim view of the SEALs and frogmen in Vietnam. SEALs were "drinkers and killers," Col. Penney told his son, immoral men who had done distasteful things during the war in Vietnam.[2]

One of Penney's BUD/S classmates who also went to UDT-21, but served in a different platoon, described the environment they entered with the Vietnam SEALs:

> Those guys from that time were pretty fucked up by Vietnam. My first platoon officer Fred Keener....We had a platoon party, a pool party at his house. We all brought our wives and our girlfriends. I brought my wife, who's liberal. Everyone's wives and girlfriends show up at Keener's house. Keener's wife didn't show up, I didn't know at the time but they were having problems. Everybody of course got drunk, a little stoned, and then he brings out the camera and he brings out those old screens and then he brought out these little slides. Had those set up in a tray. These were his Vietnam kill shots so he took pictures of everybody he could that he killed. His claim to fame was that he killed more people by the time he turned twenty-one than Jesse James did. These were pretty grotesque pictures. Of course, I didn't complain or anything, I'm the new guy. The older guys are being tough and hootin' and hollerin'. One guy was a sniper that he shot with a shotgun. He snuck up on the guy—the guy was in a tree—and [Keener] hit him in the head, blew his cranium off, then the guy was hanging upside down because his foot was caught in a V in a branch, so he's hanging upside down—and Fred's loving this, he just thinks this is the best thing he's ever done, and you could see his brains, and I didn't know this but the brains are all connected like an intestine they were hanging all the way down. And a bunch of other shots like that. When we were leaving, my wife said, "Who the fuck have you got involved with?"[3]

Col. Penney and his wife refused to discuss their son's intention to join the SEALs after Stanley brought it up while still in the Air Force Academy. Nevertheless, in September 1978, the colonel's son began the SEAL training program. BUD/S was a six-month training, headquartered at the West Coast SEAL and UDT base on Coronado Island off San Diego. It was the most demanding military training in the United States and arguably the world, and remains so today. Penney's experience there perfectly illustrated how the training course drew the most dedicated and deter-mined volunteers, even as it frequently weeded out the strongest.

There has never been a secret formula to determine who will graduate from BUD/S. Even in Penney's time, the program had an attrition rate that often oscillated between 50 and 80 percent. Statistically, the program is inefficient. The Navy isn't simply seeking the strongest, most fit men physically capable of completing a brutal training course; it wants those who would rather die than give up on their assigned task. The SEALs refer to this willingness to give their life as "putting out." Although there is a physical fitness requirement to be selected for the training, the initial phase's purpose is to find these strong-willed men who can complete their mission despite extreme stress, pain, and fatigue.

The goal of BUD/S hasn't changed since the first combat swimmers went through the original Naval Combat Demolition Unit training in Fort Pierce during the Second World War: to find a man's breaking point and demonstrate that he can go past it. But it has since become much longer and even more challenging than the program Lt. Cdr. Kauffman conducted. Trainees spend the first weeks in physical training combined with forced deprivations intended to test a SEAL hopeful's resolve. This includes open-ocean swimming, timed seven-mile runs on the sand, and physically punishing tasks like hoisting boats and telephone poles above one's head and transporting them along the beach or in the cold Pacific surf. Four weeks into this first phase, Hell Week begins. It is considered the single most grueling portion of BUD/S. The volunteers must operate with no more than eight hours of total sleep (over five days) and often less, none of it for longer than fifteen-minute increments.

"The three things that make BUD/S hard are lack of food, lack of sleep, and cold," said a retired SEAL who spent three decades in the Teams. "What you see happen over a period of time, and it has to be a week or longer for sleep or food, is if you have any physical weakness, it breaks you down mentally. If you're mentally weak, you break down immediately, and anything will weed you out. If you are good mentally and good physically, how do you break them down? The easiest way to break someone down is to deprive them of sleep or freeze their balls off....Because your mind has to go toward taking care of yourself, you start focusing on 'I'm tired, I hurt, I'm cold,' and you start to break down mentally. And then you start questioning, why am I doing this? Do I really want to do this? It's going to tear at your resolve. Do I really want to be here? Do I really want to do this? And that's really what it comes down to. What you see people do is through cold and sleep and physical abuse, like running [and swimming] forever, people will decide that they don't really want to do it. That's what you're trying to weed out at BUD/S. You're trying to weed out that no matter how bad anything ever gets, once you've made a decision that you're going to do it, no matter what happens, you will finish it. Period."

The purpose of this is not to create the world's single hardest military program, according to this SEAL, but to simulate the rigors of combat. "It gets your brain to that point where a three-day combat operation where you're taking fire, and you've got wounded, where the odds are against you; you're getting crushed, but you never fucking quit, that's how you get to that point, and you get to that point quickly in Hell Week. That's why it works. You tear down a human being all the way to his resolve, very fast....You cannot have someone's resolve get broken in combat. We put them to the point where we are testing that resolve beyond, almost, the stress of combat to make sure their resolve never breaks in combat. That's the genius of BUD/S."[4]

As it was in the first generation of frogmen, officers and the enlisted go through the same training; officers are also tasked with planning and leading some of the training exercises in later phases. After the physical activity and tests, prospective SEALs learn hydro reconnaissance, scuba diving, land warfare, and weapons. BUD/S trainees average 2 miles of ocean swimming per week to go along with running 50 miles. Before a trainee graduates, he has to complete a timed 5.5-mile open-ocean swim and a 15-mile run.

By the time Penney graduated from the six months of BUD/S, he had proved himself. According to several people in his class, many much bigger, stronger young men quit in the first phase, in particular during

Hell Week. Penney not only demonstrated he had the resolve to become a SEAL, but he also excelled during training and ended up as the only officer to graduate from his class. "He totally took control of the class," said one of his BUD/S classmates. "You had confidence in him. There was no 'if' about him. It was almost like he'd been through BUD/S before. I had total confidence in Penney."[5]

Several of Penney's classmates would later remark that he was a natural leader who took care of his men. "He always made sure his men ate first," said Michael Reiter, who attended BUD/S with Penney. "He ate last and not until we finished. He was a leader from the front. He was demanding, not a perfectionist, but he made sure we kept military bearing and [he] took no nonsense." "He was a really good guy," another classmate said. "He never cut corners. He was never afraid to take responsibility to lead. He did everything the right way."[6]

After graduation, most of BUD/S class 101 headed to Fort Benning, Georgia, for the Army Airborne School to become qualified in skydiving. Penney's time at the Air Force Academy had given him one advantage over his BUD/S classmates: he'd already completed Jump School. Penney showed up to Underwater Demolition Team 21 at Little Creek ready to serve, but also still needing to prove his toughness. He may have been the leader of his BUD/S class, but in April 1979, he was UDT-21's FNG, the Fucking New Guy. Back then, BUD/S graduates didn't get their SEAL Trident designator pin until they had completed six months in a platoon. BUD/S only qualified you to join a SEAL team or UDT and prove your worth once again, in part by going through more advanced training. Like BUD/S, there was a purpose to the engineering of a SEAL or frogman's development. You weren't really a SEAL or a frogman until you got your Trident, and only SEALs could deploy overseas.

As it happened, a platoon from UDT-21 was scheduled for dive training in Vieques, Puerto Rico. The command sent Penney to a platoon led by Lt. Joseph Maguire. Penney didn't yet have formal orders, so he would likely switch platoons afterward, but the trip would allow him to get a head start on the advanced training he'd need to earn his pin.

"He was new and we thought it would be good to go down to Puerto Rico to get worked up before he joined his own platoon," retired admiral Thomas Richards said. "He was an ensign and we wanted him to have a leg up." At the time, Richards was the executive officer of UDT-21 and paired Penney with Maguire's platoon.

Even during peacetime, SEAL training is serious business. It is said that a SEAL doesn't rise to an occasion but falls back on his training. Shooting multiple weapons, skydiving, scuba diving, reconnaissance, and survival are the tools each SEAL craftsman has to rely on during a deployment and so must be mastered. The dive training at the Roosevelt Roads naval base in Vieques, an islet off the main island of Puerto Rico, was rigorous work. SEALs would spend hours underwater, testing equipment and operating in the turquoise Caribbean Sea. They might practice getting in and out of a submarine at depth, or conduct reconnaissance exercises for hours.

After training, though, the SEALs and frogmen liked to drink. Drinking was an integral part of SEAL culture. On weekend liberty in Vieques, they commandeered an old landing craft utility boat from World War II, which was converted for offshore diving. They'd use the ship to ferry from Vieques to St. Thomas in the US Virgin Islands, a two- to three-hour trip east in good seas.

During the May 1979 training trip, Ens. Penney joined his dive-training officer in charge, Petty Officer 1st Class George Edward Leasure, and a few other men from the platoon on the trip to St. Thomas. Known as "Fast Eddie" because he was a pool hustler and had an easy time picking up women, Leasure had served several tours of duty in Vietnam with SEAL Team 2. He was a popular SEAL who'd earned several nicknames during BUD/S, including "Skill" for his hand-eye dexterity.[7] In Vietnam he'd developed a reputation as an excellent operator who'd run an intelligence collection network assigned to the PRU, part of the CIA's Phoenix Program. For the Fucking New Guy, having the thirty-five-year-old enlisted Leasure on your first liberty weekend in St. Thomas was ideal. "He wasn't good-looking, but he had a personality [that] attracted people to him," said retired SEAL master chief Thomas Keith, who served with Leasure in Vietnam. Another SEAL officer who served with Leasure put it another way: "Eddie Leasure was the devil. He had a sense of humor, was full of piss and vinegar and a hell of an operator."[8]

"There was probably between 1973 and 1979…twenty-five Eddie Leasures—wartime SEALs, they didn't want the war to stop," retired captain Tom Coulter said. "I worked with several of them. The other hundreds of SEALs were in Vietnam—they were able to let it go. But there were twenty to twenty-five Eddie Leasures that had a very black-and-white outlook at people—you either commanded their respect or you didn't."

The SEALs moored the ship in the main harbor and began their young-men's prowl through town. They checked into the Windward Passage Hotel, on the harbor, with a view across Cay Bay. That evening, Leasure took Penney and several others out for a night of drinking. In St. Thomas, every bar but one closed at midnight. In order to keep the night going, Leasure led Penney to the island's gay bar, called Fannies. SEALs and frogmen from UDT-21 drank in Fannies frequently over the years. St. Thomas had once been the winter base for UDT-21, and trade secrets such as where you could drink all night were passed down through the different eras of Naval Special Warfare. In 1979, the gay men who frequented Fannies were called "Benny Boys" by the SEALs, a derogatory term that referred to their female dress and appearance. Some were cross-dressers; others were what are now known as preoperative transgender women. It was not uncommon for the veteran SEALs to take the younger guys to Fannies and buy them enough drinks that they would become unconscious. Once blacked out, the SEALs would then "auction" the passed-out man to one of the gay patrons. Sometimes they'd put him up on the bar; other times they would strip him down, sit him in a chair, and parade him around the bar, according to a veteran SEAL who participated in and witnessed the hazing. The hazing was part of the Teams' culture then, with much of it perpetrated by the Vietnam War veterans on the younger SEALs, according to interviews with a dozen SEALs and UDT frogmen from that era.

"After training all day you go up to the bar, any bar, and drinks were twenty-five cents. Well, you get shit-faced on five dollars," one SEAL officer recalled. "St. Thomas was very liberal and well known for the gay community. Being hard-muscled, hard-charging warm bodies, the guys were certainly targets and it was common for us, when we ran out of our twenty-five-cent chits, to see who we could get shit-faced and sell him to a gay guy so we had more money to drink. Is that hazing? Do I know that it worked? Enough that they'd wake up in a strange place without knowing what happened."

The policy the next day, he said, was the SEAL version of "don't ask, don't tell."[9]

Leasure set Penney up with one of the cross-dressers and plied the ensign with drinks. Penney continued to drink and was unaware that he was flirting with a man. Then Penney went back to his room at the Windward Passage Hotel with his guest. Leasure eventually visited the hotel room to check up on the ensign.

The next day, when Penney recovered, Leasure informed the young officer that he'd had sex with a man, not a woman. Leasure told others in the platoon when the two returned to Roosevelt Roads that he'd set Penney up with a Benny Boy and that the ensign went home with a man. Leasure had told several men in Lt. Maguire's platoon that Penney had been "sold to a fag."[10] Penney, who was too intoxicated to consent, was sexually assaulted by a man, on his first professional trip in the Teams, arranged by his training chief.[11]

"Eddie Leasure orchestrated the whole thing," said one UDT-21 operator who learned of the hazing from his teammates. "You didn't want to be around that guy."

On the flight back to the mainland, Penney was upset, a teammate would later tell his family. Penney and the rest of UDT-21 returned to Little Creek during the week before Memorial Day. Shortly after they returned to Virginia Beach, Penney left the base and purchased a .22-caliber revolver and ammunition. On Saturday that weekend, Penney got his car inspected at the DMV so he could register for Virginia plates and, later, paid bills in his officer's quarters. In the afternoon, Penney sat on his bed, pointed the gun at his head, and fired. Unfortunately, the round was small, and Penney did not immediately die. He stood up from his bed, took several steps, lost a shoe, and collapsed facedown.

COL. STANLEY PENNEY AND HIS WIFE, ANN PENNEY, DROVE FROM Athens, Georgia, to Little Creek shortly after Naval Special Warfare notified them of their son's death. Col. Penney asked that Penney's room not be cleaned or cleared, and that besides his son's body, everything remain in place. The command agreed. By the time Penney's parents arrived, however, Penney's quarters had been cleaned. Lt. Joe Maguire, the platoon commander and officer in charge on the training trip, and his wife, Kathy, insisted on having Penney's parents stay with them rather than in Penney's quarters. Maguire said nothing to the Penneys about their son's liberty trip to St. Thomas, or about Fast Eddie Leasure.

"I don't think there was anything Joe could [do] to fix this," said retired captain Tom Coulter, who served at UDT-21 during Vietnam and who later became the executive officer of SEAL Team 6. "Nothing he said to the parents was going to do anything to bring their son back." Coulter acknowledged that the SEALs have a way of finding a teammate's weakness, and pushing him to see if he will break is part of the SEAL culture. "If it's determined that Penney had a problem, the commands are relatively ruthless. That's part of our group mentality."

Another retired SEAL officer, who spent twenty-five years in the Teams, described the internal team dynamics this way: "Whatever chip in the armor you have, we're going to exploit it—immediately. If you're a homophobe, we'll grab your ass. If you don't like fish, we'll make you eat fish. We get under your skin—that's what the guys do."

When the news of Penney's death got out to the others in UDT-21 and SEAL Team 2, Penney's classmates from BUD/S were devastated. "He was just a solid officer," said one of Penney's teammates. "So for him to get fucked over like that, I could see why he blew his brains out. He couldn't live with that disgust."

Two of Penney's classmates from BUD/S, who were also assigned to UDT-21, said Penney's hazing and suicide were among the reasons they left the Teams rather than reenlist. The hazing culture then could be unforgiving. "It was sad that he killed himself, but it was also kind of a joke around UDT-21 after that," said Jimmy Rowland, who didn't know Penney but was at Little Creek when he died. "Guys would take the command microphone and announce, 'Ensign Penney, come to the armory and clean your weapon.' It was some sick shit."

Rebecca Penney, now sixty-two years old, remembers vividly her brother's final visit in April 1979 as he made his way from California to Virginia Beach. "He was happy," Rebecca Penney said. "We went out one night with my friend. We had a great time." Penney recalled how thrilled her brother was to be going to his first command and—despite his father's admonition—the pride he felt with becoming a SEAL. "He was so excited," she said.

The Naval Investigative Service (now the Naval Criminal Investigative Service) conducted an investigation into Penney's death. After several weeks, they completed a report, which they refused to release under the Freedom of Information Act, that found no foul play. The report concluded that Penney took his life because he was depressed. Although investigators interviewed Fast Eddie Leasure, the report made no mention of a liberty weekend in St. Thomas, no mention of a night of drinking at Fannies gay bar, and had no details about the hazing. Penney's parents and sister found the report's conclusion that Stanley was depressed to be unbelievable.

"It didn't make sense," Rebecca Penney said forty years later. After reading the report and sifting through the photos of her brother's quarters, she believed he must have been murdered. She had no reason to believe that except that the Navy's story never added up.

Capt. Tom Coulter said Naval Special Warfare would never admit to hazing Penney. "What was the command going to say?" Coulter asked. "We drove your son to his death? Penney wasn't even the tip of the iceberg in terms of hazing in the Teams." He said he understands the Penney family's pain. "No one wants to lose a son," he said. But Coulter also suggested the possibility that Eddie Leasure saw some weakness in the young officer that might have hurt the accomplishment of a mission in which he was in command. "I want to know who Penney's instructors were at BUD/S," Coulter said. "What did they miss? They should be looking at a young officer's fitness to lead men."

The other more significant question the NIS report left unanswered was what command knew about the events leading up to Penney's death. At a moment early in his career, Maguire was faced with a difficult situation: a junior officer assigned to his platoon was sexually assaulted, orchestrated by a senior enlisted SEAL with far more experience and credibility in the Teams. The junior officer killed himself as a result. Years later, Maguire, through a spokeswoman, denied that he knew about the hazing. "He has never knowingly condoned, tolerated, or permitted the mistreatment of anyone under his command. The death of Ens. Penney was tragic, and then Lt. Maguire and his wife Kathy mourned alongside Ens. Penney's family, friends and fellow service members."[12] Members of Maguire's platoon, as well as other SEALs, questioned how an officer in charge could not know that his newest ensign had been "sold to a fag" during a training trip, which ultimately resulted in his suicide.

Rebecca Penney has spent the last forty-one years dealing with the questions surrounding her brother's death. She never believed the Navy's conclusion, and it was clear to her that there had been a cover-up of some kind, but of what she didn't know. She filled in the absence of information from the Navy with her own suspicions, including that her brother may have been murdered.

For those inside the Teams who knew of the sexual hazing and how it led to Penney's suicide, Ens. Penney's tragic end served as a reminder that in the post-Vietnam era, what made SEALs excellent on the battlefield could also make them dangerous even to their own.

CHAPTER 3

THE BIRTH OF SEAL TEAM 6

NEARLY SIX MONTHS AFTER ENS. PENNEY KILLED HIMSELF, IN November 1979, a group of Iranian student radicals raided the US embassy in Tehran, taking sixty-six Americans hostage. The Iranians ultimately released fourteen of the hostages, but held the remaining fifty-two, demanding that the United States return the country's exiled former leader to be tried, and release the country's frozen financial assets held in the United States.

The Iranian hostage crisis served as a forceful repudiation of American foreign policy in the Middle East. It was also the American public's first real reckoning with Islamic terrorism. They had watched as Palestinian terrorists executed Israeli athletes during the 1972 Munich Olympics, and followed the successful 1976 Israeli hostage rescue in Entebbe, Uganda. But the US public didn't truly confront the terrorist threat—or acknowledge what it might mean for them—until American diplomats were held hostage and paraded around the seized US embassy wearing blindfolds.

President Jimmy Carter ordered a rescue attempt. Named Operation Eagle Claw, the plan was complicated. The military planners who designed it acknowledged that it did not have a great chance of success. The Army would send in its recently created secret commando unit called 1st Special Forces Operational Detachment–Delta, but colloquially known as Delta Force. To get the Delta operators into Tehran, the team would assemble in Egypt, fly on to Oman, and then fly again by plane over the Gulf of Oman and continue seven hundred miles into Iran's Great Salt Desert, some sixty miles southeast of Tehran. Military planners code-named the staging location Desert One.

From Desert One, the Delta operators would fly in a small fleet of Navy helicopters, flown by Marine pilots, to a mountainside location on Tehran's outskirts. The Delta team would rest and then travel by truck into Tehran the next night. They would storm the embassy, kill the Iranians holding the American hostages, grab the hostages, and walk them across the street to an adjacent soccer stadium. The RH-53 helicopters would fly from the mountainside location, pick up the hostages, and transport them to an airfield sixty miles southwest, which would have been seized by Army Rangers. The hostages and their Delta rescuers would switch to C-130 transport planes, and the entire force, minus the helicopters, would fly back to Masirah, Oman.[1]

The military prepared for five months, rehearsing and refining, hoping to get the approval to conduct the mission. The operation was unprecedented in scale and difficulty. But there were minimum requirements to conduct the raid once the mission began. One of the first principles of any military operation using helicopters is that helicopters are prone to malfunction. To get all fifty-three hostages plus the 132 members of the assault force out safely, a minimum of six RH-53 helicopters would have to be operational once they reached Desert One. In all, eight helicopters would deploy, leaving them with a small, two-helicopter cushion. Conceptually, the task was overwhelmingly not in the military's favor. One of the Delta commanders put it this way: "Delta trained for operations in permissive environments with the support of local government, military, and police. Now, suddenly, we found our first mission was not only in a non-permissive environment with no support, but also the local government was going to be the enemy."[2] Grabbing the hostages from the US embassy in Tehran was a difficult task; doing so inside a hostile nation with a capable defense force added a level of difficulty and challenge for which no one in the US military was fully prepared.

In late April, Carter ordered the mission to go ahead. On April 24, a group of military planners sat inside a charmless room on the Pentagon's second floor, listening to a stream of radio transmissions halfway around the globe. The room was filled with cigarette smoke, and ashtrays with stubbed butts covered the main table. The officers, part of the Terrorist Action Team (TAT) assembled to plan Eagle Claw, occupied a room-within-a-room, a sensitive compartmented information facility that prevented any sound or other transmission from escaping.[3] They were receiving transmissions from helicopters flying off the USS *Nimitz* carrier in the Persian Gulf, heading toward Iran, Delta personnel departing from Oman in the C-130s, and a single Delta operator hidden inside Tehran—all communicating on the same encrypted frequency as the mission got under way. Supporting them were special cadres from both the Navy and Air Force, but the chain of command was convoluted and diffuse. The action team officers were listening to a series of separate transmissions simultaneously, but there was no central communication point for the complex and multipart operation. The organizational chaos was mirrored by the failure occurring on the ground as commandos secretly infiltrated Iranian territory.

Delta operators flew from Egypt to Oman, switched planes, and flew to the Iranian desert; the eight RH-53 helicopters, painted in Iranian Air Force colors, took off from the USS *Nimitz* in the Gulf of Oman and headed north toward Desert One. Inside Tehran, the single Delta operator, who had secretly infiltrated the capital to help coordinate the embassy raid, transmitted updates by encrypted radio frequency. At the landing zone, the cargo planes with the Delta team arrived safely. Six of the eight helicopters arrived, but two had turned back mid-flight with mechanical trouble. Shortly after the six helicopters landed at Desert One, one helicopter pilot reported a mechanical problem that could not be fixed quickly and deemed the helicopter unusable. That left five working helicopters.

Col. Charlie Beckwith, the Delta commander overseeing the operation, aborted the mission. Delta operators loaded into the two C-130 transport airplanes, which were also filled with fuel bladders. Beckwith's order required the helicopters to refuel for the return flight back to the *Nimitz*. All five began a delicate repositioning near the C-130s to hook up to the fuel bladders. The Delta operators had split in two, with one squadron in each transport plane, and began to settle themselves into their respective fuselage. The helicopters were almost all refueled when one, after finishing, repositioned itself in an effort to clear away from the C-130. As the pilot moved his chopper around, he lost visibility and had sudden vertigo in a vast sand cloud generated by the helicopter's rotors and a strong gale. His helicopter drifted over to the nearby C-130, clipping its fuselage, filled with fuel and half the Delta operators, in the process. The front half of the transport plane exploded into a fireball, as did the helicopter. The fire moved closer to the full fuel bladders, making it only a matter of time before the fuel ignited, turning the airplane into a bomb. The Delta team filed out of the plane quickly but calmly, one by one. When the plane finally exploded, five Air Force crewmen were still trapped inside. The explosion also killed three Marines in the helicopter and sent a ball of flames several miles into the night sky. The planners in the Pentagon heard part of the radio transmission go silent. When Desert One came back online, they reported at least eight dead and more men burned. With the fire still raging, the Eagle Claw team was forced to leave the eight dead servicemen behind. As daylight approached, all the survivors loaded into the remaining transport airplane and took off.

The remaining US members of the rescue operation made it safely out of Iran. Still, the mission's failure severely damaged America's reputation as the world's most powerful military. Images of smoldering American aircraft in the Iranian desert were televised around the world, projecting a superpower's defeat and humiliation. The US military had failed to rescue American citizens from a collection of radical university students and had been forced to leave behind their dead.

FOR THE MILITARY PLANNERS SITTING IN THE PENTAGON'S SECOND-floor room-within-a-room for the mission, the flaws in the plan were abundantly clear. The United States did not have a central command or enough elite counterterrorism units to conduct complex, time-sensitive operations using different branches of the military.

Among those on the edge of their seats in the Pentagon for Eagle Claw was thirty-nine-year-old Navy Cdr. Richard "Dick" Marcinko. A tall, broad-shouldered man with black hair and dark, hooded eyes, Marcinko's physical appearance broke with the Navy's image of a chiseled and refined WASP naval officer; he looked more like a Marine grunt. He also defied the Navy's expectations of an officer's demeanor. Marcinko was a foul-mouthed and aggressive SEAL who'd earned Silver and Bronze Stars for valor in several deployments during the Vietnam War. The men in his family had been coal miners. His grandparents had immigrated from then Czechoslovakia to Pennsylvania, where Marcinko's grandfather, and then his father, worked in the mines. Marcinko's childhood was, by his own account, blue-collar and rough—and he decided not to follow his father and grandfather underground but instead put out to sea. He dropped out of high school and enlisted in the Navy.

Shortly after enlisting, Marcinko, a radioman, saw *The Frogmen*, the 1951 film depicting UDT-4's heroics in World War II, and knew he needed to join the Underwater Demolition Teams. He would have to wait a few more years before he could secure orders to try out. He completed UDT training in 1961.[4] After several years as an enlisted frogman, Marcinko passed a high school equivalency exam and was selected into the Navy's officer candidate school to earn his commission. By the time he became an ensign, in 1965, the SEALs had been in and out of Vietnam for three years.[5] Marcinko's previous enlisted experience gave him instant credibility with the men, even if his fellow officers were leery of him.[6] Bill Hamilton, the former UDT officer who had created the Navy SEALs, described Marcinko as "rough at the edges" with "a vocabulary liberally sprinkled with 'fucks' and 'assholes.'" Marcinko was the kind of man, Hamilton wrote in his memoir, "you wanted with you in a barroom brawl."[7] Marcinko had earned a reputation as an aggressive, caustic, and savvy bureaucratic hustler inside the Navy during Vietnam. He was known as "Demo" Dick and was well regarded if not popular among his peers.

In 1979, Marcinko was assigned to the Pentagon as a planning officer for the Joint Chiefs' terrorism branch when the Eagle Claw planning began. He had initially proposed going into Iran with a small team of SEALs to throw bombs from an Air Force plane onto the Tehran airport, but was overruled. Marcinko would later write that not having any SEALs on the mission gnawed at his competitiveness, even though he believed the mission would still likely fail. But having listened as transmissions from Desert One went silent, Marcinko was unequivocal in how badly the mission failed. "From the top down," Marcinko later wrote in his memoir, "it had been one humungous goat fuck. One big waste."[8]

The internal US response was almost immediate. Two days after the Desert One failure, President Carter ordered the military to plan a second rescue attempt. The Pentagon used the planning of a second rescue operation to develop a new organization and structure to conduct hostage rescues and counterterrorism operations around the world. The new organization would conduct what the military called "special operations," intended to be thorough, decisive, and over quickly. To be named the Joint Special Operations Command, this new organization would answer to the president. It would serve as the closest thing the country had to a Praetorian Guard: an elite force authorized by the head of state to accomplish a mission of national importance. As part of this new command, both the Air Force and the Navy would get a new so-called Tier 1 team, like the Army's Delta Force. The Joint Chiefs asked Marcinko to help design the Navy's contribution to the new joint command.

Marcinko saw Operation Eagle Claw's failure and the second rescue attempt as the opportunity to create a new counterterrorism unit. To the only Naval Special Warfare officer in the planning team, the missing piece was obvious: SEALs. When he was asked for input two days later, Marcinko saw an opportunity to create the new SEAL unit he'd been imagining. The original draft described the SEAL portion of the new joint command as an "element," which translated to one or two platoons, or roughly fourteen to twenty-eight SEALs. Marcinko replaced the word "element" with "command." A command meant an entire new SEAL team, like SEAL Team 1 and SEAL Team 2. The new unit would require a commanding officer and would then be equal in standing to Delta. It would be a stand-alone national mission unit focused on maritime targets or operations, where a shoreline was used to infiltrate a land-based target. Marcinko envisioned six platoons, or an additional eighty-four SEALs, dedicated to counter-terrorism and hostage rescue. His one-word change was as pragmatic and bureaucratic as it was tribal. He understood that as initially worded, the SEAL element would serve as an auxiliary to Delta. He wanted more. The Pentagon kept Marcinko's word change and, to his delight, commissioned the new SEAL unit.

New problems led to new solutions. Terrorism, hostage taking, and non-state adversaries were the latest military problems facing the United States, just as President Kennedy had warned twenty years earlier. Marcinko and his new SEAL command would be the answer. In the spring of 1979, other SEAL officers saw counterterrorism and hostage rescue as Naval Special Warfare's next tactical evolution. Both SEAL Teams 1 and 2 already had counterterrorism training for some of their SEALs. In SEAL Team 2, at Little Creek, two platoons were already dedicated to counterterrorism and hostage rescue. They were called Mobility 6, or MOB-6. But Marcinko was in the right place at the right time to influ-ence the Pentagon's new command and help create a new SEAL team as he imagined it should look.

In September 1980, Marcinko left the Iranian hostage rescue plan-ning mission at the Pentagon and took over his new command. At the time, the chief of naval operations, Adm. Thomas Hayward, had one terse order for Marcinko: "You will not fail."

Marcinko had promised the Pentagon and the Joint Chiefs that he would have the new unit ready in six months. It was a massive task. It had taken nearly three years to build Delta before it deployed on the Iranian rescue operation. Marcinko and Hamilton decided to call the new unit SEAL Team 6. Although there were only two other SEAL Teams at the time, the two Naval Special Warfare veterans thought 6 might confuse the Soviets into wondering about SEAL Teams 3 through 5. The number also reflected how many SEAL platoons had already gone through counter-terrorism training.[9]

Marcinko raided from both existing SEAL Teams and some of the UDT's roster as well, starting with fifteen officers and seventeen enlisted SEALs. He sought men who, in his estimation, would otherwise be athletes or criminals in the civilian world. He wanted SEALs "who had combat experience," he later said in an interview, "who had a bullet go past their head with their name on it."[10] Marcinko looked for SEALs who, like himself, had served in Vietnam. Marcinko also wanted men who were adept at all the traditional SEAL skills—shooting, underwater diving, skydiving, mountain climbing—but who also had or could develop tradesman-like skills; these men had to engineer solutions to any problem standing in their way to mission success, whether it required manufacturing a quieter piece of equipment or conceiving a quieter method for a building entry.

But as Marcinko recruited for his unit, another characteristic emerged. Marcinko liked to drink, and any SEAL who wanted to serve in his new, secret, and elite team would have to be able to drink as well.

"I used alcohol as a tool," Marcinko later told me. If a prospective SEAL Team 6 operator couldn't keep up with Marcinko at a bar, he was of no use to him. "We were social misfits, and I set it up like a mafioso, a band, a brotherhood."

Ultimately, Marcinko selected men in his image, men he liked or whom his master chief, Ken MacDonald, liked, and primarily from the East Coast. Applicants did take the Minnesota Multiphasic Personality Inventory, known as the MMPI, a standard psychological evaluation tool that measures personality structure and psychopathologies. But the exam was used almost as a perfunctory device, and few selectees were barred from the unit because of their test results. Marcinko recruited a special forces psychologist, Dr. Michael Whitley, who had studied the psychology of terrorism. Marcinko told me he hired Dr. Whitley for bureaucratic reasons. "I did it to cover my ass, to say all of us had been evaluated. But it was a fallacy. We were normal, according to me. If I was fucked up, then we were all fucked up."

Whitley could discern no real effort to conduct psychological screening when he arrived in Virginia Beach to root out any SEALs with troubling personalities. Some of Marcinko's recruits even refused to take the MMPI. "There were a lot of great men at [SEAL Team] Six," Whitley said in an interview. "But there were a few sociopaths in that group. There was no psychological screening to speak of."[11]

SEAL Team 6 was, by design, to be the furthest thing from the Navy. Good order and discipline wouldn't guarantee the successful completion of the mission. Marcinko wanted pirates, rogues, outlaws, and men who would have had a hard time staying out of legal trouble as civilians if they hadn't been in the military. "If you want to call them sociopaths, you can. That's how you get the enlisted in charge. They are the talent. My priorities for the unit were Mission, Unit, Flag, Family. SEAL Team 6 is not really a military unit as much as it is a mafia. If there were problems at the command, I kept it in-house, like a padrone or mafioso," Marcinko told me. "I could send a guy to a special court-martial, or I could cut his pay. Cutting a man's pay hurt more, and I had a personal dilemma: Do I shitcan them? This was a combat environment. We were the only unit at a combat tempo. I don't have time to groom guys, and I can't afford to lose them."

As a former enlisted frogman, Marcinko was transparent about his affinity for enlisted men—and not the officer class. He intentionally designed SEAL Team 6 to be a command where an experienced, seasoned enlisted operator would effectively lead the unit beneath the commander. There would be a distinct difference between who was in command and who was in charge. The officers were in command, but the senior enlisted were in charge. The Navy had a precedent for this dynamic. A captain might have commanded a ship at sea, but it was his senior enlisted master chief who operated and controlled the vessel.

In some ways, the purpose of SEAL Team 6 was simple. If there was a hostage, their job was to reach a location and enter a building, ship, oil rig, or plane, for example, without detection. Then, in a matter of seconds, correctly identify the hostage from the hostage takers and kill or otherwise neutralize the hostage taker while saving the hostage. To train for this kind of split-second decision, the SEALs in the unit would fire more bullet rounds in their first six months than all of the Marine Corps in a year. The SEALs saw themselves not as commandos, a British military term, but as "operators," artisans of saving hostages' lives and killing their captors. For weeks, Marcinko had the team move through a "shoot house," practicing the intricate choreography of maneuvering as a group through spaces with walls, doorways, and stairs. Operators had to hit three-by-five index cards placed on the silhouettes of the "bad guy" in the training simulations. To pass, one had to hit the index card and only the index card. Failure to hit it would eventually result in being dropped from the unit.

Their training would include high-altitude, high-opening parachuting, or HAHO, where jumping required face masks with oxygen because of the lack of breathable air. They rehearsed for any scenario they could conceive of and trained as if they would be sent the next day to complete the mission.

The creation of SEAL Team 6 did not go unnoticed. Marcinko rankled his fellow officers by raiding the rest of Naval Special Warfare for SEAL Team 6 personnel. And the resources devoted to the new command drew envy. But what infuriated Marcinko's peers the most was SEAL Team 6's unique position outside Naval Special Warfare and the Navy chain of command. Marcinko, at the rank of commander, an O-5 position, the equivalent of a lieutenant colonel in other services, was able to establish a new SEAL team that overshadowed the other Naval Special Warfare teams, which were commanded by Navy captains, one rank above Marcinko. In the competitive and petty professional environment of SEAL officers, the former enlisted operator had leapfrogged over his superiors. Marcinko was immodest in assessing why he was loathed by so many of his fellow officers: "No one in naval special warfare had the balls to buck the system."[12]

The unit broke into two assault teams, designated Blue and Gold after the Navy's colors. Each team divided further into the equivalent of two platoons. Each element broke into two squads of six SEALs, called boat crews. As they were in Fort Pierce in 1943, the primary unit size was based on how many men could fit, with explosives, in a rubber boat. Both Blue and Gold Teams had four boat crews, or squads. Each boat crew was composed of five to six assaulters. These operators had one primary function: assault a position, rescue a hostage, and kill a hostile threat. Over time, SEAL Team 6 would expand to include other specialized roles like snipers and breachers, but the basic competency of men in the new unit was as an assaulter, an operator. All the skydiving, scuba diving, mountain climbing, and maritime skills were for arriving at a mission location. After that, SEAL Team 6 represented the premier assault unit in the Navy.

In interviews, several of Marcinko's predecessors came to the same overall conclusion about Marcinko's accomplishment in creating SEAL Team 6. The unit was a testimony to his force of personality—he alone had the will to bend the Navy and Naval Special Warfare to his demands in creating the team. But while the unit had talented shooters, Marcinko created a culture within the unit that resembled the mafia ethos he celebrated, unaccountable to anyone but themselves, and sometimes, not even that.

This came at a cost. Team 6 operators were required to carry out amoral acts while operating within a world governed by personality, according to a SEAL officer who studied SEAL Team 6. The SEAL told Orr Kelly, author of *Brave Men, Dark Waters*, a history of Naval Special Warfare, that this posed an inherent risk in the men selected for the unit.

You get a bunch of people, smart, strong, aggressive, and you require them to kill other people. You are requiring guys to do some really tough things. They are going in and find terrorists are women, terrorists are children, anybody. You're up close. This is very personal. The psychologist looks at whether you can blow a hole in a man two feet away and watch brains come out the other side of his head—and do it....You give them all this training and require them to kill people, not from a hundred yards away, not from thirty thousand feet with a bomb, but from three feet away.

Can you imagine that group of people together? All of a sudden in that group of 150 or 200 men, who are so highly trained, all keyed up and required to do such hazardous things, you are going to find some amoral people. They're there because they're smart and aggressive, and they have no morals. You have guys who have no morals, will do anything. That's how you get a reputation for being really bad.

But the great majority are really dedicated, straight, hard-working people. The reason the amoral man doesn't get away with more is that a lot of people watch him. He is controlled. But you are going to find that kind of person when you have a group of people required to perform what these people are required to perform.[13]

Another SEAL who spent more than twenty years in the Teams and operated with Six throughout much of his career described the psychological tension at the command this way: "You're asking guys to commit murder, turn around, fly home, and go back to their home life without missing a beat. That's not normal, but that's what we expect. Kill somebody in the morning, be home in time for dinner with the family and pretend it never happened. On some level, that takes a sociopath." In every way, and by design, the men attracted to the unit, and those who gained entry, were abnormal. They had to operate outside normal military levels of supervision, in high-risk environments, which required independent decision-making, while staying within the law. And yet Marcinko sought, as had his Naval Special Warfare predecessors, SEALs who knew when and how to break the rules. There was an inherent tension in creating a unit that required strict standards of conduct but was filled with outlaws and rogues.

Within six months of establishing SEAL Team 6, Cdr. Marcinko had successfully conceived, selected, built, trained, and launched the Navy's most secret, elite special operations unit. He wanted civilian-dressed killer SEALs, in his image, including his near-mutinous attitude, his foibles, and his fondness for gin. He got them.

In the military's lexicon, SEAL Team 6 would be a "special mission unit" and assigned to the counterterrorism joint task force. They would operate under the chairman of the Joint Chiefs' authority, the top military advisor to the president, under CONPLAN 0300, the military planning designation for counterterrorism. In effect, this meant that the unit was always on alert. In the military vernacular, SEAL Team 6, like Delta, was a Tier 1 unit, which meant that they were on immediate deployment status. SEAL Team 6 had to be ready to deploy from Virginia Beach within four hours of the president signing the military order for an operation. It is this designation that confers SEAL Team 6's elite position in the hierarchy of military units. In time, SEAL Team 6 would describe itself as the "President's Own."

Within a year of establishment, SEAL Team 6 moved from their two shacks at Little Creek to a former Navy anti-aircraft position farther south in Virginia Beach. The base, Dam Neck Annex, known as Dam Neck by its occupants, is a well-preserved three-mile stretch of oceanfront that housed a small naval intelligence training school. While Delta had a thousand-acre expanse at Fort Bragg in Fayetteville, North Carolina, Marcinko got a roughly hundred-acre section of marsh and estuary. The first headquarters was nothing more than a single building in a former parking lot facing sand dunes. In typical Marcinko fashion, he found an ingenious way to secure the real estate. Because Dam Neck had a protected watershed, any amount of land Team 6 took required an equivalent amount of water returned to the watershed. Marcinko read the regulations closely and discovered that while he took square feet, he could return in cubic feet. If he dug a one-hundred-foot hole in the marsh, he would return the water measured cubically, rather than linearly. And although the Team 6 headquarters wasn't much compared to that of the Army's elite unit, Marcinko put his own touch on the new additions. He had a pool built for both swimming and dive training on base, but he had it constructed to forty-nine meters in length, rather than the standard fifty meters used for swimming events. The purpose was to keep the regular Navy occupants on the other half of Dam Neck from using the pool for local swim competitions or practice.

In fact, SEAL Team 6 was able to expand as Naval Special Warfare imagined more and more mission sets for the unit. The command added a third assault team, named Red, and all three developed a subculture and identity. Each assault team had given themselves alternative names; their identities would develop over time and have lasting effects on the team's culture. Blue became the Pirates, with the Jolly Roger symbol of a skull and crossbones as their flag; Gold became the Fighting Lions and initially had a faux Templar-era lion as their symbol (later they would become the Crusaders); Red adopted a Native American profile with two tomahawks and called themselves the Redmen, or the Tribe. Very quickly after they formed, each assault team worked to differentiate itself from the others, a sibling rivalry of personality and culture. The result, only obvious years later, was that each assault team kept its own dark family secrets.

WITHIN THE FIRST FEW YEARS OF SEAL TEAM 6'S CREATION, THE pathologies Marcinko had built into the organization had begun to clash with the mores and hierarchy of the larger Navy and other SEAL Teams. In the winter of 1983, Blue Team, under the command of Lt. William McRaven, traveled to Lake Tahoe for its annual winter warfare training program. McRaven, a broad-shouldered Texan with a clean-shaven face and dark brown hair at his ears, was among the new, young officers who had cycled into SEAL Team 6, which was not yet two years old. McRaven was the son of an Air Force pilot who had been shot down in France during the Second World War and eventually escaped. Fifteen years after the war, a young McRaven spent Friday nights at the American officers' club in Fontainebleau, eavesdropping as his father, Col. Claude C. McRaven, and other retired Air Force officers told war stories while drinking whiskey. McRaven graduated from the University of Texas with a journalism degree, enlisted in the Navy, and graduated from BUD/S in 1978. McRaven had spent the first four years in the Teams on the West Coast, an automatic black mark on his résumé for Marcinko.

Blue Team's senior enlisted leader then was Senior Chief Petty Officer Robert Schamberger, a highly respected, combat-proven SEAL with ten years of experience on the assault team's new officer in charge. As a Team 6 plank owner, Schamberger was tailor-made for Marcinko's unit. Schamberger brokered no shit from his men. He worked hard and required the same from his men. After working hours, he expected them to drink just as hard as they worked, Marcinko-style. Schamberger was also "tough and talented," one of his Blue Team operators told me. Almost from the moment McRaven arrived at the command, he and Schamberger clashed. Schamberger, who had fifteen years in the Teams and seventeen years in the Navy by that point, disliked and mistrusted McRaven. He was not prepared to yield to McRaven.

The Tahoe schedule was typical of Team 6's training regimen. First, the team would do four to five days of downhill skiing, followed by several days of ice mountaineering. Next, they moved to cross-country skiing, going uphill, downhill, and flat with the skis and military gear, and then practiced building snow caves. Everyone was outfitted in civilian green Gore-Tex snowsuits, making them a conspicuous sight in the snow-covered mountains of Tahoe National Forest. Blue Team would end the two-week trip with a series of military operation exercises.

Before the operations cycle began, McRaven discovered anomalies in how some of the operators were filing their travel voucher claims. He brought the issue to Schamberger's attention. Schamberger defended his men and bristled, telling Lt. McRaven that he ran Blue Team the way he saw fit, not McRaven. Schamberger then tossed McRaven's gear and travel bags out of the cabin that the two men shared during the trip. McRaven moved to another cabin, occupied by one of the boat crews. Tossing the skipper's belongings out of the cabin was an act of defiance by Schamberger. The message Schamberger sent to McRaven and the rest of Blue Team was unambiguous: the enlisted were in charge; the military hierarchy didn't exist. What at first glance was a messy but minor personnel issue between a seasoned operator and a junior officer was in fact something more profound. McRaven's ejection from the cabin was an insurrection by those under his command. His senior enlisted men viewed him as insufficiently tough and too focused on the rules.

When Blue Team returned to Dam Neck, Marcinko backed Schamberger and fired McRaven. "Schamberger's way was the way I wanted it done," Marcinko said. In an interview nearly forty years after the incident, Marcinko accused the then lieutenant of treachery. "McRaven got his running orders from the West Coast," Marcinko said. "Officers more senior than me told McRaven, 'Go in there and get your ticket punched [meaning professional development],'" Marcinko claimed. "He was basically a spy."[14] (McRaven denied he was sent to Dam Neck to spy on Marcinko.[15])

The firing was more significant because it was the culmination of a culture Marcinko created and then fostered at SEAL Team 6. "Marcinko really treated the enlisted well," said the former Blue Team operator who observed Schamberger's tossing of McRaven and later Marcinko's dismissal of the officer from Team 6. Marcinko had "a real affinity for us, but he was really tough on his officers. McRaven did nothing wrong," the SEAL said. "Bob Schamberger was a hard-core guy and a complete asshole." Schamberger "was East Coast biased, and he formed a little coup to kick McRaven out because he wanted to run Blue Team."

In firing McRaven, Marcinko upended the barest semblance of order and command integrity. This sent a signal to all the operators: Marcinko was the only officer who required their respect. "Marcinko didn't expect the team leaders to follow him, and he expected the mafia to follow him," Capt. Tom Coulter said. "He wanted senior enlisted people running operations, and the officers were there because they had to be." Coulter compared Marcinko's decision to a Navy captain on a ship siding with a senior enlisted chief over a fellow officer. "It's the chain of command: you live by it, or you hang by it."

For Marcinko and Team 6's enlisted men, McRaven represented the Navy's rules; Schamberger, whom Marcinko had formerly commanded at SEAL Team 2, represented results. The tension and competition at SEAL Team 6 between the rules and results would continue to plague the unit well after Marcinko had left the command.

McRaven later wrote that the firing was one of his worst professional moments. "It was a jarring, confidence-crushing, hard-to-swallow moment, and I seriously considered leaving the Navy."[16]

It also marked a turning point for naval leadership, who had lost patience with Marcinko and the rogue culture he'd created in Team 6. A few months after McRaven was fired, senior officers in Naval Special Warfare and Pentagon officials decided to replace Marcinko. "By 1983, I'd pissed off, threatened, alienated, provoked, offended, and screwed with the [Naval Special Warfare] commodores on both coasts," Marcinko wrote about his time running SEAL Team 6. "Worst of all, I played havoc with their system. I treated my lowest-ranking seaman with more respect than I did most [Naval Special Warfare] captains and commodores. I ate and drank with my enlisted men and chief; I threw loud parties; I said 'fuck' to flag-rank officers."[17]

His replacement would be Capt. Robert Gormly, who did two tours of duty in Vietnam and had risen to commanding officer of SEAL Team 2. Gormly was eager to take over and had been warned by a rear admiral that Team 6 was "in need of some discipline."[18] But on his first day as commanding officer, he learned just how bad things were. The executive officer gave Gormly a picture of a skilled but unruly force. The executive officer told Gormly that Marcinko led the unit "in libertine style," Gormly later wrote. "Anything the troops wanted was okay by him and he routinely misled his superiors in the chain of command under the guise of [operational security]. If the officers attempted to assert themselves, Dick backed the enlisted." Then there was the alcohol. "Dick insisted upon everyone drinking with him whenever he wanted and as long as he wanted," Gormly wrote of the executive officer's assessment. The subordinate was concerned about the readiness of the command. "On exercises they seldom finished the entire scenario because as soon as things got tough, Dick would step in, abort the exercise, and take the troops drinking."[19]

In late June of 1983, Marcinko welcomed aboard the new skipper of SEAL Team 6 at a Virginia Beach bar. But Marcinko's enlisted acolytes were less accommodating that night. Gormly got his first taste of the rogue and, at times, unprofessional attitude Marcinko had fostered in three years. Gormly would later write that Marcinko's men were "insubordinate" at the bar, angry that Marcinko was being ushered out of Dam Neck.[20]

After Gormly left the bar, Marcinko decided to continue drinking elsewhere. He had a command aide drive him in a modified Mercedes-Benz sedan, one of three that he had custom built and shipped to the United States, which he frequently used as his personal car. That night, Marcinko's driver fell asleep in the early morning hours and rear-ended another car, causing significant damage to both vehicles. Marcinko ordered his staff not to report the accident or alert Gormly and his new executive officer while he had the Mercedes repaired. The Team 6 operations officer refused to comply with an illegal order and reported to Gormly both the accident and Marcinko's demand for a cover-up. When an investigation commenced, Marcinko blamed his driver.

Marcinko received a captain's mast, or what the Navy refers to as nonjudicial punishment. The term comes from a time when Navy ships were under sail and the captain handed out both punishment and accolades to enlisted crew on the ship's deck, underneath the mainsail mast. It was an era in which Navy ships were out to sea for long periods, and the captain of a ship was the ultimate authority. If a sailor or officer committed a transgression that wasn't serious enough to return to port for a court-martial, he was sent to captain's mast and sentenced to a punishment on the ship. In the modern era, the captain's mast serves as a way for a commander to punish a subordinate for a crime akin to a misdemeanor instead of a felony. The mast can be a career killer, but it often allows an enlisted operator to salvage his career if he can stay out of trouble in the future. Marcinko's captain's mast resulted in a letter of reprimand and a negative fitness report, both of which should have killed any chance of promotion to a captain's rank.

Marcinko left SEAL Team 6 embittered. The Navy had removed him before SEAL Team 6 got the chance to conduct the kind of real-world mission for which it had been created and for which they had trained. The mast added insult to injury. But even his harshest critics were in awe of what the former enlisted frogman had created. "I'm not a Marcinko cheerleader, but only Dick could have pulled Six together," said Coulter, who joined SEAL Team 6 as executive officer shortly after Gormly took command.

Marcinko was neither fired nor retired after SEAL Team 6. He drifted to a purgatory at the Pentagon, not content to complete his naval career with the creation of the unit. His advancement was possible thanks to an acknowledgment by the Navy's brass that what he had created at SEAL Team 6 was extraordinary.

Meanwhile, Gormly, Coulter, and the new leadership set about professionalizing SEAL Team 6. "Gormly's second command to me was, 'Get rid of those goddamned Mercedes,'" Coulter said. "They were such a bone of contention and were so toxic." Where Marcinko had seen the benefits of the outlaw ethos, the new leadership saw significant flaws in the unit's integrity. Among the implicit messages Gormly sent to his new command was that officers were now in charge. Training requirements were established and maintained. It wasn't enough to make it into SEAL Team 6; you had to earn the spot each day.

Marcinko's immediate legacy at the command presented more significant problems than customized European cars and drunken joyrides. The questions around how Team 6 screened for and chose their SEALs was a work in progress, though the brutal training program was considered superior to anything else in Naval Special Warfare. Coulter, for example, discovered there was no baseline standard for deciding who made it into SEAL Team 6 and who did not. "I asked, 'How did you screen for SEALs in the past?' They told me, 'We just pick who we like.' They had no screening process." Coulter set up a small group as a selection board. Coulter improved the screening process and ensured it was not just a good ol' boys' club, but there was still an inherent SEAL flaw to the screening. Although a psychologist was part of the screening board, Coulter thought him unhelpful. "I told him he was useless." Coulter frequently wondered how a shrink would know who would, or would not, make a good Team 6 operator. He got the final pick to pass to Gormly for approval.

For those who did get selected, the training process, which became known as Green Team, was established and successful. Marcinko had borrowed liberally from what MOB-6 had done and put a senior enlisted operator in charge. Still, it would take years, and several more commanding officers, before Team 6 was seen as a professional outfit. Whether Team 6 was professional, however, was irrelevant. Shortly after Marcinko's departure, it was their readiness that would be tested.

CHAPTER 4

THE ROGUE WARRIOR

IN LATE OCTOBER 1983, PRESIDENT RONALD REAGAN ORDERED US forces to invade the Caribbean island nation of Grenada, an action called Operation Urgent Fury. As part of his Cold War strategy, Reagan focused on the Communist-governed island as its relationship with Cuba and the Soviet Union grew. Unlike Carter, who had overseen a reduction in military spending, Reagan sought to reassert American military might to dissuade the Soviet Union from extending its reach in the Western Hemisphere. Fidel Castro had put Cuban military personnel on the island, and the Reagan administration feared that the Soviet Union would move to use the island as a refueling station for long-distance bombers. When the Marxist prime minister was overthrown by his deputy and subsequently executed, the United States grew concerned about the roughly seven hundred Americans on the island. Reagan authorized a seven-thousand-man force, the largest American military force assembled since Vietnam, to invade. The operation was the first test of the new Joint Special Operations Command, to whom Dam Neck belonged. Army, Navy, Air Force, as well as Special Operations Command elements were sent. But the invasion was as much about toppling the new, relatively unpopular coup and flexing military muscle after years of decline as it was a hostage rescue. Some in the military viewed the operation as nothing more than President Reagan trying to erase the memory of Carter's military failure at Desert One.

From the perspective of the military's newest elite command, Grenada was more of the same. On October 23, eight Team 6 operators, along with eight SEALs from Team 4, prepared to parachute with two boats during daylight into the sea, pick up a four-man Air Force Combat Control Team from a nearby destroyer, and insert them onto the island, where they would help guide Army Rangers once the invasion began. The SEALs' jump was delayed for several hours, moving it into the evening with zero moon illumination, and an unexpected rain squall formed in the drop zone. Despite the unfavorable change in circumstances, the SEALs jumped. The sea was rough, and there was no visibility. The pressure to do the mission despite the weather and time led to a jump that was too low. Twelve SEALs hit the water, released their parachutes, and found their boats. Four of the operators, all from Team 6, including Senior Chief Petty Officer Bob Schamberger, drowned, presumably unable to jettison their chutes and therefore sank. Neither their bodies nor their gear were ever recovered. "It was a hellish entry into the water," a former SEAL Team 6 operator who deployed on the Grenada operation said. "It wasn't one thing but many mistakes."[1]

Ultimately, the unit accomplished several of its missions, which included rescuing a Grenadian governor, seizing control of a radio tower, and calling in air strikes. But a series of tactical and intelligence failures tarnished the command's fledgling reputation as the Navy's most elite special operations unit. Their assault was neither sophisticated nor particularly smooth. One group of the SEALs had to direct air strikes by using a telephone calling card after the mission command changed radio frequencies without notifying Team 6 commanders. In both successful assaults, SEAL Team 6 underestimated the reaction forces, which led to what was supposed to be a four-hour mission lasting more than twenty-four hours.

In Washington, Marcinko was furious he missed his unit's maiden operation, and damned the poor planning that cost his men their lives. In Virginia Beach, SEAL Team 6 required all operators jumping into water to test their buoyancy with and without their weapons, known as a dip test, and changed the type of parachute they used. As with many tactical advancements in special operations, the lessons come from tragedies, not successes. "From 1980 to 1984," one SEAL on the mission said, "a lot of our rules were written in blood."

The drive Marcinko had shown in creating SEAL Team 6 was matched by his ability to survive bureaucratic battles within the Navy. His captain's mast should have been the end of his career; instead, Marcinko managed to extend his career and make even more enemies among the Navy brass. His final years in the military became an extreme example of what could happen to Team 6 if military brass and senior civilians did not maintain adequate supervision of a small band of talented criminals.

For two years, Marcinko slogged through various Pentagon bureaucratic jobs, protected by his sea daddy, Vice Adm. James "Ace" Lyons. As deputy chief of naval operations, Adm. Lyons was an influential figure in the Navy. He was able to help erase Marcinko's letter of reprimand on appeal.

With Marcinko out of trouble, Lyons gave him a new mission: to head up a second highly classified unit with even less oversight than SEAL Team 6. But lessons had been learned from Marcinko's tenure at SEAL Team 6. The admiral sought to mitigate the inevitable fallout of Marcinko's involvement in the mission by assigning a commanding officer to oversee him. Bill Hamilton, who held a commander rank, came on to lead the new unit with Marcinko as his deputy. If it was an effective demotion, it was also a resurrection.

Called Red Cell, or OP-06D in the Pentagon's language, the team would pose as terrorists and conduct staged attacks at naval installations in the United States, including ships and nuclear submarines. The idea was to demonstrate how unprepared the Navy was for terrorism at home.

The unit would be a single platoon or two squads, including Marcinko, and have no base or headquarters, which in effect meant very little oversight. All but one of the fourteen members came from the original SEAL Team 6 crew, the most committed of the Marcinko mafia.[2] Marcinko reported directly to Lyons, which made him, at least initially, untouchable.

Marcinko and team, posing as terrorists, would arrive at an installation, give the security officer a heads-up, and then disappear. When they showed up next, it was often inside a sensitive location with a fake explosive, or at the admiral's house, where they'd capture the flag officer, and sometimes his wife, throw them in a car, and retire to their base of operations. There, they'd inform the security officer they'd lost the game. There were ground rules: no real beatings, no torture, and nothing beyond the confines of the base other than the commanding officer's home, if that was a target.

Red Cell has been described as a defensive measure intended to demonstrate how unprepared the Navy was for a terrorist event. But Red Cell's security mission was also used by Marcinko to peddle the false notion that Red Cell was the next evolution of Team 6. It wasn't enough for the former enlisted operator turned officer to have salvaged his career and convinced a three-star admiral to let him create a new, highly classified unit. He needed to maintain a fantasy that he'd been allowed to resurrect his vision of a no-shit Tier 1 unit to win the next war. Marcinko didn't just leave that command embittered, he left thinking his original idea failed.

In his mind, SEAL Team 6 had grown too big, too fast during his time there. The result was that it was neither as nimble nor as clandestine as what he and Bill Hamilton envisioned as a Naval Special Warfare counterterrorism force. With over one hundred operators, SEAL Team 6 could deploy quickly and quietly by a conventional force's standards, but they were not covert. They still required military hardware and transport. Marcinko wanted an extremely nimble force of operators who looked like civilians with the ability to show up anywhere in the world clandestinely and kill a terrorist target—without direct support.

Some of Marcinko's issues with SEAL Team 6 were fair. It was a small, elite force, but within a joint operation it was still beholden to the lumbering, bureaucratic branches of the military. The Grenada operation validated the view that this hamstrung SEAL Team 6 from achieving Marcinko's concept of its potential: they were too beholden to conventional military planners who used Team 6 no differently than a conventional Marine reconnaissance unit. There was little about Operation Urgent Fury that called for special operations.

If Red Cell was to be Marcinko's success story and help rehabilitate his image, it failed. They managed to demonstrate serious security flaws at Navy installations and bases around the world, but the secrecy, elitism, and Marcinko's rogue ethos collapsed under its own unethical weight. Red Cell would eventually be shut down, a direct result of Marcinko's alcohol-fueled descent into excessive violence, boredom, lies, cover-ups, and corruption. In other words, Red Cell was the blueprint for elite SEAL operators who were left too much freedom, too much money, and too little supervision.

RONALD AND MARGARET SHERIDAN WOKE UP AT 3:00 IN THE MORNing to the phone ringing in their suburban Los Angeles home on March 20, 1986. It wasn't unusual for the Sheridans to get calls at that hour. Ronald was in charge of base security at the Seal Beach naval weapons facility thirty miles south in Orange County. The person calling told Sheridan there was a security issue that needed his attention. Sheridan usually left his house at 4:30 a.m., so he decided he'd head to work early that morning. Even though he was a civilian, Sheridan and his wife took their safety seriously. Margaret saw Ronald off to work every day with a loaded .45-caliber pistol in her hand, just in case a criminal decided to grab Ron on his way to the base. They'd never had an incident. But the Sheridans believed you could never be too prepared.[3]

As Ron left that morning, a fit and burly man with long hair and a mustache, and brandishing a pistol, jumped from behind a bush and confronted him. Ron noticed that red tape covered the pistol's nose. The intruder showed his Navy security badge and advised Sheridan that this was part of an ongoing security exercise at the weapons base. But from the front door, Margaret, who wasn't aware of the security exercise, saw only that an intruder was pointing a gun at her husband and walking toward their car. She called out and pointed her .45 at the intruder.

Ron quickly told his wife that this was a simulation and not real, and that she needed to put her gun down. Margaret hesitated, not convinced. The intruder looked like a "street thug," she later recalled, and the pistol looked real. Still, she lowered the weapon as Ron continued to assure her that he was safe and would leave with the man. She raised her pistol twice more, aiming at the intruder, before being convinced her husband was safe.

Sheridan and his "kidnapper" got into a car, where a second kidnapper was waiting, and the three drove off.

MARCINKO AND THE REST OF THE TEAM HAD BEEN IN ORANGE County for a week, pretending to be domestic terrorists and demonstrating the porous security at the facility. Seal Beach served as an inviting target for would-be terrorists: along the Pacific Ocean coastline, the facility stored highly explosive material as well as missile technology. Southern California's highway lattice and a dense residential area surrounded the weapons facility. An effective attack on the base posed a significant threat to Orange County residents, who paid little attention to their neighborhood weapons depot as they went about their daily lives.

In the week leading up to the mock kidnapping, Marcinko and the rest of Red Cell had exposed a prolific list of security flaws at the base and with Sheridan's operation at Seal Beach. Marcinko and his team had done that continually all over the world at every naval installation they tested. In one sense, Red Cell served a useful purpose: they revealed how lax the Navy's security was, how vulnerable to attack their bases, ships, and vessels could be to a determined enemy. Red Cell had even been able to sneak onto a nuclear submarine in New London, Connecticut, and plant a fake bomb in the control room.[4]

But in another sense, Marcinko and his rogue pirates—all but one of the fourteen were active-duty Navy SEALs—were playing a very unrealistic game. As operators, they were among the most skilled un-conventional warriors in the US military. Real terrorist groups, whether foreign or domestic, did not have their training and expertise, nor the resources to realistically conduct operations as sophisticated as the simu-lations Marcinko and his men devised. But in each location they surveyed, they found a distinctly SEAL perk to their job probing the security op-erations: humiliating the admirals and security chiefs responsible for any deficiencies. Marcinko called each exercise "CB," which stood for one of his favorite epithets, "cockbreath." Seal Beach was CB-10.

Sheridan was a unique quarry. He had pushed and prodded the Red Cell team during their week on-site. He'd mouthed off and pointed out the flaws in their operations, detailing how unlikely and unrealistic the simulations were. He'd also refused to provide them with an on-base op-erations center, which Marcinko and his crew viewed as spiteful.

The team instead worked from a local dive called Garf's. There Marcinko and the team plotted their next operation while drinking, day and night; this included how to terrorize Sheridan. The strict rules of engagement called for all operations to occur at the naval facility be-ing probed, and for the operators to only use force to simulate getting control of a target. Sheridan lived in Eagle Rock, a Los Angeles suburb north of Seal Beach. By the time the two operators—Frank Phillips and Arturo Farias—showed up at Sheridan's home, they had already gone too far.

Phillips had grabbed Sheridan—and narrowly averted being shot by the security chief's wife—while Farias had waited in the car. The plan was to head toward their hotel, but the Red Cell operators decided to divert and make the exercise more realistic. They passed a down-at-the-heels motor inn, the Don Quixote, and checked into a room. For most of the day, Sheridan and his Red Cell abductors sat in the room watching TV, awaiting instructions from Marcinko. During their exercises, Red Cell had a film crew on-site to document their various operations. Red Cell provided the tapes to the Navy and the security staff afterward to docu-ment what the SEALs did and help base security staff see where they were vulnerable.

Late in the afternoon, Sheridan had had enough of the charade and asked to be let go. The SEALs refused. They called Marcinko, who was drinking at the bar and told them to "tear him a new asshole." With the cameramen filming, Phillips and Farias, each wearing a balaclava, smashed into the hotel room and began striking Sheridan. They stripped his clothes off down to his underwear and socks, tied him to a chair, and fastened a pillowcase over his head. Sheridan, now terrified, protested. "You little pussy," one of the SEALs said to Sheridan. The SEALs hit and slapped Sheridan as they questioned him. Eventually, they removed Sheridan from the chair and slammed him onto the floor. Rather than slowing down after the initial assault, the interrogation became increasingly violent.

Phillips and Farias picked Sheridan up off the floor and dragged him into the bathroom. Then, lifting him by his feet, they held him upside down as they repeatedly submerged his head in the toilet. Each time they submerged his head, the SEALs flushed, effectively waterboarding him as the pillowcase gagged his mouth and nose. Next, they repeated the water torture by shoving his head into the water-filled bathtub. One of the SEALs slipped and fell onto Sheridan, who screamed that he now had a broken rib. Finally, the SEALs untied Sheridan and let him sit on the bed. The cameraman stopped filming. Under any definition but that of SEALs, what Phillips and Farias had inflicted on Sheridan was torture.

Sheridan returned home to Margaret thirty hours after the ordeal began. He was bruised and cut, with sprained ribs, and rattled. Margaret would later say that when she found him at home, seated on a living room chair, she was horrified by his condition.

Margaret regretted letting Frank Phillips take her husband, saying later, "I wish I had shot that guy."[5]

THE FALLOUT OVER SHERIDAN'S TREATMENT WAS SWIFT.

With the interrogation over, Red Cell returned to their hotel to review the Sheridan interrogation. The team knew the footage was bad. Marcinko joined them in a room as they watched. "Can we clean that up?"

Marcinko asked his men. Marcinko did not need to issue a direct order. The SEALs and the camera crew, who were all former SEALs, knew how to interpret Marcinko's words. In their culture, orders were sometimes given with just a glance or a facial expression. The next day, the video team edited the tape to remove the most violent images of what they'd done to Sheridan in the bathroom.

Sheridan, however, had immediately reported his treatment, accusing Red Cell of abusing and torturing him. The Navy opened an investigation. The Naval Investigative Service seized the interrogation's complete video recordings. With the advantage of having seen the unedited video, the Navy investigators next interviewed Marcinko. Although Red Cell had previously bound admirals and hog-tied commander's wives, the Sheridan interrogation had gone too far. The investigators asked Marcinko if anything unusual or out of the ordinary had occurred during the investigation or whether Sheridan was manhandled. Marcinko denied anything had gone wrong.

Capt. Bill Hamilton, Marcinko's Red Cell superior, later told *Soldier of Fortune* magazine that Marcinko's lie was the beginning of the end for the SEAL Team 6 founder's career. "When asked about the incident, he denied anything happened," Capt. Bill Hamilton told a journalist. "But NIS had seen the tapes and talked to some of the players, so the next thing you know, we had a federal case."[6]

Despite lying to investigators, a felony, Marcinko didn't face a court-martial. Marcinko still had juice inside the Pentagon for building SEAL Team 6. Instead, he was fired from Red Cell within a month of Seal Beach in April 1986 and sent to an admiral's mast, where he received another letter of reprimand. Even though he escaped a court-martial and, potentially, time in a brig, Marcinko's troubles continued.

A month after the Red Cell firing, the Navy opened a second investigation into Marcinko, focused on his time as commander of SEAL Team 6. The Navy received a report that Marcinko had gotten drunk and pulled a pistol while drinking on a military exchange trip to New Zealand when he commanded SEAL Team 6. A group of NIS investigators relocated to SEAL Team 6 headquarters at Dam Neck Annex to follow up on the report. One of the case agents, Ralph Blincoe, remembers the trepidation he felt when he first arrived at the base. "It was intimidating," Blincoe told me during an interview. "I was scared shitless. We were told going in, 'SEALs circle the wagons and don't rat each other out.'"[7]

That was true, up to a point. The NIS agents found that the only way to get the SEALs to implicate their own was by gaining leverage. When Blincoe discovered that several operators had taken AK-47s as war trophies from the Grenada mission three years earlier, the NIS agent got what he needed. The SEALs quietly pointed him toward a Marcinko acolyte named John Mason. Mason was a handsome man, six feet tall, two hundred pounds, clean-shaven, with straight sandy-brown hair he kept short. He had been one of the command's top snipers, an expert marksman who regularly competed in shooting contests. But everything that made Mason an ideal SEAL Team 6 operator—highly skilled, charming, and willing to break the rules—also made him a liability. Mason was a schemer. During one of the Navy's shooting competitions, Mason forged a judge's signature and gave himself a higher score. He was caught but not chastened. Mason would eventually confess to the NIS that while at SEAL Team 6, he'd stolen a new underwater breathing system from the command. "Mason had a track record of telling lies and deception," Blincoe said.

A pattern emerged over the course of the investigation. "Ninety to ninety-five percent of those guys were awesome," Blincoe said of the operators. "The mismanagement was pretty significant, aided by the fact that at that time there was no oversight, no audits." Blincoe and his team began poring over Mason's travel records. On temporary duty assignments to Washington, DC, Mason and other SEALs at the command, including Marcinko, filed reports saying they stayed at a hotel called the Mariner's Rest. They then charged the government for the lodging. But there was no such hotel. The SEALs bunked, for free, on a small yacht moored in the Potomac River, owned by Marcinko's friends. Mason, Marcinko, and others then billed the Navy for a night's stay at a fake hotel, pocketing the reimbursed funds. By the time NIS agents discovered the scheme, in 1986 and 1987, Mason had separated from the Navy. He'd been a Red Cell plank owner, a trusted member of Marcinko's inner circle, but the NIS now had what they needed to lean on Mason. Secretly, the NIS charged Mason with thirty-seven counts, including travel fraud and theft of government property. The NIS agents eventually offered Mason a suspended sentence in exchange for a guilty plea and his cooperation in their investigation of Marcinko. Marcinko's mafia experienced the same fate that would plague La Cosa Nostra: a rat within their ranks. Mason flipped and agreed to testify against his boss.

In 1987, the military formally changed SEAL Team 6's name, in part to move on from Dick Marcinko. It was renamed the Naval Special Warfare Development Group, but became known as just Development Group, or DEVGRU for short. The name reflected part of what the command did for the larger Naval Special Warfare community: experiment with, develop, test, and evaluate weapons and technology to be used by SEALs for operations. The command represented the cutting edge in military tactics and technology. It served as a proving ground for manufacturers who made military equipment. Because of the secrecy and urgency involved with the SEAL command, the procurement process was fast by necessity, with fewer layers of Defense Department bureaucracy to push through than other units. But the name change was also, in some ways, just a clerical adjustment. The unit would forever be known as SEAL Team 6, Team 6, or just Six. Technically, however, that name is classified by the US military and is never acknowledged. The Development Group, however, is unclassified. The nuance makes little sense even to those on the inside.

Of course, its role as the Navy's Development Group was precisely what made it so easy for Marcinko and his friends to exploit to their advantage. Part of Marcinko's acumen lay in his ability to skirt Navy rules to accomplish the command's primary mission. Marcinko's flair for finding ways around Navy rules and paperwork went a long way in setting SEAL Team 6 above and apart from the other SEAL and UDT commands. The setup enabled the incredible advances in military tactics and technology— and made the command susceptible to operators willing to steal government funds.

While Marcinko was still running Red Cell, he and Mason came up with a more lucrative fraud scheme. Mason had separated from the Navy and was now a civilian, but had not yet been cornered by NIS. Marcinko ordered 4,300 developmental grenades for Red Cell, using SEAL Team 6 as the "sponsor" for the contract, claiming that he had to hide his new secret unit. In theory, the grenades offered a new feature that would make them ideal for counterterrorism training. The manufacturer described them as capable of re-pinning, allowing an operator to reverse the pulling of the pin, which is used to trigger the grenade's explosion. The government accused Marcinko and Mason of conspiring with a weapons manufacturer to sell several thousands of the experimental grenade for $310,000. Prosecutors alleged that Marcinko, who was running Red Cell at the time, and Mason, who by then was out of the Navy, had padded more than $110,000 into the government contract, which the manufacturer would funnel to them. But the grenades shipped to Dam Neck were just regular fragment grenades and too numerous to be a sound contract for testing an experimental weapon. The NIS discovered that the entire deal served as nothing more than fraud: Marcinko used his position to force a contract through Team 6, which he no longer commanded, to buy substandard conventional hand grenades. The contractor made a significant profit—the grenades were basic and wildly overpriced—and in turn, paid nearly a third to Marcinko and Mason as a kickback. The contract also allowed a previously little-known weapons contractor access to Team 6, which bought and evaluated products at lightning speed compared to other commands. The NIS accused Marcinko and Mason of conspiring to take the $110,000 in the scheme. Prosecutors alleged that the two wanted the money to help establish a jointly run security business after Marcinko retired from the Navy. With Mason as their cooperating witness, federal prosecutors charged both Marcinko and the contractor with bribery and conspiracy in Virginia's Eastern District.

"Marcinko was dirty," said a second NIS agent who investigated him. "No doubt about it."[8]

A first trial ended with a hung jury after a lone juror held out against a guilty verdict. The government tried Marcinko again shortly after. Capt.

Bob Gormly, Marcinko's Team 6 successor, testified in both trials about how Marcinko had used his former command to purchase faulty weapons. The testimony ensured that details about the Navy's most secret unit and its creator were now exposed to the public for criminal misconduct. In late January 1990, Marcinko was found guilty on a single count of conspiracy. A judge sentenced Marcinko to twenty-one months, which he served at a minimum-security federal prison filled largely with drug abusers and white-collar criminals. Marcinko, a convicted felon, was now persona non grata, unable to enter through the Team 6 base gates. In the aftermath, Dam Neck would change its name and spend the rest of the next decade trying to shake off the taint of Marcinko's criminal past.

Gormly would later write of Marcinko's legacy: "Dick had once been a good naval officer. When he became a convicted felon, he shamed the uniform he'd worn for so many years. He discredited himself, the Navy, and SEAL Team Six in the process of trying to steal taxpayers' money. While Dick commanded Six, he created an aura of suspicion around the Team. The way he did business made many question his honesty. When his actions at [Red Cell] brought him under scrutiny again, his former association with Six brought the command under scrutiny, too. Six became known within the upper echelons of the Navy as 'the command under constant investigation'—Dick Marcinko's legacy."[9]

Marcinko never accepted that view. He remained adamant that he had been railroaded by the Navy because, as the Red Cell leader, he'd embarrassed and humiliated too many admirals during his security exercises. While there was some truth to Marcinko's view, much of his trouble was self-created. "It was his own community losing faith and confidence in him," Blincoe said. "They were tired of his bullshit."

But while Marcinko's reputation soured in the special operations community, he set about working to burnish his reputation with the general public. While in prison, he began writing, with a coauthor, an autobiography for the publisher Simon and Schuster. Marcinko focused much of the story on his fathering of SEAL Team 6. He hoped a successful tell-all would help him pay off his $250,000 legal debt from two trials and the conviction's restitution costs.

Rogue Warrior became an instant bestseller when it was published in 1992. The book introduced Marcinko to the public and provided the first public accounting of the Navy's elite, top-secret unit. The book perfectly captured his larger-than-life personality and his complete disdain for authority. The prose was appropriately profane, liberally salted with "fucks" and "cockbreaths," often doled out in his accounts of interactions with his fellow Navy officers, superiors, and peers alike. A media tour propelled Marcinko to celebrity status, with both a *60 Minutes* profile and an interview with CNN's Larry King. SEAL Team 6 was now a part of the American public consciousness. The book ultimately sold two million copies and made Marcinko a highly sought-after motivational speaker. It also served as the recruitment tool for an entire generation of SEALs, who would go on to fight the Forever Wars in Iraq and Afghanistan after 9/11.

A few months after *Rogue Warrior* was published, retired SEAL Capt. Larry Bailey received a call from a fellow SEAL. Bailey's friend asked him if he'd read Marcinko's book. Bailey and Marcinko had served at SEAL Team 2 together during the Vietnam War. Later, Bailey helped establish the Joint Special Operations Command when Marcinko first commanded SEAL Team 6. Bailey knew Marcinko well and thought highly of him as an officer, even if, like so many of Marcinko's peers, he didn't condone Marcinko's leadership style. Bailey's friend advised him to get *Rogue Warrior* immediately.

The book recounted an ambush Bailey had been in with Marcinko in 1967.

"He said you abandoned him."

ON THE CLEAR MOONLESS NIGHT OF MARCH 13, 1967, LT. LARRY Bailey steered a small, twin-outboard-engine boat up the Bassac River in the heart of Vietnam's Mekong Delta. That evening, Bailey's job was to insert SEAL Team 2's Bravo squad, led by then Ens. Marcinko, to a small island downriver from Vietnam's border with Laos. The islet, Dung Island, was on a well-known Vietcong smuggling route. Once evening curfew arrived, the area was considered a free-fire zone, meaning the SEALs had authority to shoot anyone they encountered. Bailey dropped Marcinko and his squad of five enlisted SEALs just off the riverbank and watched them skulk silently into a thick tangle of mangrove trees and reeds.

Marcinko's plan was simple and straightforward. He'd take his squad inland and set up an ambush on the Vietcong. In his account of the evening in *Rogue Warrior*, Marcinko wrote that he wanted to provide his men their first combat kills. "The killing was an important element," Marcinko explained. It was war, of course, but he had other reasons. "I wanted to make sure that each member of Bravo was up to the task." Marcinko and his crew snuck onto the island and got into an ambush position. They waited.

Bravo squad hid silently for about thirty minutes until they heard the creaking of a wood oar guiding a sampan toward the shore. The SEALs waited until the boat was twenty feet from their position, then Marcinko opened fire. Almost instantly, the rest of the squad followed suit, firing on what they could see were two unarmed men gliding across the Bassac River. Their gunfire was so ferocious in Marcinko's account that it effectively shredded the suspected Vietcong couriers. The SEALs quickly jumped onto the boat as it began sinking to recover the bodies and grab any intelligence they may have been carrying. As they pulled the bodies out of the boat, Marcinko wrote, gunfire rained down on them. Marcinko and his men crawled back to their ambush position, pinned down, while Marcinko tried to reach Bailey and others on the radio for help. "We took fire for maybe eight to ten minutes—an eternity—while I called and called for the [boat]," Marcinko wrote. When one of the SEAL boats finally arrived to extract the men, Bravo squad had to evacuate while under fire. "We moved down the bank, shouting for covering fire as we slithered, ducked, and rolled our way through the jungle underbrush, as VC bullets sliced the leaves just over our heads or dug divots too close for comfort as we scrambled toward the STAB [SEAL Tactical Assault Boat]."

Once Marcinko and his men were safely aboard and farther downriver, he confronted Bailey for abandoning Bravo squad, putting him and his men in danger. "I was furious," Marcinko wrote. "I wanted to kill somebody." He approached Bailey, who outranked him by two ranks, shoving him, swearing at him, and accusing him of deserting his team. "'I pleaded for covering fire,'" Marcinko quotes himself saying to Bailey, "'and you were so goddamn far upriver you were out of goddamn radio range. Is that bad enough for you, you pussy.'"

Marcinko's story in *Rogue Warrior* was unambiguous. Marcinko painted himself as the righteous hero: loyal to his enlisted men and aggressive in his operations, to the point of being insubordinate to any officer, lieutenant and admiral alike, who he believed had failed his men. Marcinko added that for legal reasons, he had asked Bailey before publication whether he remembered that evening.

But much of Marcinko's account was false, according to Bailey and at least one of Marcinko's Bravo squad teammates on the ambush.

According to Bailey, after he dropped off Bravo squad, he motored his boat downriver a few miles and tied up with a second SEAL vessel. Bailey's small team served as a backup and rescue force if Marcinko and his team ran into trouble. An hour into the wait, Bravo squad had been radio silent. Then the sky above Dung Island lit up with tracer rounds. Bailey and his small team could see the rounds were not incoming. The tracers were American, a sign the firefight was one-sided. After things quieted down, Bailey tried to reach Bravo on the radio but heard nothing. "I keep waiting for Marcinko to come up on the radio to ask for extraction, and we don't hear it."[10]

Eventually, Bailey untied his boat and headed back to Dung Island. The radio silence concerned him even if there had been no apparent enemy fire. Bailey's boat got to about three hundred yards from Marcinko's ambush position. Again, Bailey made several radio calls, with no answer. Finally, Bailey and one of his men jumped off their boat and waded ashore to pull Bravo squad out. As they crept inland, "I could hear some guys laughing," Bailey said. The laughing was unmistakably American, he recalled. "I could hear Marcinko hollerin'. They had lost all degree of military discipline in a supposedly hairy area." When Bailey reached the squad, they asked him what he was doing there. Bailey explained that he'd radioed for more than an hour with no response, so he'd come to pull them out. Bailey, Marcinko, and the rest of Bravo squad loaded up on Bailey's boat, and they made their way back to their base. "There was no problem going back."

Later, when they got back to their base, Bailey asked the radioman, Joe Camp, why he hadn't answered the radio calls. Camp told Bailey he'd turned the radio off when they got into their ambush position to maintain silence. Then he'd forgotten to turn it back on. "They hadn't come under any contact at all," Bailey remembered. "I asked Joe, 'Who'd you make a hit on?' He said, 'A couple of fishermen. We have our first war souvenirs.' He pulled out a Ziploc-like bag which had a couple of Vietnamese government ID cards and a wristwatch."

Dung Island was a free-fire zone. The rules of engagement at the time authorized Marcinko and his team to shoot anyone in the area after the nighttime curfew. The two dead Vietnamese men may have been unarmed Vietcong or sympathizers, but Marcinko's men found no evidence.

Bailey didn't think about that 1967 evening until he read *Rogue Warrior* twenty-five years later. He couldn't understand why Marcinko would fabricate a story. "Marcinko's version was absolutely false. We never had any difficulty [between us] at all until he wrote the book." Bailey began contacting Marcinko's men from Bravo squad. Each man that he spoke to confirmed that Marcinko's version in *Rogue Warrior* was false. Bailey shared his concerns with the publisher of *Soldier of Fortune* magazine, Robert Brown, a friend of Bailey's. Brown asked a young Washington, DC, lawyer, Abbe Lowell, to represent Bailey in a potential libel suit against Marcinko and Simon and Schuster.

A few weeks later, Bailey demanded a retraction from Simon and Schuster. Bailey had obtained Marcinko's after-action report from that evening—having been tipped off by one of Marcinko's men from Bravo squad—which, while light in details, contradicted parts of Marcinko's story. The publisher agreed to change the text in the paperback editions. Yet, it wasn't the retraction that Bailey sought. Marcinko's account of a withering firefight on the island went unaltered, but he changed Larry Bailey to a fictitious officer and otherwise kept the account the same. What had started as an inaccurate and embellished account of an actual event became a fiction loosely sketched from real life.

Eventually, Robert Brown took an interest in Marcinko's inaccurate portrayal of the events in *Rogue Warrior*. Brown assigned Dale Andrade, a respected military historian, to do a story. The resulting article, "Pogue Warrior," supported Bailey's accusations, confirmed by a member of Marcinko's squad.[11] The article also found another instance from Marcinko's book in which he grossly mischaracterized what was supposed to be a seminal event in his military career—losing his first SEAL in battle—and appeared to outright fabricate a scene in Vietnam.

While "Pogue Warrior" became well-known inside the SEAL Team 6 community, Marcinko's commercial success did not suffer. He followed *Rogue Warrior* with a sixteen-book fictional series and established the SEAL Team 6 brand. Marcinko had been many things in his career: a hero in combat, a felon and fabulist, and, ultimately, a celebrity. While he should have served as a cautionary tale for the generations of SEALs to follow, too many saw in Marcinko something else: a model to aspire to.

CHAPTER 5

THE ETHICAL WARRIOR

Spring 1991—Trappe, Maryland

Duane Dieter stood at ease with his arms to his sides, taking stock of his opponent. Across from Dieter was a six-foot-five-inch enlisted Navy SEAL operator, stretching his muscular arms and thick legs and hopping up and down on his toes. The SEAL not only towered over Dieter by six inches, but he outweighed Dieter by at least fifty pounds, built as he was like a stone wall.

"You better get ready," the SEAL said. "I'm the best fighter at SEAL Team 6."

"I'm OK," Dieter said. "I'm ready."

Two other SEALs stood off to the side watching.

The SEALs were in Dieter's training facility to watch what promised to be a scary and protracted brawl between their toughest teammate, Fran Rodgers, and Dieter, a civilian who was quickly becoming SEAL Team 6's favorite training guru. Dieter's training program with SEAL Team 6 was limited to a small number of operators but popular at the

77

command. He trained the SEALs in everything from how to defend themselves in a hand-to-hand fight to how to sweep a room with their weapon at the ready. In the closed and secret world of SEAL Team 6, Dieter was the rare civilian who understood how operators and assaulters needed to physically move through a hostile environment with the best possible chance for success. Most importantly, Dieter's training regimen incorporated a method of fighting and self-defense that taught the SEALs how to control and channel their aggression so it never became needlessly violent. Dieter's system became so popular that the SEALs eventually pushed for Green Team, the command's training unit, to incorporate Dieter's technique to ensure that each new member of SEAL Team 6 learned it.

When Rodgers heard about the proposal, he demanded that he test Dieter's skill. Rodgers held black belts in several martial arts and was considered the command's hand-to-hand fighter. He was widely acknowledged as the toughest member of SEAL Team 6. His teammates called him Dr. Jekyll and Mr. Hyde, a reference to his violent mood swings. When Rodgers went "dark," most of his peers were afraid of him. In the all-alpha-male community, Rodgers was at the top.

Inside Dieter's training facility, Rodgers got into a fighting stance. Dieter lifted his hands from his sides and put them up, palms outward, in front of his own face. Rodgers pounced, stepping toward Dieter while lifting his foot off the mat to begin a roundhouse kick. But before he could move more than a few inches, Dieter extended his right arm upward toward Rodgers, striking Rodgers's forehead with the palm of his open hand. Rodgers dropped instantly to the floor and lay motionless.

"You killed him!" yelled one of Rodgers's teammates.

Dieter dropped down next to Rodgers and confirmed he was still breathing. Rodgers's two teammates crowded over them.

"He's not dead," Dieter said.

Dieter massaged the SEAL's shoulders and spoke to him, and after less than a minute, Rodgers's eyes opened and he regained consciousness.

"I'm ready to listen," Rodgers said.

EACH SEAL STEPS INTO A FOUR-BY-FIVE-FOOT AREA MARKED BY duct tape in an empty room. A hood lowers from the ceiling by a pulley until the SEAL sees nothing but total darkness. A white noise rattles over a speaker, so he can hear nothing. He waits. He doesn't know for how long, and he doesn't know what he will face when the hood is lifted. All of his senses are heightened. His stress increases as the light deprivation mixed with a sensory overload combines with the anticipation of the drill. A video camera in one corner films the exercise and instructors stand above the room on a catwalk to observe.

When the hood lifts, the SEAL sees several people, some right in front of him, others in the back of the room, and perhaps others behind him. He has to determine, almost instantly, who is a threat, who is not, shoot who is, subdue who is not, and save a hostage. If there is a person who is a threat but is unarmed, he cannot shoot. He can physically strike someone only if they are attacking or refusing to get down on the ground. He has to do this in a matter of seconds, and never leave the taped area of the floor.

"The hooded box test is meant to overwhelm. It is meant to force you to make very difficult decisions, right or wrong, good or bad, life or death, all in seconds," one SEAL Team 6 operator wrote. "It wasn't until... the hooded box test, that I started to really think about how to manage stress. I learned there that the key was to first prioritize all the individual stressors and then act....Through constant practice, repetition, experience, most SEALs can prioritize stressors fast enough that it feels more like an instinct than a process."[1]

At its most basic, the hood drill, as it came to be called, is Dieter's foundational training exercise. The drill, along with another, unarmed defensive drill—which includes an open-handed strike to the head, the same move Dieter used to render Fran Rodgers unconscious—served as the starting point for Dieter's training system in Green Team. The drill helps force the SEAL into instant reaction, shutting off the conscious mind and, with practice, instinctively reacting.

The exercises are intentionally disorienting, and few SEALs, if any, can successfully complete their first drill. Even twenty years after going through a week's training, former operators can recall both the required stance and the sensation of going "under the hood."

The first time he did the drill, one operator wrote, "every second under the hood felt like a year."

"The darkness heightened your senses and tried to make you aware of your immediate surroundings," a retired SEAL Team 6 officer told me in an interview. "As the hood is lifted, your senses explode on the situation you're in. It triggered your subconscious mind to see everything at a much faster pace than your conscious mind and you're able to respond or react faster. I thought what he taught was the best thing we learned."[2]

DUANE DIETER HAD GROWN UP IN EASTERN MARYLAND'S RURAL lowlands, between the Chesapeake Bay and the Delaware state line. The son of a Wesleyan Methodist pastor, Dieter woke up on Sundays at 4:00 a.m. to join his father, who traveled across rural Maryland, ministering at a different church each week. The Dieter parents held three immutable rules they and their children adhered to: no drinking, no smoking, and no swearing. Dieter was the middle child of three, a caring and sweet kid but curious and rambunctious. During Sunday services or other church gatherings, Dieter would often wander out of the small church to explore the local woods or riverbanks along the small rivers that led out to the bay. Dieter's childhood was the picture-perfect rural American idyll, with hunting, fishing, and sports.

When he was nine years old, Dieter and his friend Dennis crept out just after the choir finished and the evangelist took his place on the podium. The two boys were headed across a field away from the tabernacle when they heard a girl screaming for help from a nearby tent. Dieter and Dennis pulled back the tent flap and saw a teenage girl being held by three teenage boys, all brothers from a local family. A fourth young man stood off to the side, directing the brothers. One of the boys holding the girl's arms covered her mouth with his hand to quiet her. She bit him. "Shut her the fuck up," one of the others said, while another boy grabbed a handful of dirt from the ground and shoved it into the girl's mouth.

Dieter watched as the girl gagged, a plume of dirt shooting out of her mouth toward the top of the tent. He looked down, grabbed a fist-sized rock, and threw it at the brother who had gagged the girl. The rock hit the teenager on the side of the head. The brothers released the girl and chased Dieter and Dennis back to the tabernacle. Inside the main tent, the two boys stopped the sermon, screaming that a girl was being hurt outside. Eventually the adults rushed to the tent, where they found the girl shaken but not hurt. The three brothers and their partner had fled in a car and were later reported to the Denton police. They were eventually charged with assault. The church elders praised Dieter and his friend as heroes who had saved the girl's life. The events of that day in 1967 would ultimately lead him to work for the US government, Dieter would later recall. "I just had a total sense that I needed to protect that girl from those boys," Dieter said.

By the time Dieter was in high school, he was a devout martial arts student, learning multiple disciplines at once. He became known in Denton as a kid who would stand up for other kids being picked on by bullies. He wasn't an enforcer, but the tougher kids in the area knew not to push Dieter into a fight. While still in high school, Dieter's martial arts mentor took his student into town bars, where, after a few beers, Dieter would test his skills by getting into fights with drunk patrons. There was only one rule: Dieter was not allowed to attack first. If a patron bullied another drinker or harassed a barmaid, Dieter would step in but always waited until his adversary struck first.

Dieter ended up with nine different black belts and started his own martial arts business to help get himself through college. And despite his fighting skills, he came across to others as earnest, sincere, and friendly.

But a chance encounter would forever change his view of martial arts—and the real skills one would need in combat. One day, Dieter stood on a street corner in Washington, DC's Chinatown, waiting for the light to change. He was headed to a bookstore that carried Chinese-language martial arts books and manuals. He sensed another man on his right, also waiting for the light to change. Dieter turned his head just in time to glimpse the man throwing a punch toward Dieter's head. Dieter bobbed his head back, and his attacker's fist just missed his face. Dieter threw the man into the intersection, slamming him onto the street. His attacker gave up and ran away. Dieter pulled himself together and made it to the bookstore, where he took stock of what had just occurred. "I was upset, my hands were shaking, and my face was all flushed," Dieter remembered. "I'd never felt the stress before that. I'd never felt the adrenaline and endorphins kick in. I had all these black belts and I didn't use any of it. None of the fighting I did prepared me for what happened that day." Dieter had an epiphany: martial arts had no real-world application. There was no magic system that could make you invincible. He'd walked away from that street corner without a scratch simply because he got lucky.

The experience pushed Dieter to turn his attention to developing a fighting system that responded to real-world situations. Martial arts were choreographed, Dieter concluded. They had no application to defending yourself from a random assault on a Washington, DC, street corner and no use on a battlefield. The key to training and defending oneself was managing stress, Dieter thought, and channeling the powerful biochemical cocktail that came from the adrenaline and endorphins when confronted with a fight-or-flight scenario.

In 1981, Dieter created a small company to train civilians and local law enforcement in defensive fighting and handling the stress of a physical altercation. After years of experimenting in his home basement and a small office building in Trappe, Dieter developed his own training system, which became popular on the Eastern Shore of Maryland. After going through Dieter's training, law enforcement officials deputized Dieter to help conduct warrant raids and arrests. Later, Dieter's reputation and methodology gained the attention of the Drug Enforcement Agency, which recruited Dieter to serve on a task force focused on drug smuggling in Maryland's Eastern Shore region.

Then, in 1989, Dieter received a call at his office in Trappe. The caller did not identify himself, saying only that he was in the Navy, in a "special team," and that they'd heard about his training. The caller said he and a few colleagues wanted to meet Dieter and tour his training facility. Dieter agreed to meet, despite being unsure that the call was legitimate. A few days later, Dieter stood on the Easton airport apron and watched as an unmarked helicopter descended onto the tarmac. Not yet convinced his visitor wasn't a revenge-seeking drug dealer, Dieter quickly took a disposable camera from his pocket and snapped several photos of the white-red-and-yellow helicopter as it landed.

As it turned out, the man on the helicopter was named Clay Sherman, a boat crew leader from Red Team. At Dieter's office, Sherman and another SEAL pulled out a small stack of nondisclosure forms for Dieter to sign. They told Dieter they were from Naval Special Warfare Development Group, a secret Navy unit, and that colleagues in the DEA raved about Dieter's training while he was on their task force. If Dieter signed the secrecy papers and submitted to the security clearance process, they wanted him to teach them his tactical and defensive system. Dieter signed the papers and agreed to train Red Team.

Dieter had never heard of the Development Group, but Sherman also mentioned he was a Navy SEAL. Dieter only knew one SEAL, his college buddy Jim Kelz. They'd met during a game of water polo at Chesapeake College, near Dieter's Eastern Shore hometown. Kelz was new, from Philly's rough north side, and carried what he described as a "chip" on his broad, defensive lineman shoulders in his new environment. Kelz wanted to show his dominance by roughing up another player, one of Dieter's friends. Instead, Dieter realized what was going on and quickly subdued Kelz, who relented.

Kelz recognized that Dieter had had an opportunity to hurt him but didn't take it. He used only the force necessary to free his friend and communicate to Kelz that there would be no more bullying. After the match, Kelz and the others headed to the locker rooms to change. When Dieter went over to Kelz to talk to him, Kelz tried to attack him. Dieter quickly wrapped Kelz up and pinned him down against the bench. Then, once more, he let him go, allowing Kelz to stand up. "We can fight if you want," Dieter said. "Or you can stop bullying my guys and we can be friends." Dieter stuck his hand out. Kelz relaxed and shook Dieter's hand. They became good friends.

After college, Kelz joined the Navy. When Kelz was stationed on the East Coast, he'd visit Dieter on his breaks and hang out with his friend.

Sometimes they trained informally in Dieter's basement, though Kelz never took one of Dieter's courses. Kelz told Dieter little about what he did in the Navy, and Dieter never asked. Kelz eventually made it to SEAL Team 6, where he joined Red Team as an assaulter. Despite never going through Dieter's operational program, Kelz respected Dieter's fighting skills and admired Dieter's ethics. He always remembered his first experience in the college pool. In the team room at Dam Neck, Kelz recommended that they go see his friend Duane, but his teammates never took the recommendation seriously. Then one day, Clay Sherman announced that they were going to be doing new combat training with a guy out in Maryland named Dieter. "That's the guy I told you about!" Kelz said.

FROM 1991, DIETER'S PRESENCE AT THE COMMAND INCREASED. He was given a small office inside the Dam Neck base, and a secure telephone at his Maryland office so he could discuss classified subjects with the command when he wasn't there. In becoming part of Green Team's required training, Dieter's methodology in close-quarters combat—which Dieter called Close Quarters Defense, or CQD—became a core competency for each operator who graduated.

Dieter was a civilian with no connections to the military who had been given access to one of America's most secretive military units and allowed to witness their tribal codes. This made him unique. He forged bonds with operators, though he never went through BUD/S or served in a SEAL platoon. Dieter knew little about the secret means the command might have to develop a target and was never privy to the latest gossip in the halls of the Pentagon about special operations, but he knew, intimately, each operator's tics. Command psychologists turned to him for tips and insights into specific operators or general observations about their ability to train under stress. In time, Dieter became a confidant to dozens of men at the command. A group of operators formed at the command who argued that Dieter's training was the best combat and tactical training they'd received in the Teams. They were called Dieter-ites, and a small fissure developed at the command between his supporters and those who championed martial arts. Even so, Dieter loved training the military's most elite.

"It was great. Ninety to ninety-five percent of the guys at the command were fantastic men," Dieter said. "But there was also a few knuckleheads who were bad."

In 1989, Dieter was approached by two operators with an offer: they asked whether he wanted to put his unarmed CQD training on VHS for commercial sale. It was the first offer of its kind, Dieter said. When he declined, Dieter recalled, the SEALs responded with a veiled threat: "Do you want to train the guys or not?" Though indirectly, the two SEALs made it clear that if Dieter was not willing to expand his training into a business opportunity in the civilian world, they would shut his training down. Dieter refused and took his chances. As an outsider, and the new guy, he didn't complain. He quietly asked Sherman if the two operators were going to be a problem. "They don't represent the command," Sherman told Dieter.

Dieter forgot about it until two years later, in 1991, a few months after he began training Green Team. One of the command's top leaders invited Dieter for a conversation in his office. There, the veteran SEAL asked Dieter to let the command film his training program. Why? Dieter asked. The SEAL Team 6 leader said he wanted to have an internal video of Dieter's training techniques. He stood up from behind his desk and walked Dieter down the hall to another room. He had set up a training room, with a camera up high in the corner, able to record the entire space. It would take no more than an hour, the master chief said. Dieter declined, telling him that he'd provide as many refresher drills—for free—as anyone at the command needed, but he wouldn't be filmed. What if the videos leak? Dieter asked. He explained that his program works best when an adversary doesn't have access to the training. He reasoned that letting the bad guys, as he said, have an opportunity to learn his skills would risk the SEALs' effectiveness. The master chief tried to assure Dieter that the videos would remain secure, but Dieter had already seen videos of his Dam Neck predecessor available for sale off-base. Dieter knew that once his program was on tape, he would lose control over who had access. By now the master chief was getting angry. "He said to me, 'Do you want to train the guys or not?' I'll never forget it because I'd heard it before."

Dieter refused. A few days later, Dieter learned that his contract for Green Team had been "suspended" and that his course would no longer be part of the curriculum. The command offered no explanation. He continued training individual boat crews, as he had before Fran Rodgers tested him, but became certain that the command had an ethics problem. If the senior enlisted leader can blackball me because I don't agree to let them brand me, Dieter thought, they have some problems here. The senior SEAL Team 6 leader retired less than a year later. Shortly after, the Green Team training supervisor informed Dieter that his training would be added back into the course list.

Dieter's drills did more than train an operator on the elemental decision of whether to shoot a target or refrain from shooting, the command's core tradecraft. The training also introduced an ethics in how a SEAL conducted himself in each scenario he drilled. And over time, an operator's performance in both armed and unarmed training, Dieter believed, revealed something about his character. The challenge for operators is that they must be capable of both applying deadly force in a split second and lowering their aggression to adjust to the threat level. This is what separated a Dam Neck operator from a regular SEAL—the ability to navigate instinctively between these extremes. If he's too aggressive, an operator can get himself or a teammate killed, but not showing aggression carries the same risk. Dieter called this the ability to "dial up or dial down"; it was foundational to the technique his system taught. It wasn't enough to simply know whom to shoot and whom not to shoot; SEAL tradecraft required an operator to know when to modify the level of violence used in a situation. These kinds of training exercises, which focused on this tradecraft, also inevitably provided Dieter, and any other instructor, a window into the operator's character. During some shooting drills, an operator might place his foot on the chest of a person who served as the threat in the training scenario. There was no operational need to do so, but Dieter noted that it served as an act of dominance by the operator. "I'd step in and explain why it was not only unnecessary but sent the wrong message. It was like a dog standing on top of his kill after a hunt." In prisoner training, operators would work on how to maneuver to grab their target, disable him, and detain him for transfer. Occasionally, a SEAL would strike the "detainee" after securing the prisoner, even though he no longer posed a threat. Dieter would quickly have the operator step off and counsel them on why they shouldn't.

"I give a lot of credit to Duane Dieter for his pioneering work on the marriage of physical and professional skill sets with the moral and ethical continuum of a complete warrior," wrote retired SEAL Dick Couch in a book about military ethics. "The physical and professional skills in themselves are valuable. The moral and ethical skills are essential."[3]

Dieter's training was based on small, specific physical movements, but it also taught operators how to process and handle stress. The training accepted the reality of the job: SEALs would kill other people, but just because you can kill someone in the confrontation doesn't mean you should. The ethics built into the training were directly connected to the ethics of the man who developed the system. What's more, the training matched SEAL Team 6's purpose: to carry out a mission quickly and efficiently and get out.

But every few years, Dieter would be reminded that a small but persistent group at the command failed to observe the connection.

One day in 1993, Dieter realized he'd entered an ethically compromised environment at the command. He'd been invited to the Virginia Beach house of a young officer, Lt. Cdr. Timothy Szymanski, a Blue Team element leader. Szymanski was handsome, with dirty-blond hair and a prominent nose. He'd been a star wrestler in high school and had the hulking posture of a man at ease grappling. Szymanski attended the Naval Academy, and although he nearly flunked out, he graduated in 1985. He graduated BUD/S in 1989 and spent the first two years in the Teams at SEAL Delivery Vehicle Team Two (SDVT-2), the East Coast unit dedicated to boats and mini-subs. He screened for Dam Neck and arrived in 1992. Szymanski had just finished a CQD training evolution at Dam Neck when he invited Dieter for dinner, telling the instructor that the command was too chaotic a place to have a meaningful conversation there.

When Dieter arrived at the home, Szymanski gave him a brief tour of his quaint two-floor clapboard house and his backyard, which ran up against the fairway of the local golf club. Dieter sat down to dinner with Szymanski and his wife and their children. After dinner, Szymanski brought Dieter into his living room, where the two sat alone. Szymanski praised CQD and told Dieter that he wanted his men in Blue Team to get more training and have them advance further along in the system. As Dieter recalls, Szymanski spent a few minutes complimenting CQD, telling him he was the "real SEAL trainer" and that he wanted Dieter to provide more written material for the assaulters so they could learn even when they were not in a training session. Dieter thought it odd, since he didn't provide that kind of material. When he declined, Dieter recalled, Szymanski responded by asking, "Do you want to train the guys or not?"

"I remember my heart going down to my foot, because I'd heard the question two times already."

This was the third time he'd been asked the question, word for word.

According to Dieter, Szymanski told him the two could go into business together. "He said he was on the fast track and that he was going to make admiral," Dieter recalled years later. Dieter told the lieutenant commander that he loved training SEAL Team 6, but they couldn't do business together. He was a civilian and Szymanski was an officer in the military; it would be inappropriate.

"I'm a golden boy," Szymanski replied. "Do you want to train the guys or not?"

He told Dieter that his idea was to make a video of the training to sell to civilians.

Dieter recalled Szymanski telling him that he could even use the cherished Trident image in the proposed commercial enterprise. With the SEAL brand, he continued, the two could franchise Dieter training schools across the country.

Dieter asked if Szymanski was explicitly asking that they sell Dieter's CQD training, which was, up to that point, only for SEAL Team 6. Szymanski told Dieter no, that he could sell the previous martial arts system he practiced before developing CQD. Dieter pushed back, telling the lieutenant commander that he wouldn't sell a product that he knew wasn't effective, and he wouldn't sell the real training if he couldn't vet each person who received the training. It was both unethical and unwise.

"It's not the product, Duane, it's the brand," Szymanski replied.

Dieter left Szymanski's house shaken.

"It was a big blow," Dieter remembered. "In order to get to SEAL Team 6 I thought they had to be the best of the best of the best and be vetted at a high level to get there."

Dieter had witnessed corruption within the local sheriff's department where he'd been put on a task force, but in many ways, Dieter's rural and religious background had made him naive. His experimental training was validated by SEAL Team 6 when he got to the command in 1989, and he assumed that its ethical guidance was a clear and recognized characteristic of the training. Szymanski's approach upended Dieter's view.

Dieter told his wife and a few operators he trusted of Szymanski's offer, but he didn't report it any further.[4] In the years after the incident, Dieter made it a personal policy to decline any invitation to visit any SEAL Team 6 home unless it was part of a group event. It wasn't just that Dieter didn't want to be put on the spot again, but if it did happen, he wanted witnesses.

CDR. ERIC T. OLSON WAS DRIVING HIS WHITE TOYOTA CAMRY SOUTH to Virginia Beach on Route 301 on Maryland's Eastern Shore one day in 1994 when he spotted a sign for Dieter's Academy near Easton. Olson had served twenty years as a SEAL officer but was new to Dam Neck as he took over as SEAL Team 6's newest commanding officer. He'd seen some of Dieter's training at the command, but he was also wary by nature and he liked to look things over for himself. And Olson was a decorated combat veteran when he joined the team.

Olson decided to take a detour and make an unannounced visit to Dieter's facility. Dieter was a civilian contractor whom he'd only recently met a few times at the base. A few months earlier, when Olson renewed Dieter's contract with the command, he made a request of Dieter and now he wanted to test Dieter's commitment. Olson made Dieter's contract conditional. He told Dieter he couldn't use SEAL Team 6 or the Navy SEALs to advertise his business. "I don't ever want to open up a magazine and see 'Duane Dieter: The Guy Who Teaches the Navy SEALs!'" Olson told Dieter.

Olson pulled into the parking lot in Trappe and entered the building. He announced himself to the staff but was told that Dieter wasn't in. Olson asked for a tour of the facility, looking to see evidence that some of the US military's most valuable assets conducted secret training in the building. But as Olson went through the building, there was nothing much to see.

"True to his word, there was no sign, no photograph, no indication of any kind that he'd ever done SEAL training," Olson said. Dieter's employees unlocked a heavily fortified unmarked door and let Olson take a peek. Only inside the secure room did the Team 6 commanding officer see any evidence, in the form of equipment, that would connect Dieter in any way to the Navy's top-secret unit. Olson was impressed. "It verified for me that Duane was telling me the truth," Olson recalled.

Olson soon became Dieter's biggest proponent in the SEAL community. "I've been exposed to a number of hand-to-hand combat techniques," said Olson. "But there was nothing there that was consistent across the force. All of them were taught by contracted instructors who specialized in a single style of martial arts." Olson found in Dieter combat training that was realistic, he said in an interview. "A lot of martial arts training is sort of move/counter-move, a series of trained responses to your opponent's series of trained actions. Dieter made it much more real than that."

In the never-ending search for the latest training or skills, SEALs sought out the best instruction for everything from mountain climbing to skydiving. Martial arts and combat fighting were just other skills SEALs would sharpen in their off-hours. But martial arts provided a different level of commercial opportunity for a motivated operator. Previous contractors had built a side market of branding their businesses with the Trident and using their connection to Naval Special Warfare to sell their products.

One former SEAL, Christopher Caracci, left the Navy and began selling videos described as a SEAL workout and BUD/S training program. What Caracci didn't advertise was that he left the Navy shortly after failing Dam Neck's Green Team.

In 1995, for example, Frank Cucci, an ex–Blue Team assaulter, appeared on the cover of a martial arts magazine wearing a wetsuit and Navy fatigues, with a small rifle hanging from his neck. Cucci and several other Blue Team operators appeared on a combat fighting video produced by Dieter's predecessor at Dam Neck. Here were SEALs in one of the military's most elite—and classified—units offering the public a glimpse into the fighting skills they claimed made them the most lethal operators in the world. Cucci left Dam Neck and separated from the Navy shortly after the command learned that he appeared in the video. Once out, Cucci started a martial arts academy in Virginia Beach, highlighting his time in the SEALs. Cucci arranged a fight billed as SEAL Team 6 versus Delta Force, featuring active-duty operators from each unit. Lt. Cdr. Tim Szymanski, one of Cucci's friends, was set to fight an enlisted Delta operator named Dale Comstock. The fight was part of a fighting-style tournament Cucci arranged in Virginia Beach. The sibling rivalry between the Army's and Navy's premier special operations units was a clever selling point for the bout, a rivalry that exists to this day. Besides the unethical nature of a paid fight between two active-duty servicemen, the promotions explicitly highlighted their military affiliations, which was the commercial appeal for a casual fighting fan. After Dam Neck senior officers learned of the planned fight, they prevented Szymanski from participating and admonished him for poor judgment. Szymanski had revealed an inclination to use Team 6 and promote the Navy SEAL brand.

Olson saw Dieter as an antidote to this new phenomenon. "The guys couldn't train with CQD and then go win a trophy on the weekend, the way there is with some of these other forms of martial arts," Olson said. "I just thought it was pure and clean, that it was an operational methodology without a recreational or a sports connotation to it and I liked that professional mindset of that the only reason people were getting it was because it was operationally valued but it had no collateral benefit."

Eventually, Olson made Dieter's system the unofficial unarmed training for Team 6. The training also helped vet operators. Olson sought
insights about his SEALs' performance during CQD from Dieter, one
measure of their overall performance at the command. Olson's outreach
came just as the command psychologists' did. At one point Capt. Olson
remarked, "The guys who give Duane trouble are the same guys that give
the command trouble."[5] The culture of the Teams rewarded performance,
but Dieter's training tied performance to a new element: ethics and mo-
rality. Tactical success, in his view, involved more than dominating the
enemy. It meant doing the right thing in the right moment, just as Dieter
had done when as a child he confronted the teen boys assaulting that teen
girl. Dam Neck was filled with SEALs who shared Dieter's ethic, but his
was one of the only forms of training where they could encounter it. Olson's support of Dieter and CQD cemented the civilian as an official part
of Team 6's skills base.

"I think he is an honorable man," Olson said.

AFTER GRENADA, TEAM 6 CONDUCTED MISSIONS, MOSTLY AS PART
of the combined Joint Special Operations Command. SEAL operators
deployed twice to Panama, including during Operation Just Cause, to locate Manuel Noriega in 1989 and 1990. That mission was among the first
times each of the various service special operations units worked jointly
as the main element of military action, and was among the first times
the military began calling each unit as a color-named task force. Team 6
became Task Force Blue, for example, while Delta was called Task Force
Green, and "vanilla" SEALs from Team 2 and Team 4 became Task Force
White. The colored names became standard in the years ahead.

Dam Neck operators also deployed to Somalia in 1993 for Operation
Gothic Serpent, which became known as the Battle of Mogadishu or the
Black Hawk Down incident. A team of Dam Neck snipers ultimately
earned Silver Stars for their roles, but the mission was led by Delta and
Army Rangers.

From 1980 until the 1990s, Team 6 was considered less mature and less capable than Delta, which later changed its cover name to Combat Applications Group, or CAG. Part of the reason Dam Neck failed to get missions stemmed from service rivalry and simple geography. Since its creation, the Joint Special Operations Command had only had an Army general as its commanding officer. That, plus the fact that JSOC, based at Pope Air Force Base in Fayetteville, North Carolina (now Pope Army Airfield and operated by the Army as part of Fort Bragg), was in the same location as Delta. Team 6 had a seat at the table, but Delta sat at the head of it. But there was another reason Dam Neck couldn't gain the internal respect necessary to be given the lead on missions: a distinct lack of overall maturity. During Olson's tour as commanding officer, for example, a Red Team boat crew lost an opportunity to deploy to the Balkans, in part, after Capt. Olson learned they had been involved in a drunken bar fight in south Florida during what was supposed to have been a dive-training trip. After the Navy helped the Red Team operators avoid legal ramifications, Olson discovered that far from being a training exercise, the trip had no operational purpose.

But Team 6's reputation changed in 1997. Although the Somalia mission had been considered a political disaster by the Clinton administration because of the images of a smoldering downed Black Hawk helicopter in the streets of Mogadishu, and the eighteen US military casualties, the president authorized a robust special operations effort in the Balkans a few years later.

Working with NATO, the Clinton White House authorized a secret deployment of both Delta and Team 6 for the location and capture of persons indicted for war crimes in the Bosnian war. In a first, Dam Neck deployed entire assault teams for a long-term mission. Their efforts proved to be successful, and their overall performance gained the respect of both the Joint Special Operations Command and their internal rivals, Delta.

In 1997, the SEALs began tracking Goran Jelisić, a Bosnian police officer who served as guard at the notorious Luka prison camp. After Bosnian Serbs forced Croats and Muslims from their homes starting in 1992,

they rounded up many of the displaced and sent them to the camp in a town called Brčko. Jelisić, who was notorious for his beating and killing of prisoners at the camp, referred to himself as the "Serb Adolf Hitler." In 1995, he was indicted by the International Criminal Tribunal for the Former Yugoslavia for genocide, crimes against humanity, and violating the customs of war. In the two years after his indictment, Jelisić had lived fairly openly in the northeast Bosnian town of Bijeljina. Team 6, working with the CIA, tracked Jelisić to his apartment and surveilled him for weeks. Finally, they were authorized for capture operation in late 1997.[6]

At Dam Neck, the Gold Team operators who were assigned the operation began training with Dieter on how best to capture the wanted war criminal. For six weeks, Dieter rehearsed the entire operation with Clark Cummings, Sean Sheehy, and Dave Kent. In the early morning hours of January 22, 1998, a van with more than a half-dozen operators parked on a small Bijeljina street. When Jelisić left his apartment on his way to his girlfriend's place, the door to the van slid open. Sheehy and Kent jumped out, grabbed the Bosnian Serb, and hooded, cuffed, and hustled him into the side of the waiting van, which then took off. The entire operation took roughly sixty seconds. At the White House, aides woke President Clinton up in the middle of the night to inform him of the successful capture. Jelisić was flown to the Hague to stand trial. He was convicted of crimes against humanity and violating the customs of war for his role at the Luka death camp in 1999 and sentenced to forty years in prison. For Dam Neck, the successful capture was one highlight among several during the years the command participated in the Bosnia mission. For Dieter, it was validation that his training system worked.

PART II

Forged by Adversity: The Wars

[2001–2011]

CHAPTER 6

ROBERTS RIDGE

THE MORNING OF MARCH 4, 2002, ATOP TAKUR GHAR BEGAN with an ominous sign: footprints stretching in the snow toward the ten-thousand-foot peak. The Chinook helicopter pilot who spotted them as he prepared to insert Master Chief Britt Slabinski's sniper reconnaissance team had only a moment to register what that meant: the aerial surveillance that had detected no enemy presence on the mountaintop was wrong. Moments later, the pilot spotted a pop of light, followed by a muzzle flash. Within seconds an RPG slammed into the helicopter, exploding and shredding electronics and hydraulics that helped the pilot control the fifty-thousand-pound helicopter. The Chinook lurched violently. The SEALs from Dam Neck's Red Team, call sign Mako 30, were suddenly in a fight for their lives.

The first to fall was Petty Officer 1st Class Neil Roberts. He'd been perched on the loading ramp of the Chinook nearly ten feet from the ground when the explosion tossed him out of the aircraft. A crewman had grabbed him, but the additional hundred pounds of gear strapped to

Roberts had turned him into dead weight. He slipped from the crewman's grasp. He landed on his squad automatic weapon with enough force to bend the rifle at the stock. Roberts was alone on the peak and the helicopter was spinning down the mountain face, with the pilot fighting for control.

The pilot tried putting the Chinook down to recover Roberts but couldn't adequately control the damaged helicopter and ultimately managed a crash landing some two thousand feet beneath the mountain's summit, only six minutes after they first tried to insert up top. Realizing Roberts was missing, Slabinski, Air Force combat controller Chapman, and the four remaining SEALs considered pushing back up to the summit on foot to get to Roberts. But with knee- and thigh-high snow, and a steep climb in difficult conditions, Slabinski recognized making it to the top would require a helicopter. Fortunately, a nearby helicopter knew that Mako 30 was in trouble, picked up the SEALs and their air crew, and returned them to Gardez.

Meanwhile, up top, Roberts had suffered injuries from his fall and lost the use of his rifle. A small group of al Qaeda fighters eventually advanced from two sides, surrounding him. One enemy fighter fired a final, fatal round into Roberts's head just a few minutes after he fell from the helicopter. Other enemy fighters stripped Roberts of his boots and part of his Gore-Tex snowsuit. A predator drone circling above Takur Ghar captured one of the al Qaeda fighters retrieving a knife, sitting on Roberts's chest, and beginning to cut his neck. Whether because of the cold or a dull blade, the Islamic militant quit without finishing and left Roberts's mutilated body near a bunker just before 4:30 a.m.

THE SEPTEMBER 11, 2001, ATTACKS FUNDAMENTALLY ALTERED THE American national security state, closing the door on a post–Cold War period of relative quiet for the United States and ushering in the War on Terror, an era that has not ended. Within two weeks of the attacks, Secretary of Defense Donald Rumsfeld wrote in the *New York Times* that the war on terror, as it would soon be called, would be different than any previous war the United States had waged. "Forget about 'exit strategies,'" Rumsfeld wrote. "We are looking at a sustained engagement that carries no deadlines."[1] The US military was not set up to chase diffuse, non-state terrorist networks across the world, though it had been trying to learn how since Vietnam and Desert One.

The war would have neither temporal nor geographic limitations. For the military in particular, the War on Terror would truly be unprecedented. The structure of the military had been conceived, built, and operated around the idea of nation-state adversaries. After the humiliating loss in Vietnam, the US military tried to forget the lessons it learned and shifted attention back to the Soviet Union, China, Iran, and North Korea. In the years since the failure of Desert One during the Iran hostage crisis, first the Joint Special Operations Command (JSOC) in 1980 and then the Special Operations Command (SOCOM) in 1987 were created to address unconventional, asymmetrical, and irregular warfare. Even so, until al Qaeda turned commercial jets into weapons of mass destruction, the US military had only limited experience or success in the manhunting business. The special operations forces were little more than a small, expensive tool three successive presidents occasionally took out of the shed to admire and make sure it functioned. No administration had yet used it to actually fix a problem. That all changed when Osama bin Laden and others planned and executed the attacks on 9/11. Officially, the US government professed that the war was meant to root out terrorist networks like al Qaeda and any country that sponsored or harbored such organizations. And while the George W. Bush administration explicitly described this new era as a "long war," which was about more than bin Laden or al Qaeda, many of the operators at Dam Neck wanted retribution.

Those in SEAL Team 6 understood that they would be among the first to seek vengeance for the deaths of more than three thousand Americans. Despite being one of only two special mission units dedicated to counterterrorism, however, SEAL Team 6 would have to wait to enter the fight. Rumsfeld was furious to learn in the weeks after 9/11 that neither SOCOM nor its subordinate command, the JSOC, had an existing list of terrorists or locations to pursue militarily. The military posture had been almost strictly reactive. Rumsfeld quickly assigned a special operations expert to study the problem. Rumsfeld wanted to know why, with a $315 billion annual budget, his department couldn't generate a list of places to bomb or people to kill in the weeks after September 11.[2] The study concluded that the national security community had drawn the wrong lessons from the Battle of Mogadishu in 1993. Broadly, the Pentagon had not viewed terrorism as a "clear and present danger." Terrorism had previously been classified as a crime, rather than considered as a form of war.[3]

While Team 6 and Delta had occasionally been called in to look at pre-9/11 proposals to kidnap or kill bin Laden, those plans never went anywhere, and always relied on intelligence provided by the CIA and the National Security Agency. Inside the national security apparatus of the US government, the CIA was the lead agency on Afghanistan, a legacy of the Reagan administration's covert action to help the mujahideen expel the invading Soviet army. Since the Soviet exit in 1989, the few military personnel who had been to Afghanistan went on assignment for the CIA. Afghanistan was largely a blank spot on the Pentagon's strategic map, even while they spent years working with neighboring Pakistan and monitoring that country's nuclear weapons program.

One week after September 11, a small team of CIA paramilitary officers landed in Afghanistan to prepare for an American invasion. Because the CIA had maintained a small but consistent contact with the Northern Alliance, a renegade Afghan militia, and its leader, Ahmad Shah Massoud, it was the agency that deployed into Afghanistan first. But the agency's paramilitary group, the Special Activities Division, which was made up almost exclusively of former special operations personnel, did not have a force big enough to work with Northern Alliance forces alone. Rumsfeld did not turn to the Navy SEALs. Instead, he authorized as many as seventy-five Army Green Berets to serve under the agency's authorities and surge into Afghanistan, doubling the size of the force.

On October 7, the Bush administration declared the start of Operation Enduring Freedom, the official military campaign to remove the

Taliban and eliminate bin Laden's organization. The paramilitary officers, working with Green Berets, helped guide US bombers flying over the country to Taliban targets. In one month, the Army Special Forces and the CIA routed the Taliban in the country's north, moving south toward the capital, Kabul. On November 13, the Northern Alliance and US forces pushed into Kabul and took control. Osama bin Laden and a sizable entourage of foreign al Qaeda fighters fled Jalalabad, a city east of Kabul, and moved to the Tora Bora mountains along the Pakistan border. The Taliban fell in the capital and retreated to Kandahar in the south, the heart of Afghanistan's ethnic Pashtun region. Mullah Omar, the Taliban's leader, had already fled Kandahar to try to assess the options for survival.

Meanwhile, a small group of CIA and Green Beret forces moved into the country's south, toward Kandahar, the Taliban's seat of power. While Kabul fell under a Northern Alliance ground force backed by US air support, the Taliban more or less abandoned the city. Instead, the Pashtun forces spread out south and east, melting into the indistinguishable border area with Pakistan, ensuring their survival. By early December, bin Laden, too, fled, decamping to the Tora Bora mountains. The Taliban and Arab al Qaeda forces that hadn't already filtered into Pakistan atomized into Afghanistan's Pashtun rural and mountainous heartland in the south and east.

In a matter of weeks, this small US force had replaced the Taliban and installed a new government. But the SEALs, much to their frustration, were not an integral part of this early victory. Members of Team 6 assigned to Task Force 11, the new special operations component in Afghanistan, were part of what became the JSOC unit whose new mission was to help find and kill bin Laden once the situation in Afghanistan settled. But even those involved with the task force were forced to watch from the sidelines as a small team of Delta operators worked with the CIA and Green Berets in an attempt to kill bin Laden with a massive bombing campaign. US forces tried pinning the al Qaeda leader into a network of caves and calling in ordnance while Afghan allies blocked any attempted escape. The Afghan support failed, and there were too few US forces to stop bin Laden and his associates from walking into Pakistan. Instead, the al Qaeda leader disappeared into Pakistan, out of reach of US forces.

As the limited US forces crushed al Qaeda and Taliban forces, the rest of SEAL Team 6, and Red Team in particular, began to prepare in Virginia Beach for a January 2002 deployment to Afghanistan. At that moment, the Teams represented some of the best-trained men in the US military. Yet they had little combat experience. Those who had carried out operations in the Balkans in the mid-1990s were older and in some cases had to quickly get in shape in time for deployment. No one had fought a war at altitude. Red Team's three elements, two assault and one sniper/reconnaissance, conducted training as they would for any mission. In an effort to prepare for winter warfare in the mountains at high altitudes, the Red sniper element did a week of CQD training with Duane Dieter. The snipers were led by Britt Slabinski. Dieter had known Slabinski since he had trained Green Team in 1993, when the lanky SEAL first joined the command. Dieter liked Slabinski, but in the years since he'd initially instructed him, he noticed the SEAL was less committed to training than some of his teammates.

Dieter recalled an incident in 1995 when he had Slabinski again for a weeklong training course. One day, during a lunch break, Slabinski waited for his teammates to leave. Now alone, Slabinski approached Dieter. "He told me the guys were getting tired and asked if I might ease up a bit on the instruction," Dieter recalled later. "I told him sure, no problem." After two days of Dieter releasing the SEALs early, one of Slab's teammates asked Dieter after class why they weren't doing full eight-hour days. "I told him I thought they were tired and wanted to do a little less." "Did Slab say something to you?" Dieter recalled the operator, who used Slabinski's nickname, asking him. "He's always doing that. Don't listen to him; he doesn't speak for us. We want more training, not less. Slab's just lazy."

In the six years between that training and 9/11, Slabinski had risen to sniper team leader and been promoted to senior chief petty officer. Given that few SEALs had deployed into hostilities, Slabinski was by then a veteran presence, with several trips to the Balkans hunting Bosnian war criminals under his belt.

Also training with Dieter that fall was an Air Force technical sergeant, John Chapman of the 24th Special Tactics Squadron. Chapman was a combat controller, a key role in Tier 1 missions. Combat controllers were a product of the joint command, highly trained operators who attached to Team 6 and Delta squads. They were responsible for communicating with any air assets either for air strikes or exfiltration and served a crucial role for mission success. Known as CCTs, the controllers were respected members of the team, even if they did not share the unit's tribal identity. Chappy, as he was called, was older than all but one of the SEALs. Though he'd been through CQD plenty of times when he was part of Gold Team, he'd moved to a less operational assignment in the subsequent years. Immediately after 9/11, he was transferred back to Team 6 for war.[4]

Slabinski's recon troop, along with Chapman and the other Redmen, practiced maneuvering and worked on everything from the hood drill with live fire to shooting accurately while under stress.

The command, like others in the military, started transforming to meet the new wartime needs. At Team 6, they had a straightforward problem with no straightforward solution: they needed more SEALs. Going to war would mean each of the assault teams would have to be fully manned on each deployment. They couldn't reach in and borrow an operator here, or a sniper there, from the sister teams, as those teams would follow on the next deployment. Dam Neck didn't have a hidden stash of screened, Green Team–qualified SEALs waiting for their chance to join the command.

But despite manpower issues, the operators at the command, like Slabinski, were almost universally eager to deploy. The comparison between the 9/11 attacks and Pearl Harbor was frequently made by both the Bush administration and the US media, and for an entire generation of Americans, but especially for the SEALs, it was a galvanizing event. The SEALs, like so many in the military, wanted revenge.

January 2002—Bagram, Afghanistan

The roughly fifty men of Red Team arrived in Afghanistan with their skipper, Capt. Joseph Kernan. Kernan is a brown-haired, barrel-chested Irish American with a sharp, angular nose and bright blue eyes. Kernan was well liked and had, unlike most of his officer peers, served several years in the Navy fleet as a young officer out of the Naval Academy. He was a political heavyweight inside the Naval Special Warfare community, more political operator than SEAL operator. Kernan had a deep ambition to be a SEAL admiral, and to help other SEAL officers get there as well. In his previous commands, he'd worked to move officers he favored into billets he thought best positioned them for their potential promotion to flag. In doing so, he generated favor among the younger SEAL officers he lifted up. Kernan had done a previous tour at the command as the chief of staff, but like most at the command, he had little experience in a war zone.

At Kernan's side in Bagram was now Cdr. Tim Szymanski, who was now the operations officer for Team 6. Although Kernan and Szymanski were Dam Neck's two most senior officers in Afghanistan, they were not, ultimately, in charge. They worked for the special operation task force commander, Air Force Brig. Gen. Gregory Trebon. In the two decades that followed, the chain of command for Team 6 and other special operations forces would streamline, making it easier for a Team 6 commanding officer to oversee and control how his men were used on the battlefield.[5] The SEALs entered Afghanistan as part of Task Force 11 for a straightforward mission: to kill or capture bin Laden, his deputy, Ayman al-Zawahiri, and another ten or so al Qaeda leaders on the strike list. As far as they knew, their targets were still in Afghanistan: bin Laden had last been seen in Tora the previous month, and Zawahiri too. The mission set was called the "Ten and Two," and though the SEALs were hunting in Afghanistan, the task force was going global. Along with the CIA, Team 6 and Delta could be utilized anywhere they could find their target.

Their mission would not be easy or straightforward. Bin Laden had a long history in Afghanistan. He had been in and out of the country since the early 1980s and had forged relationships with Afghan and Pashtun tribes throughout the country's east, along the Pakistan border. He'd arrived as a young Saudi scion seeking to support Afghanistan's holy warriors, the mujahideen, in their resistance against the Soviet-backed Afghan government and the Soviet army. And although his wealth and contributions had not changed the course of that fight, they were nonetheless appreciated. He became a fixture in the country, and when Mullah Omar, a one-eyed Pashtun mujahid, became the leader of the Taliban, bin Laden forged a financial relationship with him. His fledgling terrorist organization settled into the country, establishing an ad hoc network of training camps for like-minded foreigners to train and occasionally serve with Taliban units in their battles against Massoud and the Northern Alliance.

In the east, in Afghanistan's Nangarhar province, bin Laden had brought equipment from his family's construction empire to build a network of caves and safe houses in the Tora Bora mountains, along the Pakistan border. And it was there that bin Laden and his entourage fled from Jalalabad as the Northern Alliance, with US support, made their move toward Kabul. Bin Laden's eventual escape from the mountain redoubt, during what became known as the Battle of Tora Bora in December 2001, came only a month before Red Team arrived in Afghanistan.

While most of the hard-core al Qaeda cadre exfiltrated after the Battle of Tora Bora, US intelligence believed that as many as two thousand Islamic militants remained in Afghanistan. These militants, a collection of Afghans, Arabs, Uzbeks, and a smattering of other foreign fighters, had temporarily settled into a valley near the Pakistan border called Shah-e-Kot, in Paktia province. Afghanistan's Paktia province is about the size of Delaware, with ten-thousand-foot ridgelines and arid valleys with dry riverbeds below, nestled along the border with Pakistan's Federally Administered Tribal Areas. The valley had been the scene of intense fighting during the Soviet invasion of Afghanistan, a well-established hideout for Afghan mujahideen because of its high, rugged terrain—the valley basin rests at seven thousand feet above sea level. The two most prominent mountain ranges often served as the last geographic refuge for retreating forces entering Pakistan. The Shah-e-Kot, which means "Place of Kings" in Pashto, had been the protected gateway for escaping and/or defeating invading forces for centuries.

For the SEALs who landed in Afghanistan, the valley of Shah-e-Kot would be their first major test of the war. Under the planning of Maj. Gen. Franklin Hagenbeck, commander of the Army's 10th Mountain Division, US forces would make a surprise assault early on March 4 into the valley, in the hope of wiping out what was left of the remaining Taliban and foreign al Qaeda fighters. The mission was named Operation Anaconda. The plan was to insert special operations forces, including the SEALs and Delta, onto the mountaintops along the valley's eastern ridgeline. With control of the peaks overlooking the valley, Task Force 11, including SEAL Team 6 recon elements, would help direct air strikes and overlook the Army's 10th Mountain Division and 101st Airborne troops, who would move into the valley and block any escaping forces fleeing to Pakistan.

SEAL Team 6 arrived in Afghanistan as a formidable fighting force. The team consisted of two assault elements, a reconnaissance element and sniper team, plus additional operators to help augment a frequently undermanned roster. They were transported by the Army's 160th Special Operations Aviation Regiment, which had the world's best helicopter pilots. They were supported by the CIA and the task force, who provided intelligence and surveillance information, and their combat controllers, who stood at the ready to bring B-1 and F-18 bombers in to neutralize any target. They were a small unit, designed to deliver outsize results using their superior training, skills, and access to the joint capabilities of the US military. But in truth, few of the men had direct combat experience—and none of them had fought at the altitude of the mountains where the enemy was believed to be hiding.

Unfortunately, the SEALs' reconnaissance mission was flawed from inception. For one, the chain of command was attenuated, both by the geography of the US military's new footprint in Afghanistan and by the parochial divisions of the branches. On paper, Gen. Trebon oversaw the mission; he'd flown from the United States to Oman and then Bagram so he could oversee the task force's role in the mission. But the SEALs worked from a small forward operating base in Gardez, more than one hundred miles to the southeast, under the authority of an Army Lt. Col.,

Peter Blaber. The SEALs found themselves under the command of an Air Force general with no special operations experience, and it didn't help that their most immediate commander, Blaber, was Delta. When Slabinski and the Red Team arrived, the commander back in Bagram, Gen. Trebon, decided that the authority of the forward operating base in Gardez should fall to the SEALs.

The action had already kicked off by the time Slabinski and his team got there, however. Blaber had already inserted a squad of Team 6 snipers a day or so before Slabinski arrived in Gardez. The snipers were half of Slabinski's team, which he dispatched from Bagram to Gardez days earlier. Before Anaconda started, Slabinski and much of Dam Neck's leadership believed the operation would be largely a conventional military affair. Considering the mission less vital than an opportunity to hunt bin Laden or his top deputies, Slabinski sent half his team, with the call sign Mako 31, to work for Blaber in Gardez. In the lead-up to H hour for Anaconda, Blaber had sent the Mako 31 SEALs into the same ridgeline as Takur Ghar, to establish an observation post a few kilometers away. Mako 31 were inserted along the same mountain range, and patrolled by foot to their objective, an observation post not far from Takur Ghar. They discovered a well-fortified al Qaeda position at the peak, and eventually killed the militants they found occupying it, which afforded them a good view down and across the valley. What was becoming clear to Blaber and the recon unit was that al Qaeda had already assessed the best vantage points for a battle and had occupied the peaks along the ridgelines well before the American forces.

In the military, senior officers are responsible for what is called command and control—the organization and structure for communicating between units on a battlefield. Anaconda did not remedy the communication issues—if anything, it revealed divisions of command that made sense at the Pentagon but created problems on the ground in Afghanistan. Trebon had only partial authority and little situational awareness at the front. His role was largely confined to pre-mission reconnaissance of the special operations forces, a small portion of what was expected to be a multiday assault on the valley. And while Kernan and Szymanski had access to Trebon because they were in the same Bagram operations

center, each ran his own line of communication to his men: Trebon to
Blaber, and Kernan to Slabinski. This redundancy undermined rather than
reinforced the efforts of each commander. But even when Trebon, Kernan,
and Szymanski did have a full picture, they did not always share it with
the men at the front. The lines of authority and communication were a
mess, the unfortunate result of a new war with senior officers who'd never
commanded in a war zone.

While Slabinski's team waited to launch at Gardez, the Team 6 officers
at Bagram asked the Mako 31 team to leave their observation post and
make their way the three kilometers along the ridgeline to Takur Ghar.
The request, if accepted, would spare Slabinski and his team from having
to insert. Mako 31 reported back to Capt. Kernan and Cdr. Szymanski
in Bagram that Takur Ghar was already occupied by enemy fighters. The
evening after they settled into their observation post, the SEALs could
see the outline of several men coming in and out of a bunker, as well as the
outline of a tree that they later described as a bonsai. The Mako 31 team
reported back to their superiors at Bagram that they could not take the
position, and alerted them to an enemy position on top of Takur Ghar.[6]
Moreover, they told Kernan and Szymanski that even with a helicopter
insertion, they would need to return to Gardez for resupply before flying
to Takur Ghar. Even then, they would have to land at an offset location
distant enough from the al Qaeda fighters so that the approaching helicopter wouldn't be heard and they would be able to patrol up on foot with
stealth. Slabinski, in Gardez, was telling his commanders the same thing.
"When we declined the mission," Andy Martin, the combat controller
attached to Mako 31, later told an author, "they moved it on to Slab's team
instead."[7]

As Anaconda's launch hour neared, Trebon decided he wanted a
SEAL recon unit up on Takur Ghar. Blaber resisted, telling the Air Force
general that Slabinski's team needed as much as a full night to insert
somewhere much lower than the mountaintop and then patrol on foot
to the peak. Trebon was unmoved. Kernan and Szymanski separately
pressed Slabinski to take Takur Ghar as well. "The pressure was on us to
get bombs on target by sunrise," Slabinski would later say. The only way to

do so would involve a direct insertion—the loud and lumbering Chinook landing on the mountaintop. It is unclear when Kernan and Szymanski received or read Mako 31's report. But the SEALs on the nearby observation point had provided the crucial information Team 6 needed before launching Slabinski and his Mako 30 team: if they flew to the mountaintop, they'd fly into an ambush. That Slabinski's teammates knew Takur Ghar was occupied by the enemy and relayed that information back to their commanders in Bagram who either didn't see it in time or didn't convey it to Slabinski was no different than the command-and-control failure that occurred in 1943 at Tarawa with the neap tides.

Finally, after 11:00 p.m., Slabinski and Mako 30 left Gardez to Takur Ghar. But within ten minutes of their approach the Chinooks turned back because their F-16 air cover had to leave for another area. Back at Gardez, Slabinski tried to get a delay to the insertion because the longer it took to launch, the closer to the top he would have to land. If the position was occupied by the enemy, there'd be no element of surprise. Kernan and Szymanski pushed Slabinski to accept Trebon's timeline and get to the top of Takur Ghar to establish an observation post. Despite his asking for another twenty-four hours, his Team 6 commanders told him he "really needed to rethink" his request. "To me," Slabinski would say later, "that was: 'Hey, you gotta go [to Takur Ghar].'"[8] Kernan and Szymanski overruled Slabinski, who had more combat and tactical experience, anyway.

"This was already eating at my gut," Slabinski said about his orders. "You don't do this. I know you don't do this, you don't go in there."[9] Still, Slabinski followed his orders, despite knowing that he no longer had time to land lower on the mountain and patrol on foot, increasing the risk of an ambush by the enemy. His team, including Chapman, would go "light," meaning they would leave Gardez with as few provisions as possible. No body armor, little or no water, in an effort to keep the weight on the helicopter down, giving it a better chance to get up to the top in the cold weather. Slabinski told Chapman to pack smaller radios with less range and bring fewer extra batteries. Every ounce would count.

At 2:30 a.m., Slabinski, Chapman, and the rest of Mako 30 took off from Gardez, headed for the top of Takur Ghar. Despite the chaos and confusion between Bagram, Gardez, and Takur Ghar, Team 6 commanding officer Capt. Joe Kernan and his operations officer, Cdr. Tim Szymanski, had sent their men on an operation that violated one of the fundamental rules of a reconnaissance mission: always patrol to your destination from a safe distance to preserve any element of surprise. "Everything [at that point] is pointing to the fact that I need to say no," Slabinski later told the author Malcolm MacPherson. "No one wants to fail their mission." In fact, as the mission commander, and a senior enlisted Team 6 operator, Slabinski was supposed to contradict his officers. That was Marcinko's vision for SEAL Team 6: experience and knowledge should outweigh rank.

Around 3:00 a.m., the telltale sound of the Chinook's twin rotors echoed across the valley below the summit. In that moment, it was apparent to the men of Mako 31 that something had gone terribly wrong. Soon after, the rattle of gunfire joined the cacophony—and Mako 31 could hear the failure of the command and control between Trebon and the task force senior officers in Bagram play out with fatal consequences for the other team of SEALs in Mako 30. The disaster caught their counterparts of Mako 31 by surprise—they hadn't been alerted to the Takur Ghar mission. And they were helpless to do anything in the disaster unfolding down the ridge. They were close as the crow flew, but might as well have been in Pakistan for how little they could help whichever unfortunate American forces were trying to land on Takur Ghar.

Roughly 3:20 a.m.

When Slabinski, Chapman, and the team of four other SEAL snipers arrived back at their forward operating base, they had narrowly survived the mountaintop ambush and the crash of their helicopter. Yet, they clamored to return to the fight. Roberts was alone on the mountaintop, surrounded by an unknown number of enemy forces, Slabinski reported. He wanted the command to sign off on a rescue mission.

Back at Bagram, Kernan, Szymanski, and other Team 6 officers faced a challenging situation. Roberts remained alone on the mountain with enemy fighters who were dug into a well-defended post. The officers had little visibility into the conditions on top of the mountain beyond those facts. They might as well have been back in Virginia Beach, given the deficit of intelligence in the Shah-e-Kot. A debate erupted about whether to scramble together a rescue team, called a quick reaction force.

Kernan and Szymanski wanted more clarity about who and what were at the mountain's summit before they released the rescue team. From their perspective, sending a team onto an enemy-controlled post as the sun was rising would risk further disaster. But the junior Red Team officer, a fellow Naval Academy graduate, Lt. Jeromy Williams, pleaded with his superiors to approve their departure. He argued that they needed to immediately send the rescue force from Bagram to Gardez—that leg alone was a two-hour flight. The move would save precious minutes and allow the senior officers to gather more information in the meantime. Kernan and Szymanski dismissed Williams's plea. Williams started to raise his voice to the point where he was nearly screaming, telling his superiors they were wasting precious time. Williams argued that the helicopters served no purpose sitting at Bagram; an effort to get back to Takur Ghar would require stopping in Gardez for more fuel, and by the time they arrived there, Kernan and Szymanski would be in a better position to know what Roberts's status was. At that point, the Rangers would be significantly closer to the mountaintop. If not, there would be no downside. Williams, losing his temper, banged on a table. His superiors ordered him to leave the room.

While the officers debated, a rescue force composed of nearly twenty US Army Rangers waited, at the ready, in two Chinooks on the Bagram flight line for permission to depart. A mid-career Navy SEAL, Lt. Cdr. Vic Hyder, was also waiting in one of the helicopters. Hyder was one of only two junior officers deployed with Red Team at the command, and he, like the rest of the rescue force, desperately wanted Kernan and Szymanski to order the choppers east to Gardez and then to Takur Ghar.

The men waited in the predawn darkness for two hours after the first reports of Roberts's abandonment. Then, finally, Kernan and his operations officer authorized the quick reaction force to save him.

A FEW MINUTES BEFORE 5:00 A.M. SLAB, CHAPMAN, AND FOUR OTHERS of Mako 30 departed Gardez and landed near Roberts's last known location at Takur Ghar. Again, the team flew directly into an ambush. Slabinski led the charge off the rear ramp, falling in the snow. Chapman was off the helicopter next, and because his team leader fell, he was now the point man. His teammates poured out behind him, scrambling to find cover. As they split into three groups of two, Chapman and the SEALs came under fire.

The SEALs found themselves in the worst tactical position possible, fighting up a steep slope in deep snow against multiple fortified enemy positions with bullets coming at them from three directions. Chapman led the charge up the mountain alone toward a tree, which, if secured, he could use as cover to begin calling in air strikes as instructed by Slabinski. As he made his way uphill, he came under fire from what turned out to be a bunker, which sheltered two militants firing directly at him. He put himself in the open, alone, drawing automatic weapons fire to his position and away from the rest of Mako 30. The two other pairs found cover and took defensive positions. Slabinski eventually followed Chapman through his path in the snow toward the bunker. Chapman assaulted the position and killed the two enemy fighters inside at close range as Slabinski caught up with his combat controller.

Militants with a heavy machine gun now fired down on Chapman and Slabinski. The enemy occupied yet another previously hidden bunker, about twenty feet away from the Americans and farther up the slope. Slabinski took cover next to a small outcrop of rocks. Chapman did the same behind a small tree. Two other SEALs made their way to the opposite end of the outcrop where Slabinski held cover, firing at the second bunker but from a different direction. Slabinski heard Chapman yell out, "Where did that come from?" over the machine-gun fire. Slabinski turned to look at Chapman, who was now down, lying on his side. At least one round had hit him, but Slabinski could not see where.

Slabinski later reported what he first saw when he looked over at Chapman: on his side, his gun and its unmistakable red laser beam going up and down as it lay across his abdomen. The movement made it clear to Slabinski that Chapman was in distress but still breathing, rapidly. The team leader continued taking fire from the second bunker while unloading a grenade launcher at it with no success. The other four SEALs, still split in two pairs, fired at the al Qaeda fighters from positions near him, but they too failed to stop the enemy's attack. As Slabinski ordered his teammates into different positions to try to hit the second bunker, a second teammate, Brett Morganti, was hit by enemy fire. Morganti's thighs received two bullet wounds. The SEALs were taking fire from three directions now. Chapman was down and Morganti was hurt. A few moments passed and Slabinski looked back over to Chapman. He would later say he noticed that his combat controller's gun laser sight was no longer moving up and down across his chest. The laser, like Chapman's torso, was still.

Slabinski took in his situation, he would later recall. "I remember taking a look around," Slabinski said, "and going, 'Hey, OK, there is way more than six dudes [enemy fighters] up here. I am pretty sure Chappy's gone. I don't have Neil [Roberts] anymore and I got Morganti wounded with his .60 [caliber machine gun] gone.'" Still under heavy attack, Slabinski moved toward the combat controller's position. Next, he scanned Chapman's chest again and saw still no signs of breathing. He would later say he got close to Chapman. "I know I don't have time to check his pulse," Slabinski said. "It's kind of like, 'Hey, I've got no movement on him, and there's nothing from him.' I take a last look at him…I can't drag him. I have to worry about Brett and I'm fairly certain that [Chapman is] dead." Slabinski did not call out to Chapman, afraid of giving his position away. "I just thought he was dead."[10]

Slabinski decided he had to break contact. He would claim he crawled over part of Chapman's legs or feet as he moved back down toward two of his four remaining teammates and noticed no movement or indication that Chapman was still alive.

Slabinski tossed smoke grenades and tried to provide cover fire for the last two SEALs, so they could retreat to his position. As the last two SEALs moved through the smoke away from the second bunker, one of them yelled out. Stephen Toboz, known as Turbo, had been hit by a bullet above his ankle, which was now nearly severed from his leg. With the five SEALs now together, one asked, "Where's Chappy?" Slabinski recalled. "He's gone," Slabinski replied. "He's dead."

Slabinski made the decision to break contact, leaving Chapman and Roberts, whom they didn't find, on the mountaintop, and retreat in an effort to save other injured teammates. No soldier or SEAL wants to face that scenario in combat, and Slabinski, as team leader, had to make the decision under heavy enemy fire. For three and a half minutes, with cover from a boulder and terrain, just beneath the mountaintop and Chapman's body, Slabinski waited with his remaining teammates, the Predator drone video would show. He was just feet from Chapman but did not attempt to retrieve his body or check his vitals. Instead, he tried calling the AC-130 gunship flying above but failed to establish communication. He hoped that if he could get air support on the mountaintop, he and his remaining team could recover Chapman and Roberts.

Then, twenty minutes after they'd exited the helicopter to enemy fire, the SEALs aborted the rescue mission for Neil Roberts. Slabinski and the four other SEALs tossed more smoke grenades and slid down the steep, snow-covered summit. Unable to carry the wounded down because of the snow and the terrain, Slabinski and his two healthy teammates had to pull their fellow SEALs at different points to get away from enemy fire. To cover their retreat, Slabinski called for fire on the summit, in an effort to kill the al Qaeda fighters or, at the very least, prevent them from trying to maneuver to stop their escape.

"We are no longer on top of the ridge," Slabinski said over the radio. "Need you to put effective fire on top of the ridge ASAP. Have troops down, possible KIA. Fire on top now."[11] The team leader told the gunship overhead that he had all his men and that they were clear to fire.

Slabinski was the only American on Takur Ghar to see his teammate fall. He believed that Chapman died and, to prevent further losses, led the surviving SEALs to safety. He would later be asked whether it was possible that the body Slabinski brushed across on his way down was Roberts, not Chapman. Slabinski dismissed the possibility, noting that he knew the difference between his longtime teammate and Chapman. "I crawled over the top of that guy," Slab would later say about Chapman. But drone video of the firefight revealed that Slabinski was closer to Roberts's body, and that he never made it closer than twelve feet from Chapman. In either case, Slabinski didn't take a pulse or check for other vital signs and so he couldn't have been certain if Chapman was dead.

WHILE SLABINSKI WAS LEADING HIS TEAM OF FIVE, WITH TWO SERIous injuries, down the mountain, Chapman found himself alive and conscious where Slabinski had left him for dead. Chapman was alone, and despite wounds, had managed to engage one of the militants near his position. Video shot from a drone circling overhead would later reveal that Chapman maneuvered to several positions on the mountaintop, engaging multiple enemy fighters. For roughly fifty-four minutes, Chapman fought alone and waited for backup. As his team's radioman, he knew what was likely occurring: some kind of quick reaction force was on the way. He took his MBITR radio and, using a frequency and call sign unique to combat controllers in the 24th Special Tactics Squadron, he radioed out for help. "Any station, any station, this is Mako Three Zero Charlie."[12]

Several kilometers north of Takur Ghar, on an American-occupied observation post above the valley, one of Chapman's teammates from the 24th STS heard the transmission. Tech Sgt. Jason Hill knew Chapman's call sign, as well as the way he made the call. There was no mistaking Chappy. Hill responded, but Chapman didn't seem to get the transmission. From inside the bunker, Chapman kept putting out the same transmission. Then enemy fire erupted toward Chapman.

In fact, there was a pitched battle going on at the mountaintop. Al Qaeda had as many as two dozen fighters scattered in fortified and entrenched positions along the ridgeline. After the SEALs retreated, several of the militants attacked Chapman's position. Chapman successfully fought them off, and at one point killed an enemy in a hand-to-hand fight after the militant was able to sneak into Chapman's position. By daylight, Chapman was in another gunfight with an enemy moving toward him, no farther than twenty feet away.

Finally, at 6:11 a.m., Chapman could hear the first of the two Chinooks that had come to find Roberts (no one yet knew Chapman was left behind). With the daylight, Chapman exited the bunker and began moving toward the enemy in the second bunker uphill, shooting as he moved. He laid down cover fire on the militants to protect the incoming Chinook. It was Chapman's only hope for survival. The enemy fighters waited for the Chinook to prepare to land, then fired a rocket-propelled grenade, or RPG, striking one of the engines. The helicopter heaved with the explosion, then fell onto the slope; it had been low enough that the crash didn't cause catastrophic injuries to the force inside. Chapman turned around and began firing at any militants who had a line of sight on the crashed Chinook. As he did, an enemy fighter from the second bunker moved toward Chapman, who was facing downhill. The fatal shot came from behind, entered his back, and pierced his aorta, killing him instantly.[13] The American was finally dead.

WHEN THE RANGERS FINALLY EXITED THE CHINOOK, SLABINSKI and the SEALs were an hour into their escape. With daybreak, the entrenched force of militants on the mountaintop could now clearly see this new team of approaching Americans. The al Qaeda fighters had already faced two helicopter-borne assaults that day and were prepared for the inbound Rangers. After a few minutes, the rear ramp lowered, and the Rangers charged out into the snow. Two were killed within a few steps, struck by enemy rounds, as the other American soldiers tried to establish a perimeter behind the Chinook. The American force made its way toward the summit, taking the same heavy fire Slabinski and his team had faced earlier. None of them knew it at the time, but Chapman had been providing cover fire for them until just moments before they came off the Chinook.

At 7:00 a.m., the second Chinook carrying Hyder and ten Army Rangers about a half mile from where the previous quick reaction force helicopter had crashed. The second team of Rangers rushed out, wading into the same snow and fighting their way uphill toward incoming fire. Hyder didn't follow the Rangers. He knew that Slabinski and his team had escaped off the summit, and he immediately cut across and then down the mountainside in search of his fellow SEALs. When Hyder finally found Slabinski and his team, he communicated back to Bagram with a status update and a location. The Rangers who'd flown with Hyder, meanwhile, trudged their way up to the mountaintop to reinforce their teammates. It took them nearly three hours to get there. Reinforced, the Rangers took the mountaintop, but only after losing several soldiers to casualties. One final counterattack by a few remaining militants wounded an Air Force pararescueman. The battle between the Rangers and the remaining al Qaeda fighters lasted nearly four hours.

Finally, around noon on March 4, some nine hours after Neil Roberts first fell from his helicopter, the battle of Takur Ghar was over. All remaining survivors, including Mako 30, as well as the dead were lifted off the mountain around eight that evening. Slabinski arrived back in Gardez at roughly 9:00 p.m., nearly a day after he'd initially departed for the mission.

The next morning, Slabinski and the two uninjured snipers returned to Bagram. By then, the day's toll was becoming clearer. Roberts was dead, mutilated by the enemy. Chapman was also dead. Five others—Snr. Airman Jason Cunningham; Army Rangers Pfc. Matthew Commons, Sgt. Bradley Crose, and Spc. Marc Anderson; and Sgt. Philip Svitak of the Army's 160th Special Operations Aviation Regiment—also died. Two of Slabinski's sniper team were seriously wounded, with Turbo eventually losing his right leg beneath his knee.

Slabinski, nose swollen, limped into the tactical operations center where Capt. Kernan and Cdr. Szymanski were waiting.

"Good job," they told him.

IT WOULD BECOME APPARENT IN THE YEARS AFTER THE BATTLE OF Roberts Ridge, as it would come to be called, that no one came down

Takur Ghar the same as they'd gone up. Red Team lost two of their own, including the first SEAL casualty of the war. Neil C. Roberts died at age thirty-two, leaving behind a wife, Patty, and a son, Nathan, who was eighteen months old. John Chapman, thirty-eight, left two daughters, Madison and Brianna, and his wife, Valerie. Red Team also had to contend with something they hadn't imagined before they deployed: the desecration of Roberts's body. It felt like a silent message from al Qaeda to a group of SEALs who had believed themselves invincible. The day after the battle ended, Roberts's body was located and brought back to Bagram to be processed. Many of his teammates and friends viewed his mutilated body. The descriptions were passed to everyone else on the team who hadn't. Several of the men on the deployment and up on Roberts Ridge made the battle their last, transferring out of Team 6 or leaving the Navy altogether. Those who remained in the SEALs would later take stock of what transpired and draw their own conclusions.

One of Slabinski's teammates told me that Red Team operators did their own internal assessment of where the mission went wrong. "We were pissed off that Britt was forced to go to the top of that mountain when he had said, 'Hey, I think this is a bad idea.' But he relented. You know, he compromised, and he owns some of that failure." SEAL Team 6, according to Dick Marcinko's vision, would always rely on the expertise of the enlisted operators. On Takur Ghar, the enlisted team leader bowed to his officers, who had no battlefield experience, and tragedy ensued. The Red Team operator, who spent more than two decades as a SEAL and later became a senior leader in Naval Special Warfare, also told me that Slabinski's effort to return to the mountain to find Neil Roberts was "one of the most heroic things I've ever seen."

Another Team 6 leader, who studied Takur Ghar for the command, disagreed. He described Slabinski's actions as the equivalent of "recovering his own fumble." Slabinski would carry psychological scars from the failed mission from almost the moment he returned to Bagram the next day.

At the time, very few had any solid inkling that Chapman had survived his initial wounds and kept fighting. In the years afterward, there would be recriminations and bad blood between the Navy and Air Force special operations communities as some of the chaos and confusion of the night became clearer. But at Bagram, some already had a sense of what had gone wrong. What was well understood at Team 6 at the time was that on an awful day, their man had left Chapman's body at the top of the mountain.

In the hours after Red Team gathered at Bagram, one of their leaders, the master chief, huddled them together. "We will refer to this as Roberts Ridge," he said. "One day, they will make books and movies about what happened up there."[14]

A bit later, one of Chapman's fellow combat controllers took possession of Chapman's kit and weapon. His magazines were empty, his chest rack was bloodied, his rifle's grip had been blown off from a bullet. He was part of Red for the deployment, part of the team. He took Chapman's gear to his hooch. On his way, he saw Slabinski outside a tent for the first time since the battle ended. He went over to the team leader. "What happened?" the combat controller asked Slabinski. Slabinski refused to look up.

CHAPTER 7

THE WEDDING PARTY

R ED TEAM HAD BARELY PROCESSED THE TRAUMA OF ROBERTS Ridge when they were again called into action. On March 6, with Lt. Cdr. Vic Hyder still wearing his stained and dirty uniform from the battle on Takur Ghar, he and more than a dozen Red Team operators boarded two Chinook helicopters and took off from Bagram, en route back to Paktia province, near Gardez, hoping that within hours they would kill or capture Osama bin Laden.

Earlier that evening, Gen. Trebon and Task Force 11 had scrambled together the Red Team element after watching a Predator drone video feed of a man in white flowing garb set off in a convoy of three or four vehicles from the Shah-e-Kot. Although the initial video feed had revealed no weapons, and the generals had only tenuous intelligence that the convoy was al Qaeda—just suspicions based on the color of the man's clothes and the deference showed him by others in an area associated with al Qaeda forces—they were nervous that bin Laden might get away again, as he had a few months earlier at Tora Bora. The convoy was headed east, toward the Pakistan border, as if they were trying to escape. The mission was called Objective Bull.

As the special operations helicopters approached the convoy from the north and west, Air Force jets dropped two five-hundred-pound bombs, halting the vehicles and killing several people instantly.

That was not how the SEALs had wanted the mission to develop. Inside the helicopters, some of the operators had pushed to hold off any air attack, arguing that they had plenty of time to intercept the convoy before it reached the Pakistani border. "The reason SEAL Team 6 exists is to avoid bombs and collateral damage," said a retired SEAL Team 6 member who was on the mission. "We said, 'Let us set down and take a look at the convoy to determine if it's al Qaeda.' Instead, they dropped several bombs."

The bombing stopped the convoy along a dry wadi, or ravine, with two of the trucks approximately a kilometer apart. Survivors began to flee the wreckage, and over the radio Hyder and the rest of the team heard the order that the convoy was now in a free-fire zone, which allowed the Chinooks' gunners to fire at anyone still alive and deemed to be a threat. The SEALs had no authority over the helicopter gunners. One of the helicopters' miniguns fired at a man standing on the top of a large hill with a weapon.

The two Chinooks landed separately, one near each end of the convoy. Both teams exited the helicopters to find a grim scene. The SEALs with Hyder came out and separated into two groups. One, led by an enlisted operator, took in the damage to one of the vehicles. Men, women, and a small girl, motionless and in the fetal position, appeared dead. Inside the vehicle were one or two rifles, as is customary in Afghanistan, but none of the men wore military clothing or had any extra ammunition. "These were family weapons," said the retired SEAL. This wasn't al Qaeda, they realized, but civilians tragically killed by a series of mistaken inferences by senior officers several hundred miles away.

The SEALs from the other helicopter immediately headed up a steep hill to locate the armed man whom the minigunners shot before landing. It became clear to the SEALs that the now dead man had been attempting to protect the women and children, survivors of the initial bombing, who now lay dead or mortally wounded from the helicopter fire.

Other SEALs on the ground proceeded as though the survivors were combatants. Hyder and an enlisted operator, Petty Officer 1st Class Monty Heath, had gone in a different direction and saw a survivor flee the bombed vehicle toward a nearby berm. Heath fired once, hitting the man and sending him tumbling down the back side of the small rise.

At that point Hyder began assessing the damage and surveying the dead. "I was going around to the different [killed in action] with my camera to take photos," Hyder told me. "It was a mess."

Hyder said that he and a few other SEALs began to bury the casualties near a ravine by piling rocks over them. As they did so, he approached the man that his partner had shot. "He was partially alive, facedown, his back to me, and he rolled over. I shot him, finished him. He was dying, but he rolled over and I didn't know whether he was armed or not. That was the end of that." Hyder said that his single shot had blasted open the man's head.

What followed Hyder's shooting of the wounded man is in dispute. It turned out the man was unarmed. The premature attack by the Air Force jets on the convoy was widely viewed within the team as a tragic military error. But what came next, according to a retired SEAL on the mission, was a sickening, intentional act. Heath later reported to his team leader that he watched Hyder mutilate the dead man by stomping in his already damaged skull. When Heath reported Hyder's actions, "several of the guys turned and walked away," said the retired SEAL who was on Objective Bull, but who did not witness Hyder's alleged mutilation. "They were disgusted." He quoted Heath as saying to his team leader, "I'm morally flexible but I can't handle that."

Hyder told me that he did not desecrate the body during Objective Bull. "I deny it," he asserted, adding that he didn't understand why his partner would have claimed to have witnessed it. "Why would I do that?" he asked. "Somebody else is making this up. Memories get distorted over fourteen years. They're telling you how they remember it. There was a lot of chaos. I'm telling you the absolute truth." In the days after the operation, however, Hyder bragged and told others about the mutilation while show-ing off photos he'd taken.[1]

The retired SEAL, who spent the better part of two decades at the command, said he never asked Hyder why he mutilated the corpse. It wasn't necessary. He assumed it was a twisted act of misplaced revenge over the previous day's events—specifically, the gruesome death of Neil Roberts.

By THE TIME THE TWO DOZEN OR SO RED TEAM OPERATORS HAD departed for Objective Bull, tension had already grown between Hyder, a commissioned officer, and the enlisted operators under his command. The situation was not particularly hard to understand.

One of the inviolable rules at Dam Neck since its inception was that to gain entry, a SEAL had to pass Green Team. Even in the early years under Marcinko, when SEALs were selected because they were popular or could handle their gin, they still had to meet the training and per-formance standards. No exceptions. For officers specifically, the only way you could command Red, Gold, or Blue was to have passed the training course. Just as officers and enlisted went through the same training at BUD/S, so too did SEAL Team 6 officers and enlisted pass through the same training crucible. It was the same at Delta as well. The officers were unlikely to need these skills in an operation; their main role was instead to command and communicate during an operation. But Marcinko under-stood that an elite force of operators would never respect an officer who couldn't demonstrate the same skill level at shooting, diving, and jumping. Historically, some SEALs who did not select for Green Team served at the command in the boat division, called Gray Team. In a maritime oper-ation, officers and enlisted SEALs would drive and man the boats. If they wanted to join an assault team, they had to pass Green Team.

But shortly after 9/11, when it became clear Team 6 would be de-ploying, Capt. Kernan was faced with the dilemma of going from peace to war: he needed more manpower. With few options, Kernan took Gray

Team officers and enlisted operators and surged them to the assault teams, skipping Green Team. Kernan had, in effect, lowered the standard at the command. It would become one of the most consequential decisions at the command, one that would have effects stretching for two decades afterward. Kernan, in an effort to fulfill the Pentagon's request for a new war, had upset Team 6's delicate culture of performance.

With the Gray officers in particular, Kernan favored SEALs who fit his image: Naval Academy graduates. There was no formal or official policy change, but in the years Kernan was in command at Dam Neck, no officers who were not from the academy were selected or otherwise brought into Dam Neck.

Lt. Cdr. Hyder, a Gray Team officer and academy graduate who had never been to Green Team, fit both Kernan's preferences, and he moved to Red Team. Kernan's bureaucratic adjustment did not necessarily mean that Hyder was unworthy to lead a group of assaulters, but in the eyes of the enlisted operators, he'd taken a shortcut in a world where SEALs earned their position through talent and hard work. As they saw it, putting Hyder, or any of the other Gray Team officers who "fleeted up," into the assault teams was unfair. He might not have seen the eye-rolling his presence provoked among the enlisted, or the quiet derision from operators who rarely accept an officer they don't view as an equally skilled, if not as experienced, craftsman. But the eye-rolling and quiet derision existed nonetheless.[2] The enlisted mafia's feelings about officers in Hyder's situation ran from suspicion on one end to contempt on the other, just as Richard Marcinko had designed it twenty years earlier. The standard was part of their code, and their code had been violated.

Even before the attack on the Objective Bull convoy and the alleged mutilation of the dead Afghan's corpse, Hyder had committed at least one killing with questionable justification. Just a few weeks into the deployment, on January 18, Hyder killed an unarmed Afghan man north of Kandahar during the unit's first ground assault of the war. In that operation, Hyder was leading a team on a nighttime mission to capture suspected al Qaeda militants in a compound. After securing several detainees and cordoning off the area, Hyder and his men waited for their helicopters to arrive and extract them. During the mission, the SEALs reported receiving small arms fire from exterior positions, though no one was hit. After ninety minutes, as the helicopters were nearing the rendezvous point, one of the SEALs alerted Hyder that a man who had been lying in a ditch nearby was walking toward the SEALs' position.

In an interview, Hyder later said the man had approached his position with his arms tucked into his armpits and did not heed warnings from other SEALs to stop. Hyder acknowledged that the man likely did not understand English and probably couldn't see very well. Unlike the SEALs, the man was not wearing night-vision goggles. "He continued to move towards us," Hyder said. "I assessed he was nearing a distance where he was within an area where he could do damage with a grenade." Hyder said that a week earlier, a militant had detonated a concealed grenade after approaching some American CIA officers, seriously injuring them. "He kept moving toward us, so at 15 meters I put one round in him and he dropped. Unfortunately, it turned out he had an audiocassette in his hand. By the rules of engagement he became a legitimate target and it was supported. It's a question, why was he a threat? After all that activity, he'd been hiding in a ditch for 90 minutes, he gets up, he's spoken to, yelled at in the dark...it's disturbing. I'm disappointed he didn't take a knee."

Hyder faced no discipline for the shooting. The rules of engagement allowed the ground force commander to shoot anyone he viewed as a threat, regardless of whether they were armed at the time of the shooting. But in the eyes of the enlisted SEALs of Red Team, Hyder had killed a man who didn't have to die. Five or six operators stood in a semicircle, their lasers trained on his chest as the old man approached their position. All of them were closer than Hyder. They perceived no threat. It was cold; he was old and underdressed and kept his hands in the only reasonable place to warm them. Two of the operators who had been with Hyder reported afterward that the man was not a threat. One of those operators was Neil Roberts. "We watched him execute the dude with no cause," an operator who witnessed Hyder's shooting told me. After that day, the enlisted started calling Hyder "Waingro," after the serial killer in the movie *Heat* who killed impulsively.

AFTER OBJECTIVE BULL, RED TEAM GATHERED BACK AT BAGRAM. Most of the operators held a meeting. No officers were present at the meeting. The discussion covered battlefield ethics, according to the retired SEAL who was present. Inside a heated tent, as many as forty SEAL Team 6 operators asked themselves how they wanted to treat their fallen enemies. Should they seek revenge for Roberts? Was it acceptable to desecrate the dead?

"We talked about it," said the retired SEAL. "We said, 'This is not who we are. We shoot [enemy combatants]—no issues with that—and then we move on. There's honor involved…and Vic Hyder obviously traipsed all over that.…Mutilation isn't part of the game.'"

Despite the internal unit discussion over how to treat dead bodies on the battlefield, Red Team did not report Heath's allegation of Hyder's battlefield mutilation, a war crime that if substantiated was punishable by up to twenty years in prison under US military law. In what would become part of a pattern of secrecy and silence, the SEAL operators settled the issue on their own and kept the incident from their chain of command.

Senior leaders at the command knew that the grisly circumstances of Roberts's death had unsettled Red Team. "Fifi was mutilated," said a retired enlisted SEAL leader, using Neil Roberts's nickname, and who was involved in internal discussions about how to prevent SEAL Team 6 from seeking revenge. "And then we had to address a very important question, how do you get the guys' heads straight to mitigate any retaliation for Fifi? Otherwise, we knew it's going to get out of control."

In the twenty years since each assault team developed names and flags, each had developed a group personality around those identities. Many in Red Team had appropriated the Native American warrior self-image. As they saw it, the attempted beheading of Roberts was an unmistakable message of brutality from the enemy. "A third of the guys literally think they're Apache warriors, then you had the Muslim way of removing a head," the retired SEAL leader explained. "I understand the desire, I don't condone it, but there was definite retaliation."

After the deployment, SEAL Team 6's leadership examined Hyder's actions during Objective Bull. The review took place in the weeks after Red Team redeployed to Dam Neck. Like nearly everything at Team 6, the review was internal and unofficial. Tactical lessons would be shared within the special operations community, unofficially, but behavioral or leadership failures would never be discussed outside headquarters. To some of them, what was most troubling about Hyder's deployment was not that he may have taken gratuitous revenge for Roberts's death on an unrelated civilian, but that on more than one occasion, as ground force commander, he had fired his weapon at all. "If you have multiple incidents where the ground force commander pulls the trigger on a deployment, you have a total breakdown of operational tactics," said one retired SEAL leader. "It's not their responsibility—that is why we have DEVGRU operators." In one deployment, Hyder had demonstrated a detrimental consequence of Capt. Kernan's decision to drop a standard.

Beyond the mutilation allegedly committed by Hyder, the sight of the dead civilians, especially the women and children, killed during the opening air strikes of Objective Bull left an indelible impression on members of Red Team. "It ruined some of these guys," said the former SEAL operator on the mission. One of the children hit in the attack was medevaced back to Bagram. The child survived and lived at the US air base for some time after, cared for by members of JSOC and SEAL Team 6.

Six days after Objective Bull, the Pentagon announced at a press conference that an air strike had killed fourteen civilians, who a spokesperson said were "somehow affiliated" with al Qaeda. Sources at SEAL Team 6 present during the operation estimated the number of dead was between seventeen and twenty. At Team 6, the incident became known as the "Wedding Party bombing" after it was learned that the convoy was driving to a wedding.

"The SEALs believe that they can handle the discipline themselves, that's equal to or greater than what the criminal justice system would give to the person," said Susan Raser, a retired Naval Criminal Investigative Service agent who led the agency's criminal division. "They have an internal process that they think is sufficient and they are not inclined to cooperate unless they absolutely have to." Raser, who conducted investigations into both regular SEAL units and SEAL Team 6, said that in her experience SEALs simply didn't report wrongdoing by their teammates.

Despite the disapproval the Red Team assaulters may have had for Hyder, there was another code, which they would not violate. None of Hyder's teammates would rat him out to the Navy. Some of that code could be the result of how Marcinko designed the unit's ethos. But as much of it, if not more, was an almost sacrosanct rule in the military overall. Every young soldier, no matter which service they join, learns from the first days of boot camp that snitching is a cardinal sin. Gen. Douglas MacArthur, explaining why he didn't rat out West Point classmates who hazed him, said, "My father and mother have taught me these two immutable principles—never to lie, never to tattle."

SLABINSKI'S TEAM—OR WHAT REMAINED OF IT—SAT OUT OBJECtive Bull. The snipers recovered at Bagram, then returned to Gardez to wait for their next operation. It came a week later. One of the task force's Predator drones spotted a convoy departing Shah-e-Kot, moving toward the border with Pakistan. Red Team had been chastened by the Wedding Party incident and the limits of aerial surveillance, but the images coming back from the drone appeared promising: heavily armed men could be seen mingling with the vehicles, apparently acting as a security escort for someone important enough to require one.

Two Red Team elements, including Slabinski and Kyle Soderberg from Takur Ghar, loaded onto Chinooks and headed toward the Pakistan border, hoping to intercept the convoy before it got into the Tribal Areas. The mission was code-named Objective Wolverine.

When the helicopters caught up to the convoy, one Chinook strafed the three trucks on the road, forcing them to stop. Meanwhile, the second Chinook, carrying Slab and his sniper crew, landed several hundred yards away, out of view from the road. Once off the helicopter, Slab and the snipers made their way toward a rise above the road, where they established a firing position hidden from the militants' view.

The scene below was chaos. The militants fled their bullet-ridden vehicles, scrambling to get away from two additional Chinooks headed in their direction. From his vantage point, Slab fired rounds from his SR-25 sniper rifle at the fighters trying to escape. Slab and his sniper crew killed nearly twenty foreign al Qaeda fighters. The bodies lay across the roadway and the slope, cut down before they could reach cover from the SEALs' fire. It had been roughly a week since Slabinski lost Chapman and Roberts at Takur Ghar. But now he found himself with the higher ground, able to target the enemy with impunity. Slabinski and some of his teammates had discussed getting revenge for Takur Ghar. Now he had the opportunity.

"After I shot this dude in the head," Slabinski later said, "there was a guy who had his feet, just his feet sticking out of some little rut, I mean he was dead but everyone's got nerves. I shot him about 20 times in the legs and every time you shot him his body would kick up, you could see his body twitching. It was like a game. Like 'hey look at this dude,' and the guy would just twitch again. It was just good therapy. It was really good therapy for everyone who was there."[3] It took an officer's order to get Slabinski to stop firing.[4]

And, unlike the Wedding Party, the SEALs hit a hostile enemy. When the SEALs searched the dead, they found US military equipment and gear on the bodies: it had come from Takur Ghar.

Slab would describe the operation as "good payback" in an unpublished interview with an author of a book about Roberts Ridge. According to Slabinski, "We just slaughtered those dudes....We needed that. The guys needed that [after Takur Ghar] to get back in the saddle because everyone was gun shy."

The operation was referred to by some in Red Team as a "revenge op" and passed down as a war story told to all the new operators who arrived for years to come. The story usually came after questions about Neil Roberts's squad automatic weapon, or SAW rifle, bent from his fall out of the Chinook. It was placed on the wall of Red Team's room at the Dam Neck base in Virginia Beach, a visible reminder of their teammate, their first deployment, and the troubles that would follow.

Slabinski returned to Dam Neck shortly after Takur Ghar and Objective Wolverine. He was awarded a Navy Cross, the second-highest battlefield award for heroism. For a year afterward, the leaders at the command limited Slabinski's battlefield exposure—assigning him to Green Team as an instructor, for example—hoping the psychological wounds from Roberts Ridge would heal.

A few months after the 2002 deployment, Team 6 held a ceremony for Chapman's widow and daughters, celebrating his heroism on Takur Ghar. During the ceremony, the SEALs unveiled Chapman's name etched into their wall of heroes, the only non-SEAL to be included, and just under Neil Roberts's. The SEALs credited him with saving their lives by engaging the enemy in the first bunker after they exited their helicopter. "If John hadn't engaged the first enemy position, it would have surely killed us all before we reached cover," Slabinski said in September 2002. "John died saving us from enemy fire, which was effective from three sides when he was killed." The statement was included in Chapman's Air Force Cross citation, which was awarded in 2003.

CHAPTER 8

SEAL TEAM 6, 2.0

I N DECEMBER 2004, SOME OF THE LATEST GREEN TEAM GRADU-
ates filed into a room on the second floor of the Team 6 base at Dam
Neck, each carrying a case of beer. This was their first day at the command,
the day they joined their assault team. Each had been drafted, like professional athletes, and had come to meet their teammates. Among the "rook-
ies" were Matthew Bissonnette and Robert O'Neill. The two operators
were part of a new generation at Team 6, among some of the first SEALs
at the command since the wars in Afghanistan and Iraq had begun. Bissonnette, a college-educated son of missionaries from Alaska, had come
to Dam Neck from SEAL Team 5. O'Neill, a beefy, red-haired Montana
native, had served at SEAL Team 2 and Team 4 before being selected. The
two were dissimilar in many ways—Bissonnette was tidy and reserved,
O'Neill was scruffy and gregarious—but each was a talented operator who
arrived at Red Team as part of a new generation shaped by the legend and
legacy of Takur Ghar and the first deployment in the Afghan war. They

were not just Team 6 operators, they were Redmen, part of what was referred to as the Tribe.

Around the table, the Tribe stood, most long-haired and heavily tattooed, waiting to meet the newest additions. Up on the walls around them were memorabilia and mementos from previous deployments. One item in particular stood out: an MK 46 light machine gun known as a SAW, or squad automatic weapon. This particular SAW had a bent stock; it had belonged to Neil Roberts. The gun served as a prominent reminder of what everyone at Team 6 referred to as Roberts Ridge. Joining Red Squadron meant an indoctrination into the history of Roberts's death and mutilation, Slabinski's heroics, and the resolve he and the Redmen showed in the days after. O'Neill would later write that joining Red Team meant he could "avenge" the death of Neil Roberts as well as the victims of 9/11. Bissonnette, O'Neill, and other new Team 6 members would learn to value "revenge ops" like Objective Wolverine, where Slabinski had fired his sniper rifle two dozen times to watch an al Qaeda fighter's dead body twitch. They were joining a unit that had established its own myths about its war experience but had not reckoned with the realities of the new wars and how they would shape these men and their unit.

As the sharpest tip of the spear in the US military, they hunted an enemy that had only grown and metastasized. In the nearly three years since Objective Wolverine, the command had changed, first subtly and then less so. The demands of two simultaneous wars altered Team 6's mission. While they were still required to hunt for bin Laden and the rest of al Qaeda's leadership, they were no longer planning and training for single missions, one-off counterterrorism raids, and hostage rescues. The needs of the Forever War meant that deployment after deployment, the SEALs were rarely conducting missions that were considered traditional military special operations. Team 6 had transformed into an elite group of storm troopers.

THERE WAS SOME INTERNAL ACCOUNTABILITY FOR TRANSGRESSIONS in Afghanistan. Vic Hyder finished his tour at SEAL Team 6 shortly after returning from the 2002 Afghanistan deployment and was later promoted to the rank of commander, the Navy equivalent of a major. He was awarded the Silver Star for his efforts at Takur Ghar to save Roberts and the rest of the Red Team recon element. Despite that, a few years later, after Hyder's name was mentioned for another rotation in Red Team, some of Hyder's former operators informed SEAL Team 6 leadership that he was not welcome back in the unit.

The violence the SEALs experienced and participated in during their first wartime deployments had a lasting effect on nearly everyone in Red Team. Their reactions varied from repulsion to an embrace of brutality. Some, like Hyder, were quietly sidelined from the unit. Others self-selected out of the unit. Among those who remained, there were those who reveled in the violence. And wanted more.

"Experiencing, seeing real violence affects guys differently," a retired SEAL officer who served at the command during Takur Ghar said. "Some recoil. Others see war and violence as an art form—they're the great ones. Others are so overcome by violence they get more violent in response."

Sadism crept into the SEALs' practices, with no apparent consequences. A few months after Objective Bull, for example, a Red Team operator began taunting dying insurgents on videos he shot as part of his post-operation responsibilities. These "bleed out" videos were replayed on multiple occasions at Bagram Air Base. The SEAL, known as the Mad Turk, would gather other members of Red Team to watch the last few moments of an enemy fighter's life, counting down the last five or so seconds until an enemy fighter expired. "It was war porn," said the retired officer, who viewed one of the videos. "No one would do anything about them."

During the same deployment, the Mad Turk and a teammate got drunk one evening in the unit's Bagram quarters. An argument ensued. Turk hit his teammate in the face with a pistol. He was sent back to Virginia Beach and was then quietly pushed out of the Navy, but the experience didn't chasten him: he later bragged to Duane Dieter that he'd used on his teammate a CQD "muzzle strike" technique from their training. He joined the CIA's paramilitary branch.

New missions also meant new training. One of the consequences of the war was that Duane Dieter and his CQD training were removed from Green Team. In fact, Bissonnette and O'Neill were among the first new generation of Team 6 who would not meet Dieter during the selection course. For a year after Dieter was no longer invited to lead his CQD training, the unit still did the hood drills taught by CQD instructors. Bissonnette and O'Neill were among the last to receive the training at Team 6. At the time, Dieter was told the hood drills and the hand-to-hand defense were no longer as vital for the kinds of assaults the operators were conducting in Afghanistan and Iraq. And while he was never explicitly told why his contract wasn't renewed, Dieter believed Szymanski led an effort to replace CQD with mixed martial arts, known as MMA, which was becoming increasingly popular as a sport in the United States. The impact of removing Dieter from Team 6 in 2004, though, was glaring. At a time when Team 6 began a cycle of constant deployments, one of the few, if only, ethical guardrails at the command was removed. While CQD would continue to be taught at BUD/S and the regular teams for another decade, the decision to remove Dieter had lasting consequences.

Team 6 adapted to the new wars, adjusting their training and learning lessons about the realities of war. After Takur Ghar, for example, no Team 6 reconnaissance element would ever conduct an insertion at the location of their target, known as "landing on the X," where X is the target—a potentially perilous tactic that is faster than patrolling stealthily on foot but eliminates the element of surprise. But no amount of training could prepare Dam Neck SEALs for leadership failures.

June 28, 2005—Kunar Province, Afghanistan

Chief Petty Officer James Hatch scanned the smoldering remains of the MH-47 Chinook helicopter on the mountainside. Little remained: a rotor, part of an engine, and black charred earth where the helicopter—with sixteen Americans, including eight SEALs, aboard—crashed after being shot down by a single rocket-propelled grenade. Hatch, a Red Team operator, had climbed with his troop over one side of a nearly vertical mountainside and down the other, searching for survivors. He and his teammates could see there would be none.

The Chinook had flown in a day earlier, part of a quick reaction force trying to rescue four conventional SEALs who had inserted on the mountaintop for a reconnaissance mission. The four had landed on a moonless night on a mountain ridge, perched above and near a village that sheltered a local insurgent. The SEALs were trying to locate their target, mark his position, then exfiltrate back to their base. A larger team of SEALs and Army Green Berets would return twenty-four hours later for a raid. But within an hour or so of making their way from their drop-off point, the four SEALs—Lt. Michael Murphy, Petty Officer 2nd Class Danny Dietz, Petty Officer 2nd Class Matthew Axelson, and Navy Hospital Corpsman 2nd Class Marcus Luttrell—were ambushed.

The SEALs' target, a local insurgent named Ahmad Shah, had been alerted by the unmistakable noise of a twin-rotor helicopter flying over a steep and narrow canyon. Shah grabbed his small force, as few as seven but no more than ten, and quietly stalked up the ridgeline in the early morning hours as the SEALs settled into a covered observation post. Shah and his men had the advantage of both the high ground and familiarity with the terrain. They hit the Americans with an overwhelming attack, from AK-47 rifles, a PK machine gun, and rocket-propelled grenades, which forced the four SEALs down the nearly sheer mountainside. The SEALs fought and survived for more than an hour, but struggled to contact their base for air support or a rescue. Eventually, Lt. Murphy exposed himself to use a satellite phone to reach a Bagram operations center and request help. Video footage shot by Shah's men captured a thunderous gunfight between the Afghan insurgents and the Americans. At one point, during a lull in the fire, the cameraman trailing Shah can be heard shouting to the SEALs in English, "If you don't fight, we don't kill you."

The quick reaction force, which consisted of eight additional SEALs, including the SEAL task unit commander, Lt. Cdr. Erik Kristensen, and another eight members of the Army's 160th Special Operations Aviation Regiment (SOAR), flew to Murphy's last known location. As the SEALs in the Chinook were preparing to fast-rope down and search for their teammates, Shah's fighters hit the helicopter from close range. The Chinook fell within moments, killing everyone aboard.

The mission for Hatch and his team was to look for not just survivors of the helicopter but also any sign of Murphy and his recon team. Another team of Redmen was making its way by foot up the other side of the mountain. Among the group was Robert O'Neill on his first deployment with Team 6. As he and his team struggled up the steep mountainside, searching for Murphy, Axelson, Dietz, and Luttrell, it dawned on him that he was experiencing "real" war for the first time. The longer it took to find the SEALs, the less likely they would find them alive. But on June 28, no one in Red Team knew where the missing SEALs were or what condition they were in.

Three of the four, Murphy, Dietz, and Axelson, were already dead, their bodies scattered around the mountain bowl. But Luttrell, a massive six-foot-five-inch former high school football player from Texas, was alive. In the middle of the battle, he'd later admit, he'd dropped his weapon and run. He was eventually hit by an RPG, his body thrown down the mountainside. When he regained consciousness, he hid under a rock ledge until Shah's fighters moved beyond the gully and dispersed. Luttrell, with a gunshot wound in his leg, three broken vertebrae and a broken nose, and hit with shrapnel from the RPG, walked and crawled with his broken back and heavy blood loss through the cedar trees and ferns for several hours, until he was eventually found by a man from a village on the other side of the Sawtalo Sar ridge.

For seven days, the villager, Mohammed Gulab, gave Luttrell sanctuary. Each day Shah's men appeared in his village, threatening Gulab and his neighbors for harboring the American and demanding they turn over Luttrell. Gulab and his village refused, and eventually a village elder snuck a handwritten message from Luttrell to the nearest American military outpost.

A few hours later, US forces flew into Gulab's village, where they found Luttrell and Gulab hiding from Shah's militiamen in a wooded area. They quickly ferried Luttrell to safety. He was the lone survivor of the disastrous Red Wings operation.

James Hatch, Rob O'Neill, and the rest of both Red Team squads searched the area the entire time Gulab sheltered Luttrell, leaving only when they had received word Luttrell was alive. They had scoured the ravine for every piece of American-made equipment to find their fellow SEALs and to understand what had taken place near Sawtalo Sar. Hatch would later write in his book, *Touching the Dragon: And Other Techniques for Surviving Life's Wars*, that he found one of Shah's ambush sites, a dug-in spot behind a cropping of boulders, with what he estimated were hundreds of spent 7.62 mm brass casings from AK-47 rifle fire. There was no question his fellow SEALs had been overwhelmed with firepower. The American rescue and recovery efforts found no evidence of any enemy fatalities. The Afghan fighters, with double the manpower and the advantage of the terrain, had the tactical upper hand over the four-man SEAL reconnaissance element. Years later, Gulab would tell a *Newsweek* reporter that when he found Luttrell, the SEAL still had all eleven of his rifle magazines on him, full. Unless Luttrell had used one of his fallen teammates' weapons, Luttrell was unable to fire many rounds, if any, at Shah's men.

Luttrell would later tell Anderson Cooper in a *60 Minutes* interview that Murphy took fire as he made the emergency satellite phone call. Luttrell was close, but protected by rocks, and he listened as Murphy, dying with multiple gunshot wounds, called for Luttrell to come save him. "He took two rounds to the chest," Luttrell told Cooper. "It dropped him. I tried to make my way up to him....I was out in the open, waving my hands. I was like, 'Just come down to me'....I heard his gun go off and a lot of gunfire in his area. I was trying with everything I had to get to him, and he started screaming my name. He was like, 'Marcus, man, you gotta help me! I need help, Marcus!' It got so intense that I actually put my weapon down and covered my ears. 'Cause I couldn't stand to hear him die. All I wanted him to do was stop screaming my name....And I put my weapon down in a gunfight while my best friend was getting killed. So that pretty much makes me a coward....I broke right there, I quit right there."[1]

Luttrell's candor broke with SEAL tradition, which celebrated quiet professionalism. But his experience and actions during the operation reflected the full spectrum of human behavior under wartime duress. Luttrell had also been wounded, and if he had not hidden in a crevice and covered himself in debris, he too would have likely been killed. His determination to crawl down the mountain and evade Shah's forces was miraculous. His rescue and protection by Gulab, at the threat of death, was heroic.

Red Team witnessed everything but the initial ambush and understood what occurred that day. In the days after Luttrell was recovered, the SEALs at Team 6 could see clearly how a series of poor leadership decisions by several SEAL officers had played out in tragic proportions. The failures began with the mission itself. The operation to go after Ahmad Shah had been proposed several times by previous SEAL commanders based in Jalalabad before Team 10 had arrived in the country. In fact, once the unit composed of SEAL Team 10 and the SEAL Delivery Vehicle Team One arrived, SEAL Team 6 had again been approached about conducting the operation. Each time, SEAL Team 6 officers and senior enlisted declined to participate. Shah wasn't worth the risk, they assessed. Shah was a local commander, neither al Qaeda nor affiliated with the Taliban. The SEAL Team 6 officers went so far as to discourage other special operations units from conducting the mission. The Dam Neck planners thought the better approach was to wait Shah out. Eventually he'd want to leave the valley, and when he did, US forces could target him.

The terrain worried the Team 6 planners. It would minimize the likelihood of success of the operation, they reasoned. The Korengal Valley was perhaps the most dangerous place for US troops in Afghanistan. The topography made it a place few outside forces, if any, had ever controlled. The Soviets didn't bother, and though US forces would try for more than a decade to deny the Taliban, al Qaeda, and Islamic insurgents like Shah a foothold in the valley and its neighboring canyons, the Pashtuns of the area have never endured a successful foreign occupation. The Americans came to call it the Valley of Death.

The mission concept bore a striking resemblance to Takur Ghar: it involved dropping an inexperienced reconnaissance team on the top of a mountain by helicopter as had happened more than three years earlier with Slabinski and his men—and this time in even less traversable terrain. And yet, despite that and the misgivings of SEAL Team 6 as well as the CIA, the conventional SEALs were approved to conduct the mission. The military rewarded officers who were viewed as aggressive. This was a war, after all. The result was both catastrophic and avoidable: nineteen American servicemen dead, among them eleven SEALs, in what became the most fatal operation in Naval Special Warfare's history at the time, and the worst day for American forces in the Afghan war at that point. Plus, a young SEAL was scarred for life. For the Dam Neck SEALs, the leadership failures were clear.

But before any of the awful details about what had transpired on the Red Wings operation came to light, Chief Petty Officer James Hatch and his teammates made it to the gulch beneath the Sawtalo Sar ridgeline just as Luttrell was loaded into a helicopter and flown to safety. Hatch turned to one of his teammates and said, "That guy is going to write a book and make a million dollars."

CHAPTER 9

THE HATCHET

B Y THE TIME O'NEILL, HATCH, AND THE REST OF RED TEAM RE-
turned to Virginia Beach in 2005, the unit was in the midst of a transformation. Lt. Gen. Stanley McChrystal, the commanding officer of the
Joint Special Operations Command, was in the process of expanding his
task force to fight two wars. To do so, the mission, scale, and tempo would
radically change. "[T]he escalating war on terror in the aftermath of September 11," McChrystal wrote years later, "compelled the relatively small
hostage-rescue and counterterrorist force to adapt to new, more ominous
threats. [JSOC] needed to become a more complex organization with unprecedented capability, and we needed to employ that on a daily—and
nightly—basis, year after year."[1]

For SEAL Team 6, a new mission required an expansion. The command, whose force had fluctuated between one hundred fifty and two
hundred operators, was asked to grow. The Navy elevated SEAL Team
6 to what was called a major command. The unit would add a hundred
more operators, each assault team would become known as a squadron,

and each squadron would add another assault troop. Team 6 also added a new intelligence component to the three assault squadrons. Called Black Squadron, it gave Dam Neck four major squadrons. A SEAL captain, the Navy equivalent of a colonel, would command the unit, with officers at the commander rank leading each squadron. The change, while bureaucratic, was seismic. Just as Capt. Kernan had responded to the needs of the new war by filling his assault teams with SEALs who had not completed Green Team, the new expansion meant the SEALs were diluting the quality that had made Team 6 their premier unit. At the time Team 6 was asked to expand, Naval Special Warfare did not expand with it. That meant that for several years, starting in 2005, the command would allow more operators into the unit from the same size pool of candidates in the regular teams. Team 6 was, in effect, lowering its standards.

This also meant that Dam Neck diminished the experience level at key leadership positions. This was a secondary consequence of adding operators to the command and expanding the assault teams to squadrons. An assault team boat crew leader, as they were called, usually had seven to eight years' experience at Team 6 when they were promoted into the position. When the Teams expanded to squadrons, the newly named commanding officers had as few as three years' experience at the command. Likewise, the officers leading the troops and squadrons were now a rank or two lower, while having more authority on the battlefield. Combined with Kernan's decision to move several Gray Team officers into the assault teams at the outset of the war, some Team 6 leaders warned Naval Special Warfare that the expansion would have terrible consequences. "Once the squadrons were granted [commander rank] command authority," a retired senior Team 6 leader said, "it decentralized accountability and oversight. I was a vocal critic against the change. It set the stage for much abuse, which DEVGRU is suffering the consequence of today." By granting greater authority to lower-ranking officers and less experienced enlisted SEALs, the command reduced its own internal oversight on battlefield conduct. At a time when the command had forced an ethical trainer like Duane Dieter out and increased the frequency of its missions, it needed greater scrutiny and oversight. Instead, it had less.

This was the Dam Neck that Bissonnette and O'Neill returned to following their first deployments. The Redmen, now Red Squadron, were led by a mid-career SEAL officer who would come to have more influence on Team 6 than any other officer for almost two decades, and would come to define the unit's identity as lethal and violent. Hugh Wyman Howard III is as blue-blooded as a SEAL officer can get. He is the descendant of several admirals and was the fourth generation to attend the Naval Academy. Howard is almost six feet, trim, and viewed by his peers as a mediocre physical performer. In fact, Howard, known as Wyman throughout Naval Special Warfare, should not have been at Dam Neck at all, several Team 6 officers and operators told me. Howard graduated BUD/S in 1991 and then was assigned to SEAL Team 8 at Little Creek. Howard, who is consistently described as an intelligent, ambitious, and hardworking officer, was still among the lowest-ranked junior officers on the East Coast. The distinction disqualified him for Dam Neck, yet in 1998, Howard found himself screened for Green Team. Howard's naval pedigree had earned him a sea daddy in then Cdr. James O'Connell. When O'Connell moved to Dam Neck as the second-in-command, he got Howard a slot in Green Team. O'Connell convinced Capt. Albert Calland, the Team 6 commanding officer, to let Howard into Green despite failing selection. "Bert agreed to bring Wyman in because O'Connell told him Wyman was great with paperwork," a retired SEAL who worked for Calland told me. Once in Green Team, the Team 6 leadership made it clear to the training cadre that unless Howard committed a serious safety violation, he would be allowed to pass training and join Team 6. Howard was considered a competent operator, but without the push by O'Connell, he would never have made it to Team 6. Howard hadn't cheated, but two senior SEAL officers had bent rules and lowered the standard to get the younger SEAL into Dam Neck. Howard's ascension into the SEALs' most elite unit was a paradox: by letting Howard in, the unit was violating the inviolable standard Marcinko had set, especially for officers, while simultaneously doing so in a manner that reinforced Marcinko's notion that the leader of the command could choose whomever he liked to join. Howard was drafted into what was then Red Team, joining the Tribe and subscribing to the Native American identity as the command's most elite warriors.

WHILE MUCH OF THE TRIBE SEARCHED THE WRECKAGE OF RED Wings, Petty Officer 1st Class Matthew Bissonnette was on his first deployment in Iraq as a member of SEAL Team 6. Bissonnette was a twenty-nine-year-old rising operator. He'd started carrying a rifle by the end of elementary school in Alaska. Bissonnette enlisted in the Navy after graduating from college, and eventually served his first two tours with Team 5 in Coronado, California.

Bissonnette was, in many ways, what Marcinko envisioned: a highly gifted enlisted SEAL who used any and every available angle to gain an advantage. One of Bissonnette's superiors would later say that he first encountered the young team leader in Afghanistan and asked Bissonnette to walk him through how he planned a raid. At the time, McRaven's new rules of engagement required that SEALs conduct "callouts," where operators announced they were outside and ordered the target to surrender or they would commence an attack. The goal was to avoid civilian casualties by allowing women, children, and the elderly to flee before the SEALs began their attack. The SEALs had scoffed at giving up the element of surprise, allowing their targets to hide weapons and gain a tactical advantage on the impending raid. Bissonnette's solution was simple: ignore the rule in situations where they were certain their target was inside the building. The superior was impressed with both Bissonnette's willingness to break the rules and his up-front justification. It was precisely the kind of question-and-answer that candidates for the command might receive during their selection board, and Bissonnette showed a glimpse of what made him an effective Team 6 operator.

Iraq was a different kind of war. There, US special operations forces were called upon to kill at rates unseen in previous wars. Their exposure to daily violence was unprecedented. For his first deployment, Bissonnette was sent to Iraq, where he was added to a Delta squadron. With Delta, Bissonnette would get his first kill as a SEAL operator and conduct dozens of raids in Baghdad. At the time, many of the Delta operators in the squadron had an unusual weapon attached to their uniforms: a fourteen-inch hatchet, or tomahawk, with a smooth mahogany handle.

The Delta operators had been using the hatchets on operations for several deployments. They had them thanks to Kevin Holland, one of their most senior operators, who had been a member of SEAL Team 6's Redmen. Holland was an avid outdoorsman from rural North Carolina and had fixated on the Native American warrior identity. He asked a friend, Dan Winkler, a bladesmith who made custom knives, for a tomahawk. Winkler replicated historically accurate Native American blades—the authenticity of his work was acknowledged when he was hired to make the weapons used in the film *The Last of the Mohicans*, starring Daniel Day-Lewis. Winkler made a tomahawk for Holland, who put it up in the Red Team room as the group's symbol. A few years later, Holland left the Navy. After the September 11 attacks he asked to return to active duty and rejoin Red Team. He was rejected but was told he could return after completing one tour with a regular SEAL team.

Insulted, Holland joined the Army and applied directly to Delta Force. At Delta, the only requirement for admission is passing their rigorous selection course. One need not even have served in the military. If a prospective operator can pass their selection and meet the standards, Delta doesn't discriminate. The openness of their selection process is one reason Delta's culture is now seen as less insular and their operators more mature than those of the SEALs from Dam Neck. Holland passed selection and returned to active duty as an elite assaulter for the Army. Shortly after the war in Iraq began, Holland asked Winkler to make tomahawks for his assault team, which they could bring to the war zone. Holland and Winkler found a group of private donors to pay for their procurement. Winkler initially made six tomahawks for Holland's assault team within C Squadron, each branded on the handle with a number from the first production. The tomahawks soon became popular.[2]

What had started as a tool to break a lock or bash a doorknob soon evolved into a secondary weapon. After several deployments in Iraq, the Delta operators had a discreet competition among themselves over who could score the most kills with the weapon.[3] One retired three-star general who served at the Pentagon at the time told me senior officers and civilian officials received reports from the field that Delta operators were committing war crimes. The view from the higher levels of the Pentagon at the time, however, was that Iraq was a nasty war, the enemy didn't follow the laws of armed conflict, and the limited atrocities served as a psychological deterrent to al Qaeda and the Iraq insurgency.

"We made it clear they needed to keep it quiet," the retired general said. Delta kept track internally of who within the unit desecrated the dead or otherwise violated the laws of armed conflict, he said, and once the pace of the war slowed down enough that the individual operator could be replaced, the assaulter was quietly pushed out of Delta. "It served a purpose for a limited time during the war."

One former SEAL Team 6 noncommissioned officer said that he and others at the command were concerned that the scale and intensity of the violence in Iraq were so great that US operators might be tempted to engage in retaliatory mutilations, a tactic al Qaeda and the Iraqi insurgency sometimes employed. "Iraq was a different kind of war—nothing we'd ever seen," said the now retired Team 6 senior leader. "So many dead bodies, so many, everywhere, and so the potential opportunities for mutilations were great."

After the summer 2005 deployment, Howard became Red Squadron's first commander. When Bissonnette and others came back from their time in Iraq with Delta and the Winkler hatchets, the new commander decided the Redmen should have their own hatchets.

In keeping with Red Squadron's appropriation of Native American culture, Howard started a procurement scheme to purchase Winkler hatchets for each SEAL who had a year of service in the squadron. Winkler sold the tomahawks commercially for more than $600 each, making it an expensive tool for an enlisted SEAL paying out of pocket. Following the model of Delta's C Squadron, the hatchets were paid for by private donations solicited by Howard and others. They were stamped with Red Squadron's symbol: a Native American warrior in a headdress with crossed tomahawks.

At first the hatchets appeared to be merely symbolic, because such heavy, awkward weapons had no place in the gear of a special operator. "There's no military purpose for it," a former Red Squadron operator told me. "But they are a great way of being part of a team. It was given as an honor, one more step to strive for, another sign that you're doing a good job."

For some of Howard's men, however, as in Delta, the hatchets soon became more than symbolic. The SEALs began to use them to mutilate dead fighters in Iraq and Afghanistan. Others used them to kill militants in hand-to-hand combat. A template for battlefield misconduct had been established. The enlisted and junior officers were to keep any criminal activity from reaching the squadron commander or the two captains running the unit. This type of secrecy was made possible by the expansion of the unit—and the relatively junior commanders who had been put in place—inadvertently paving the way for the suppression of war crimes and atrocities.

The hatchets soon became a rallying cry. Howard frequently exhorted his squadron and others to "bloody the hatchet"—a send-off before missions and deployments. One SEAL I spoke with said that Howard's words were meant to be inspirational, like those of a coach, and were not an order to use the hatchet to commit war crimes. Others understood it differently. Howard was often heard asking his operators whether they'd gotten "blood on [their] hatchet" when they returned from a deployment. In motivational speeches, Howard told his SEALs that they were "national treasures," better than just SEALs, and that they "bleed red, white and blue."[4]

In 2007, after Howard, Bissonnette, O'Neill, and the rest of Red Squadron showed up with their hatchets in Iraq, the phrase took on a new meaning. The commanding officer of SEAL Team 6 at that time, Capt. Scott Moore, and his deputy, Capt. Tim Szymanski, received reports from the battlefield: their operators were using the weapons to hack dead and dying militants. The reports were not limited to Howard's Redmen. Small groups within the command were skinning the dead, and others practiced mixed martial arts on detainees. The news that American servicemen were engaged in such senseless brutality would seem to shock the conscience. But at the command, no one said or did anything about it.

BEGINNING IN 2005 AND CONTINUING THROUGH 2008, AS US SPE- cial operations forces became more central to the American military strat- egy, the number and frequency of operations in both Iraq and Afghanistan increased dramatically. "On my 2005 deployment in Afghanistan, we only went on a handful of ops," said a retired SEAL who served under Howard. "By the time we moved over to Iraq, we were doing missions as much as five nights a week. Iraq was a target-rich environment, and Wyman allowed us to be more aggressive." Howard, according to two of his former operators, was more willing than previous officers to green-light operations based on "weak" intelligence, leading to more raids and strikes. But according to several formal SEAL Team 6 leaders, it was JSOC commander Lt. Gen. Stanley McChrystal who ordered the increased operational tempo and pushed SEAL Team 6, including Howard, to conduct more frequent raids to help wipe out the insurgency in both Iraq and Afghanistan.

Three years into the Iraq War, al Qaeda and the Sunni/Baathist in- surgency threatened America's success in toppling Saddam Hussein. The prevailing military theory of counterinsurgency, proposed most by Army Gen. David Petraeus, whom the Bush administration supported, argued that any chance at stabilizing the country and helping usher in a new democratic state would require a decrease in the bloodletting. But the killing machine McChrystal created with special operations provided an easy metric to claim success: enemies killed or captured. The country was filled with extremist networks, and McChrystal's notion was that it was better to conduct raids that may fail to locate their original target but nonetheless generate more leads than to wait until US forces confirmed a target's location. "McChrystal's idea was that hitting a dry hole was a good strike," a retired Team 6 officer told me. A transformation was taking place: although the global War on Terror had been put on the military's shoulders, much of what JSOC was doing in both Iraq and Afghani- stan resembled police work. McChrystal urged his commanders to hit

suspected terrorist and insurgent safe houses and anywhere else even only
nominally connected to a target, the same way an urban police force would
send a SWAT team out, hoping their unannounced visit would generate
more leads and ultimately help them track an organization's leaders. Action would generate intelligence, which would generate action, and so on.
Pushing Team 6 and other JSOC units out on a nightly basis worked,
insofar as McChrystal could report how many enemy combatants were
removed from the battlefield. The problem was it had no long-term effect.
"As soon as you kill one network," a retired SEAL Team 6 leader said,
"another network would take over and it would build back up. It was just
this self-licking ice-cream cone, and everyone recognized it."

For the Bush administration, more operations conducted and more
enemy combatants killed served as tangible metrics of success at a time
when each month brought a new record of American soldiers killed in
action. A dead Iraqi insurgent or a dead al Qaeda financier was seen as
a bipartisan success. It might not ultimately deliver victory, but it seemingly prevented defeat. The body count also served as a bulwark against a
Democrat-controlled Congress, which supported withdrawing US troops
from Iraq.

The SEALs, however, were all too happy to play their part. For the
operators, nothing was worse than a three-month deployment to a war
zone where there was little war. SEAL Team 6, which had been designed
to conduct limited kill-or-capture missions and hostage rescues, now had
the most elite manhunters in the war zones, and they didn't want to sit
around all night playing video games. As the most visible leader, Howard
became popular among the enlisted SEALs under his command, several
of whom defended and praised him. He had created and encouraged a
warrior culture under his command, during the unit's steepest descent
into excessive violence. And Howard's enlisted men loved him for it. Robert O'Neill called him "a true warrior."

Not everyone agreed. One of Howard's former superiors who tried
to prevent Howard from advancing into assault leadership positions
said, "Wyman should never have been a squadron commander period,
let alone higher positions of influence. The best, most effective squadron

commanders to ever serve at that unit were all collectively solid SEALs operationally. Kind of like an aviation squadron on an aircraft carrier. Great pilots make great commanders. Respect, trust, confidence—all trump any false narrative of camaraderie. Operators at [Team 6] thrive under competency. Wyman is not that kind of SEAL or leader. That is largely why he is the way he is. He is forced to resort to bravado and theatrics." At a small unit equivalent in size to a small high school, one leader or personality can have an outsize effect on the rest of the group. Howard was just that personality.

Howard's critics saw the hatchets as symbols of something more sinister. They emblematized the rogue, at times criminal, conduct on the battlefield that the commander encouraged. As one former senior SEAL put it, "The hatchets say, 'We're above the law and we can do whatever we want.'" For those who favored them, he continued, the hatchets could be justified as being no more than knives. "It's a great way to explain it away, but they have the hatchets to flaunt the law. Our job is to ensure that we conduct ourselves in a way befitting the American people and the American flag. The hatchet says, 'We don't care about the Geneva Conventions.'"

But there was another factor. Gen. McChrystal had a tenet: if you're not going out on operations, you're doing it wrong. Cdr. Howard repeated to his men what McChrystal and the JSOC leadership were preaching: more operations begat more operations.

Critics inside the command were troubled by the combination of battlefield aggression and Howard's lack of military discipline. A retired noncommissioned officer said Howard's encouragement and provision of Winkler hatchets pushed a warrior ethos that strayed far from any ethical or moral line. The power of the Native American mascot, he said, was not to be dismissed. Since Red Team was first created, there were many operators in the unit who had experienced a "metamorphosis of identity and persona" into Native American warriors. O'Neill, for example, took the Redmen identity seriously. He had a Native American headdress with two white feathers tattooed on his arm. O'Neill told me in an interview that he began getting the edges of the white feathers tattooed red after he got his first "scalp," to signify each enemy kill, in Red Squadron. For six years, beginning when he joined the squadron in 2005, he'd covered much of the two feathers' edges in red. Others would also refer to their kills as "scalps" after their deployments, and in a few cases, they meant them literally.

"Guys are going out every night killing everything," a retired SEAL Team 6 leader told me. "The hatchet was too intimate, too closely aligned with a tomahawk to have been a good idea." The former SEAL, who himself had served in Red during his career, said that by giving operators the weapon attached to their battlefield persona, Howard sent an unmistakable message to his men: use it. And that should have made clear to Howard's commanders that the symbol had taken on a dangerous reality within the unit. "That's when you take away a hatchet," the retired SEAL said. "Not provide them."

Another former SEAL who conducted operations with SEAL Team 6 told me there was an evolution to the battlefield atrocities that followed the command's organization. "It started with Red, then Gold and Blue followed. Where we went wrong is when it was institutionalized." Referring to the purchasing of the hatchets, he said, "This was a failure of leadership."

During one Iraq deployment, Howard returned from a raid to an operations center, his hatchet and his uniform fresh with blood.[5] He had not stopped to clean himself before he addressed a group of analysts and nonoperational officers. Howard made no apologies for his appearance; he told them that the blood demonstrated what leadership looked like for a battlefield commander. The message was received. One operator, who confirmed Howard's remarks, added his own: "That's the business we're in."

2006—Ramadi, Iraq

In the summer of 2006, Senior Chief Petty Officer James Foreman arrived in Ramadi, a city of four hundred thousand on the Euphrates River in Iraq's western Anbar province. Foreman, a fit, highly regarded Team 6 sniper from Gold Squadron, had been sent into Ramadi for what would be strictly an observation mission. He was not there to fight, but to observe US forces conducting missions, in particular a regular SEAL unit. Foreman had been asked by his boss, Gold Squadron master chief David Cooper, to assess whether Team 6 should send any of its operators at Balad Air Base, north of Baghdad, to Ramadi to work with the two SEAL Team 3 platoons taking part in the battle there.

At the time, Ramadi was perhaps the most dangerous city in Iraq, the heart of al Qaeda in Iraq's stronghold and a key base of operations for the Sunni insurgency in the rest of the country. As much as three-fourths of the city's population had fled as fighters who'd once laid siege to Fallujah, to the north, had moved into Ramadi after being routed by US Marines in 2004. Ramadi's remaining civilians were stuck between an increasingly horrific campaign of terror perpetrated by al Qaeda and the Sunni insurgency, composed largely of remnants of Saddam's military and dissolved Baathist party. A year earlier, US generals had told Congress they thought the US forces should be reduced, but the violence in Anbar, and in Ramadi in particular, had changed the composition of the war. The conflict had shifted from sporadic acts of terrorism to a full-blown insurgency. The US military determined that winning in Ramadi held the best chance of preventing Iraq from dissolving into a failed state. By the time Foreman showed up, parts of the city looked like a World War II hellscape, especially the city center, where several streets had been decimated after months of fighting between US forces and Iraqi insurgents. "We don't need the Battle of Stalingrad, man," one US soldier told CNN at the time. "We got the Battle of Ramadi right here in modern times, baby. Stalingrad ain't got nothing on us."[6]

The SEALs from Charlie and Delta platoons were led by Lt. Cdr. John "Jocko" Willink, who led what was called a task unit, a small special operations force that supported a conventional force in the area, composed of Army and Marine battalions. Although they both became SEALs only a year apart, Foreman and Willink were a study in sharp contrast. Foreman was a small, trim, lithe assaulter who was strong but otherwise looked more like an Olympic long-distance runner than the elite SEAL operator he was. Foreman had fourteen years as a SEAL at that point, nine of them as a member of Team 6. He was aggressive but quiet and discerning, and his tactical judgment and overall cool demeanor were the reason Cooper had sent him to Ramadi. Foreman was a seasoned operator, with multiple deployments prior to Ramadi, and was a top candidate to one day serve as the command's top enlisted SEAL, the command master chief.

Willink, on the other hand, was a giant block of a man; at five feet eleven inches and 240 pounds, he looked every bit the MMA enthusiast he was. Called "Helmet Head" because of his large, closely shaved skull and muscular face, Willink was an intense former enlisted SEAL. He had graduated BUD/S a year before Foreman and had become an officer while Foreman remained an enlisted operator. Nonetheless, he had considerably less combat experience. Ramadi was only his second wartime deployment, and his first as a leader. Willink, unlike Foreman, was also prone to dramatic, almost biblical speeches to his men before missions. In his deep voice, he would tell the men that they were going to be "dropping the Sword of Damocles" on the enemy. Willink was theatric and inexperienced but he had a powerful ally. He had served as an aide to Adm. Joseph Maguire, which, in effect, insulated him from criticism and professional scrutiny in the Naval Special Warfare officer corps. Maguire had risen in the years since he was a platoon commander at UDT-2, in charge of Ens. Penney. He was now a two-star admiral, and as commander of Naval Special Warfare had followed Adm. Eric Olson as the first group of SEALs to ascend to flag officer.

Initially, what Foreman observed of Task Unit Bruiser—as Willink had named his force—appeared to be relatively benign. Willink's primary mission was to help develop a special operations–like unit of Iraqi soldiers. It was considered a necessary mission if the US was ever to leave Iraq with the confidence that government forces could protect the civilian population, but it was not a traditional SEAL mission. SEALs didn't do what is known as foreign internal defense. That was a mission purposefully given to Army Special Forces, who use language, medical care, and engineering to bond with their foreign understudies and win the "hearts and minds" of a local populace. SEALs are at their best when doing direct actions, kill-or-capture missions, or combat engineering, where finding an enemy is the goal.

In addition to serving as trainers, Willink and his SEALs served as a sniper force, an overwatch unit when the soldiers and Marines swept through Ramadi's most violent neighborhoods. The SEAL snipers would climb onto residential rooftops and work in pairs, trying to protect US forces conducting combat operations. Beyond that, Bruiser was part of the larger effort to protect Ramadi's civilian population from al Qaeda's terrorism and the Sunni insurgency. Again, the SEALs were doing police work more than special, targeted operations. And with the city's level of violence peaking, the US military in Iraq loosened the rules of engagement, the battlefield guidelines that governed when US personnel could legally fire on targets. The insurgencies in both Iraq and Afghanistan bedeviled occupation military forces because the enemy did not wear uniforms and instead blended seamlessly into the civilian population. Iraq, in particular, posed a difficult challenge. Many of the areas US forces operated in were cities with dense population centers, making the task of distinguishing an enemy from an Iraqi civilian harder.

As Foreman's assignment continued, what he witnessed troubled him, according to two Team 6 leaders at the time, including one with direct knowledge of Foreman's assessment in Ramadi. One tactic Foreman observed involved snipers taking over a building rooftop at night. By morning they would raise or hang an American flag from the building, serving to identify their position to insurgents. The goal was to be fired upon by the enemy. The idea was that by being fired at, the SEALs could then target an enemy they otherwise couldn't find. Rather than using intelligence to track a cell or conduct missions targeting a specific terrorist, Willink had his men provoke the enemy into revealing their location. In what was a departure from typical SEAL tactics, Willink also sent his Charlie and Delta platoons out on daytime patrols in insurgent-controlled sections of the city in an effort to draw fire. By provoking the enemy to fire first and expose their position, in theory the SEALs could use their superior tactics, training, and support to wipe out the insurgency.

On some level, Foreman was sent to Ramadi to see if all the action there—the violence—provided a rich hunting ground for Dam Neck SEALs, who were based north of Baghdad. Willink and the conventional forces were racking up a significant enemy body count in their near-daily operations. Cooper wanted to know if the city provided a target-rich environment for their elite operators. The problem, according to the two retired Team 6 leaders, was that Willink and the SEALs were interpreting the rules of engagement too loosely.

What troubled Foreman most, however, was what he witnessed once the SEALs got into contact. After being fired upon, the SEALs could make individual determinations as to who presented a threat, and that could include unarmed Iraqis, frequently women and children. In the chaos of Ramadi, an unarmed individual fleeing gunfire could be seen as a civilian—or an insurgent who had just hidden his weapon. A child walking to the store as SEAL snipers engaged a nearby insurgent could, through the sniper's scope, appear as a potential enemy maneuvering in some manner and therefore engaged in the battle. An Iraqi mother standing on a nearby street, holding a cell phone and a bag of groceries, could be shot because an IED had been set off down the street and the SEALs concluded her cell phone was the detonator. The judgment was left to the SEALs—to determine who was a threat and, by extension, who lived and who died. Foreman reported to a superior that Willink's young SEALs shot unarmed men, women, and children the SEALs declared threats, according to the two Team 6 leaders.[7] A retired senior SEAL officer told me that Foreman's account of Ramadi was seen inside Team 6 as an ominous sign that SEALs had lost their moral compass and that the United States may have lost the war. "There was no discretion over who they were killing," this officer told me. "Their assumption was that because they were dropped into a war zone, everyone in the city was the enemy. After they shot a woman, who is going to say she wasn't going to set off a bomb? Once they shot a kid, who is going to say he wasn't serving as a spotter for the enemy?"

According to the two Team 6 leaders, what Foreman later reported back to Team 6 was that Willink's SEALs were trying to draw enemy fire, which would allow the snipers to justify any shots they took, regardless of whether they were appropriate. "That's what happens when you do not have an officer in charge," the retired SEAL officer said. "[Task Unit

Bruiser SEALs] had no supervision and they were looking for body count because they thought it was cool."

The enemy understood the rules of engagement. SEALs, and most other US forces, had faced scenarios where insurgents and terrorists sought to pass themselves off as civilians by dropping their weapons to mix into the local population. The insurgents also sought to raise doubts whether these unarmed men were combatants. But the purpose of SEAL training was to determine who was a legitimate threat and who was not. And while fighting a counterinsurgency, the distinction had tangible consequences beyond the loss of life. If the local population viewed a killing as unjust, it made the occupied force less popular, and made the US effort to win over the population instantly harder. Iraqis were already facing foreign terrorists and Sunni insurgents who had no compunction about killing civilians to achieve their aims of taking power in the country.

In Ramadi, much of the population had fled. The rules of engagement there were predicated on the notion that most of those who remained were connected to the insurgency and attacks on US military and Iraqi government forces. There was some merit to this in certain sections of Ramadi. But it could not be applied across the entire city. For one, it ignored the fact that only Anbaris with the financial means to flee the city were able to do so. The poorest residents were stuck, caught between a foreign occupation force and insurgent interlopers who often coerced locals to provide sanctuary or aid in attacking the Americans.

Foreman's report painted a brutal picture of Task Unit Bruiser's deployment in Ramadi. He told Cooper and the other SEAL Team 6 leaders that Willink's snipers were shooting unarmed civilians, including young boys. But, according to the two Team 6 leaders, one SEAL sniper stood out. He told his Team 6 leaders that one Charlie platoon sniper in particular was shooting unarmed Iraqi civilians: Chris Kyle. Petty Officer Chris Kyle, the platoon's senior sniper, was a big man, six feet two inches tall with big hands, who grew up on a Texas ranch. Before entering the Navy, Kyle was a professional cowboy on a bull-riding circuit. He'd earned four Bronze Stars, including one for saving the life of a Marine during the 2004 Second Battle of Fallujah, and along with it a reputation for both

bravery and braggadocio. When he arrived in Ramadi for his third deployment to Iraq, Kyle was known in the SEAL Teams as a lethal sniper. But
within SEAL Team 3, he also had a reputation for self-aggrandizement
and embellishment. He had even earned a derisive nickname from some
other SEALs: "the Legend," as in Chris Kyle, a legend in his own mind.
During the Ramadi deployment, a former SEAL turned author, Dick
Couch, documented the Battle of Ramadi for a book he later published,
The Sheriff of Ramadi. In it, and using a pseudonym, Couch described Kyle
as an elite sniper and a "legend" in the Teams. Couch asked Kyle how
many kills he had, and though Couch wrote that Kyle gave him an exact
figure, "I'll just say it was well over a hundred in Ramadi," Couch wrote,
"and this was in addition to the nearly twenty he accounted for in Fallujah." Couch quoted Kyle, "These were confirmed kills, the ones who were
shot dead on the street. We don't count the ones who managed to crawl off
and probably bled out. But I didn't have too many of those."[8]

A senior SEAL leader who spoke with Foreman and later told me
about his Ramadi assessment disputed Kyle's description. "Jim comes
back [to Balad Air Base] and is appalled with what they're doing," the
retired Team 6 leader told me. "He said, 'They're shooting kids as spotters.
Whoever was used as a spotter, [Kyle] shot.'" Foreman reported one of
Kyle's engagements that painted a horrific picture for his superiors. A
young, unarmed male had been forced by insurgents to spot the SEALs.
Kyle's teammates manning the sniper rifle and the scope refused to shoot
the young male because he was unarmed. "They would not take the shot,"
the retired SEAL leader recounted. "So he"—referring to Kyle—"just
jumps on the gun and plugs the dude in the street. When the guy's family
runs out to help him, he shoots them too, only he misses. But then he calls
four enemy killed in action for his confirmed kills. He was lying about the
number of his kills."

While shooting the unarmed spotter could be a justified shot, firing
on unarmed civilians trying to render aid is a war crime. At least twice,
Kyle was accused of shooting unarmed civilians. In both cases, Army officers in Ramadi investigated afterward and did not find evidence to support Kyle's claims. Kyle was never charged with a crime, but one of the

shootings led military leaders to remove the SEAL snipers from Ramadi until their deployment ended.

When Foreman returned to Balad and delivered his assessment, according to the two Team 6 leaders, he provided a clear and simple picture: Willink's SEALs were killing civilians in Ramadi, and Gold Squadron should have no part of their operation. Although SEAL Team 6 did not join the Bruiser mission in the summer of 2006, there was a shared symptom of failure. No one from Team 6 reported Task Unit Bruiser's activities to higher command. The Navy awarded Kyle the Silver Star for his "conspicuous gallantry and intrepidity in action against the enemy" in Ramadi. Foreman later confirmed that his 2006 Ramadi assessment recommended that Team 6 work with Willink and Kyle. He denied witnessing any unjustified targets during his time in Ramadi, describing Kyle as his friend and a "good man."[9]

CHAPTER 10

HEAD ON A PLATTER

 N 1971, RANDOM HOUSE PUBLISHED AN OBSCURE WAR TITLE, *Devil's Guard*, by a relatively unknown author named George Robert Elford. The book purported to be the true account of an SS officer who with dozens of other soldiers escaped Germany after World War II, joined the French Foreign Legion, and spent years in Vietnam torturing and brutalizing the insurgency. It glorified Nazi military tactics, describing counterinsurgency methods such as mass slaughter and desecration and other forms of wanton violence as a means of waging psychological warfare against Vietnamese "savages." The savagery the book depicted, and the unlikely story line, raised questions about whether the account was fiction:

> Dominating every hill, we proceeded systematically to exterminate the guerrillas. We spared only small children and women. Everybody taller than four feet was gunned down or burned to ashes. Our aim was not to cause casualties but to exterminate; gaining territory was of little importance to us. We could not hold an inch of land for any length of

time. The destruction of the enemy manpower was our principal aim. We gunned down every man in sight regardless of whether he carried a weapon or not. They all belonged to the same snake pit. And if they were among the guerrillas we shot down twelve-year-old boys, too. We regarded them as the terrorists of the coming years. The golden reserve of Ho Chi Minh! ...It was not a senseless act of brutality. It was tit for tat. We wanted to plant such terror in their hearts that they would run, head over heels, when they heard us coming.[1]

The author went on to publish two sequels—*Devil's Guard II: Recall to Inferno* and *Devil's Guard III: Unconditional Warfare*—all but ruling out the possibility that anything in the original could be read as fact.

But that didn't stop the book from finding a new audience within SEAL Team 6.

In late 2007, Britt Slabinski was deployed to Afghanistan as the senior noncommissioned officer in Blue Squadron. The war was entering its seventh year and had become intractable, with no clear path to victory. Early in the war, the SEALs' mission was to hunt down al Qaeda's senior leaders, who had largely vanished into Pakistan, but Lt. Gen. Stanley McChrystal, the JSOC commander, extended the mission to target the Taliban, which along with al Qaeda was moving back and forth across the Pakistani border with impunity. It was the same expansion of targets that McChrystal had authorized in Iraq. "We had just been ordered to hunt Taliban," one former operator later wrote, "and I should say that single order changed the course of the command's history forever."[2]

The SEALs were now going after low-level Taliban financiers and shadow governors. The SEALs shifted further away from their original purpose and were becoming something closer to an elite strike force that was always on call and out on deployment as much as half the year. The command was less a counterterrorism force and more of a counterinsurgency force, except they only conducted raids. The command's target expanded, but they were still limited to the same skill set.

Blue Squadron was led at that time by Cdr. Peter Vasely, a Naval Academy graduate who came into the command assigned to Gray Team.

Vasely, like Vic Hyder, was one of the Annapolis officers whom Capt. Kernan moved into the assault teams even though he hadn't selected for, or completed, Green Team. He was an outsider, despite having been at the command for many years. Like Vic Hyder, he didn't have the commensurate skills as the operators he commanded, a dynamic that was reinforced by his war-hero master chief. Slabinski—experienced, charismatic, and by now legendary—bridged the gap. Slabinski had spent time in Green Team, and had deployed in 2003 to Iraq at the start of the war as a sniper leader. He was promoted to master chief petty officer, waited his turn, and was now leading a Team 6 squadron, if not commanding one.

Still, the leadership dynamic in Blue Squadron was a failure.[3] By 2007, the command's leadership was aware that some Blue Squadron operators were using specialized knives to conduct "skinnings."[4] As operators in other squadrons had done, Blue assaulters initially used the excuse of collecting DNA, which required a small piece of skin containing hair follicles, but began taking large strips of skin. According to one of the former senior leaders with direct knowledge, the two leading officers at the command, Capts. Scott Moore and Tim Szymanski, were informed that small groups in each of the three squadrons were mutilating and desecrating combatants in both Iraq and Afghanistan.[5]

"These fucking morons read the book *The Devil's Guard* and believed it," said one of the former SEAL Team 6 leaders who later investigated Slabinski and Blue Squadron. "It's a work of fiction billed as the Bible, as the truth. In reality it's bullshit. But we all see what we want to see." Slabinski and the Blue Squadron SEALs deployed to Afghanistan, the former leader said, were "frustrated, and that book gave them the answers they wanted to see: terrorize the Taliban and they'd surrender. The truth is that such stuff only galvanizes the enemy."

One telling illustration of what had gone wrong with Blue Squadron occurred on December 17, 2007, just before a raid in Helmand province. Slabinski had previously told his operators that he wanted "a head on a platter."[6] Although some of the more seasoned SEALs took the statement metaphorically, at least one operator took Slabinski at his word, interpreting it as an order.

Later that night, after Blue Squadron's assaulters had successfully carried out the raid, killing four militants and recovering weapons and explosives, Vasely and Slabinski conducted a walk-through of the compound. Vasely, who was wearing night-vision goggles, looked through a window and saw one of his operators, his back turned, squatting over the body of a dead militant. Vasely saw the operator moving his hand back and forth over the militant's neck in a sawing motion. Alarmed at seeing what he believed was a decapitation, he told Slabinski to go inside and see what the young operator was doing. By the time Slabinski entered the room where the dead militant lay, the operator had severed much of the dead man's neck.[7]

Slabinski stopped the operator before he finished the decapitation but did not report it. He told Vasely that the operator had been trying to remove the dead fighter's chest rack, a small vest that can hold ammunition and clips. Slabinski told Vasely, and Navy investigators later, that there had been "no foul play."[8]

After leaving the compound and returning to their base in Kandahar province, Vasely reported to his superior officer, Capt. Scott Moore, that he believed he had witnessed a war crime, a mutilation. Vasely told Moore he wanted an investigation into the incident. Moore, sitting in his office in Virginia Beach, pressed Vasely: What had he actually seen? Could there be another explanation?[9] Vasely would later change his account for investigators so that he offered more ambiguity about what he saw.[10]

Moore then told his deputy, Capt. Szymanski, who was in Afghanistan, to sort things out.[11] Ten days later, the senior leaders at JSOC closed an internal investigation. The Naval Criminal Investigative Service then opened an investigation. But since the crime scene was an inaccessible area of active hostilities, the investigators were forced to rely on photographs and witness statements. When investigators approached the operator accused of mutilating the dead fighter, he "exercised his right to remain silent, and to his right to counsel."[12] A few days after the attempted interview, investigators obtained photos they believed to be of the dead fighter. No cuts were visible in the photos, according to a military official who reviewed the file. Three weeks after the incident, NCIS closed its investigation, concluding that no evidence had been found that the SEAL had violated the laws of armed conflict. But according to multiple SEAL sources, the incident did in fact occur.[13]

Szymanski, according to these sources, was directed by Moore to make the episode disappear. "Tim took a dive," said a former noncommissioned SEAL officer, and it was "at Moore's direction."

The NCIS investigator on the case, John Smallman, a lawyer and a retired Navy captain himself, said it was clear from the moment he landed in Afghanistan that the case was rigged. "When we concluded, I told the captain [Szymanski], 'Sir, we didn't find anything, just as you set it up for us.' I knew we were only shown what they wanted us to see, not what had occurred in Helmand," Smallman said years later.

Although Blue Squadron had avoided criminal charges, their battlefield conduct continued to set off alarms within the command. Some SEAL Team 6 leaders were appalled by how easily Vasely and Szymanski had folded under Moore's pressure.

Within two weeks of the near beheading, Moore deployed to Afghanistan. While he was there, he confronted the Blue Squadron troop and the operator who'd tried to behead the Taliban fighter. One retired Team 6 leader told me that, at the time, Capt. Moore shamed Slabinski and the squadron for their conduct. That was the only punishment. "The investigation is so conventional it's not really going to turn up anything," said the retired Team 6 leader about the challenges NCIS faced trying to pierce the unit's code of silence. "Or, it's not going to correct anything. What's gonna correct it was a guy like Scott [Moore] walking in and getting right in their faces and saying, 'Hey, is this what we've become?' I think that woke some guys up."

But even Moore's admonishment had limitations. In a previous deployment, Moore gave his men pep talks before they left on operations. Dam Neck operators had mastered the art of vague language, code used to express what everyone who heard it would understand. The political environment in Afghanistan was fraught at that moment; Moore told the operators to "Keep it clean, boys," according to a SEAL who witnessed the remarks. "To 'Keep it clean' means, implies, they know it usually isn't clean. It's scary, to think of a senior leader encouraging war crimes."

One of the former SEAL Team 6 leaders who investigated several Blue Squadron incidents, including the mutilation of bodies, said he repeatedly asked the operators why they felt the need to commit such acts. "Often we'd hear, 'Well, they're savages,'" the former noncommissioned officer said. "'They don't play by the rules, so why should we?'"

Justin Sheffield, a Blue Squadron operator and part of the troop involved in the decapitation in 2007, would later write a book about his experiences at the command. His book is at times crude and violent, but it is also perhaps one of the more honest accounts of the perspective of the post–September 11 SEALs from Dam Neck.

For Sheffield, SEAL Team 6 assaulters had a simple purpose, and their collective success was undeniable. "We've been called everything," Sheffield wrote, "savages, sociopaths, serial killers, whatever. In a way, it's all a little bit true. What we are not is the guy who is gonna hand out a soccer ball to the kids and make sure everyone's got medical attention in the village and shit like that. We were the guys who were gonna go and kill people, period. In fact, we killed more bad guys during [Operation Enduring Freedom in Afghanistan] and [Operation Iraqi Freedom] than all the other groups combined."[14]

Years later, Team 6 operators would reveal small glimpses of their mindset as they deployed year after year and counted their kills. Eddie Penney, a Gold Squadron assaulter, described his thrill in killing. "It's almost like a drug," Penney said in a podcast. "I mean, just the feeling of taking out a bad guy. I remember the feeling that came with killing a bad guy, knowing that they're responsible for this and trying to kill you, was the greatest feeling I've ever experienced in my life."[15] Penney, who completed five deployments while serving at Dam Neck, had his entire left calf tattooed with skulls to commemorate one of his deployments. "There's a certain number of skulls on there, there's eighty-seven. That's how many kills we got on deployment—without air support."[16]

The military built a killing machine after 9/11, and the SEALs started to take pleasure in their role serving the country as the government's most lethal tool.

June 12, 2007—New York, New York

Five days after he was discharged from the Navy, Marcus Luttrell sat on an upholstered chair across from Matt Lauer in the *Today Show* studio in Rockefeller Center. Luttrell was there to promote *Lone Survivor: The Eyewitness Account of Operation Redwing and the Lost Heroes of SEAL Team 10*, his account of Operation Red Wings. He'd received the Navy Cross for his heroism two years earlier from President George W. Bush, a fellow Texan. Now he was ready for a media blitz to sell the book.

The book was almost an immediate success, becoming that summer's blockbuster nonfiction title: it remained number one on the *New York Times* bestseller list for much of the summer and would spend twenty-five weeks on the list that year. In the midst of two unwinnable wars, Luttrell and his coauthor, novelist Patrick Robinson, had delivered to the public what they wanted: an unambiguous story of survival and heroics. During the promotional campaign, Luttrell told the *New York Times* that he wrote the book because "[p]eople were writing these stories, and anything they didn't know how it happened, they just made it up."[17]

The book wasn't just a bestseller, it redefined a genre. Part tragedy and part political rant, it would serve as a template for future SEAL bestsellers. It painted the War on Terror in stark black-and-white terms, decrying the Geneva Conventions and the uproar over the torture of Iraqi prisoners by US soldiers at the Abu Ghraib prison in 2004 as nothing more than humiliation, which did "not ring my personal alarm bell."[18] But the book was wildly misleading and inaccurate, a nearly fictionalized version of what transpired near the top of Sawtalo Sar (Luttrell's coauthor was a novelist who wrote war fiction). Luttrell described Ahmad Shah as "one of Osama bin Laden's closest associates," and "the kind of terrorist who would like nothing better than to mastermind a new attack on the US mainland," despite any evidence the Afghan had any connections to al Qaeda, let alone to its leader.[19] When Shah's men started their attack, Luttrell wrote, the SEAL spotted "between eighty and a hundred heavily armed Taliban warriors, each one of them with an AK-47 pointing downward."[20] Luttrell's account described "140 men minimum" overwhelming his four-man reconnaissance team, a claim he would repeat over and over again in public interviews and speeches.[21] The number fluctuated between 80 and 200 fighters, numbers that appeared to add to the miraculous nature of his escape and survival. In Luttrell's account, the SEALs had killed "fifty or more" of Shah's men.[22] A gleaming gold Navy SEAL Trident emblazoned the book's cover. The public could be forgiven for believing that the Navy had certified Luttrell's account. Indeed, Naval Special Warfare Command said next to nothing, their silence a tacit confirmation of Luttrell's story.

The men from Red Squadron and the rest of SEAL Team 6, however, knew different. "It was very clear that it was bullshit," said the former Red operator who helped search for Luttrell in the Korengal Valley. Some of the Red Squadron operators would refuse to shake Luttrell's hand in the years afterward, disgusted that he had dropped his weapon and fled. "The hero was the local who saved him," the retired Red Team operator said.

In the aftermath of Naval Special Warfare's deadliest day, Team 6 conducted an internal examination of what went wrong on Red Wings. After several weeks, their conclusion was straightforward: nearly everything. The command's success and battlefield dominance lie in large part with their objective study of tactics and unsparing assessment of risk. "There is a reason we didn't do the mission," a retired Team 6 officer told me, confirming that Team 6 had turned down a chance to go after Ahmad Shah on multiple occasions. The planning for Red Wings made a series of false assumptions and reflected the eagerness of a new SEAL commander just starting a deployment, he said. "Every part of their plan gave away the tactical advantage."

An inexperienced but aggressive SEAL commander on his first deployment, a small team outmatched and underequipped, a series of tactical errors, a disorganized and convoluted chain of communications, poor planning and leadership, an enemy target that didn't justify the risk, and the misfortune of a helicopter filled with Americans trying to rescue the SEALs led to the worst day in SEAL history.

In the immediate hours and days after Luttrell's rescue, military commanders in Afghanistan interviewed him and asked him to write down a step-by-step accounting of what took place on the mountain. Luttrell gave three separate accounts of his ordeal, all within a few weeks of his rescue. Each account was considered so important they were all transmitted to the Pentagon and then verbally briefed to Defense Secretary Donald Rumsfeld. In Luttrell's telling, according to two people that read each of the reports, the number of enemy fighters increased. What had started as possibly fewer than a dozen grew to perhaps more than fifty. "Each account changed, and not in any way that made sense," said a person who read the accounts. "The interviewers didn't want to push him too hard—he'd been through a hell of an ordeal. They didn't want to question the changes, but at some point, we said, 'You don't get blasted fifty feet from a rocket-propelled grenade. That's just Hollywood shit.'"

In the years afterward, the myth surrounding Operation Red Wings persisted. A *Daily News* article in 2010 described the battle: the four conventional SEALs "fought it out for almost an hour, killing dozens of the enemy before he and two of his men were cut down."[23]

"There is a very significant problem with the fact that nobody in the community ever stood up and said, 'Let's have a fucking after-action report,'" said the SEAL Team 6 operator who helped search for Luttrell and his teammates in 2005.

There is little doubt that Luttrell suffered extraordinary anguish as a result of Operation Red Wings. The book's description of watching his teammates die violent deaths in a foreign war zone is harrowing and tragic. In his *Today Show* interview, two years after the event, Luttrell wore a hollow and haunted expression. Lauer pressed Luttrell to describe the "wounds" for the "rest of your life. Is there also...that survivor's guilt as to why are you the one who survived when the three others with you died, and those sixteen who were coming to get you died?"

"Oh, I died on that mountain, too, sir," Luttrell responded. "I mean, I left a part of myself up there, and I think about it every day. There's not a day that goes by where I don't wake up or I don't go to bed that—you know, if I do sleep." In the book, Luttrell described being haunted by Lt. Michael Murphy screaming at him for help, with the Texan unable to reach his dying friend because of the terrain and enemy fire.

But Luttrell also wove a singular story about the horrors of war with something else: a near fantasy of personal heroism laced with speculation that the "liberal media"—and not failures of mission planning—caused the disaster. In the book, he describes how his teammates were discovered by passing shepherds and that the SEALs opted to not kill the two Afghan civilians to avoid a media fallout. The shepherds, Luttrell claimed, later gave the SEALs' location to Ahmad Shah, thus setting off the attack on the Americans. Although evidence emerged almost immediately that Luttrell's account was not only exaggerated but in some places outright false, no military officials or members of the SEAL community called into question his version or the content of his bestseller.

Instead, the Navy authorized awards for battlefield valor. Lt. Murphy was awarded the Medal of Honor, based on Luttrell's account, ignoring a two-witness requirement for the award. The award citation claimed Shah's force was "more than 50" in size and that the SEALs had killed "an estimated 35" of them.[24] Luttrell, Dietz, and Axelson were each awarded the Navy Cross, also based on Luttrell's story. Luttrell's award was made public when the book was released. It helped establish an unassailable narrative around the failed mission. And just as awards for battlefield heroism had with Takur Ghar, Murphy's and Luttrell's awards ensured that failures of senior SEAL officers' leadership were ignored.

For SEAL Team 6, what rankled most was that the Naval Special Warfare Command refused to conduct a proper postmortem, known in the military as an after-action review. Instead, retired SEALs said the force commander, Rear Adm. Joseph Maguire, believed having a report about any failures during the operation would be "insensitive" to the families of the dead.

"Maguire sold it to our community as a way to preserve their dignity," the retired SEAL officer told me. "They handed out a bunch of awards—just like Roberts Ridge—and swept it under the rug. There was never any accountability. It's absolutely leadership's fault because we condoned it. And we absolutely set the precedent because when it came to the SEAL community and it came to our careers, we would rather have a falsehood put out there than actually deal with the consequences of our bad behavior. And because we don't want to hurt the brand and we don't hurt the families, we will go ahead and lie and cover it up.

"Maguire does it to the NSW community for Red Wings," the retired SEAL officer said, "and Kernan does it on top of Takur Ghar. What are the guys learning?

"We condoned it and therefore we condoned the distrust between the enlisted and officers. We condone their behavior. We condone the behavior after they get out of the military. The books, everything. The officers are the ones that failed the community.

"And Maguire is the worst because he's been doing it since he was a lieutenant with Ensign Penney."

Decisions in war had consequences, and when tragedy prevailed, few, if any, of the SEAL officers in leadership positions were interested in holding themselves accountable for dead SEALs. Each bad decision was justified, and any question or scrutiny of their command performance was made silent with the recognition of battlefield valor by those who were poorly led.

ON THE SECOND FLOOR OF THE SEAL TEAM 6 HEADQUARTERS AT the Dam Neck Annex, a computer, known as the "ops computer," stores the classified data on every mission the unit has completed for the past decade. Here, commanders returning from a deployment leave their hard drives with technicians who transfer PowerPoints, after-action reports, and photos of each operation a squadron conducted abroad. The database contains a variety of documents, including photographs of people killed by SEAL operators during their missions.

Some of those photographs, especially those taken of casualties from 2005 through 2008, show a grim consistency: deceased enemy combatants with their skulls split exposing their brain matter—the telltale marking of a 5.56-caliber rifle fired in close proximity at the upper forehead.[25] The foreign fighters who suffered these V-shaped wounds were either killed in battle and later shot at close range or finished off with a "security round" while dying. Among members of SEAL Team 6, this practice of desecrating enemy casualties was called "canoeing."

The canoeing photos provide dramatic documentary evidence of the extreme and unnecessary violence that the SEALs had embraced. The practice began during the SEALs' multiple high-risk, exhausting, and traumatizing tours of duty in Iraq and Afghanistan that followed Roberts Ridge. "There is and was no military reason whatsoever to split someone's skull open with a single round," said a former SEAL Team 6 leader. "It's sport."

The former SEAL Team 6 leader said that he first noticed canoeing in 2004, and though it does occur on the battlefield, it only happened rarely and accidentally. But canoeing, he said, became "big" in 2007. "I'd look through the post-op photos and see multiple canoes on one objective, several times a deployment," the retired SEAL said. When SEAL Team 6 operators were occasionally confronted about the desecration, the SEAL leader said they'd often joke that they were just "great shots."

Canoeing was just one of several acts of mutilation frequently carried out by SEALs. Nor was the lack of battlefield discipline limited to a single squadron. Unlawful violence, aberrations from rules of engagement, mutilations, and disrespect of enemy casualties, actions that had been isolated at the beginning of the Afghan War, had by this point spread throughout SEAL Team 6.

In the early years of the war, SEAL Team 6 had an inflexible standard: shooting people who were unarmed was forbidden. Anyone who did so had to demonstrate that the target had displayed hostile intent. Operators and officers prided themselves on their ability to kill only those who were deemed hostile or a threat. If a SEAL couldn't justify the threat after a shooting, he was quietly removed from the unit. But even that rule evolved over time. SEALs were given wide berth as long as they could explain why they made the decision to shoot an unarmed person. In 2007, for example, a Gold Squadron sniper was pushed out of the unit after he killed three unarmed people—including a child—in at least two different operations. He was, nonetheless, allowed to return to the regular SEAL Teams.[26]

No investigation into an unjustified killing ever resulted in formal disciplinary action against a SEAL. Between 2001 and 2018, battlefield reports and accounts of atrocities, particularly mutilations and taking of trophies, were ignored by SEAL Team 6 leadership, according to two separate sources. One said that it wasn't simply a matter of looking past isolated incidents in the midst of an ongoing war. His superiors repeatedly refused to address allegations of the SEALs' barbarism.

THE SEALs' CONDUCT DIDN'T OCCUR IN ISOLATION. IN THE JOINT nature of combat operations in both theaters, Afghanistan and Iraq, the outside intelligence and paramilitary teams that worked with the unit were confronted by the brutality that had become routine for the SEALs. In 2008, this hit a flash point. Paramilitary officers from the CIA, including a covert joint unit under the agency's command called the Omega program, were working closely with the SEALs in Afghanistan. These small teams of CIA, SEAL Team 6, and Afghan commandos operated under the agency's Title 50 authority, which governs covert activities. This meant there was less oversight over their missions—and less accountability if things went wrong.

Late that year, the CIA joined operators from Gold Squadron for an operation near Jalalabad. It was to be a predawn raid targeting a local insurgent cell that had targeted a US base. According to a CIA officer with direct knowledge of the incident, the CIA requested that the SEALs capture, rather than kill, their militant targets. During the raid, a small team from Gold Squadron breached a compound. Inside, they found six militants, four of which were in one room, all sleeping with weapons near their beds. Despite orders to detain the men, the SEALs killed all six. In the room with four of the suspected insurgents, four SEALs counted down and canoed each sleeping man with a shot to the forehead. One of their teammates killed the other two targets in another room. The SEALs photographed the bodies, then left.

The killings infuriated the CIA team on the operation. They had lost an opportunity to interrogate the suspected militants. "These were guys who were running a cell near our base," the CIA officer said. "We could've used the intel." Outside the compound, the SEALs were quick to show the photos to others on the assault team. "They were smiling, almost gleeful," the CIA officer said. "Canoeing them was funny."

Shortly after that operation, a CIA paramilitary officer named Richard Smethers wanted to do something about the incident. He was a retired SEAL Team 6 officer and understood the culture of the Teams, but he also knew the boundaries of conduct. Smethers complained to his CIA superiors in Kabul that SEALs were committing atrocities, threatening to expose the SEALs for what he believed was a series of war crimes.[27] The canoeing incident was just one of several operations in which Smethers alleged that Gold Squadron operators violated the laws of war. Smethers's allegations triggered a confrontation between senior SEAL Team 6 officers and CIA counterparts in Afghanistan. The SEAL command quickly intervened and made a deal with the CIA station in Kabul. Gold Squadron was set to redeploy to the United States anyway, and Dam Neck promised to rein in their operators. In exchange, Smethers, who never filed an official allegation or complaint, was sent back to the States. Smethers declined to comment for this book.

According to multiple members of SEAL Team 6, the fight with the CIA was one of the few instances in which the command's battlefield misconduct was in danger of being exposed. One retired noncommissioned officer recalled his failed efforts to police the unit, saying the command suffered from "unspoken oaths of allegiance" among both the officers and the operators—the omertà that Marcinko cultivated with the founding of the unit. The first instinct when misconduct surfaced was not accountability and discipline, it was to "protect the command and then the men." Team 6 had by then an established code of conduct built into its inception.

The lack of accountability didn't rest on SEAL command alone. The special operations and intelligence communities rationalized the excesses—and, in some instances, cosigned on them with their official silence. Multiple people told me the CIA station chief in Kabul at the time of Smethers's allegation had known about and condoned the same Team 6 conduct in Iraq earlier in the war. Now that he was dealing with President Karzai, these SEALs told me, he found the operators' conduct to be troubling.

"It's important that you put this stuff in context," a retired SEAL and former CIA officer who participated in Team 6 raids said. "I'm not going to tell you this didn't happen. Yes, we, they committed war crimes. It happens in war. War is an adrenaline rush. After three or four deployments in, you need more to get that stimulation. We didn't hit women or kids. We killed bad guys. And afterwards, we added the psychological warfare."

There was a reality to the war these special operators were fighting. They were far from home, with little supervision and empowered with the authority to make life-and-death decisions at a moment's notice. They often saw what they viewed as the worst of humanity in their adversary and experienced repeated physical and psychological trauma. The three hundred SEAL operators at Team 6 were among the only Americans in on a secret: violence creates its own parallel universe.

AROUND THIS TIME, THE JOINT SPECIAL OPERATIONS COMMAND took on a new commander: Vice Adm. William McRaven. The position represented something of a role reversal for McRaven. Since Marcinko flushed him from SEAL Team 6 twenty-five years earlier, McRaven had quietly risen in the ranks at the Pentagon, with the pedigree of the Navy's most elite unit but disassociated from the scandals that marked the end of

Marcinko's career. He was the first SEAL to lead JSOC—and, in his new command, he was again in a position of authority over SEAL Team 6.

It wasn't long before McRaven began receiving reports that pointed to SEAL Team 6. Just six months after taking over JSOC, a series of complaints from the Afghan government over special operations night raids and civilian deaths prompted McRaven to pull Team 6 back from the nightly raids across the country targeting the Taliban. He ordered a pause in most SEAL and JSOC operations over a two-week period in February 2009. McRaven promulgated a new set of guidelines on raids to address the concerns raised by the Afghans. Although the stoppage was not limited to the SEALs, his former unit pushed back against this new set of operational rules.

First, the SEALs would now be required to do callouts before entering a compound. The intention was to permit women and children to get out of harm's way before operators conducted their assault. The operators were unhappy about the new restriction, arguing that callouts gave up the tactical advantage of surprise. McRaven's other directive required a more extensive post-operation review to document and justify combatant deaths.[28] Previously, the command had required only frontal and profile photographs of each dead militant. The new rule required a full photographic accounting of who was killed, images of the entire body, where they were when they dropped, what weapons they held, the vantage point of the operator when he fired, and other atmospherics.

This directive served one primary purpose: to protect US forces from accusations by Afghan government officials of unjustified killings.[29] The proliferation of cell phones and social media meant that any Afghan accusation of war crimes had a nearly instant ability to delegitimize the Karzai government and inflame everyday Afghans' views of the US presence in their country. The new photos and other review documents could now be shared with local officials to justify operations. But the directive had another benefit. With the requirement of more extensive photographic documentation, SEAL operators now had to account for anything that could be construed as gratuitous violence. As a result, photographs of canoed enemy fighters virtually ceased to appear in after-action reports.

"Several of us confronted the officers," said one former noncommissioned officer who tried to stop the criminal behavior. "We knew what needed to be done to police the kids." The former senior enlisted leader said he pressed several commanding officers to address the war crimes.[30] "We failed to fix the problem," he said. "It wasn't complex, and had it been several one-off events—a guy chopping a head off—it wouldn't be such a failure. But this started in 2002 and continued through the wars. Our leadership punted and I'm not sure it will ever be corrected."

The excessive violence, atrocities, and criminal conduct were not so hidden that the senior enlisted leaders of Team 6 were unaware. The opposite was true, and some made efforts to push officers in charge to uphold the waning good order and discipline at Dam Neck. Instead, the problems worsened.

The absence of accountability carried lasting effects. "No one prepared our guys for the collateral damage and the second- and third-order effects of this war," one former SEAL leader said. "Night after night of kill or be killed. [There was] so much savagery. I'm not condoning the behavior—there's no justification to hacking a body—but we didn't prepare them either. If I told you I cut off a head after an operation—explaining that I got caught up in the moment, went over the line one time—you'd have sympathy for me. War is awful and it's human to go too far, but this isn't one time. This is multiple times on each deployment."

Contributing to the lack of accountability was an uncomfortable truth: the SEALs were winning on the battlefield. And despite McRaven's directives, there was no serious internal scrutiny of the SEALs' most excessive conduct. As long as the body count grew, no one in a position of authority would ask too many questions about how the SEALs got the results. History is frequently written by the victors, and SEAL Team 6's is no different.

ON JUNE 4, 2009, IN HIS FIRST MAJOR FOREIGN POLICY SPEECH, President Barack Obama addressed the Muslim world from Cairo University. After eight years of the War on Terror, the newly elected president sought to reset and reframe how the Muslim world had come to see the United States. With simultaneous wars in two Muslim countries and operations in several others, the US military went wherever in the world they gathered a hint of Islamic militancy. President Bush had once claimed the United States was on a crusade against Islamic terrorists. Obama wanted a new public relations campaign for the Forever Wars: "America is not—and never will be—at war with Islam." But while the rhetoric coming from the commander in chief changed, war's reality on the ground did not. President Obama moved to end the occupation of Iraq, and would do so within his first two years in office. The war in Afghanistan, however, expanded, and Team 6 played a key role in trying to turn the conflict from a stalemate to a path for withdrawal.

CHAPTER II

HOSTAGES—BACK TO BASICS

April 8, 2009—Indian Ocean, Three Hundred Miles Southeast of Somalia

Five thousand feet over the Indian Ocean, the rear cargo ramp of a C-17 lowered to reveal a clear sky and the almost-still blue waters below. The SEALs of Red Squadron leapt out, one by one, to parachute into their next operation.

Five days earlier, four Somali pirates had hijacked the *Maersk Alabama*, an American-flagged fourteen-thousand-ton cargo ship, as it made its way from Oman to Kenya via Djibouti, along the Horn of Africa and through one of the most dangerous maritime corridors on earth. The Somalis, operating a hijacked Taiwanese fishing vessel, had caught up to the *Maersk*, and armed with AK-47s boarded the hulking ship, which was three hundred miles off the eastern coast of Somalia. The pirates, led by Abduwali Abdukhadir Muse, quickly headed for the ship's bridge. There, the *Maersk*'s captain, Richard Phillips, waited for them. Most of the twenty-person crew were hiding in the ship's engine control room while

179

he tried to negotiate with the pirates. Phillips and his men settled on a plan to cut the bridge's control of the ship and the vessel's power. After a series of struggles between the pirates and the few members of the crew that remained on the bridge, Phillips offered himself plus $30,000 in the ship's safe in exchange for releasing the *Maersk* and her crew. The pirates agreed. They shuttled Phillips onto the *Maersk*'s lifeboat, dropped into the sea, and started toward the Somali coast.

President Obama, facing his first serious international crisis, quickly authorized a military operation to secure the captain's release. Obama had agreed to send one SEAL Team 6 squadron—roughly fifty SEALs—to a Navy destroyer in the Indian Ocean. The mission was called Operation Lightning Dawn. Although SEAL Team 6 had not been involved in a hostage rescue since recovering Jessica Lynch at the start of the war in Iraq, the *Maersk* operation was the type of high-stakes mission the command had been created for: on the president's order, and with much of the world watching the drama unfold on television, four small boats and fifty highly trained men would parachute into the ocean, join the crew of the USS *Boxer*, an amphibious assault ship, and wait for an opportunity to save an American hostage. Not only was this what SEAL Team 6 had been designed to do in 1980, it was also the first time the command would conduct a hostage rescue at sea. Despite its maritime origins, the unit had never conducted a full-scale operation at sea, let alone a hostage rescue.

Adm. McRaven, who was in Afghanistan, commanded the mission from an operations center at Bagram Air Base. As was the case for the president, the *Maersk* operation was also McRaven's first major operation of national priority. As the overall commander, McRaven was in a position that would have seemed impossible twenty-six years earlier when Marcinko had fired him from the command. He was in charge of the force designated to carry out the operation.

The SEALs, who were led by Capt. Scott Moore and Red Squadron's commander Roger Ullman, were working against the clock. The pirates atttempted to blindfold Capt. Phillips in the hold of the lifeboat and slowly headed toward Somalia. For McRaven and the US military, it was critical to prevent the pirates from making landfall and moving their hostage into Somali territory. As long as the pirates were in a small vessel in international waters, McRaven and the SEALs retained some advantage, though not much. In one sense, the situation was lopsided. The Navy had two frigate destroyers and an amphibious assault ship, drones, and a piloted surveillance aircraft trailing the *Maersk* lifeboat. The USS *Bainbridge*, a guided missile destroyer, was 509 feet long, with a crew and staff that rivaled the number of operators at SEAL Team 6. The four pirates had a 28-foot lifeboat, several AK-47s, and an American captive—their only piece of leverage in the unfolding drama. For all the firepower brought to the situation, everything rested on keeping the pirates' fingers off their triggers.

McRaven agreed to have a small sniper element lie across the *Bainbridge*'s fantail, their rifles and optical scopes aimed at the pirates. Then they waited. The Indian Ocean is a forbidding place for a small, ill-equipped boat. Soon enough the pirates and Phillips were in distress. They had run out of food and water—and their leader, Muse, needed medical attention. The SEALs used the opportunity to lure Muse aboard the *Bainbridge* to receive treatment as they ferried water to the lifeboat. Once aboard, he was detained, leaving three pirates watching over their hostage.

In the United States, President Obama authorized McRaven to use deadly force only if Phillips's life appeared to be in imminent danger. McRaven transmitted the president's authorization to Capt. Moore and Cdr. Ullman aboard the *Boxer*. The authority is known as an "emergency assault," and like the lethal authorities given to a ground force commander in a war zone, the emergency designation allowed the SEALs' snipers, all enlisted, to fire on the pirates without seeking permission from a commander if they believed the American hostage's life was at risk. But McRaven did not want the snipers to use the authority. He hoped that given enough time, the pirates could be persuaded to release their hostage.

McRaven later wrote about his directive to Moore, who was on the USS *Boxer*. "[L]et's just move slowly and deliberately," McRaven told the Team 6 commanding officer. "We don't want anything to compromise the hostage. Keep up the pressure, own the tempo, and look for opportunities. I know the boys will do the right thing when the time comes." While McRaven viewed himself as in charge, he was too far away to do more than relay the situation from the Indian Ocean to the Pentagon or White House. While he advocated caution and deliberation from Afghanistan, the SEALs sought a resolution.

Then, on April 12, the lifeboat ran out of fuel. To the SEALs' surprise, the pirates agreed that the Navy could hitch a towline from the *Bainbridge*, in order to prevent them from drifting farther out to sea. Slowly, the *Bainbridge* created a heavy wake with its engines and dragged the lifeboat through the wake. The pirates became seasick. The SEALs then offered to winch the towline in so that the lifeboat was closer to the *Bainbridge* and no longer in the wake.

As the sun set, the pirates on the lifeboat grew increasingly agitated. Their already desperate situation had deteriorated. It was dark; they had no khat, a leaf commonly consumed by Somali men, which has narcotic effects and leaves users in a state of withdrawal; they were at the mercy of the rough seas, they were out of fuel, and their leader was on the Navy ship enjoying food and cold drinks. They had unknowingly been dragged to within one hundred feet of the *Bainbridge* fantail, where the SEAL snipers lay watching. The pirates were irritable, and the SEALs could see and hear them abusing and hitting Phillips.

Every few minutes, one of the three Somalis would pop his head out of the hatch to get a little fresh air or relieve himself in the sea. The snipers monitoring the lifeboat determined that the risk to Phillips's life was increasing the longer the negotiations went on. The SEALs agreed that if they had an opportunity where all three Somalis were within their scopes at the same time, they should take the shot. It wouldn't be easy; they would need to fire from nearly one hundred feet away and into a small, covered lifeboat while it rocked in the bigger ship's wake.

The SEALs got their chance. For a second, the three pirates appeared in the snipers' sights—the SEALs didn't hesitate. They fired, nearly simultaneously, hitting the pirates. As soon as the snipers stopped firing, two operators grabbed onto the towrope and began shinnying their way to the lifeboat. With a bit of theatrics, one of the operators carried a knife in his mouth, gripping it with his teeth and preparing to stab any pirates who may have survived. They found the two Somali pirates dead, and one still alive. The operator who carried a knife in his mouth killed the remaining Somali.[1] Phillips was alive and unharmed.

SEAL Team 6 had stepped into an international crisis and settled it with the lethal precision that had come to be expected of them. The Capt. Phillips rescue was real-life drama, and the three SEAL snipers delivered a Hollywood ending. The crisis did, in fact, become a Hollywood movie, starring Tom Hanks as Phillips.

NOT EVERYONE SAW THE PHILLIPS RESCUE AS A DECISIVE VICTORY. At the Afghanistan command center, McRaven learned of the killings after he'd been told that the captain was safe. He was incensed that the snipers took the shot without his approval.[2] The rescue was the most high-profile mission that SEAL Team 6 had undertaken up to that point, and McRaven, a source close to him told me, wanted to be able to tell the president that he personally gave the order, if it had to come to that. Neither Capt. Moore nor Cdr. Ullman had given the order to fire, and no one in the chain of command came back to Adm. McRaven seeking permission. The risks of the pirates killing their hostage or of an errant sniper shot were high. The admiral would later write about how proud of his former unit he was, omitting any details about his simmering concerns with how the *Maersk* operation transpired. McRaven was glad that Phillips was safe, but the incident only highlighted his continued conflict with Team 6's enlisted culture. "When you put a team of guys who've been shooting people for seven years into a situation where there are armed folks holding an American hostage," said a retired SEAL operator who was there that day, "they are going to kill them given the chance."

The tension between McRaven and the operators perfectly captured the delicate position of every senior leader in the SEAL command: no enlisted personnel in the military are given as much leeway and authority on tactical matters as Tier 1 operators because of their masterful performance and unqualified experience. But officers are commissioned to uphold the good order and discipline of the force. In the end, an officer is legally responsible for his men. McRaven was furious, but the enlisted Red Squadron snipers seemed to have made the right call. In any event, they got the results President Obama wanted. The way they behaved in the aftermath of the rescue, however, revealed just how little control McRaven had over Team 6 culture, and how little had changed since 1983.

FBI agents inspected the lifeboat after it had been towed up to the *Bainbridge*, documenting the crime scene and evidence. Capt. Phillips told investigators he'd seen the $30,000 in cash he'd given his captors during the ordeal on the lifeboat, and at one point felt it when his captors gave him a bag to lean against.[3] Yet the FBI agents couldn't locate it aboard the lifeboat. The vessel had been monitored second by second throughout the standoff and no one had seen anything go overboard. No one could account for the disappearance of the cash. Investigators zeroed in on two SEALs—the operators who first boarded the lifeboat. The FBI and NCIS conducted an investigation, during which the two operators submitted to a polygraph. The results were inconclusive. The SEALs were never charged and the money was never recovered.

The celebrated operation seemed to take on the conflicting SEAL pathologies: the heroism and the exceptionalism, the insubordination and the deceit. McRaven was most upset about the missing $30,000 and the cloud of suspicion that fell over the command, recalled the veteran operator who was there that day. The SEALs had executed perfectly, yet somehow still managed to raise questions about the integrity of their unit. While the public saw the results of American snipers freeing a fellow citizen and marveled at the purported three immaculate shots, they would never get an inkling about the darker transgressions, which shook McRaven's confidence.

And yet Team 6 was the only unit capable of mission success, so McRaven continued to call on it for sensitive operations.

October 8, 2010—Dewagal Valley, Kunar Province

Shortly after midnight in a moonless sky, a Chinook hovered over a small collection of earthen structures built into the side of a mountain rise, at roughly eight thousand feet above sea level. Pilots with the 160th Special Operations Aviation Regiment had no flat ground on which to set their helicopter down, so assaulters from Silver Squadron's Alpha team stood on the rear ramp preparing to fast-rope to their target below. The insertion was what's known as "landing on the X," but unlike Takur Ghar and Red Wings, this was a rescue operation and required speed over stealth. The Chinook announced its presence as it weaved through the canyons and ridges of Kunar's Dewagal valley, giving the SEALs' adversaries valuable minutes before the helicopter perched on top of the buildings. In preparation for battle, a few minutes can be an eternity. The SEALs were aware that they would be an exposed target as the helicopter hovered low enough for the team to rope down. But on this night, as the bird sent its rotor wash sweeping over the single-room structures built into the mountainside, the SEALs took no enemy fire. Instead, as they prepared to infiltrate the location, they spotted two Afghan sentries armed with AK-47s scrambling into defensive positions.

The mission that night was not to kill, hopefully, but to rescue a British woman being held captive by a local Taliban group, who'd kidnapped her for a ransom. Linda Norgrove was an aid worker in neighboring Nangarhar province, from Scotland's Western Isles, fluent in Dari and Farsi. Norgrove was well-known in the Kunar Valley region because of her language skills and her gentle demeanor. Norgrove was small, with strawberry-blond hair and blue eyes. She was well liked by her Afghan colleagues and frequently prayed with the locals who hosted her during her development work. Most assumed she was a Muslim convert.

Two weeks earlier, Norgrove and Afghan security personnel left Jalalabad for a village along the Kunar River, where her nongovernmental organization, Development Alternatives Incorporated (DAI), had helped build an irrigation canal. The canal was one of several sustainable agriculture and infrastructure programs in Afghanistan, which Norgrove helped manage in the previous five years. She was a popular foreigner in the area, unafraid of sitting on the floor with the Afghans she worked with and helped. A local group of Taliban fighters knew she planned to attend the canal opening ceremony and saw a business opportunity. Western hostages could be worth a few million dollars each, and in addition to the financial gain, a local militant gang could make a name for themselves within the insurgency if they successfully kidnapped a foreigner.

On September 26, a Sunday, Taliban militants wielding AK-47s abducted Norgrove at a checkpoint on the road south of the canal and headed northwest into Kunar's mountainous interior. For almost two weeks, US, UK, and Afghan government forces set up a cordon around Kunar province in an effort to locate Norgrove. Within a day of her abduction, the Joint Special Operations Command task force in Afghanistan began looking for her. Silver Squadron was given the mission to help rescue her if the coalition of Western forces could locate her. As a UK citizen, Norgrove was a high priority, and the British government pressed the task force for updates.

During the first week of her abduction, the British were able to pass specific GPS coordinates for Norgrove's location as she was moved farther into Kunar's mountains. The intelligence was unusually detailed. The area where Norgrove had been taken was only accessible by foot or pack animals. Team 6, as a guiding principle, typically refuses to undertake missions without knowing the provenance of their intelligence. When they pressed for details, the British made an admission: Norgrove secretly worked with the British intelligence agency, MI6.

After more than a week of hunting for Norgrove, phone intercepts began to fill out a picture of her situation. A local Taliban facilitator, known as Maulawi Basir, or Mullah Abdul Basir, had ordered Norgrove's abduction, the conversations showed, but ran into trouble almost as soon as he took her hostage. First, he had little connection or sway with more senior figures in the Taliban, either in the country's southern Pashtun heartland or across the border in Pakistan, where parts of the Taliban were based. The US and Afghan government forces' movements in Kunar as they searched for Norgrove put pressure on Basir, and he moved her farther into a deep mountain valley. Once he decamped to the small hamlet latticed on the side of a mountain, intercepts revealed that the village elders were also pressuring Basir to kill Norgrove, in an effort to avoid a US raid on the village. By early October, the SEALs began receiving indications that Norgrove would soon be executed or moved across the border, beyond the reach of US military forces. Communication intercepts also revealed that Kunar's shadow Taliban governor wanted Basir to hand Norgrove over to him. The intelligence put the SEALs on a timetable and set the stage for an operation to rescue her.

The SEALs began chipping away at the kidnapper's network. On October 4, they launched a raid to hunt down one of Norgrove's captors. They didn't find their target but engaged in a firefight, killing several militants. The next day Silver Squadron's 1 Troop launched a mission to capture an insurgent who had helped kidnap Norgrove and was with her during part of her captivity. The assault team captured their target, Amin Gul, an associate of Mullah Basir, and killed several militants during the raid. For the SEALs it was a clear indication that they were getting closer to Norgrove or, at least, Mullah Basir. The same day, October 7, drone surveillance revealed a small cropping of single-room structures in a ravine deep in the Hindu Kush foothills. After twenty-four hours of drone and other aerial surveillance, the SEALs came up with a plan to raid the small buildings. The surveillance did not confirm that Norgrove was there, but it was clear that one of her captors was staying in the dwelling. The Silver Squadron operators had differing assessments of the likelihood that Norgrove was there. Some estimated that if she was, there was an 85 percent chance that she would be executed once her captors heard the Chinooks approaching. Every SEAL understood that by flying the Chinooks, they were taking a risk of being shot down by an RPG, as the SEALs and the 160th had five years earlier in the Korengal Valley trying to rescue Marcus Luttrell and his teammates.

Nearly two weeks after Linda Norgrove was abducted, the British government authorized a rescue mission to save her. SEAL planners called the operation ANSTRUTHER, named after a coastal town in Scotland, a nod to Norgrove's Scottish background. Overall, one squadron officer said, the mission shaped up as perhaps the most difficult and daring rescue in the command's history. "I think it was a lot of risk and that's our job,"

Lt. Cdr. Jon Fussell, who served as the ground force commander on the mission, would say later. "It is worth the risk to send the message that you don't ever do this to our people."[4]

As MOST OF 1 TROOP LANDED ON THE MOUNTAINSIDE AT 12:35 A.M., just below the houses built into the mountainside, the Alpha team leader, Greg Andrews, pushed up, leading as some of his teammates fell in directly behind him, while others flanked his position toward two distinct building rows. Greg was, by the command's standard, a grizzled veteran. A senior team leader, Greg was drafted into Red Team in 2002 and was on his eleventh wartime deployment. His specialty was as a sniper, but when Silver Squadron was created, the command moved him over to be an assault team leader. He was highly respected by both his peers and his subordinates.

Greg moved over the roofs of the lower row of buildings, spotted an armed military-age male, and fired three shots. The man fell. The team leader stepped back from his position and called on the inner "troop net," an audio communication system for just the assault team on the ground: "Shots fired, shots fired. They have weapons." Greg kept moving until he could peer around one building's corner. The SEALs, who were wearing night-vision goggles on a dark evening, could see clearly while the enemy fighters were practically blind. Greg saw a second Taliban fighter and fired twice, killing the man, all the while holding his position along the building's edge. He turned his head and saw a third armed fighter and fired a single shot into him.

As Greg was moving across the lower row of buildings, another assaulter, Tom Oliva, moved along the same row of buildings, but beneath Greg, at the floor level, farther on the slope. Tom was on his third deployment with the command, and as he scanned his field of vision, he too saw an armed male exiting a building and moving away from his position. A moment later, the fighter reversed his direction, back toward Tom, before turning a second time and heading away. Tom called out in Pashto for the fighter to stop. The man ignored the call and inexplicably changed course again, climbing stairs built into the mountainside, which allowed for access between the rows of buildings and terraces. Tom fired several shots into the man, who dropped. Tom then moved onto the terrace of a building, heading toward another mud-and-stone compound from which he had earlier seen fighters leaving. He turned back toward the stairs and saw a second man with an AK-47. He managed to shoot him before the fighter noticed Tom. Tom held his position, which gave him some cover but also allowed him to peer into a group of one-room buildings on the lower row.

Tom was joined by another teammate, Ben Ives, the troop's newest operator. Ben had been a SEAL since just before 9/11 and had done multiple deployments, but this was his first as a member of SEAL Team 6. As Ben pushed up beside Tom, Tom saw a third armed man walking toward them from a perpendicular pathway, an alley-like space between two buildings. Greg, meanwhile, was positioned on one of the buildings' roofs. Tom could only see the man's left side, which included his AK-47, and fired two more rounds at him. As Tom fired, Ben called, "Frag out, frag out," meaning he was deploying a fragmentary grenade. Tom pushed off to one side, seeking cover from the blast along a building wall. As the grenade landed in the alley, Greg fired a single shot into the same fighter's right side. At the moment Greg fired, something detonated and the blast threw him back against a rock.

With the three fighters dead, Greg pushed uphill to the higher row of buildings. It was here that the drone video had suggested Norgrove might be held. In the twenty-four hours prior, the two buildings had shown the most activity, with men, women, and children seen coming and going. Greg made it into one of the two structures, saw a final armed man, and shot him. As the rest of the assault team moved through the buildings, they called out that everything was clear. The hostilities were over, but they hadn't seen Norgrove yet. One of Greg's teammates asked the team leader if he had seen the female down, near the alleyway in the lower row of buildings. Greg had not and made his way in that direction.

There, a small, fair-skinned woman with reddish-brown hair was lying on her back, her head uphill. A dead fighter, who was missing most of his left torso, lay across one of her legs. Greg leaned down to remove a shawl from near her face. It was clear it was Norgrove. He asked one of his teammates, an Air Force pararescueman and trained medic, to examine her.

Lt. Cdr. Jon Fussell, the troop commander, made his way to the body. "Jackpot," he called back to Bagram, meaning they had located their hostage. A quick cheer in the operations center went out. A moment later Fussell announced, "We are administering CPR at this time."[5] The operations center went silent.

On the mountainside, the Air Force pararescueman listened for Norgrove's breath, checked her pulse, and watched closely to see if her chest rose or fell with air. Nothing. Then he noticed a small piece of her left earlobe missing and what he assessed was brain fluid draining from the ear. Lifting her torso up to examine her back, he could see significant blood staining her shirt. He cut her shirt and saw ten to fifteen nickel-sized wounds, which started at her lower back and appeared to move upward toward her neck. The Air Force sergeant told Greg that she had massive frag marks and that she was expectant, a technical term meaning that while he would not declare her dead, he judged that even with immediate emergency care, she had a 99 percent chance of dying.

"Jackpot is KIA," Fussell told his commanders at Bagram.

Norgrove's body was wrapped, placed in a body bag, and hoisted up to a helicopter. Meanwhile, the team gathered all the weapons and explosives, including a pipe bomb, into a pile and detonated them. They took pictures of each of the four men who were killed, from multiple angles, and prepared to exfiltrate the compound. Fussell pulled his senior enlisted SEAL, Senior Chief Phil Ryan, the troop chief, and asked him to gather Greg and the other team leaders. He needed to find out if anyone had unintentionally shot Norgrove. Ryan was shocked at the order, but Fussell explained that he wasn't making an accusation, he just wanted to gather all the facts. Fussell would later say that given the high profile of the mission, he wanted to be able to tell the medical examiners and his superiors what they could expect during a proper examination of Norgrove's body.

When Greg first showed his troop commander her body, he explained that his shot had set off a suicide vest or a grenade rigged to the militant's ammo vest. On his previous deployment, he had fired at an enemy, which appeared to then set off an explosive vest the fighter wore, exploding less than thirty feet from where Greg was standing. From Greg's vantage point now, it seemed to have happened again. For Greg's teammates, many of whom had been on that operation a year earlier, the explanation made sense. The fighter who died next to Norgrove had most of his left side blown off, and his AK-47 was destroyed from the blast as well. After he heard Greg's explanation, Lt. Cdr. Fussell radioed back that Norgrove was killed by an apparent suicide vest worn by one of the captors.

Greg and the other operators couldn't understand why they were unable to see Norgrove until after she was found dead. Each team member had covered their area of responsibility during the assault, which left them with little visibility on each other's actions. Most missions end up this way: no one can see the entire choreography play out. Each operator is limited to his narrow vision—often with little to no periphery because of his night-vision goggles—and the terse exchanges between teammates over the troop net.

As the SEALs waited for their helicopter to take them back to their base, Tom retraced his steps. Norgrove's body was already being hoisted by the time he returned to the alleyway where he'd engaged the last fighter. He'd overheard two of his teammates remark that the fighter he'd shot had set off an explosives vest and a cursory glance at the body appeared to confirm it. But Tom also heard Norgrove was found in the same area and was surprised because he hadn't seen her there. Tom found Ben and pulled him aside. "I'm just trying to retrace my steps," Tom later recalled asking his teammate. "You did throw a frag, correct?" Ben confirmed the grenade and said it came on the initial "shootout" in the alleyway. "I'm not suggesting anything at all," Tom said, "but we need to talk to Greg about that." Ben agreed.

When the squadron landed in Jalalabad, they immediately began to download the mission. At Bagram, at the British embassy in Kabul, in Washington, and in London, British and American officials were anxious to learn the full details of the failed mission.

The assault team conducted what they call a "hot wash," a post-mission debrief around a firepit at the base. The mood was somber. The operators

were expert tradesmen, yet they had not managed to bring Linda Norgrove back alive. "They'd trained their whole lives for this scenario and
they failed," a Team 6 leader told me. Led by the troop chief, Phil Ryan,
the debrief was informal, almost casual, despite the fact that a national priority mission had failed. Given the stakes and the result, Greg described
his engagement with the fighter and the suicide vest, concluding that on
this, his second consecutive deployment to Afghanistan, he had encountered a Taliban militant who had set off a rigged vest rather than be killed
by an American. But Tom and Ben said nothing about the grenade. The
gathering ended after fifteen minutes and everyone dispersed.

Not long after, Tom went to Greg's sleeping bay and told his team
leader that Ben had thrown a grenade during the operation. He walked
Greg through what he'd seen and gathered. Ben joined Tom and Greg
and confirmed that he threw the grenade. "I will take care of this," Greg
told them.

Later that night, Silver Squadron's administrative team processed the
post-mission photos and evidence, concluding that Norgrove was killed
by her captors. The report was quickly passed to senior military officials,
including David Petraeus, then the commanding general of US forces in
Afghanistan. American officials informed the British government that
Norgrove's captors had killed her before she could be saved by her rescuers. President Obama called Queen Elizabeth II to inform her that
Norgrove was dead, killed by her Afghan captors, despite the SEALs' efforts.[6] Within hours of the operation, the US military had announced to
reporters in Afghanistan that a rescue operation to save Norgrove ended
when her captors killed her.

"Afghan and coalition security forces did everything in their power
to rescue Linda," said Gen. Petraeus in a statement given to the media.
"Linda was a courageous person with a passion to improve the lives of
Afghan people, and sadly she lost her life in their service."

AT BAGRAM, COL. ERIK KURILLA, THE TASK FORCE COMMANDER IN
charge of all special operations in Afghanistan, sat in an operations center

the following day, watching and rewatching the drone footage. Col. Kurilla was an Army Ranger with twenty-two years of service who had commanded special operations forces in both Iraq and Afghanistan. Kurilla was a Gen. McChrystal acolyte and a veteran of JSOC's hunter-killer teams that the general had built earlier in the war effort. In the live feed, the images were low resolution, and just as the operators hadn't seen Norgrove being dragged from one of the houses by her captor, neither had the command center watching as the operation had unfolded. Now Kurilla wanted to figure out where Norgrove had come from, and how she was killed. He had examined post-raid photos of the militant the SEALs believed had blown himself up. But there was something wrong with the SEALs' account, Kurilla thought. It wasn't that he suspected they were lying or covering something up—their conclusion that a grenade or a vest had detonated had some merit. Grenades and a pipe bomb were found on the target; the team leader, Greg, saw the explosion from close range; and although the self-detonation attack was more common in Iraq, it was not out of the range of tactics the Taliban might use. But the injuries from the Norgrove mission were also inconsistent with self-detonating. "I have seen hundreds of grenade injuries and I have seen dozens of suicide vest blasts," Kurilla later told military investigators about his assessment of the photos. The commander asked the Silver Squadron commanding officer, Cdr. Matt Burns, if his men had thrown any grenades. The SEAL told him they had not.

The next day in Jalalabad, troop chief Phil Ryan called Greg, Tom, and Ben into his quarters to review the low-resolution drone footage. Ryan wanted to know why no one from Alpha team saw or heard Norgrove until she was dead. Greg described the operation as he had previously, narrating as Phil played the video. Greg said nothing about the grenade. Ben and Tom stood in the background, silent as Greg described his assessment of the video. The low-resolution video did not show which building Norgrove came from, nor did it show Ben throwing the grenade.

On Sunday morning, Col. Kurilla was still troubled, and he ordered the drone video hard-drive downloaded so he could view high-resolution video of the operation as well as see it from additional angles. In the afternoon, the British ambassador flew to Jalalabad to personally thank the SEALs for their rescue attempt. The entire troop sat in a hangar, including Greg, Tom, and Ben, as Phil Ryan recounted the operation. As they had the day before, the three Alpha team operators remained silent. But at Bagram, Kurilla was scrutinizing the high-resolution footage, and what it showed was unmistakable. The video clearly captured Ben, on one knee, throw something underhand, followed by an explosion four seconds later in the space where Linda Norgrove fell. The video was unmistakable: the SEAL killed Norgrove.

Kurilla was stunned and now contemplated something almost unthinkable: Team 6 was covering up how Norgrove died. The Ranger was unsure how high the cover-up went. He called the Silver Squadron commander, Matt Burns, to Bagram. Kurilla wanted to see how Burns reacted when the SEAL viewed the high-definition video. Despite having a good relationship with Burns, Kurilla feared the SEAL was in on the cover-up. Burns watched and, like Kurilla, understood instantly the gravity of what was afoot. Burns told Kurilla that he didn't know the SEALs had killed Norgrove with an errant grenade. Kurilla was satisfied that Burns was telling the truth.

Next, Burns dispatched his master chief, William King, to Jalalabad to confront the troop who'd conducted the mission. King arrived in Jalalabad, found Phil Ryan, and brought Greg Andrews into an office, now nearly forty-eight hours after the mission had ended.

"Did you know anything about this?" Phil asked Greg. "At first," Phil recalled later, "he was like, 'No, I don't.'" A moment later, Greg admitted the truth. "'I did,'" Ryan quoted Greg telling him. "'My guys came to me and told me.'" Phil said later about his reaction to Greg's confession, "I got sick to my damn stomach."

After Greg's admission, the command confirmed for Col. Kurilla that Ben, against all basic hostage rescue tactics and protocols, had deployed a grenade. Gen. Petraeus called the British government to amend the story. President Obama called Queen Elizabeth II to amend the account. It was the SEALs, the American president told the British monarch, who had mistakenly killed Norgrove.[7]

Gen. Petraeus ordered an investigation and assigned a top special operations officer, Maj. Gen. Joseph Votel, to lead it. The impact of Votel's investigation, which was later made public, was immediate and devastating for the command. Much of it focused on the tactical challenges and complex choreography during the mission. But Votel's interviews, which were given under oath, also revealed the culture of impunity and the lack of integrity that had thrived at the command. One senior Army special operations officer who helped conduct the investigation and oversaw dozens of SEAL Team 6 operations during the war described what came out of Votel's investigation as an "I-told-you-so moment." Because both the US and UK governments were watching the mission closely, the SEALs' mistake and subsequent misconduct had provided a level of outside scrutiny that the SEALs had not previously experienced. Suspicions about the command's criminal behavior and lack of accountability were finally exposed, even if behind the classified curtain of an elite military unit. What troubled many within the special operations community was that if Team 6 would lie on a mission when so many others were watching, how did they conduct themselves when outsiders were not?

The investigation was, in fact, the first and only time that outsiders had knocked down the command's wall of silence and been given an opportunity to peer inside. The interviews made plain how devastated Silver Squadron was that they were unable to rescue Norgrove. Several senior SEALs, including Lt. Cdr. Fussell, broke down mid-answer, in tears, as they described finding Norgrove dead. Even in dry military transcripts, their emotion, dedication, and courage come through. "We knew going in it was very high risk," Fussell told Votel. "I gave us about a 20 percent chance of having a bird shot down that night." Later, Fussell described the pre-mission assessment he presented to his superiors. "I think if she is there, I give her 15 percent chance of survival. I think there is a really strong chance they will execute her and I think we have a 20 percent chance of something catastrophic happening going into this valley." Fussell was asked if the mission was too risky to be approved. "No, I don't think that it shouldn't have been launched, sir. I think it was a lot of risk and that's our job and we go do it," he answered. The command became so good at conducting raids that when it came to an operation where they would have to land a helicopter and then traverse a steep mountainside with loose shale and boulders and push uphill toward their target, they went out with the complete belief that they would prevail, even when the odds were nearly impossible.

While Votel and a small team of investigators tracked the movements and perspectives of each operator and senior leader on the mission, much of the investigation centered on why Ben threw a grenade. His use of the weapon was a blatant violation of basic hostage rescue tactics, which dictate that the only scenario in which you might deploy a grenade would be after you have secured the hostage, and even then, only as a last resort. The potential for collateral damage is considered too high. Ben's peers understood why, based on what he was seeing at that moment, he deployed the grenade. He was trying to protect his teammates, concerned that he and they were trapped in what is known by the operators as a "fatal funnel," where assaulters are moving into a narrowing location with no cover, which the enemy can easily attack. Ben was scared and panicked, and the difference between taking a momentary breath and pulling a grenade became the difference between saving Norgrove and killing her.

But testimony from the subsequent investigation revealed more than just the dissonance in how the command viewed tactical errors versus ethical ones. The interviews revealed the divide between the officers and the enlisted, a relationship marked by respect as well as plenty of suspicion. In this case, the suspicion came from an officer. Fussell seemed most upset about Ben's choice of throwing the grenade. The veteran commander had a theory that had not yet surfaced: the newest member of the SEAL team had shot Norgrove by mistake, then tossed the grenade to cover up his error. Fussell was horrified, not only by the idea that this occurred, but by what it revealed about the SEALs as a team, as indicated by his testimony:

> Our selection process is not perfect. No one's is. You are always going to have problems. The [lack of] integrity thing is just absolutely inexcusable. The selfishness of the individual who did this, who shot her

and threw a grenade on her. I'm not convinced a grenade wasn't thrown as a cover up when he realized he had shot her.

That is just me speculating. I am highly disgusted by the whole thing and the integrity issue is mind blowing there....I don't know how you screen for that but I think it is a symptom of an overall sickness that, you know, that guy, whether we missed him on [redacted] or I don't know what the issue is but...[i]t is disrespectful and then try to justify and make stories up....

I mean I think we are going to take a seriously hard look at how we are vetting, how we are screening, how we are selecting and at the team level I feel horrible for the guys who went out and did what, in my opinion, not to toot anyone's horns, but one of the more daring [hostage rescues] ever. No one is going to remember who did what and where, what environment and under what risk level they [*sic*] are just going to remember that somebody botched it.

Votel could not substantiate the accusation that Ben threw the grenade to cover up unintentionally shooting the hostage. But when the investigator told Fussell that they found no evidence of this, the lieutenant commander was unmoved. Fussell conceded that he had no proof, but he doubled down. He was confident that, with all he had come to know about the Teams, it was in the realm of possibility. Lt. Cdr. Fussell, who'd commanded and planned the mission, took little personal responsibility for his men. In fact, he savaged the lowest-ranking operator, stood up and defended his team leader, and offered little apology for how he commanded his troop. Fussell, the SEAL officer in command, played the same game as senior Pentagon officials and politicians in Washington do: pass the buck.

Ben's mistake, although tragic, could be understood in the context of an extremely difficult mission. But Greg's decision to withhold the information from his superiors was both willful and unbecoming, especially from such a senior, seasoned SEAL Team 6 operator.

"At that moment," Greg told investigators, "when they told me about that grenade I just, I already had a problem because I had to stand in front of my [command] and tell them how this went wrong, that I didn't save her. Then on top of that they come to me with this [grenade], I was lost. I ain't going to lie. I panicked; I had no idea what to do."

Greg had done thirteen deployments and, according to his teammates, countless acts of bravery. But when he faced scrutiny, he could not summon any moral courage. The SEALs represented an inherent contradiction. For all their specialized training and elite capabilities, many struggled with foundational, almost rudimentary, ethical actions: to not steal, to obey authority, to tell the truth. They were ill-equipped to confront failures and the accountability that came with them.

AFTER SEVERAL WEEKS, THE INVESTIGATION CONFIRMED THAT NOR-grove "likely" died from wounds suffered when Ben—who did not see Norgrove—tossed a grenade in her vicinity. Among his findings, Votel concluded that the grenade use, "though understandable given his perception of the threat," was "in direct contravention" of hostage rescue tactics. The investigation also concluded that Greg was "derelict" in his "performance of duties" and made a "false official statement," both violations of the Uniform Code of Military Justice. Votel acknowledged and commended Greg for his "absolutely courageous" performance during the rescue attempt. "He led his team with distinction on a high-risk operation to which he and his team members were exposed to danger and hostile conditions in perhaps the most challenging terrain US forces currently operate."[8]

The investigation into the operation identified the failures and recommended that only Greg, alone, be punished. Adm. McRaven personally traveled to Dam Neck and made his own determination: all three SEALs involved in the cover-up should be removed from Team 6.[9] The admiral's mast was an unprecedented disciplinary action at the command, which had always been allowed to discipline itself. Normally, the Team 6 commanding officer, a captain, would conduct a mast, a form of nonjudicial punishment. McRaven's message to the command's leadership was clear, according to a former SEAL leader who attended the proceeding. "What you're saying is you have no faith in the commander," he said. "All of us were upset."

After the Norgrove investigation, McRaven also held a meeting with a group of dozens of senior officers under his command. He told them that SEAL Team 6 had effectively made lying to protect a teammate an honorable course of action, according to a person who attended the meeting. "He told us they had put unit and self before mission and country," the retired officer said. "He reminded us all that our first loyalty was to the Constitution. McRaven told us, 'You're fighting for your country, not your partner. Your job is to defend the Constitution.'"

But for the enlisted, the Norgrove mission wasn't about an errant grenade or a cover-up. They saw the punishment for three enlisted operators but none for any officers as a double standard and a dereliction of their duty as commanders. Greg and Tom later returned to the unit. Ben went back to the regular Teams. Both Greg and Ben were pushed to spend time retelling their failures on the mission to SEALs and other special operations units.[10] The idea was to provide ethics training, but the Team 6 enlisted saw something else: forced humiliation. No Silver Squadron officers were counseled; none had to relive their failures. After ten years of war, the enlisted, entitled as they were, received a clear message from the command's officer corps: we don't have your back. One Team 6 officer involved said the enlisted operators were right to identify the double standard of having the team leader and two junior assaulters receive punishment while both the troop commander and troop chief escaped punishment. The officer explained that what the assaulters could not recognize was the gravity of their lies. "When the president has to call the Queen of England and tell her, 'Sorry, ma'am, I lied, our guys killed your citizen,'" said the officer, "it's a big fucking deal."

McRaven was wrestling with an organization that he would later say had lost its moral compass. But it wasn't clear whether the Teams had a moral compass to begin with. McRaven's conflict at Dam Neck was much the same as it had been with Bob Schamberger nearly three decades earlier, in 1983. The command in 2010 was noticeably more professional than it was in the Marcinko era, but it still was unable to hold itself accountable for anything other than operational mistakes. When confronted with ethical or moral transgressions, the institutional instincts were to cover up. For as much as the War on Terror had changed the command, so much remained the same: SEAL Team 6 still behaved like a crime family, above the law, often accountable only to themselves.

TEAM 6 BRISTLED WHEN THEY WERE HELD IN CHECK BY SENIOR OFficers outside the unit, but struggled to police themselves. A few months before the Norgrove mission, Dam Neck showed the limits of their self-governance. Britt Slabinski was up for a promotion at the command, and for the first time, SEAL Team 6 leaders expressed concerns about Slabinski's past conduct as a squadron master chief. Before recommending Slabinski for a promotion, the command conducted two secret inquiries into the Navy Cross winner's time as the Blue Squadron enlisted leader. Almost immediately, the issue that received the most scrutiny was the December 2007 attempted beheading. According to two former SEALs, Slabinski told his teammates and superiors that his remark about wanting a head was figurative and not a literal order. By then, there was no question about whether the attempted beheading had occurred; the question was why.[11]

"We didn't debate whether Slab had told his guys he wanted a head on a platter—he copped to that. The only issue was, was his order real, or just talk?" said one of the retired SEALs involved. "It didn't make a difference. He said it and one of his operators did it because he believed he was following an order."

Ten officers and master chiefs voted unanimously against allowing Slabinski to return to the command. At that point, the second inquiry was commissioned by the SEAL Team 6 commanding officer, Pete Van Hooser. Evidence was presented that Slabinski gave an order to shoot all the men they encountered during another raid, whether or not they were armed. According to the *New York Times*, Afghans accused Blue Squadron of killing civilians during that operation, but a subsequent military investigation determined that all those killed had been armed and hostile.[12]

When Slabinski was confronted by the command's senior enlisted leader about whether he had instructed Blue Squadron operators to kill all males during the operation, code-named Pantera, Slabinski acknowledged that he had done so.[13] The second inquiry also uncovered the "head on a platter" remark as the instigation for the beheading in December 2007, but the command's senior enlisted leader told Slabinski he would not get the promotion or be allowed to serve at the command again because of the Pantera order. Overall, it had become clear that Slabinski's run as a leader on the battlefield caused Blue Squadron to come "off the rails," according to a former SEAL Team 6 leader.

Slabinski has not responded to multiple queries and requests for comment, though he did deny to the *New York Times* in 2015 that he gave the illegal pre-mission guidance to kill all males.[14] In his interview with the *Times*, Slabinski asserted that it was he who had witnessed the operator slashing at the dead fighter's throat, saying, "It appeared he was mutilating a body." Slabinski portrayed himself as trying to police his men and said that he gave them "a very stern speech." He claimed to the *Times* that he told his men, "If any of you feel a need to do any retribution, you should call me." In the *Times* story, Slabinski said nothing about Vasely ordering him to investigate the scene or the remark about a head on a platter.

"To this day, he thinks the guys turned on him," said one of the former SEAL Team 6 leaders. "Well, they did. What we didn't do was turn him in. You will step over the line and you start dehumanizing people. You really do. And it takes the team, it takes individuals to pull you back. And part of that was getting rid of Britt Slabinski."

Two other SEAL Team 6 leaders with a combined thirty-five years at the command said the removal of Slabinski and the failure to pursue official punishment was an indictment of the senior officers—they had failed one of their most basic duties, to hold themselves and others accountable for wrongdoing. "If a guy cuts off another guy's head and nothing happens, that becomes the standard," said one of the former SEAL Team 6 leaders. "You're moving the bar and buying into an emotional justification, 'War is hell.'"

When then Commodore Tim Szymanski, commanding officer of all regular East Coast–based SEAL Teams, heard that Slabinski had been rejected by Team 6, he requested him as his senior enlisted adviser. The request was approved and Slabinski was promoted.[15]

February 2011—Indian Ocean, near the Somalia Coast

Tensions with McRaven reached another level just a few months later, when the SEALs were once again sent on a daring hostage rescue mission. Two American couples, sailing a yacht in the Indian Ocean, were hijacked by armed Somali pirates. The couples—Jean and Scott Adam, and Phyllis Macay and Bob Riggle—were in open seas nearly three hundred miles from Oman, on a Christian missionary trip delivering Bibles by boat. President Obama again authorized Adm. McRaven and JSOC to send Team 6 to try to rescue the Americans. Gold Squadron deployed to sea, assembling on Navy vessels.

But this time, McRaven refused to give Team 6 the emergency assault authority as he had during the Capt. Phillips rescue two years earlier. "McRaven told us we had manipulated him on Lightning Dawn [the *Maersk* operation] and it wasn't going to happen again," said a retired SEAL Team 6 leader who took part in the *Quest* mission. As they had with the *Maersk* lifeboat, the goal was to keep the pirates from getting the four American hostages and their vessel, the *Quest*, to the Somali coastline. McRaven commanded the operation from the JSOC headquarters in North Carolina. The SEALs sat helpless as they watched the *Quest* make its way into Somali waters, where the pirates' comrades prepared to bring the captives ashore. SEAL snipers watched through their scopes as the pirates became agitated and began shooting at both a Navy vessel and the SEALs, who were not allowed to fire back. McRaven ordered the USS *Sterett* to pull alongside the *Quest*, blocking the fifty-eight-foot yacht.

Inside the *Quest*'s cabin, the pirates responded to the American maneuver. In the fallout of the *Maersk* operations, the Somali pirates were instructed to kill their hostages if their commander did not return from US custody. With their commander still aboard the *Sterett*, and fearing that its repositioning was the beginning of an American assault, two of the pirates pointed their AK-47s at their hostages and executed the four Americans. From the smaller Navy vessel, the SEAL team snipers watched through their rifle scopes as the Somalis executed the hostages. The SEALs stormed the boat, hoping to save the Americans. They killed all but two of the pirates, but were unable to save the missionaries. The mission had failed, and this time the SEALs blamed McRaven. He had micromanaged the operation from half a world away and, from the SEALs' per ective, emasculated them, leaving them unable to respond to the situation.[16] Four Americans were dead, and while the pirates had pulled the trigger, Team 6 operators saw McRaven's oversight as the killer. The SEALs believed McRaven had failed. The retired Team 6 leader involved paraphrased McRaven's last message to the SEALs in the aftermath of the mission: Who would have thought the Somalis would have done that? "Well, I can tell you who would have thought that," the retired SEAL said. "Every operator on that boat watching those Somali pirates on that sailboat knew what was going to happen."

But even when the SEALs may have been too boxed in by officers, their propensity for excessive behavior made an appearance during the mission. After the SEALs stormed the sailboat, one of the snipers decided to use his knife to kill the captors. When one of the pirates on the deck, who initially appeared to be dead, suddenly moved, the SEAL used his knife to end the Somali's life.[17] Medical examiners later documented ninety-one stab wounds on the dead Somali pirate.[18] The SEAL was required to see the command's psychologist afterward but was cleared to operate.

THE BATTLE GOING ON BETWEEN ADM. McRAVEN AND TEAM 6 continued to represent the same struggle between Navy commanders and the skilled but undisciplined operators at Dam Neck, as it had when Marcinko was commander. The enlisted men wanted the glory but not the responsibility; the officers frequently provided little input for operational success and blamed the enlisted when the mission failed. In both successful and failed high-profile operations, Team 6's lack of integrity was exposed to McRaven. He understood the problem and was trying to fix it, but he often had to turn to Dam Neck to accomplish the most difficult of missions. He just had to hope they could succeed without revealing the ugly truth to his higher command: Team 6 skirted the line between being criminals for the state and just old-fashioned criminals.

PART III
Recognition for My Actions: The Brand

[2011–2016]

CHAPTER 12

THE BIG MISH

IN THE PREDAWN HOURS OF MAY 1, 2011, THE THUMP OF INBOUND helicopters woke the residential neighborhood in Abbottabad, Pakistan, where Osama bin Laden, the al Qaeda leader and architect of the September 11 attacks, had hidden out for nearly five years. When a stealth UH-60 Black Hawk helicopter crashed inside the walls of his three-story compound, it would have eliminated any doubt that he was the target of a night raid. In the courtyard below, a short burst of suppressed gunfire killed his courier, who was staying in a building adjacent to the main home. Then sounds of more suppressed shots and an explosion echoed from the floors below. Bin Laden waited with one of his wives and daughters in the top-floor bedroom, given a few moments to contemplate what was happening. For the SEALs racing each other up the stairwell, there was no question bin Laden would be killed. They had come to kill bin Laden. The only question was who would get to do it.

THE SEALs WERE THE OBVIOUS CHOICE. DESPITE ALL THE PROB-
lems between McRaven and Team 6, the three-star admiral was still a
SEAL, and the unit had spent a decade as the lead Tier 1 unit in Afghanistan. The operation itself would shape up as a relatively straightforward
assault raid, the kind Team 6 had conducted hundreds, if not thousands,
of times over ten years.

The SEALs at Team 6 had been waiting for the bin Laden mission
since the Saudi terrorist had escaped from Tora Bora in 2001. At the command, a raid for bin Laden was known colloquially as "the Big Mish"—the
Big Mission. Nearly everyone at the command had gotten on a helicopter
in Afghanistan at one time or another and been told the operation could
possibly involve bin Laden. The Big Mish had become mythical, and always felt just out of reach. Like anybody else who asked the question
"What happened to Osama bin Laden?," plenty of Dam Neck operators
speculated he was dead or wasting away in an Afghan cave. When the
twenty-three SEALs from Red Squadron were pulled from training and
briefed on the mission, many thought they were going after Libyan dictator Muammar Gaddafi. Once CIA briefers made clear the Big Mish had
indeed arrived, the Team 6 operators set about preparing to launch.

But Obama's national security team had no visibility on who the individual SEALs were. Or that under the veneer of quiet professionalism,
there were members of the strike team with grand ambitions to use the
raid as the crowning achievement of a military career—and a launchpad
for their next one.

The careers of Rob O'Neill and Matthew Bissonnette were closely
aligned. They'd each entered Red Squadron in 2005 and were both recipients of the Winkler hatchets handed out by Wyman Howard. They were
both talented and competitive, and they were determined to profit from
their experiences as SEALs.[1]

Bissonnette was viewed as the prototypical SEAL Team 6 operator: a
college-educated enlisted man with a savvy understanding of tactics and
technology. O'Neill, by contrast, was not considered as clever as his teammate, but he was a deadly sniper and had had a successful tour as a team

leader in Red Squadron. Both had risen to become team leaders, a position that, although the lowest enlisted one in authority, was nonetheless highly sought after and a requirement for further promotion.

Both men were also known among their teammates for their self-promotional tendencies—a trait not well suited for a "team-first" environment. In the end, their inclusion and their roles in the bin Laden raid defined where they fit in: Bissonnette worked closely with the CIA and SEAL Team 6 superiors during the planning phase to help plot out the assault, and would lead a team of operators to find and kill bin Laden's courier. O'Neill was chosen as a team leader for a group providing external security but ultimately traded that leadership role for a junior spot on the team he believed would get the first shot at bin Laden.

The twenty-three operators assigned to the mission prepared constantly for the entire month of April 2011, practicing on two different full-scale mock-ups of the bin Laden compound. Tactically, there was little about the upcoming raid that was complex. Unlike the hundreds of other assaults SEAL Team 6 had carried out in Iraq and Afghanistan, in which the operators would plan and carry out a raid within a matter of hours, this time they had weeks to prepare. They had detailed plans of the Abbottabad compound provided by the CIA, and knew where they could expect to find bin Laden. The SEALs' biggest concern was how much time they would have, which was dictated by the amount of fuel the two Black Hawks could carry for the round-trip.[2]

The obsessive planning and attention to detail were Adm. McRaven's hallmark. His master's degree thesis had been a study of successful special operations missions from World War II, Vietnam, and the Israeli hostage rescue in Entebbe, Uganda. The thesis, which was later published as a book, argued that each special operations mission needed six principles of operation, and McRaven applied them to planning the raid. Unlike the hostage rescues, McRaven had time to consider every detail and possibility the SEALs might face in the bin Laden operation. Speed, surprise, security, simplicity, repetition, and purpose were the key factors in success. With as much as a month to rehearse and repair, McRaven would maintain the ability to keep his attack dogs on a leash until the precise moment he needed to let them off, and hope they did not bite him afterward.

After initial training at a CIA facility in North Carolina, the team traveled to Nevada, where they rehearsed every element of the raid on an exact model of the compound. The Nevada location best replicated the weather, terrain, and altitude in Abbottabad, which helped both the SEALs and the 160th SOAR pilots who would fly them get a feel for what the mission would require.

The planning was so meticulous, one retired SEAL Team 6 leader told me, that a helicopter pilot warned mission planners that one of the two stealth Black Hawks they were to use would likely experience a "vortex ring state," which means air disturbed by the rotors would prevent the helicopter from getting the lift necessary to continue hovering. The pilot noted that the two mock-up compounds had chain-link fences around the buildings, allowing the air to disperse, while the real compound had thick concrete walls. The pilot dropped out several weeks into the planning because he was so disturbed by McRaven's continued insistence on using the high-tech helicopters despite knowing there was a high probability that one would fail on the mission.

Less than a week before the assault, Bissonnette and O'Neill got into a shouting match at the Dam Neck base over who would sell the inside story of the raid. Several of their teammates on the mission had to intervene, according to a former SEAL Team 6 operator. A former Team 6 leader told me that O'Neill and Bissonnette originally agreed to cooperate on a book or movie project after the raid was over, but later had a falling-out. The former SEAL said the extensive amount of training for the mission, combined with Bissonnette's planning role, gave both men ample opportunity to find ways to locate themselves on the third floor of the Abbottabad compound, which would allow for a good position from which to kill bin Laden.

Despite claims by John O. Brennan, then president Obama's chief counterterrorism adviser, that the raid was a "capture or kill" operation, the SEALs were told explicitly to kill bin Laden. There was no plan for capture, and no contingency for a surrender. "They were told, 'Go in, kill him, and bring the body back,'" said a former SEAL Team 6 leader with direct knowledge of the order.

ON MAY I, TWO STEALTH BLACK HAWK HELICOPTERS TOOK OFF from Jalalabad, Afghanistan, and headed east toward Abbottabad. The flight took ninety minutes, and as the Black Hawk that Bissonnette rode in approached the compound walls, it effectively slammed on the brakes thirty feet above the ground. The pilot who had warned that one of the helicopters would stall was right. Bissonnette's helicopter crashed into bin Laden's side yard. Bissonnette and his teammates were nearly killed, and most of the dozen or so operators aboard ended up with serious injuries.

Bissonnette and a small team of SEALs moved from the helicopter to a small building adjacent to bin Laden's main house. After the SEALs tried but failed to blow up the building's gated front door, someone inside fired several rounds out a window. One of Bissonnette's teammates then put his gun through the front door, which was now slightly ajar, and shot the gunman in the head. The man was Abu Ahmed al Kuwaiti, one of bin Laden's couriers. His would be the only shots fired by anyone but the SEALs during the raid.

After the SEALs killed the courier, his wife, who was inside near her husband, opened the gate and confirmed to the SEALs that bin Laden could be found on the third floor of the main building, just as the team had been briefed. Bissonnette and his team then moved into the main house.

Once inside, the SEALs proceeded slowly and methodically. O'Neill's teammates shot and killed al Kuwaiti's brother and his wife on the first floor. After blowing open the iron gate blocking the main stairway, the lead assaulters, among them Bissonnette and O'Neill, followed an operator known as Red up the stairs. Red encountered and shot bin Laden's son just before the second-floor landing, and the SEALs following behind him fanned out into the hallways and rooms on the second floor to search and secure the area. It was then that both Bissonnette and O'Neill hung back on the stairway.[3] Standard procedure dictated that after Red killed bin Laden's son, each should have joined their teammates fanning through the second floor to secure each room. Instead, as Red began his ascent to the third floor, they followed him up, hoping to get in on the kill.

As Red approached the third-floor bedroom, he saw bin Laden standing in the doorway, peering out. He was unarmed and wearing pajamas. A few of his female relatives were nearby. Red came to a stop and fired two shots with his suppressed rifle. One shot hit bin Laden in the chest, and the second shot glanced off his hip or thigh. Bin Laden stumbled backward into his room and fell toward the foot of his bed.[4]

Red watched bin Laden fall. He later told his teammates that it was possible one arm was twitching reflexively as he died, but otherwise he was effectively dead and not a threat. The distinction was crucial. As the lead assaulter, it was Red's job to make the most important tactical judgments because he largely blocked the view of the SEALs behind him. According to several former members of SEAL Team 6, the most basic principle of assault training is "follow your shot," meaning that an operator who has fired on a target must ensure the target no longer poses a threat. Your teammates beside and behind you will cover all the other possible angles and areas of a room as you move forward.

Red could see bin Laden bleeding out from his chest wound, but he still had not entered the bedroom.[5] Then, as two of bin Laden's eldest daughters began to scream, Red quickly pushed them into a corner of the hallway, a move considered heroic by other SEALs on the mission. Had the daughters been wearing explosives, Red would have died while shielding his teammates from much of the blast. Instead, he corralled them in the corner long enough for his teammates, including O'Neill, to enter the bedroom.

Several more SEALs, including Bissonnette, entered the bedroom as bin Laden lay on the ground, bleeding out. O'Neill then fired two rounds.[6] According to his own description, the first two rounds hit bin Laden's face and forehead. Then O'Neill canoed bin Laden with a final shot.

Conflicting accounts have emerged about how many other SEALs fired rounds into bin Laden's lifeless body, though one former SEAL

Team 6 leader who viewed the body in Jalalabad told me the body appeared to be intact aside from the chest wound and obliterated face.

The SEALs had been specifically asked to avoid shooting bin Laden in the face.[7] O'Neill's decision to canoe the al Qaeda leader made bin Laden unrecognizable. A SEAL who spoke Arabic interviewed bin Laden's wives and daughters until he was able to get two positive identifications. O'Neill later claimed that he shot bin Laden because he wasn't sure Red's shots had hit the target. He also claimed that bin Laden had been standing when he fired and that a weapon was visible nearby. But the weapons found on the third floor were not discovered until the rooms were searched.[8] Neither was loaded.

O'Neill's canoeing of bin Laden cost his teammates precious time. The SEALs placed bin Laden's body into a rubber body bag, dragged him down the stairwell and out of the building, and loaded him onto one of the helicopters. Other SEALs ransacked the compound for documents and media for intelligence, left the survivors inside the compound, and returned to Jalalabad Air Base.

THE RED SQUADRON ASSAULTERS LATER GATHERED IN A PRIVATE area of Bagram Air Base and debriefed the mission in front of a military lawyer. The squadron's commanding officer recorded it on a cell phone. Bissonnette claimed he shot and killed al Kuwaiti and had fired bullets into bin Laden on the third floor. But according to three sources familiar with the debrief, Bissonnette never fired his weapon at al Kuwaiti. At least two of Bissonnette's teammates who were with him when al Kuwaiti was killed were angry about the deception—taking credit for a teammate's actions on a mission was unprecedented and dishonorable—but refused to contradict him in the presence of a military lawyer. Several of Bissonnette's teammates later informed their superiors that he had lied about his actions.

During the debrief, Red was identified as having hit bin Laden with a fatal shot, and O'Neill was credited with putting security rounds into him after bin Laden had already gone down. There was no discussion of a visible weapon, no claims that one of bin Laden's wives had been used as a shield or a threat. The raid, several of the SEALs said afterward, was one of the easiest missions they'd ever conducted. There were no heroics, and, apart from al Kuwaiti's shots, no firefight.

Once the lawyers left, another post-operation review transpired. Some of the assaulters on the mission were also annoyed that O'Neill defied instructions, which cost them precious minutes in the compound. The SEALs were also frustrated that Bissonnette and O'Neill both headed to the third floor, hoping to get a chance for the historic kill, instead of helping search and secure the second floor. Both were accused by some of their teammates of breaking with standard operating procedure to get themselves in position to be among the first to see or kill bin Laden.

When the C-17 carrying Red Squadron back from Afghanistan landed at Naval Air Station Oceana, Capt. Wyman Howard was waiting for them on the tarmac. Howard frequently celebrated when the command killed an al Qaeda target, but bin Laden's death was a historic moment, and the deputy commander wanted to party. As Bissonnette, O'Neill, and the others exited the aircraft, Howard rushed to them, hugging and cheering his men. Howard held a fervent belief that SEAL Team 6 was the best, most lethal military unit in the world and naturally felt that the Redmen were the best within the command. Howard congratulated everyone from the mission. In fact, many operators from Red Squadron and the command were waiting to greet the team upon landing. At one point, after some beer and cigars were passed around, someone asked the team who had gotten bin Laden. The SEALs on the mission turned and pointed at Red.[9]

SEVERAL MONTHS AFTER THE BIN LADEN RAID, IN OCTOBER 2011, SEAL Team 6 held its annual "stump muster," a reunion of current command members and their families, as well as past leaders and senior operators. That year's reunion, the first under Wyman Howard as commanding officer, was held at their new headquarters. It was a monument to the SEAL's ascendance during the War on Terror: a $100 million, state-of-the-art facility, a command center befitting a force known as the "President's Own," a clandestine global force capable of striking anywhere, killing anyone, reaching out as the tip of America's military spear. Outside the main entrance a thirty-foot steel trident had been placed, sculpted from a fragment of the World Trade Center.

At the reunion, a few hundred yards from the Atlantic Ocean, a small group of current and former master chiefs stood around drinking and telling war stories. Among them was one retired senior SEAL Team 6 leader who had led the unit during the early days of the wars in Afghanistan and Iraq. Over the years, he had worried about battlefield discipline and retaliation after Neil Roberts had been nearly beheaded, and he had feared his men would seek retribution in Iraq during the height of the violence there. He'd left the SEALs before the worst of the war crimes had taken place, though his former teammates would occasionally call him to report what was happening on deployments. He'd been told that Blue Squadron had collected ears and that mutilations had become common. He wasn't surprised. After more than thirty years in special operations, he knew that elite forces would inevitably cross ethical, moral, and legal boundaries if they were given too long a leash. But he also knew of the lasting impact these transgressions could have. When he'd first arrived at Dam Neck, operators in the unit who had served in Vietnam warned him that war crimes and battlefield atrocities hung like a cloud over the entire unit—even if only one SEAL had participated.

Sitting with old friends, the retired SEAL was handed a ring-bound portfolio. Opening it up, he saw a collection of photographs, graphic documentation of more than a dozen men: each had been canoed. The photographs were part of SEAL Team 6's "greatest hits" of terrorists killed since 9/11, he was told. The images did not belong to the private collection of some individual operator. These were the command's official after-action pictures.

The old sailor put the portfolio down. This wasn't his command anymore. His former command was now the most famous and recognizable military unit in the world—an unfortunate position for a clandestine organization composed of what are supposed to be "silent warriors." In the ten years since the global War on Terror was launched, SEAL Team 6 had arrived at a place where their skills and reputation had become legendary and undeniable while simultaneously undercutting their purpose. They were now a global brand and there would be no turning back. After a short while, he quietly left the base.

CHAPTER 13

"YOU CAN'T EAT HONOR"

Matt Bissonnette entered the offices of Dutton, a storied imprint of the Penguin book-publishing company, in Midtown Manhattan a week before Christmas. Bissonnette was a newly promoted senior chief petty officer, but he'd arrived for this meeting with his civilian life in mind. Dutton set up the meeting after the publisher offered Bissonnette's agent $1 million for Bissonnette's firsthand account of the bin Laden raid seven months earlier. Dutton's vice president and publisher, Ben Sevier, wanted to meet the SEAL in person, put eyes on him to be sure he wasn't being conned, Sevier would later recount. He couldn't Google Bissonnette and SEAL Team 6, and there was no hotline to call to confirm one's membership in this exclusive club. A month earlier, Bissonnette had contacted Elyse Cheney, a New York literary agent, after a former teammate from Team 5 suggested her. She agreed to meet with him and discuss a book about the raid.[1]

But Bissonnette was still an active-duty Team 6 team leader, and a few days after his call with Cheney, he traveled with the rest of his squadron to Tucson, Arizona. The squadron practiced high-altitude, high-opening skydiving, jumping from altitudes of twenty thousand feet or higher, in air so thin that the SEALs require masks pumping oxygen to breathe while they free-fall at more than two hundred miles per hour over the open Arizona dust lands north of Tucson. During the training, Bissonnette had clashed with his superiors and sported what they viewed as a bad attitude. Several days into the trip, Bissonnette asked to speak with his squadron commander and his master chief, collectively referred to as the Head Shed by the Team 6 enlisted operators. Bissonnette told them he did not intend to reenlist for another four-year commitment. "I had talked about it my last deployment while we were overseas. My guys all knew I was done with my team leader time," Bissonnette later said about his decision to quit the Navy. "I joined to be the guy on the ground, and that's what I've done my whole career. And I was having family issues at home. That was not going well. So, I had done 13 straight deployments and [it] just seemed like it was time to get out." He knew, he said, that "it was time to hang up the guns."

His time as team leader was over, which meant that, after thirteen deployments, he would no longer be an assaulter. If he remained in the Navy, he would have to rise into a senior noncommissioned role filled with paperwork and politics and fewer gunfights. He also wouldn't be able to write a book about the bin Laden raid. His marriage was in the process of dissolving, and his neck injury from the stealth helicopter crash in Abbottabad would require more surgery and rehab. In fourteen years, he'd skyrocketed to a rank of E-8, the second-highest enlisted in the Navy, and had done it at Team 6, no less. It was an impressive accomplishment, but perhaps after America's number one enemy has been killed, an elite operator loses his motivation. In 2012, a SEAL Team 6 senior chief petty officer with fourteen years of service earned less than $100,000 a year, even with all the extra pay for being in a Tier 1 unit.

It would not have been easy for an operator who helped kill the country's most wanted man to wait another six years for retirement and a chance to earn substantially more. Enlisted operators leaving military service found themselves entering an economy where their highly specialized skills were of little use. Many gravitated toward the security industry, working for private security companies like Triple Canopy, Constellis, and Academi, where they consulted for large corporations doing business in areas of the world where SEALs had experience or were working. Many signed on to work as contractors for the CIA, returning to the same war zones they'd deployed to in uniform. A select few channeled their competitive instincts into equally demanding academic and professional pursuits, becoming surgeons or even astronauts. Bissonnette had something that the others did not, though: a story—perhaps the greatest story of the early twenty-first century. Either way, after making his desire to leave clear, Bissonnette was sent back to Virginia Beach two days early and told he was no longer a Redman.

Free from constraints, Bissonnette plotted his next move. He flew to New York a few days later. He visited the 9/11 Memorial at the former World Trade Center site, hung out with actor Robert De Niro, and met his literary agent, Cheney.[2] In her office, Bissonnette told Cheney he was an operator on the bin Laden raid and was interested in writing a book. How much of an advance would a book like that fetch? She told him she thought half a million dollars was a reasonable estimate. Bissonnette's former teammate had first told Cheney that Bissonnette was on the raid, but besides his word, Bissonnette brought nothing to prove he was there or even a member of SEAL Team 6. Cheney didn't have much experience with an elite serviceman, so, she would later say, she looked for cues and body language to sense whether Bissonnette was who he said he was. After a short meeting, Cheney became confident that Bissonnette was who he claimed to be and that she had a bestseller in the making.

Cheney quickly called Sevier, to whom she'd sold several books over the years, and asked if he was interested in the first tell-all from inside the bin Laden raid by a SEAL on the mission. Sevier didn't mince words; he would buy it. He offered Cheney $800,000, but she rejected the offer. The next day Sevier came back with a second offer for $1,000,000, and Cheney accepted. But as excited as Sevier was to get the book, he wasn't giving seven figures to a man sight unseen. He told Cheney he wanted to meet Bissonnette to discuss what the book would be. And so, a week before

Christmas 2011, Senior Chief Petty Officer Matthew Bissonnette found himself sitting in Sevier's office.[3]

When Sevier took the meeting, portrayals of the raid were widely published—in the *New Yorker*, for example—but none of the accounts were firsthand or from the perspective of the men who killed bin Laden. The executive couldn't tap his network to find journalists or editors to confirm Bissonnette's identity because the members of SEAL Team 6 were a closely guarded national security secret. After he sat down across from Sevier, Bissonnette pulled out from his backpack a brown *pakol*. It was Osama bin Laden's hat, Bissonnette told Sevier. He'd grabbed it in the aftermath of the raid. Bin Laden frequently wore the hat in his video messages denouncing the United States for its foreign policy in the Muslim world. Bissonnette took it as a war trophy—a perk of the job, but also a crime.

Bissonnette told Sevier and Cheney two things. First, that he wanted to write under a pseudonym to protect his identity, and second, that he intended to donate all the proceeds to military charities. Although he was willing to give his firsthand account of the raid, he wouldn't describe or otherwise confirm any classified technology or tactics. The publisher agreed, and the two sides came to the previously accepted terms for a $1 million advance.

Shortly after the meeting, Cheney helped Bissonnette plot a future in Hollywood as well as publishing. Bissonnette sought deals for movies and television, video games and toys, all based on his career as a Navy SEAL. The book was his platform to create a content empire, a brand built on SEAL Team 6. If the transformation of the bin Laden raid from national security mission to media property seemed swift, it was because the process was well worn. Bissonnette was charting the same course that Richard Marcinko had laid out with *Rogue Warrior*.

TWO WEEKS LATER, AS BISSONNETTE AND DUTTON HAMMERED OUT a formal contract and put together their plan to publish the book by

September 11 of 2012, Chris Kyle's book, *American Sniper: The Autobiography of the Most Lethal Sniper in U.S. Military History,* was published.

The book, published in January 2012 by William Morrow, covered Kyle's ten years in the Teams and his four combat deployments. It was an instant bestseller and spent fourteen consecutive weeks on the *New York Times* bestseller list. The memoir contrasted Kyle's battlefield accounts with that of his wife, Taya, offering her perspective on raising their two children alone while her husband went off to war and returned with post-traumatic stress disorder. The back-and-forth point-of-view sections between Chris and Taya softened Kyle's account of the war in Iraq and his claims of record-setting kills.

But its central claim was that Kyle was the "most lethal" sniper in military history. For operators at Team 6, the claim was, at best, misleading and, at worst, a false marketing ploy. "The Pentagon has officially confirmed more than 150 of Kyle's kills," the publisher asserted, "but it has declined to verify the astonishing total number for this book." What was marketed as a coy signal to the reader was, in fact, a giveaway that Kyle's story was inaccurate and self-serving.

Ultimately, the book served as a testament to Kyle's killing prowess and another milestone in America's culture war, the portrayal of the war in Iraq as a direct response to the September 11, 2001, attacks and justified to defend American democracy. "Savage, despicable evil. That's what we were fighting in Iraq. That's why a lot of people, myself included, called the enemy 'savages.' There really was no other way to describe what we encountered there."[4] In some ways, Kyle's book was a continuation of the right-wing talking points about the post-9/11 wars that Marcus Luttrell had used in *Lone Survivor*, but with more religious overtones. In a section called "Evil," Kyle writes that he knew little about Islam beyond the history of the Crusades and the historical conflict between Muslims and Christians. "But I also knew that Christianity had evolved from the Middle Ages. We don't kill people because they're a different religion. The people we were fighting in Iraq, after Saddam's army fled or was defeated, were fanatics. They hated us because we weren't Muslim. They wanted to

kill us, even though we'd just booted out their dictator, because we practiced a different religion than they did. Isn't religion supposed to teach
tolerance?" Kyle wrote.[5] "I only wish I had killed more. Not for bragging
rights, but because I believe the world is a better place without savages out
there taking American lives. Everyone I shot in Iraq was trying to harm
Americans or Iraqis loyal to the new government."[6]

Kyle's message and tone were pitch-perfect for the culture wars. He
was a gunslinging hero, a Texas cowboy, writing a book, almost forced to
declare that he held the record for most kills in US military history. The
central claim was impossible to verify and, therefore, impossible to refute.
According to the book, Kyle was the recipient of two Silver Stars and five
Bronze Stars with "V" devices for valor, an impressive number of awards
for a SEAL who'd served ten years in the Teams. "I'm not a numbers guy.
SEALs are silent warriors, and I'm a SEAL down to my soul. If you want
the whole story, get a Trident. If you want to check me out, ask a SEAL."[7]

But most readers, let alone most Americans, do not know a SEAL,
nor do SEALs speak out publicly against their own. It is a violation of the
Brotherhood. ("Long Live the Brotherhood," or LLTB, is a community
saying, and many SEALs have it tattooed as a tribal tribute.)

The book raised questions about Kyle's—and his publisher's—
accounting. The sections about his four deployments to Iraq described at
least 76 different sniper kills, using the term "confirmed kill." According
to the book, a confirmed kill is one where a second uniformed service
member witnesses a death. The kill had to be both justified by the rules of
engagement and witnessed. Kyle wrote that kills where his target moved
out of sight after being hit didn't count. Early publicity for the book cited
255 sniper kills, a number his publisher supplied. This accounting rested
on a false premise: there is no such thing as a "confirmed kill" in the US
military. War frequently presents situations in which no other teammates
or American service members witness a shooting. Instead, many snipers
keep a private, unofficial tally of their dead; there is no ledger of kills, confirmed or otherwise. "Confirmed kills are a comic fallacy," James Hatch,
the Red Squadron SEAL, wrote in his book *Touching the Dragon*.[8] They
are self-reported, unofficial, and prone to error and exaggeration. "[T]o

this day," Hatch wrote, "I still haven't found the office in the Pentagon that's responsible for confirming kills."[9]

This was more than a marketing point, embraced and leveraged by one of the leading publishing houses in the country. It was a grim milestone for the war in Iraq, which the American public had widely rejected as worth fighting by the time the book was released in 2012. Kyle and his publishers sought to turn death into a selling point—and in particular, as the author clearly stipulated in the book, the death of Muslims. Nearly a decade into the war, at a moment when the United States had failed to secure anything resembling a victory in Iraq, Kyle's narrative offered something else: revenge.

Kyle acknowledged in the book that some in his chain of command questioned his exploits. On at least one occasion, his commanders pulled him from the battlefield while he was investigated. But the assessment of Task Unit Bruiser and Chris Kyle by the Gold Squadron sniper who went to Ramadi never made it past the classified perimeter of the Dam Neck base. Kyle references James Foreman's observation mission in the book, though not by name, in a section about Team 6. "They had heard we were out there slaying a huge number of savages, and so they sent one of their snipers over to see what we were doing. I guess they wanted to find out what we were doing that worked."[10] It's unclear whether Foreman's warning to his chain of command about Jocko Willink and Chris Kyle in Ramadi ever made it back to them, but *American Sniper* suggests that Kyle didn't see any problem with what he was doing. Kyle wrote that some of his men joked that he kept the silhouette of a gun on the end of his sniper scope so that anyone he saw through the lens appeared armed. But he claimed that he was always justified when shooting, because "the truth was, my targets were always obvious, and I, of course, had plenty of witnesses every time I shot."[11]

Three months before the publication of *American Sniper*, the Naval Special Warfare Command received a copy of the manuscript. It was sent as part of a prepublication review process required by the Department of Defense for any book written by a service member. The policy is meant to ensure that no classified or otherwise sensitive information is disclosed.

After reviewing the book, the command asked now-retired Jocko Willink to read the draft as well. Willink didn't find anything in the manuscript that was classified. Instead, Willink found material that, he warned Kyle, "was going to make the Teams and you look bad."[12]

In an email dated October 18, 2011, Willink wrote to Kyle after reviewing the manuscript: "[W]hat concerned me the most was the amount of questionably inaccurate information that the author put in there. I am not sure why he did this. Your real story is truly amazing. Your actual documented sniper achievements are unmatched. Maybe when you were telling him stories he got confused or decided to exaggerate things. Again, I have no idea why he did this because the facts of what you did in the Teams are incredible enough—there is no reason to stretch the 'truth'.... The nay-sayers are going to try to find errors, exaggerations, and misrepresentations and they are going to expose them. If they do that, and prove one thing wrong, the whole book will come into question. In fact, everything you have done will come into question."

After listing several anecdotes and depictions that appeared exaggerated, including sixty-five confirmed kills on Kyle's first deployment in 2003, Willink continued, "I am sure that these are based on some reality, but they are too far from the truth now to know what is real and what isn't....exaggerating heroic events, numbers of confirmed kills, awards, and other things of that nature is totally different and totally dishonorable. They will be researched and disproven....Again, remember, people are going to attack this book because they are jealous of you/or the SEAL Teams, and they might be anti-war, anti-christian [sic], and anti-American. So the more things you give them to tear apart, the more they will attack you."

And at least one significant claim was outright wrong, Willink informed Kyle. "[Naval Special Warfare Command] was asked to confirm your awards; the book says you have 2 silver stars, 5 bronze stars with V, and some others. Navy records show that you actually have 1 silver star and 3 bronze stars. This is a huge difference and this will be terrible if the book gets published this way. Trust me, people will dig into the records and it will not look good at all."

Kyle appeared to get the message. He wrote back to Willink, telling him that he had already heard from another of his former officers, Leif Babin. "After talking with Leif I started reading a little more, and I do know what you are talking about." Kyle explained that his ghostwriter, Jim DeFelice, was the fiction author who wrote the Rogue Warrior series of novels with Richard Marcinko, based on the success of his autobiography, "so there is some over dramatization." Kyle added, "There are also some flat out lies. We spent several weeks together discussing my deployments, and him jotting down notes. The book has not turned out the way I intended. I was hoping that DOD would do more as far as getting rid of BS, but they just took out the name DevGru." He told Willink he would "fix the book," but that the inaccurate award count was a reflection of what he had on his service record form, called a DD-214, and that the numbers in the book "came from me. I am not trying to exaggerate that, but put in what the DD 214 says." Kyle insisted, "The teams were a huge part of my life, and I don't want to do anything to bring shame or disgrace on the community…I will fix the errors in the book."

Kyle did make changes based on Willink's and Babin's comments. Several of the anecdotes Willink listed did not appear in the published manuscript, though Kyle kept the inaccurate award count. Even so, there were troubling and questionable scenes from his Iraq deployments. In one that Willink had flagged, Kyle described a mission on a stretch of a street in Baghdad that had been nicknamed "Purple Heart Boulevard" for all the US servicemen injured by insurgent attacks. From a high-rise, Kyle watched an Iraqi teenager waiting at a bus stop several stories below his position. When a bus arrived, several teenage and young adult men exited the vehicle. Kyle noticed the teenager turn and walk in the opposite direction. "The group caught up quickly," according to Kyle's account. "One of them pulled out a pistol and put his arm around the kid's neck. As soon as he did that, I started shooting. The kid I was protecting took off. I got two or three of his would-be kidnappers; the others got away." As described in the book, the incident was a questionable killing. Kyle was in a building down the street, in a sniper's nest, completely hidden. By his own account, Kyle was neither targeted nor even seen. There was no threat or hostile intent toward Kyle or an American. Kyle then makes the point, briefly, that the Iraqi insurgency kidnapped family members of Iraqi politicians as a tactic to terrorize the population and discourage the new US-installed democratic process in Iraq. Among Willink's list of dishonest anecdotes was "the shooting of kidnappers that just happened to be kidnapping the election official's kid." In the final version, Kyle appears to have altered the anecdote by separating the election official detail from the kidnapping, raising questions about the truthfulness of the alleged incident and whether it occurred at all.

Toward the end of the book, Kyle has a final thought on his four deployments in Iraq. "Everyone I shot was evil," he writes. "I had good cause on every shot. They all deserved to die."

American Sniper sold more than two million copies.

A year after *American Sniper* was released, Kyle took a young Marine veteran struggling with PTSD to a shooting range. The young veteran opened fire on Kyle and another man, killing them both. Seven thousand people attended Kyle's funeral, held in Cowboys Stadium in Arlington, Texas. The next day, hundreds of Texans lined the highway as Kyle's funeral procession traveled two hundred miles from his home in Midlothian to the Texas State Cemetery in Austin.

A MONTH AFTER *AMERICAN SNIPER* WAS PUBLISHED AND SHORTLY after Bissonnette signed the contract for his book on the bin Laden raid, an eighty-five-year-old retired veteran stood up from a row of chairs in a Washington, DC, Marriott ballroom to address Adm. McRaven. In the nine months since the mission in Abbottabad, McRaven had earned a fourth star and a promotion. He was now commander of the Special Operations Command. McRaven was the keynote speaker for an annual special operations conference, and after his remarks, the audience asked questions. The retired veteran who rose was no former grunt. He was retired Army Lt. Gen. James Vaught and had served in both the Korean and Vietnam Wars. More importantly, he'd been the overall commanding general for the failed rescue attempt at Desert One in 1980. "You've been splashing all of [your SEAL Team 6 operations] all over the media, and I flat don't understand that," the retired general said. "[If] you keep publishing how you do this, the other guy's going to be there ready for you, and you're going to fly in and he's going to shoot down every damn helicopter and kill every one of your SEALs," Vaught warned Adm. McRaven. "Mark my words, get the hell out of the media."[13] McRaven, the former journalism major at UT, was polite but pushed back. "It is not something we actively pursue, as I think a number of the journalists here in the audience will confirm. But the fact of the matter is with the social media being what it is today, with the press and the twenty-four-hour news cycle, it's very difficult to get away from it."

Two weeks later, a Hollywood film starring active-duty Navy SEALs was released in more than three thousand theaters nationwide, nearly one theater for each Navy SEAL in the service. The movie, *Act of Valor*, was a fictionalized account of actual events and missions and used footage from real SEAL training exercises. The footage was originally part of a Pentagon-required push to increase recruitment. The video was initially intended for ads—official Navy propaganda—but the production company doing the filming thought it should be a feature film. After the Naval Special Warfare Command signed off on the idea to make it a Hollywood film, they also allowed a platoon from SEAL Team 7, who'd done the training exercises, to star in the movie. During filming, the Team 7 platoon left their deployment in Iraq to finish scenes for the film. *Act of Valor* was the biggest-grossing film in the country the weekend it was released and ultimately earned roughly $100 million in gross receipts. The film generated media buzz and hype and consternation among the special operations community, which caused only more media coverage. Peter Travers, a *Rolling Stone* magazine film critic, wrote, "I don't know what to make of *Act of Valor*. It's like reviewing a recruiting poster."

McRaven defended the film at the same conference without acknowledging the contradiction with his earlier response to Lt. Gen. Vaught. "We think it accurately represents a number of the acts of valor that have occurred over the last 10 years with respect to the SEAL teams. We're conscious of the fact that there are active-duty Navy SEALs here. I can

tell you they all volunteered," McRaven said. "The film company that produced this had a very collaborative effort with the Navy and with U.S.
Special Operations Command."[14]

There was an unambiguous message in this. Adm. McRaven and
the senior officers of Naval Special Warfare made clear to the rest of the
SEAL community that as long as you make the SEALs look good, you
can sell the brand. The Navy happily offered a full-throated defense of
using active-duty SEALs for a Hollywood movie, but confronted with errors and misrepresentations in Marcus Luttrell's *Lone Survivor* and Chris
Kyle's *American Sniper*, there was only silence. For the SEALs, the hy-
pocrisy of senior officers was unmistakable—and potentially dangerous.
Then retired admiral Joseph Maguire, who allowed Luttrell time off while
on active duty to write his book, told *Newsweek* that year: "Hollywood,
money, and politics were never part of the success of SOF [Special Operations Forces], but they very well could be part of its demise."[15]

The SEAL brand, including that of Team 6, had arrived. "I've been
doing these kinds of books for 15 years," an executive editor at St. Martin's Press, which published a book by a SEAL Team 6 sniper shortly after
the bin Laden raid, told the *New York Times*. "They've crossed over into
the mainstream, and you have a general reader taking interest. You're not
going to sell 400,000 copies of SEAL Team Six only to a military read-
ership."[16] A second publishing executive told the *Times* that there was a
"whole generation of readers who are growing up with the military. And
particularly the SEALs are larger-than-life heroes."[17]

What Bissonnette and Kyle understood was that writing books about
their elite military accomplishments was a lucrative business model. They
didn't invent the SEAL-to-bestselling-celebrity career model. Marcinko
had done that twenty years earlier. Being a SEAL author, though, isn't
enough to ensure a bestseller. In a country where so few serve in the military, there is more appeal in reading about elite soldiers than actually
being one, a way to experience the military superhero fantasy. Few military
memoir bestsellers tell the first-person accounts of the grunts who make
up the statistical majority of uniformed personnel, however. And because

the books are exaggerated, misleading, or outright false, the reader doesn't ever get to see what the authors' teammates, colleagues, and superiors see: all their moral and ethical flaws.

ON APRIL 20, 2012, BISSONNETTE OFFICIALLY SEPARATED FROM the Navy after almost fourteen years of decorated service. He had earned a Silver Star and five Bronze Stars, all with valor, for what was by any measure a laudable career in the military. He would later complain to his former teammates that all he got for his service was a neck injury from the Abbottabad helicopter crash and a plaque with his name misspelled. Still, Bissonnette's plan for a post-military career in entertainment was well on its way by the time he separated from the Navy.

His book was scheduled to be published on September 11, and his vision of a content empire came into view. That summer, Bissonnette met Steven Spielberg, who signed on to make a television show based on his career in the Navy for HBO. He'd sold the film rights to the upcoming book for an additional $600,000. In fact, he was so prepared for the financial windfall that he decided he would establish two pseudonyms, one for publishing and one for television and movie projects. He also consulted with Electronic Arts, maker of the video game *Medal of Honor*, helping film a series of promotional videos of SEAL Team 6 tactics with several of his teammates who were all still on active duty.

Bissonnette, acting on the advice of a lawyer, did not submit his book for review, despite explicit rules that all veterans do. But in August, a copy of the book made its way to the Special Operations Command and the Joint Special Operations Command, sounding alarms across the bureaucracy.

On August 30, Jeh Johnson, then the Pentagon's general counsel, sent a letter to Bissonnette, care of Penguin Putnam, of which Dutton was an imprint, notifying him that he'd violated both a secrecy agreement and the requirement to submit the manuscript for prepublication review. In failing to submit, Johnson warned, Bissonnette was in "material breach and violation of the non-disclosure agreements you signed" and that any money resulting from the book's publication would go to the US government as a result. The warning did little to quell the momentum surrounding the book's release. The Pentagon led a media storm of coverage about Bissonnette's book. Dutton moved the publication up a week to catch the buzz. *No Easy Day: The Firsthand Account of the Mission That Killed Osama bin Laden*, by Bissonnette under the Mark Owen pseudonym, was published September 4 and almost immediately became the bestselling book in the United States.

The media buzz around the book included a *60 Minutes* segment featuring Bissonnette in disguise. The show devoted most of its broadcast to Bissonnette, his book, and the raid. "This operation was one of the most significant operations in US history," Bissonnette said. "And it's something I believe deserves to be told right and deserves to go in a book and stand for itself."[18] The *60 Minutes* correspondent, Scott Pelley, presented Bissonnette as a humble hero and the first person who had direct knowledge of bin Laden's last moments to speak. *60 Minutes* still had an average audience of 8.18 million viewers, and Bissonnette's episode had more than 12 million. The commodification of the bin Laden raid was now part of the SEAL Team 6 brand.

Bissonnette's account in *No Easy Day* largely hewed to what the Obama administration had already disclosed publicly: that a team of CIA analysts had tracked al Kuwaiti to the Abbottabad compound, and that based on nothing more than an educated deduction, the CIA believed bin Laden lived with several of his wives on the third floor. *No Easy Day* was the first eyewitness account of the operation, and it contradicted the Obama administration and media accounts of one significant detail: Bissonnette described bin Laden as unarmed and posing no threat. In the book, Bissonnette also implies that he was directly behind Red on the third floor when bin Laden was shot and was one of the two SEALs who followed into bin Laden's bedroom. His account credits Red with the shot that felled bin Laden, but he claims that he and a third SEAL fired several rounds into bin Laden as he was lying on the floor. Bissonnette repeated the false claim that he'd shot and killed al Kuwaiti in his exterior apartment on the compound but otherwise described the events of the raid accurately.

In Virginia Beach, the command opened multiple investigations, first into the book and then into Bissonnette. According to a retired SEAL leader who oversaw the review, the book had not disclosed any serious classification concerns, but the investigation into who at the command may have known that he was writing a book led to an investigation of Bissonnette's business contracts while he'd been assigned to Dam Neck.

Operators whose personal hobbies or interests overlap with their professional responsibilities fill the Team 6 universe. Some spend their free time as skydiving aficionados, others scuba dive, race motocross bikes, or compete in martial arts, and nearly all are gun collectors. A smaller group focuses on tactical gear and military equipment. During his time at SEAL Team 6, Bissonnette served as Red Squadron's tactical gear and equipment evaluator, which meant working with the outside contractors who sold gear to Team 6 for specific missions or tasks.

Bissonnette was a self-professed gear junkie, obsessed with the intricacies and minutiae of everything from guns to shoes. His interest in the tech and gear was not particularly noteworthy—the command was filled with SEALs just like him—but his involvement in the manufacturing and design of some of the equipment made him unique. Years earlier, Wyman Howard encouraged Bissonnette to pursue outside business opportunities to "take care of your family."[19] Howard's only proviso was that Bissonnette clear his plans with the command's lawyers. Bissonnette, still on active duty, then created Chief Consulting LLC as an entity that could handle any contracts or consulting outside his work for the Navy. Operating as Chief Consulting, Bissonnette helped one company improve a helmet strobe light and received a patent for the modification. Later, with four other teammates, Bissonnette helped establish Element Consulting Group, known as Element Group. On paper, Element worked like his personal corporation, Chief Consulting. The active-duty SEALs would use their expertise to advise and consult with tactical gear companies on products the companies were developing. In theory, as long as the products they consulted on were unrelated to the US Navy or the command,

and the work was undertaken when the SEALs were off duty, the arrangement was legal.

EACH JANUARY, THOUSANDS OF GUN ENTHUSIASTS FLOCK TO LAS Vegas for the most American of professional functions: an industry conference. The annual Shooting, Hunting, Outdoor Trade Show, known as the SHOT Show, serves as America's largest consumer weapons exhibition. Put on by the Firearm Industry Trade Association, the SHOT Show is among the largest twenty trade conventions in the United States.[20] The vendors are gun and ammunition makers and related gear and equipment manufacturers. The event is held annually at the Sands Expo Center, with nearly seven hundred thousand square feet of vendors selling weapons, ammunition, and tactical gear like knives, night-vision goggles, and nylon balaclavas. The SHOT Show, which is heavily attended by men in the gun industry, law enforcement, and military, happens each year at the same time as an annual adult video award show and expo. The gun show attracts more than twenty thousand attendees each year, and over two thousand vendors put on displays for their products.

For years, the SHOT Show attracted a small group of Tier 1 operators seeking the latest military weapons technology and tactical equipment. In some regards, the expo is an annual prom for Team 6 and Delta operators. They spend their time networking with gun industry executives for their civilian careers while testing the latest bullet or an upgrade to a favored assault weapon. "[W]e would go every year to meet with vendors and see what kind of new guns and equipment were on the market," Bissonnette wrote about the SHOT Show in *No Easy Day*. Bissonnette also inadvertently revealed the friendly relationship between Team 6 operators who attended and industry leaders, who, like much of the military's rank and file, idolized anyone or anything associated with the two Tier 1 military units. Bissonnette wrote that he introduced a teammate to vendors he knew at the show, and the teammate quickly became popular. "At a bar after the show the third night," Bissonnette wrote, "I found Walt [a Team 6 teammate] holding court with executives from the National Rifle

Association. He had a cigar in his mouth, and he was slapping backs and shaking hands like he was running for office. They all loved him."

During the Team 6 preliminary investigation into Bissonnette and Element Group, the command discovered that some of Bissonnette's teammates flew to the SHOT Show on a private jet belonging to Luke Hillier, CEO of Atlantic Diving Supply (ADS), a violation of military rules. The investigators discovered pictures of the operators inside the private jet on their social media accounts. The operators are each the Prom King during the event. Their choices in clothing, weapons, and anything they endorse by taking them on the battlefield ultimately become popular, first with lower-tier special operations units, then with the regular military and law enforcement communities, and finally with the larger gun enthusiast subculture.

But when, after the publication of *No Easy Day*, the command opened an investigation into Bissonnette, Element Group, and Chief Consulting, they quickly identified potential areas of legal and ethical concern. Bissonnette, as Red Squadron's evaluator, or "supply representative" in the command's nomenclature, had direct contact with military contractors who presented their products to the command, and he could thereby influence which products were eventually purchased. Through Chief and Element, Bissonnette was paid to help design or consult on military and nonmilitary gear, including flashlights, "event tactical nylon," and strobe lights. Four primary tactical gear manufacturers paid Bissonnette, including a company called London Bridge Trading. One of the critical issues raised in the preliminary investigation was whether Bissonnette had improperly influenced command purchases of gear or equipment made by the companies from which he received outside payment. "[E]vidence also supports," the report stated, that Bissonnette and a second SEAL were "always trying to push London Bridge Trading equipment," which was a "big supplier" of Team 6 equipment.

The preliminary investigation found that a retired senior command member had reported that Bissonnette had possible ethical conflicts with civilian companies that sold equipment to Team 6. The former command master chief, Steve Rose, had contacted Team 6 leaders and alleged that

Bissonnette received kickbacks for equipment being sold to the command.[21] When the command followed up with Bissonnette about the allegation, Bissonnette told the Team 6 command master chief David Cooper that he had sought and received an okay from the Team 6 judge advocate general for his arrangement with Element and the manufacturers, just as Wyman Howard had advised Bissonnette to do a few years earlier. The preliminary investigation faulted the command for never following up on what Bissonnette told the command's attorney and for not making him do any of it on paper, as required. "Unfortunately, due diligence by leadership to follow up and ensure employment was properly requested and vetted did not happen," the preliminary inquiry determined. Ultimately, the command's internal inquiry into Bissonnette's business dealings, which were never shared with the inspector general or, later, the Naval Criminal Investigative Service, found that Bissonnette misled the command's lawyers about the details of his activities. A Team 6 leader told me that the command quickly concluded that given the military lawyer's sign-off on Bissonnette's request, any criminal or judicial remedy against Bissonnette would require that they first prosecute the command's judge advocate general for failing to do due diligence. In either case, Team 6, then commanded by Capt. Howard, would have to acknowledge that senior leaders had failed. They would have to hold themselves accountable for Bissonnette's profiteering.

It wasn't worth the trouble. According to a former command leader at the time, with Bissonnette discharged and few concerns about the presence of classified information in the book, it was easier just to end the investigation and counsel active-duty operators on their ethical obligations.

In *No Easy Day*, Bissonnette dedicates an entire section to the detailed description of the gear and equipment he wore during the raid, including at least one of the companies he consulted for. The chapter reads like a print product placement. One company mentioned was Daniel Winkler, the bladesmith who made the Red Squadron tomahawks. One military equipment manufacturer, who requested anonymity because he feared he would lose contracts with the SEAL command if he spoke publicly, said he met with Bissonnette while the latter was on active duty and claimed that Bissonnette insisted on a $50,000 cash bribe to get the manufacturer's product into the command. In all, Bissonnette earned $247,039.33 through his Chief Consulting work while serving as an active-duty Navy SEAL.[22]

Bissonnette's profiteering served as a reminder that, in some ways, SEAL Team 6 was still very much what Richard Marcinko had created thirty years earlier. Capt. Wyman Howard and other Red Squadron officers had encouraged and empowered Bissonnette during his time as an assaulter at the command because he was a talented operator. The enlisted mafia at the command was what Marcinko had screened for in 1980. But operational brilliance did not come with ethical training. Howard lectured junior officers and senior enlisted SEALs that Bissonnette was the prototype of the world's most lethal and effective operator in the world.[23]

Bissonnette and *No Easy Day* had borrowed plenty from Marcinko and *Rogue Warrior*. In the days after the bin Laden raid, ABC News aired a television piece by Chris Cuomo about how to "spot a Navy SEAL." In it, Cuomo asked Marcinko about the SEAL Team 6 operators on the raid. Marcinko, who remained a pariah at the command after his felony conviction, did not know any of them. Nonetheless, he could still imagine, accurately, their psychological makeup. "They are individual egomaniacs that make music together," Marcinko told ABC News. "They learn to depend on each other. When they are bored they play with each other to keep pushing. Otherwise, they get in trouble."

After the segment with Marcinko aired, Bissonnette and his teammates laughed their "asses off," he wrote in the book. "I know he was the founder of DEVGRU, but he was hopelessly out of touch with the modern force. I didn't know a single SEAL who fit his profile. We'd evolved past being egomaniacs....It wasn't part of our ethos. We were team players who always tried to do the right thing."

Bissonnette appeared to be in denial. A former teammate summed up Bissonnette's decision to cash in on his career: "You can't eat honor."

CHAPTER 14

THE POLITICS OF BRAVERY

S EALs like Bissonnette and Kyle were certainly skilled self-promoters, but they also believed they were getting in on a game that their command and their president were already profiting from. Vice President Joe Biden stood onstage at the Democratic National Convention on September 6, 2012, his arms bracing the lectern. He had accepted his party's renomination for vice president and was now filling the role he'd become so good at: he was the hype man for Barack Obama, making the case why Obama deserved reelection. "Ladies and gentlemen, I'm here to tell you what I think you already know," Biden told the party delegates seated in Charlotte's Time Warner Cable Arena. "Bravery resides in the heart of Barack Obama, and time and time again, I witnessed him summon it," Biden declared, gesturing with his index finger to emphasize his point. "This man has courage in his soul, compassion in his heart, and a spine of steel. And because of all the actions he took, because of the calls he made, because of the determination of American workers and the unparalleled bravery of our special forces, we can now proudly say what you've heard me say the last six months." The delegates clapped louder with each beat as they followed the speech's crescendo. Biden lowered his voice an octave, looked straight ahead, and declared, "Osama bin Laden is dead, and General Motors is alive."[1]

As political poetry, the slogan was much more Biden than Obama: short and straightforward, workmanlike prose rather than lyrical verse. It had none of the lofty, inspirational tones of the 2008 campaign's "Yes We Can," but it was succinct. Like all good political messages, it delivered a clear image summing up what the Obama campaign viewed as its argument for reelection. The Obama campaign had been using the bin Laden raid as a defining moment since the previous September on the tenth anniversary of the 9/11 attacks. Then, too, Biden was the messenger. *New York Times* columnist Maureen Dowd quoted Biden previewing how the bin Laden raid would feature in the Obama reelection campaign. "He knew what was at stake," Biden said. "Not just the lives of those brave warriors, but literally the presidency. And he pulled the trigger."[2]

Biden's job as a messenger also served a purpose: it allowed someone else to boast on Obama's behalf about killing an adversary. Much of Obama's successful 2012 campaign for reelection included surrogates calling Obama what no Democratic presidential candidate in more than a generation had been able to boast against a Republican nominee: Obama was a hawk, a Democratic candidate who was strong on national defense.

Seven months before the election, Bill Clinton did an entire television ad about Obama's decision to send the SEALs into Pakistan to kill bin Laden. Highlighting what he described as the risks, including bin Laden not being there and the SEALs being killed or captured during the raid, Clinton said that Obama "took the harder and the more honorable path" in authorizing the operation. The video then asked what Mitt Romney, the 2012 Republican candidate, would have done. It showed a quote from five years earlier in which Romney questioned the utility of spending billions of US taxpayer dollars on finding and killing one man.

But the selling of Obama's heroism had a secondary effect. The 2012 campaign brought Navy SEALs into the political spotlight. There was nothing unique about former military personnel and service members using their veteran status to make a political point for or against a candidate. A group of veterans had attacked Senator John Kerry's Vietnam record during his 2004 run against George W. Bush, in what then became known as "swift boating." But for the first time, Navy SEALs had the cultural authority to enter the fray.

While Obama won reelection, in part, because of the SEALs' success in Abbottabad, former Navy SEALs used their new public popularity to bash Obama during and after his campaign. One political group, Veterans for a Strong America (VSA), ran an ad attacking Obama for "excessive" celebrating about killing bin Laden. The video claimed, "Heroes don't seek credit…heroes don't spike the football." The video went viral on social media. The chairman of VSA told *Mother Jones* magazine at that time that the ad was "the swift boating of the president in the sense of using what's perceived to be his greatest strength and making it his greatest weakness." Then, before Election Day, the group aired an ad featuring retired or former Navy SEALs, their Tridents on their suit lapels, including Cdr. Ryan Zinke. The four SEALs sat on a stage with an American flag imposed as a background while answering questions about how the SEAL community viewed Obama. Each of the four offered "guesstimates" that 95 to 99.9 percent of their SEAL teammates would not be voting for Obama. "America needs to take back our country," Zinke said. "And America is us," referring to veterans and active-duty service members. As the video ended, the text read, "America's Bravest Are Not Voting For Obama."

Zinke himself, near the time the VSA ad ran, started a SEAL political action committee, Special Operations for America, before running for Congress as a Republican. In an interview with journalist Hunter Walker, Zinke explicitly called out the Obama campaign's bin Laden ad. "I think when the commercial came out with President Clinton and President Obama, and they talked about the political ramifications of failure, they didn't talk about the families that would be left without a father. They talked about political consequences—that was a bridge too far."

The status and myth of the Navy SEALs, and especially Team 6, continued to grow. They'd successfully entered the political fray during the 2012 presidential campaign, the next rung on the celebrity ladder. If war had become something like a video game or Hollywood action for most Americans, SEALs were the stars, the larger-than-life protagonists. First, they dominate a battlefield, then media, and from there the political land-scape, all built on the Trident.

IN THE DAYS AND WEEKS AFTER THE BIN LADEN RAID, CHIEF PETTY Officer Rob O'Neill caught the attention of senior leaders at the command. And it wasn't for good reasons. O'Neill's drunken antics off-base became difficult to ignore. While Obama administration officials leaked out various and sometimes contradictory details about the raid, O'Neill took his victory lap through Virginia Beach leaking his own version. The Red Squadron operator had publicly declared while drunk in several bars that he was the man who shot bin Laden, Team 6 leaders were told. It wasn't the first time, according to several of his former teammates, that O'Neill had professional problems related to his alcohol consumption. O'Neill had a reputation for being late or absent on training trips, where he was in charge, due to excessive drinking. The reaction inside the command for bragging about the bin Laden raid was swift. O'Neill was re-lieved of his team leader position and removed from Red Squadron. He ultimately transferred to Silver Squadron, completed a final deployment to Afghanistan in winter 2011–2012, and separated from the Navy in August 2012, just as the controversy over *No Easy Day* broke in the press.

Immediately after he became a civilian, O'Neill followed Bissonnette's lead. There was money to be made from his first-person account, whether it was about the raid or how to lead men into battle. He began giving paid speeches not long after his departure. Fortune 500 companies, leading financial institutions, and trade groups hired O'Neill to tell his story in person. In the presentations, O'Neill demonstrated an easygoing, affable charm as he told the story of the *Maersk Alabama* raid and played video of himself and his teammates jumping out of a C-17 into the Indian Ocean.

A rivalry had formed between the former teammates. O'Neill viewed Bissonnette's book as a betrayal of the deal the two had discussed in the days before the raid, according to several Team 6 members at the time.

Additionally, Bissonnette's claim that he was behind Red up the stairs, and thus second through bin Laden's bedroom door, left O'Neill in a bind. The marketplace had specific demands: if O'Neill was going to make money off his participation in the bin Laden raid, he could not just be an eyewitness to history, someone who fired a few rounds into a dead man's body. To top Bissonnette, O'Neill would have to be the man who killed bin Laden.

O'Neill had learned the lessons of Bissonnette's failure. He did not immediately reveal that he participated in the bin Laden raid. Instead, in February 2013, a month after the release of a feature film about the raid, *Zero Dark Thirty*, *Esquire* magazine published an approximately fifteen-thousand-word profile of an unnamed man they referred to only as "The Shooter."[3] The article claimed that "enough people connected to the SEALs and the bin Laden mission have confirmed" that this man—O'Neill—was the first through bin Laden's bedroom door, and that there, he confronted bin Laden not only alive and without gunshot wounds, but standing, "pushing his youngest wife, Amal, in front of him....The Shooter's is the most definitive account of those crucial few seconds, and his account, corroborated by multiple sources, establishes him as the last man to see Osama bin Laden alive."

Sections of the report are written in O'Neill's voice, presenting a supposed firsthand account of how he moved through bin Laden's compound. (Although he wasn't named in the article, SEALs who knew him confirmed to reporters that it was O'Neill.) In his telling, he, not Bissonnette, was behind Red, and the two of them were alone on the top floor as their teammates continued sweeping through the second floor where bin Laden's son was killed. In O'Neill's account, he did not see Red fire his shots at bin Laden because he looked back down the stairs for reinforcements. When he finally entered the bedroom, alone, bin Laden was standing uninjured, a weapon nearby, his wife in front of him like a human shield. "There was bin Laden standing there," O'Neill told *Esquire*. "He had his hands on a woman's shoulders, pushing her ahead, not exactly towards me but by me....He looked confused....He had a cap on and didn't appear to be hit. I can't tell you 100 percent, but he was standing and moving. He was holding her in front of him. Maybe as a shield, I don't know."

O'Neill then explains his thought process, how he identified a threat, which gave him the authority to kill bin Laden, and how his face was about ten inches from bin Laden's face as the Saudi terrorist stood behind his wife. "He's got a gun on a shelf right there, the short AK he's famous for. And he's moving forward. I don't know if she's got a vest and she's being pushed to martyr them both. He's got a gun within reach. He's a threat. I need to get a headshot so he won't have a chance to clack himself off. In that second, I shot him two times in the forehead. Bap! Bap! The second time as he's going down. He crumpled onto the floor in front of his bed, and I hit him again, Bap! same place....He was dead."

This account did not sit well with some veterans of the mission. Word spread quickly that O'Neill was the SEAL in the article, since his personality, even when anonymous, was obvious to his teammates. Some were outraged that he had been so brazenly inaccurate and self-serving in his account. For many on the raid, including those who had been present in bin Laden's bedroom with O'Neill, it was the first time they'd heard anyone say the terrorist leader was standing or posing a threat of any kind after Red's shot. O'Neill offered a false scenario where bin Laden threatened the SEALs. O'Neill's teammates had in fact located bin Laden's famous short-barreled AK after he was killed, on a shelf that was not visible from the bedroom; there were no bullets in it. The team had been given the mission to kill bin Laden—regardless of how they found him. As it turned out, he was killed leaning his body out of his bedroom door. The last thing he would've seen was the darkened hall or his bedroom ceiling, if not a glimpse of a muzzle flash.

O'Neill also used the story to generate pity and point a finger at the military. He described himself as a newly retired SEAL who'd been given nothing for his sixteen years of military service, beyond his awards and memories. "He's taken monumental risks," O'Neill's father told *Esquire*. "But he's unable to reap any reward." The portrayal omitted the fact that it was O'Neill's choice to separate from the Navy four years before he'd earn a lifetime government pension, choosing instead to capitalize on the bin Laden raid. As a public relations campaign to portray himself as a downtrodden hero, the *Esquire* article was brilliant theater. (*Esquire* was forced to issue a correction later acknowledging that O'Neill was eligible for health-care benefits for the first five years after his discharge.)

O'Neill eventually published his own book, *The Operator: Firing the Shots That Killed Osama bin Laden and My Years as a SEAL Team Warrior*, repeating his false account from the *Esquire* profile, in 2017. In the book, he also describes the Operation Red Wings disaster in 2005, during which he was sent to search for Marcus Luttrell and the rest of the missing SEALs. O'Neill repeats Luttrell's distorted and inflated accounts of parts of the ambush and battle, despite knowing otherwise. O'Neill had scoured the Korengal Valley looking for Luttrell, but the main lesson he seems to have learned from Luttrell and his *Lone Survivor* template was how to use a false and misleading portrayal of events for financial gain.

In November 2014, O'Neill unveiled himself as the man who killed bin Laden in an hour-long Fox News special; he later became a paid Fox News contributor. A day earlier, Bissonnette published a second book, *No Hero: The Evolution of a Navy SEAL*. The former teammates both hit the press circuit, each telling reporters off the record that the other was a liar.

A retired Team 6 operator tried to put his former teammates' dishonesty in perspective. "Think about the fucking ego it takes to lie like that and to prop the rest of your life up with those lies," he said. "Think about Biss lying in the fucking debrief with the guy who actually shot [bin Laden's courier] sitting right there. The temerity is beyond comprehension."

As ethically compromised as Team 6's code had become, Bissonnette and O'Neill still managed to violate it. To cause shock and disgust within their peer group was as notable a feat as killing the world's most wanted terrorist.

"The beauty of what they have constructed," the retired Team 6 operator continued, about how Bissonnette and O'Neill cornered the market on the bin Laden raid, "is that there is only one guy, essentially, who can come forward and say they're lying—and he won't ever talk." The Team 6 operator asserted that the real shooter had too much professional integrity to publicly take credit for his actions.

THE BUSINESS CYCLE OF AMERICAN CULTURE IS EXTRAORDINARILY predictable. Most bestselling books become films, but that is especially true of military books. As Rob O'Neill was taking credit for killing bin Laden, a film version of *Lone Survivor* was released, starring Mark Wahlberg as Marcus Luttrell. The movie stuck to the book's misleading and at times fictional depiction of events. Luttrell did a new round of media interviews for the film. Seven years after the book was first published, Luttrell had become more comfortable talking about what he viewed as his failure on the battlefield, part of the story he left out of the book. Although he has never admitted to exaggerating portions of *Lone Survivor*, he did begin describing his conduct in this ambush more accurately while doing interviews about the movie. "I put my weapon down in a gunfight while my best friend was getting killed," Luttrell told Anderson Cooper for *60 Minutes*. "So that pretty much makes me a coward."

Cooper interrupted Luttrell. "How can you say that? Why do you think that? That putting your weapon down makes you a coward?"

"'Cause that is a cowardice act, if you put your weapon down in a gunfight," Luttrell responded. "They say every man has his breaking point. I never thought I'd find mine. The only way you break a Navy SEAL is you have to kill us, but I broke right there, I quit right there."[4]

The movie ultimately made more than $150 million in theaters and continued the SEAL myth. The film introduced a new generation of Americans to Luttrell and his story, making him a celebrity. He earned several million dollars from the book and film, and more giving paid speeches. As he became wealthier and better known, he also became more overtly political; he would later give a prime-time address during a Republican National Convention. He also established a nonprofit organization called Team Never Quit, a support group for military veterans and the families of veterans who died. His fellow SEALs, many of whom knew the truth of what happened on Operation Red Wings, accepted his misleading story because his nonprofit helped fellow SEALs.

Then, in 2015, Clint Eastwood directed *American Sniper*, with Bradley Cooper as Chris Kyle. Eastwood and Cooper described the film as a character study rather than a war film, trying to limit any political criticism for how it portrayed the Bush administration's false link that Iraq was in some way responsible or involved in the 9/11 attacks. Outside the battlefield scenes, the movie showed Kyle struggling with post-traumatic stress disorder and his relationship with his wife. The movie made $110 million in its first weekend of wide release and $547 million worldwide, and was nominated for Best Picture and Best Actor, among six nominations at the Academy Awards that year. *American Sniper* is the most successful American war film in history and achieved for Kyle what he'd always wanted: a legendary status.

IN 2014, THE JUSTICE DEPARTMENT OPENED AN INVESTIGATION into Bissonnette over his failure to submit *No Easy Day* to the Defense Department before publication. That inquiry led to a federal investigation into whether Bissonnette violated the Espionage Act, then into his contracts with military manufacturers while serving as an active-duty SEAL. While the government scrutinized him, Bissonnette filed a civil suit against the lawyer who had advised him he did not need to submit his book before publishing. Bissonnette signed a consent decree with federal prosecutors forfeiting all money he earned from *No Easy Day* and any future earnings. In his civil suit, Bissonnette submitted financial details to demonstrate how much money he lost due to not submitting the *No Easy Day* manuscript. By 2016, *No Easy Day* had generated more than $7.8 million in royalties for Bissonnette, which the government seized in installments. In court documents, Bissonnette said that after the Justice Department investigation was announced, Steven Spielberg and HBO canceled their television project and dried up his speaking engagements. Still, he made a healthy living as a speaker in the years after *No Easy Day* was published. In 2014, Bissonnette earned $1.2 million from his speaking events. The following year, despite losing speaking engagements, he still managed to make $500,000.

Although Bissonnette managed to sell a book and tell his story first, O'Neill arguably got the better deal. Already a popular motivational speaker, O'Neill now charges up to $75,000 per speech. O'Neill used the bin Laden raid, including false and self-serving accounts, to establish a commercial brand, just as Marcinko, Luttrell, Kyle, and Bissonnette had done before him. He started a clothing brand called RJO Apparel, with his signature as the logo. His Instagram account, which has several hundred thousand followers, frequently shows him on private jets and partying with celebrities such as Kid Rock.

The SEALs had become a cultural phenomenon: their books were bestsellers, their stories were seen in movie theaters across the country, and one Long Island high school football player died during a team conditioning exercise replicating a BUD/S routine.[5] The trend was worrisome for Naval Special Warfare. "[T]he cultivation of celebrity status," wrote Navy SEAL Lt. Forrest Crowell, "has incentivized narcissistic…behavior within the SEAL community."[6] Crowell's master's thesis, "Navy SEALs Gone Wild: Publicity, Fame, and the Loss of the Quiet Professional," was published in December 2015 by the Naval Postgraduate School in Monterey, California. The thesis served as an internal critique of how far SEALs had moved from their origins as "quiet professionals." "In essence," Crowell argued, "U.S. Navy SEALs have become celebrities, and the SEAL brand has been transformed into a lucrative and powerful currency in the marketplace of things and ideas." Crowell was troubled by how much cultural capital former SEALs had in their post-Navy civilian life. "There appears to be a strong 'halo effect' whereby society deems that if the SEALs can kill bin Laden, then their opinions must be worth listening to on a plethora of unrelated issues."[7]

Crowell noted that, in 2015, O'Neill offered signed American flags to donors of then Rep. Ryan Zinke's SEAL PAC, asking, "How can a symbol of an apolitical military unit be used in such a partisan way without any protest from society or the military?" Crowell quoted a fellow SEAL who summed up why the enlisted were untroubled with profiting off their time in service. "Until we can officially acknowledge our mistakes and have the leadership apologize to the community, we will never be able to hold others' feet to the fire for Ethos violations."[8]

Bissonnette and O'Neill did suffer unofficial consequences for their brazen dishonesty. In 2016, they were unofficially banished from SEAL Team 6 headquarters. The command's top noncommissioned officer at the time, Master Chief Petty Officer Scott Keltner, placed their names on a so-called SEAL Team 6 Rock of Shame, the unofficial list of unit pariahs. Joining them on the list was Britt Slabinski, who had retired in 2014. He was added following a 2015 New York Times article that quoted him denying he'd ever ordered his men to kill unarmed Afghan targets. What SEAL Team 6 found dishonorable was that he spoke to the press, and that he lied. "That's what's wrong with my community," a former SEAL Team 6 leader told me. "Our sense of what's right and what's wrong is warped. No one was upset that he ordered a beheading or all the men shot even if they were unarmed. They were mad because he spoke to the New York Times and lied."

Some consequences of Team 6's lack of accountability are less visible for others who didn't meet pariah status. The operator who followed Slabinski's direction to give him a Taliban head experienced psychological difficulties in the years that followed the 2007 incident. In 2016, the command determined that he was medically unfit to deploy. His superiors believed he had become "unglued" over the 2007 deployment.[9] The SEAL was quietly removed from Dam Neck and returned to NSW Group 2 at Little Creek. There, he came under the command of Peter Vasely, then a commodore, the officer who first witnessed him decapitating a dead enemy in Afghanistan. The enlisted operator told at least one former Team 6 teammate he hoped never to deploy again.

"He's just beginning to suffer for what he did," said one of the SEAL's former superiors. "He's young, and he has so much more to go through."

WITH THE OSAMA BIN LADEN RAID AND THE HIGH-VALUE-TARGET kill list, Team 6 gave Obama a clear and decisive victory in the Forever

Wars; they'd completed their mission. What did it matter, ultimately, if those involved in the raid lied about parts of the story to inflate their heroism, or that some looted the compound in violation of military laws? Team 6 had delivered Obama a second term, as they'd predicted, and their operational success made them famous. America's special operations forces delivered tangible "victories" even as US military officials acknowledged that the United States could not kill its way to victory. Their successes insulated Team 6 from oversight and scrutiny and perpetuated a system that rewarded covering up misconduct. They could kill anyone they targeted, delivering a potent message about American power.

But what did their successful killing achieve? Bin Laden's death did not bring an end to terrorism or even al Qaeda. The body counts in Iraq and Afghanistan brought no victories, and while Obama ended the war in Iraq, the Afghanistan War was in year sixteen when he left office. What were the costs, then, of the supposed victories? They are many and endlessly human. As the Obama administration ended, no one in the military appeared to ask what would become of a generation of SEALs who'd done the bulk of the nation's two decades of killing. The leaders who gave the SEALs their orders readily asked them to go out, night after night, to take lives. But when the killing was done, they did not ask what it does to a man.

PART IV

My Word Is My Bond: Reckoning

[2017–2021]

CHAPTER 15

MEDALS OF HONOR

I N A WAR THAT HAS NO END, THE BEGINNING CAN BE EASILY FORgotten. In September 2016, such was the case for all but those who'd participated in the battle on top of Takur Ghar in March 2002. Seated in a conference room in a Crystal City, Virginia, office, the surviving SEALs of Mako 30 listened to a presentation and watched a video of the battle. Representatives of the Air Force Special Operations Command were briefing the SEALs on a development. After applying newly created video technology and reviewing the battle, the Air Force had concluded that Tech. Sgt. John Chapman had survived his initial wounds; alone, he'd fought off as many as twenty al Qaeda militants for nearly an hour, before being killed. The Air Force intended to nominate Chapman's Service Cross for an upgrade to Medal of Honor. The now retired Team 6 SEALs of Mako 30, led by their former team leader, Britt Slabinski, were incredulous. The Air Force presentation made it clear that Slabinski had been mistaken in his assessment that Chapman was dead when he ordered his team to retreat down the mountain.

Slabinski was trying to establish a civilian career as a leadership consultant, relying on his résumé as a decorated war hero who had risen to the top of America's most famous military unit. He appeared here and there at corporate events, where he shook hands and posed for photos. But he still carried Takur Ghar with him everywhere he went. He had "visions" of the battle, he told the *New York Times* in August of that year, images of blurry, slow-motion enemy fighters on the Afghan mountaintop. He heard the gunfire and grenades from the battle. After fifteen combat deployments, he had trouble sleeping and had been diagnosed with post-traumatic stress disorder.[1]

Slabinski's account of what happened at Takur Ghar remained largely consistent from the first days afterward. He saw Chapman go down, saw teammate Brett Morganti get hit by enemy fire, and then saw Chapman prone and, as he interpreted it, no longer breathing. He then retreated down a slight slope, sliding past or just over Chapman's feet. He didn't check his pulse and kept going.

In 2004, Naval Special Warfare asked Slabinski to participate in a book about Takur Ghar, published in 2005 as *Roberts Ridge: A Story of Courage and Sacrifice on Takur Ghar Mountain, Afghanistan.* The author, Malcolm MacPherson, interviewed Slabinski for several hours. Slabinski's account to MacPherson was consistent with his previous statements in the days and months after the battle. "I know I don't have time to check his pulse," Slabinski told MacPherson, "but it's kind of like, hey, I got no movement [from] him…I take a last look at him." Slabinski explained his dilemma: "I can't drag him [because] I have to worry about Brett…I'm fairly certain that he's dead."[2]

Later in the MacPherson interview, Slabinski described the moment again. "I remember going over him, but I don't remember checking his pulse," Slabinski said. MacPherson asked Slabinski if he had yelled out to Chapman, given that he couldn't check for vital signs to see if he was alive. Slabinski said he did not. "I was really apprehensive of giving our position of my team [away]…I remember looking at him, thinkin', in the position he was layin' in, I just thought he was dead, so I throw the smoke [grenade to retreat]."

Slabinski had not outright dismissed the chance that Chapman lived but suggested it was unlikely. "There probably is a possibility that, yeah, sure, maybe he got wounded in the leg, and he was just laying there regaining his breath because his leg hurt like a motherfucker." Still, Slabinski doubted that. "I mean, heck, I crawled right over the top of that guy." If Chapman was alive at that moment, Slabinski suggested, he would have reacted. "[Give] me a grunt, a groan, give me some sign of life. Nothing… there was nothing there."

In the SEAL culture, leaving a teammate behind in battle violated a sacrosanct and governing principle. It was, in fact, part of the official Navy SEAL Ethos, which Slabinski had helped write. In preparing for the interview, Slabinski read a draft of MacPherson's manuscript. The draft concluded that Chapman had survived the initial firefight. Slabinski told MacPherson he wanted that changed. "That's the thing that hurts me the most," Slabinski said about the draft of *Roberts Ridge* he'd read. "That tells me that I'm borderline incompetent by leaving somebody behind." Slabinski continued, "That's the thing I have the biggest heartache with, you know, it's basically now telling the world that I left somebody behind when in the very beginning I went back up there to not leave somebody behind."

By Slabinski's own standard, heroes don't leave their teammates for dead on the battlefield. But the Air Force presentation concluded that Slabinski had unintentionally done just that. In fact, the video analysis determined that Slabinski had never been closer than twelve feet from Chapman's body at any point after Chapman suffered the initial bullet wounds to his torso.[3] The enhanced drone video, along with the AC-130 footage, made it clear that Slabinski's memory from a moment of great stress and trauma was unreliable.

At stake in the Medal of Honor upgrade was more than just whether Slabinski had checked Chapman's body before he decided to escape. Chapman's award would shatter Team 6's self-image. If the rest of the military and the public knew Chapman had lived, then they might begin to catch on to all the other lies and cover-ups as well. SEAL Team 6 culture prized heroism over honor and myths over truth. But the myth of

Takur Ghar could not outrun the truth of what happened there. It also threatened the edifice on which the myth was engraved.

THE AIR FORCE'S JOURNEY TO AWARD JOHN CHAPMAN A MEDAL OF Honor had begun three years earlier. In 2013, Frank Dailey, a veteran intelligence analyst with the Air Force's 720th Special Tactics Group, discovered the Predator drone video footage of the battle at Takur Ghar. The video was thought to be lost, but Dailey found the footage in a windowless room at the Hurlburt Field Air Force base near Fort Walton, Florida. Dailey had been an enlisted analyst for the 24th Special Tactics Squadron, Chapman's unit, when the battle had taken place, and like many of Chapman's teammates, he had unanswered questions about what happened to him that day.

Viewing the long-missing footage from the CIA drone circling above the mountaintop, Dailey saw in the video what those who had watched it at the time had described: an extended firefight. The problem was, the official account was that when the SEALs had descended from their position up top, Chapman was dead. If he had died, who was shooting the al Qaeda militants over the next hour? Now a civilian, Dailey watched and rewatched the footage dozens of times and compared it to the official narrative of the battle. When he cross-referenced the AC-130 video footage, Dailey came to believe that Chapman had lived and continued to fight. When he asked a colleague at the National Geospatial-Intelligence Agency (NGA), the government's premier imagery analysis agency, to take a look, the colleague concurred, and mentioned a new software developed in the intervening years since Operation Anaconda. The classified computer software took an image and identified a unique visual signature for each pixel in a video. Why don't you have the Air Force use the software on the footage to test your theory? Dailey's colleague suggested.

So Dailey did. Because Dailey could identify which small black dot Chapman was in the video the moment he exited the Chinook, the software could mark the combat controller as he moved around the mountaintop. The technology also differentiated all of Chapman's teammates, as well as the enemy forces on the mountain. Again and again, Dailey viewed the video with the new tool, and each time he was sure Chapman was the blurry mark moving on Takur Ghar, fighting alone, waiting for backup. Eventually, Dailey told his superiors that he was certain Chapman had lived to fight off al Qaeda fighters after he'd been left for dead. If Dailey was right, there was no doubt that Chapman's Air Force Cross deserved an upgrade to the Medal of Honor. But going from the pet-project assessment of an intelligence analyst in a room at Hurlburt to the president's White House desk was further than the geographical distance from the Florida Panhandle to Washington: the Air Force had not had a Medal of Honor awarded since the Vietnam War.

Then, in 2015, Obama's secretary of defense, Ash Carter, directed each military service to review all post-9/11 Service Crosses. Consideration for an upgrade required that new information be presented to the Pentagon. With the proliferation of new technology and media, Carter believed each award deserved a new look.

A year later, the Air Force had conducted a review and agreed with Dailey: Chapman had lived an additional hour and fought to his death on the top of Takur Ghar. Thanks to the new imaging software, it was clear that Chapman had participated in several firefights, during which he killed several more militants, eventually engaged in hand-to-hand combat with one, survived, and then engaged with his rifle again. Nearly an hour after he recovered from his initial gunshot wounds, he heard the rescue MH-47 Chinook making its landing nearby and exposed himself to provide cover for it as it tried to land. While the new video technology alone suggested that Chapman had lived, there was some ambiguity about the tiny black dot moving around the mountain peak in the video footage. The angles, topography, weather conditions, and camera angles from the circling drone all made positively identifying Chapman a challenge. There were also brief gaps in the footage—one or two seconds here and there—and the video had no sound.

The Air Force then shared the video with four defense and intelligence entities for an independent analysis. The National Geospatial-Intelligence Agency, the Joint Special Operations Command, and the

Pentagon's Southern Command came to the same conclusion: the little blurry dot fighting on Takur Ghar was John Chapman. SEAL Team 6 was the fourth group asked for their analysis; they concluded it was not Chapman. Their intelligence analyst, George Hartwell, contended that the pixel software the Air Force was relying on was not conclusive, and that its inventor's claims were "bogus."[4] In Hartwell's conclusion, Chapman died within three minutes of exiting the helicopter, and the idea that he survived to fight later was "completely inaccurate and fictional."

Then the Air Force reinterviewed witnesses and reviewed after-action reports and other video footage from an AC-130 gunship. Chapman's autopsy was reviewed, and the original medical examiner was interviewed. A forensic pathologist conducted an independent autopsy review. Once the investigation expanded beyond Slabinski, who was the only eyewitness to Chapman's initial wounds, the picture of what occurred on the mountain became clear. While Chapman had been struck twice by bullets below bunker one, his body had seven more bullet wounds by the time it was recovered. The forensic pathologist also determined that his death was near instant, caused by a bullet to the aorta, which had entered from a direction that would have been impossible when the SEALs were still on the peak. The autopsy showed that he had abrasions and cuts on his forehead, hands, and arms, all of which came before his death. The injuries matched what the video now showed: Chapman had ended up in a hand-to-hand fight with one of the militants and survived. If Chapman had died as Slabinski and the SEALs insisted he had, Chapman could not have ended up with all his additional wounds.

Once confident, Air Force secretary Deborah Lee James submitted the upgrade proposal to the Office of the Secretary of Defense in early 2016 and waited. She was sure their new conclusion was not just solid but provable beyond a reasonable doubt. "This wasn't just my eye," James told me later in an interview. "This was forensic experts who make a career out of studying images."

The medal upgrade package for Chapman was distributed and briefed through the Pentagon. The Air Force submitted two citations for the award, an unprecedented step that reflected what they now understood as two different battles on Takur Ghar's peak. The first citation would be the same as the Air Force Cross and reflected Chapman's attempt to recover Roberts until he was first shot and lost consciousness. The second citation detailed what the review had determined: Chapman had regained consciousness, fought on the mountain, and then, in daylight, fired his last rounds to protect the incoming helicopter carrying reinforcements.

Sitting in the Crystal City conference room in September 2016, Slabinski listened as the Air Force finished their presentation on Chapman. The video, in particular, provided further evidence that Slabinski had made a mistake. The retired SEAL didn't accept the Air Force conclusions that he hadn't checked Chapman's body and Chapman had lived. It was at odds with the story he'd been repeating for fourteen years. Now, however, he went a step further: he changed his account. According to two senior special operations leaders at the time, Slabinski was distraught after the video presentation and offered a new version of the events. Slabinski was certain Chapman was dead, he said, because he had kneeled on top of the combat controller's body and checked his pulse.[5] Both the video and Slabinski's previous accounts contradicted the new story but became, along with Slabinski's anguish with the Air Force effort to get the medal upgrade, part of the Navy's new narrative.

Slabinski wasn't the only SEAL whose legacy and career rested on the original version of events. Several weeks after the Crystal City meeting, Lt. Gen. Marshall "Brad" Webb found himself in a heated conversation at a military conference in Tampa, Florida. Webb was the Air Force Special Operations commanding officer, and though he had not initiated Chapman's award package, his team was handling it for the service branch. Standing in front of Webb was Rear Adm. Tim Szymanski, now the commanding officer of Naval Special Warfare Command. Szymanski had tracked Webb down at the conference and had a message: stop pushing for Chapman's upgrade. The SEAL admiral told the former helicopter pilot that the rehashing of Takur Ghar was devastating Britt Slabinski. The former wrestler and Naval Academy graduate demanded that Webb's team end their efforts. Slabinski, the SEAL commander told Webb, can't find closure. Webb held firm, telling Szymanski that Chapman deserved the medal and that his command would continue to press for it.

Later, Webb acknowledged being taken aback by Szymanski's hostility and aggression. "Tim was shaking so much I thought he was going to punch me," Webb told his aides shortly after the confrontation.[6]

Over the previous fifteen years, Tim Szymanski had sought to protect Slabinski, choosing the SEAL code of loyalty above all else. Those who knew both men believe that their close bond was forged by the events of Takur Ghar. It was then Cdr. Szymanski, the Team 6 operations officer, who, along with Capt. Joe Kernan, had ordered Slabinski and Mako 30 to land on top of Takur Ghar. Five years later, when one of Slabinski's men attempted to cut off a dead Taliban fighter's head, it was Capt. Szymanski who helped Slabinski navigate an investigation so that no one was held accountable. When SEAL Team 6 later blocked Slabinski from returning to the command over it, hoping the move would end Slabinski's career, it was Commodore Szymanski who hired Slabinski as his senior listed advisor, tossing him a career lifeline. Yet again, Szymanski was protecting his man. "Tim has always felt guilty about what happened on Roberts Ridge," said a retired Team 6 officer who served with both men.[7]

Another retired SEAL Team 6 leader, who worked with Szymanski for fifteen years and had once mentored him, described his effort to get Slabinski the Navy Cross in 2003 and later the upgrade to the Medal of Honor this way: "Sometimes what they do is throw valor at it and decorate it and leave it for history. It takes the scrutiny off leadership. That's one of the essential thought processes for a guy like Szymanski. He [is] still by and large one of the top three scrutinized leaders of Roberts Ridge." The former Team 6 leader said that even before the upgrades were contemplated, Slabinski's Navy Cross relieved "a lot of the scrutiny" on Szymanski. "It's the ultimate distraction, and [it] takes away from the gravity of [his] poor decisions."[8]

Szymanski's confrontation with Webb was just the beginning of the SEAL effort to stop Chapman from getting a medal. SEAL Team 6 produced its own, dueling video of Takur Ghar for Pentagon leaders, which asserted that Chapman did not survive his initial injuries. This was known as the Redbeard video, named after a dead al Qaeda fighter with a long red beard found among the deceased on Takur Ghar. The SEALs contended that Redbeard grabbed Chapman's weapon after Chapman was killed, and that he was the one who got into the firefight seen on the Predator drone video. A 2003 after-action review had first suggested an enemy-on-enemy fight as one of the two leading possibilities. (The other was that it was Chapman, but the pixel technology did not exist at the time.) The central problem with this theory was that for it to have been true, Redbeard, or any other al Qaeda militant for that matter, would have had to have taken several pieces of Chapman's equipment with identifying infrared markings and strobes (which were invisible to the eye and useless unless you had American air support above you), put them on, and engaged in a sustained firefight in daylight from not more than twenty feet away, because neither Redbeard nor his fellow militants seemed able to properly identify each other. Then, after Redbeard's comrades killed him, they would have had to strip Chapman's gear off Redbeard and place it back onto Chapman (Chapman was found with all his gear and equipment including his M4, and all the rifle's magazines were empty). Ultimately, the Defense Department dismissed the Redbeard theory. "It was clearly an [American] operator," said a retired senior Pentagon official who was involved in determining whether Chapman got a Medal of Honor. "You can see him maneuvering. Three bursts, then move. Fire, then move. It was Chappy."

Once the SEALs lost the debate over whether Chapman had lived, they shifted their approach. The Navy and SEAL Team 6 now contended that Chapman did not deserve a Medal of Honor even if he had survived. The SEALs argued that Chapman had disobeyed orders and that his actions on the mountaintop had put Mako 30 in danger. Chapman's "actions were inconsistent with the orders given," according to a Team 6 note first published in *Newsweek*. "He neglected his primary responsibility of establishing comms with air support, which, had he consolidated initially with the team and established comms, would have enabled positive identification of the team, their location and allowed for CAS [close air support] fires which could have saved Chapman and prevented the wounding of the other two team members."[9] The implication was that Chapman had gotten himself killed and wounded his teammates due to his own ineptitude.

Again, Slabinski and Team 6 were changing their story. Slabinski and the surviving SEALs of Mako 30 had stated the opposite for Chapman's Air Force Cross in 2003. At the time, Chapman's willingness to expose himself to enemy fire while heading toward the bunker was lifesaving: "John died saving us from enemy fire," Slabinski said.[10]

Meanwhile, the Chapman family waited for word on the upgrade. Lori Chapman Longfritz, Chapman's sister, said the Air Force kept her family updated on the citation upgrade efforts. It was difficult for her to hear reports about the Navy's attempts to block the medal and denigrate her brother. "It disgusts me," she said later in an interview. "They could have just said, 'We made a mistake, this is what happens in war.' And our family would have been like, 'Okay, thank you for telling us the truth.' That's all a family wants."[11]

"I was sorely disappointed with their effort to block the upgrade," former Air Force secretary Deborah Lee James told me in an interview. James believed the reason they fought Chapman's medal was straightforward. "Deep down, it was an embarrassment for them. They unintentionally left a teammate behind. They did their very best on their very worst day."

In December 2016, Defense Secretary Ash Carter approved Chapman's medal upgrade over the Navy's objections and sent it to the White House for President Obama to sign. But with the unprecedented turmoil that came during the transition to the incoming Trump administration, it did not get signed. With a new administration, the upgrade would be sent back to the Pentagon, to decide whether to bring it forward for signature again.

FOUR MONTHS LATER, ON APRIL 21, 2017, MARINE GEN. JOSEPH Dunford, the chairman of the Joint Chiefs of Staff, presided over a twenty-foot-long mahogany table in a conference room on the Pentagon's third floor. Seated along the table were a small group of senior officials from the Air Force, Navy, and the secretary of defense's office. A few enlisted personnel and administrative staff sat behind them against a wall. The Navy had submitted a package to upgrade Slabinski's Navy Cross to the Medal of Honor earlier that month. After Chapman's upgrade had been recommended, the SEALs decided to change their tactic. If they couldn't stop Chapman from getting a Medal of Honor, then their man deserved one too. Team 6 went so far as to produce their analysis with a new statement from Slabinski in which he reverted back to his original story, claiming he had not checked Chapman's pulse.

Even so, as the debate continued between the Air Force and the Navy during the first months of the Trump administration, representatives from Team 6 kept insisting in meetings that Slabinski had left a position of cover, kneeled on Chapman, and checked his pulse. Each time, the Air Force waited for an opportunity to show the Predator video to dispute the story. The fight had been ugly, and now Dunford and Deputy Secretary of Defense Robert Work had to decide whether either upgrade recommendation should be sent to Defense Secretary James Mattis for his approval. The Air Force would present their case for Chapman, and the Navy would present their case for Slabinski.

By April 2017, the Air Force had made a well-documented case that Chapman had survived his initial injuries and fought with heroism to earn the award, not once, but twice. Chapman's award package contained two parts. Material Finding One covered the events from the initial attempt to land on Takur Ghar until he was wounded and passed out. Material Finding Two described everything that occurred after Slabinski and the SEALs descended from the mountaintop. If Dunford and the others approved both findings, the Pentagon would explicitly and officially acknowledge that Chapman had lived.

The politics of giving Chapman the medal, however, came with risk. Approving Material Finding Two would also imply that Navy SEALs had left a surviving comrade behind. Any award for Chapman that suggested the SEALs were less than heroic had the potential to create a scandal. A tribal conflict between two elite military units would inevitably invite further scrutiny. Each failure in the Team 6 chain of command, in discipline, in leadership, in consistently choosing brand over true honor, could spill out past the Dam Neck base gates. The Navy, and the Pentagon, had another reason to avoid questions: American men join the Navy to become SEALs, even though the odds are low that they will make it. The SEALs are the most recognizable brand the US military has.

In the third-floor conference room, the Air Force presented their case once more. It took roughly thirty minutes. Afterward, Deputy Defense Secretary Work called for a vote. The group unanimously agreed to recommend Chapman for the Medal of Honor, approving both material findings.

Next, the Navy presented their case for Slabinski. Luckily, the SEALs had a supporter in Gen. Dunford. In previous meetings, Dunford had made clear that, in his view, both Chapman and Slabinski were deserving of the Medal of Honor for their actions at Takur Ghar.[12] His case for Slabinski was straightforward: he broke all military protocols to lead an unauthorized mission to save Roberts. On at least one occasion, Dunford said that he couldn't see giving out one Medal of Honor for Takur Ghar without giving out both.[13] "Dunford told us that Slabinski's heroism was for the entirety of the engagement, not just one moment," said a retired senior Pentagon official who participated in the medal reviews.

Despite having support from the chairman of the Joint Chiefs, Slabinski's package had flaws. For one, his peers—both at Team 6 and the Special Operations Command—voted against the upgrade. Their argument against Slabinski had two points. First, the Navy did not present any new information, a prerequisite for the awards review Ash Carter had ordered two years earlier. Second, Slabinski had mistakenly left Chapman behind.

Nevertheless, Dunford overruled the views of the Special Operations Command and the Team 6 commanding officer on these concerns. But Pentagon officials had another potential problem with Slabinski's upgrade. In 1956, Congress passed a law preventing the Medal of Honor, or any other military awards, from being given to anyone whose service afterward "has not been honorable." A few months before the meeting, a news investigation of SEAL Team 6 had made public Slabinski's record, including the audio of his description of continually firing on a dead combatant for fun. A person who had attended the meeting quoted Gen. Dunford asking, "Is there anything in Slab's past that would give us pause?" A Team 6 senior officer, Capt. Kenneth Neiderberger, answered senior Pentagon officials' questions. Had Slabinski ever been sent to a captain's mast? Capt. Neiderberger was asked. No, he had not. Had Slabinski ever been "removed" from the command? Neiderberger again said no. For some in the room, the questions for Neiderberger felt preplanned.

Even when the leaders of Team 6 banished Slabinski from Dam Neck, they had let him off easy. "When we voted to keep Slabinski from coming back to the command, we knew what we were doing," said a retired Team 6 leader of the 2010 decision. If Slabinski had been allowed to return as Dam Neck's operations master chief, he said, Slabinski would have been promoted to command master chief afterward. "We didn't kick him out officially. We blocked him, knowing that unofficially it meant he could never return to Dam Neck. We actually thought it would end his career because he wouldn't get a meaningful slot anywhere else. But we didn't 'fire' him, and we didn't kick him out. It was a subtlety that allowed us to make our point but gave him top cover. Don't get me wrong, we weren't going to let him ever return."

At the Pentagon, however, the move was paying off for Slabinski. Had any senior official chosen to peer into Slabinski's record as the Blue Squadron master chief, they would have found it disqualifying. Dunford and the Pentagon brass were not interested in investigating the beheading or the cover-up. They did express some concern about Slabinski's description of shooting a dead fighter. But because it had never been reported to higher-ups and thus never investigated, Slabinski was never disciplined for the incident. Despite Slabinski's own words describing a war crime, the Pentagon hung the decision on whether the SEAL had been officially punished for the episode. In Washington, senior leaders preferred the hero myth over the truth, just as it was at Dam Neck.

After three hours of debate, Dunford, Work, and the others voted to approve Slabinski for the Medal of Honor. "We tried our best to say these guys are two heroes," said a senior Pentagon official who approved both awards. "The command and control at Takur Ghar was a complete shit-show. You can't hold Slab responsible for that."

Gen. Dunford and the group had one last dilemma. How would they deal with Material Finding Two, which implied Slabinski left Chapman to fight alone on Takur Ghar? If President Trump awarded both medals, how could they explain giving one award to the man who left the other medal winner for dead? Dunford proposed a solution: the Pentagon would classify Material Finding Two, even though there was nothing classified in the description of Chapman's hour-long firefight. "It was a cover-your-ass arrangement," said a senior noncommissioned officer who had been at the meeting. This person described the Pentagon's logic classifying the second citation: "If we classify the second citation, no one can go to the media with it. What they didn't want was some reporter to ask the president any questions at the ceremony. This took care of that." In other words, the classification would placate the Navy SEALs.

Defense Secretary Mattis sent both medal upgrade recommendations to the Trump White House in October 2017. "When it went to Trump," former deputy defense secretary Robert Work said in an interview, "we had no idea how he would take it."[14] But ever since Trump first posed with pictures of Robert O'Neill during his 2016 presidential campaign, the president had championed the Navy SEALs. They were, like him, winners. Trump approved both medals, and in April 2018, the president put the medal around Slabinski's neck in the East Room of the White House.

Meanwhile, the Chapman family waited for John's ceremony. It had been nearly two years since they were first informed that the SEALs were trying to stop the award. "What I've said from the very beginning is I cannot blame [Slabinski] for what happened on the mountain," said Chapman's sister Lori. "I wasn't there. I've never been in deep snow in the night with people shooting at me. So I can't blame him for the decisions that were made. But I can blame him for the lying. And trying to cover things up and then eventually, later, for his part in trying to squash John's medal."[15]

Four months later, on August 22, 2018, President Trump awarded John Chapman the Medal of Honor. Although Material Finding Two would remain classified, President Trump described Chapman's actions from the first insertion attempt until he was finally killed trying to provide cover fire for the rescue helicopter. Standing on the East Room podium, President Trump highlighted Chapman's courage. After he was initially shot, he "lost consciousness," President Trump said. "Even though he was mortally wounded, John regained consciousness and continued to fight on—and he really fought. We have proof of that fight. He really fought"—Trump gestured to Chapman's daughters, Madison and Brianna—"good genes, you have good genes." Chapman, Trump continued, "immediately began firing at the enemy who was bombarding him with machine-gun fire and rocket-propelled grenades. Despite facing overwhelming force, John bravely and fiercely battled on for over an hour." In all, Trump said, Chapman helped save the life of twenty Americans that day. Then President Trump presented Valerie Chapman, John's widow, with John's posthumous Medal of Honor, on what would have been their twenty-sixth wedding anniversary.

CHAPTER 16

OUT OF CONTROL

June 4, 2017—Bamako, Mali

Staff Sgt. Logan Joshua Melgar lay in his US embassy-quarters bed, Face-Timing his wife of eight years, Michelle, who was in their Fort Bragg, North Carolina, home. For Logan, it was late, almost 2:00 a.m. in Mali. A five-year veteran of the Army Special Forces, Melgar was on his third deployment and fortunate enough to text and have video calls with his wife daily. His first two deployments were in Afghanistan, where cell service and Wi-Fi were harder for soldiers. Although this was deployment in a semi-permissive environment, Melgar and his wife were able to stay in frequent communication. Logan and Michelle were a close, intimate couple who had fallen in love more than a decade earlier. Michelle, a petite, blond-haired forty-year-old, had Hollywood looks and a straight-to-the-point demeanor. Logan was three years younger, a tall, handsome, dark-haired Green Beret with caramel-colored skin and dark eyes.

The couple had met at a clothing store in Lubbock, Texas, where Logan worked and sold Michelle a pair of pants. Shortly after leaving the store, Michelle went back in to ask Logan out on a date. She couldn't get Logan's easy, handsome smile out of her mind. In many ways, each had been the other's salvation. Michelle was coming off a divorce and bankruptcy and had two toddlers, both boys, from her marriage. Logan had difficulties with his family, and after college had drifted, unsure of his professional direction. Logan took to her boys and was serious about being a strong father figure in their lives. They eventually married, and Logan became the boys' dad, raising them as his sons. They called him Dad, and he served as their Cub Scout leader, their soccer coach.

Logan and Michelle's romance started in Texas but moved to North Carolina when Melgar joined the Army Special Forces as part of their "18 X-Ray" program, allowing volunteers to join the Green Berets without prior enlistment. Melgar was a typical but ideal recruit: a graduate of Texas Tech, he was twenty-nine years old when he joined the military, a mature adult, committed to one of the Army's more elite units. Melgar was assigned to the 2nd Battalion, 3rd Special Forces Group based at Fort Bragg in Fayetteville, North Carolina, after graduating from the Army Special Forces qualification course in 2013. Logan and Michelle and the boys resettled there, as he started his career. He'd done two deployments to Afghanistan with 3rd Group in a war that by the time he entered it was already more than a decade long. Melgar was "unflappable" when facing enemy fire, his teammates later said.

The Mali deployment would not be like his previous two. He would work from the embassy in Bamako and was unlikely to see military action on a battlefield. The US embassy in Bamako sits near the Niger River, which divides the city in half. Landlocked, Mali is naturally divided by its geography, with the northern portion of the country occupying a great expanse of the Sahara's southern band. The country borders Mauritania, Algeria, and Niger to its north and four countries along its south, including Senegal and Ivory Coast. A former French colony, Mali serves as a corridor between North Africa and West Africa.

In recent years, the corridor has served as a waypoint for Islamic militants traversing between the central and western edges of the Sahara and sub-Saharan region of Africa. Bands of militants operate through the country's sparsely populated north, and in 2012, one of al Qaeda's regional offshoots took over Timbuktu.

Al Qaeda's presence is what made Mali an outpost in America's Forever War and the reason for a classified counterterrorism task force run out of the US embassy on Rue 243, in the heart of Bamako. Most Americans could be forgiven for not being able to identify Mali on a world map, let alone its capital. Even fewer had any notion that US forces were deployed to the country to fight terrorism against the northwest African al Qaeda affiliate, known as al Qaeda in the Islamic Maghreb (AQIM).

Melgar was part of a classified and clandestine team of elite US military personnel working out of the US embassy. Their overall mission was to help train and advise Malian government military forces on how to conduct counterterrorism missions and to help the CIA gather intelligence about terrorism threats in Mali. Melgar and his team were also there to provide additional manpower in any attack on the US embassy. Formally, Melgar worked for the United States Africa Command's special operations command, referred to as SOCAFRICA. Still, his day-to-day orders and oversight came from the Joint Special Operations Command, which had its personnel assigned to the counterterrorism task force, and the CIA's station chief, who oversaw all foreign intelligence collection in the country.

Melgar and his teammates were not in a war zone. The closest conflict was several hundred miles to the north, where the Islamic militants had taken control of a vast swath of a sparsely populated region of Mali. But their mission was still deemed essential and sensitive. Working from the embassy and living in the embassy compound quarters afforded Melgar a luxury he hadn't had in his two Afghanistan deployments.

Melgar had revealed to Michelle that he was having many problems with his teammates on the counterterrorism task force. Melgar was discreet in his description to his wife—he rarely shared with her details because he said he wanted to shield her—but he had painted a clear enough picture for her in the months previous to that night. What he didn't tell his wife was that he had discovered that two of his task force teammates, SEAL operators from Silver Squadron, were stealing money from a cash fund used to pay potential informants for intelligence about AQIM and other terrorist threats in the country. The SEALs had also solicited prostitutes and brought them to their shared embassy housing for sex. Melgar had informed some of his fellow 3rd Group teammates but did not make an accusation to the chain of command. Instead, the tension between Melgar and the SEALs increased. Melgar didn't tell Michelle any details but had intimated that he would report the SEALs to his command once he returned from the deployment.

Michelle was suffering from a migraine on June 4, and Melgar called her to check in on her and say good night. He told her there had been some drama with his teammates again but didn't elaborate. Michelle took a screenshot of their video call, which she did routinely at the end of each call. They each said "I love you" and hung up.

A FEW MILES AWAY, PETTY OFFICER 1ST CLASS TONY DEDOLPH, AN operator from Team 6, nursed a drink at the Byblos nightclub. DeDolph was handsome, with dark hair, delicate facial features, and a square jaw, and physically fit. In many ways, DeDolph fit the profile of an American hero: he'd grown up in Waukesha, Wisconsin, a middle-class exurb of Milwaukee. He played high school football and later was a Division III track-and-field standout at the University of Wisconsin Oshkosh. After college, he tried to make a career as a professional mixed-martial-arts fighter before enlisting in the Navy to become a SEAL in 2003. Although it took him nearly three years before graduating from BUD/S, he was eventually assigned to SEAL Team 7. After five years at Coronado and with several combat deployments, DeDolph, by then a corpsman, screened for Dam Neck. Silver Squadron drafted him in 2014.

By June 2017, he was a decorated operator, with a Bronze Star with a "V" for valor, and a Purple Heart. He'd taken a bullet in his shoulder during a firefight in Afghanistan and continued to fight for another ninety minutes. After his injury, he refused to leave his teammates and completed the deployment. One of his former superiors said the assignment to Mali was a typical test to see whether DeDolph could handle the responsibility of working outside the SEALs off the battlefield. If DeDolph was successful, he'd be in line to get promoted to team leader within his squadron. "It's a sink-or-swim position," one of his former superiors said.

In Bamako, DeDolph was the unofficial leader of the task force; despite holding an E-6 rank, his age and Team 6 status designated him as the group's alpha male. With the workweek over, DeDolph took his colleagues out for a night on the town. He was joined at the nightclub by a second Team 6 operator, Chief Petty Officer Adam Matthews. Matthews had arrived in Mali twenty-four hours earlier, preparing for his eventual rotation on the team. Three Marine special operators, called Raiders, from the intelligence team were also there: Gunnery Sgt. Mario Madera-Rodriguez, Staff Sgt. Kevin Maxwell, and Staff Sgt. Eric Miller.

Earlier in the evening, DeDolph and the three Marines drove through Friday traffic headed to a party at the French embassy. They followed Melgar, who had his own vehicle. At some point, DeDolph lost sight of Melgar's car and became lost. Melgar continued to the embassy and joined the party. But DeDolph and the Marines believed Melgar had ditched them, a personal slight, and a dangerous one: Bamako suffered occasional terrorist attacks against Westerners.

Now at a restaurant, the SEAL then began to discuss giving Melgar a "tape job," a gentle hazing. A few others joined DeDolph and the three Marines, including a British security contractor, Alan Pugh. Most of the team viewed Melgar as an "asshole," Maxwell would say later. What if we haze Logan by breaking into his room and choking him out? DeDolph suggested. From there, the plan evolved, a joke, some of them thought, to get the Green Beret back in line.

Over several hours, the team moved from a restaurant to a nightclub, drinking. The group of task force teammates, led by DeDolph, traded ideas for what initially took the form of a hazing while the group drank and ran into other embassy personnel. A rough outline of a plan took shape: the group would break into Melgar's room, they'd tape him up, DeDolph would apply a choke hold to render him unconscious. Pugh would film it on a cell phone. Afterward, the video would be used to keep Melgar in line, in what Matthews would later describe as "professional remediation."

As the group kept drinking, the plan took a more severe turn. At first, DeDolph suggested that they hire a prostitute to fondle and sexually touch Melgar while he was unconscious. Then someone mentioned that one of the embassy security guards, a Malian called Big Man, had a sexual fetish. Let's see if he'll take part, the group suggested. Even if they only pretended to sexually assault Logan while he was being filmed, their married teammate would be humiliated.

At roughly 4:00 a.m., DeDolph, Matthews, Madera-Rodriguez, Maxwell, and Pugh made their way back to the embassy compound. There, an incoherent plan coalesced into something "operational." Operation Tossed Salad (slang for the sexual act of anilingus) was a go. DeDolph recruited Big Man and another Malian guard from the embassy. The Marines, who lived separately from Melgar and the SEALs, stopped by their quarters to grab duct tape and a sledgehammer.

Meanwhile, Matthews told DeDolph to get Melgar's immediate superior's permission to conduct the hazing, under the misguided notion that what was about to occur was part of Melgar's professional development. DeDolph woke the Army Special Forces soldier, Staff Sgt. Jamie Morris, who agreed and went back to sleep.

The group, led by DeDolph, was now seven strong. They lined up outside Melgar's locked bedroom door in what assaulters refer to as a "stack." At roughly 4:30 a.m., Madera-Rodriguez hit Melgar's door twice with a sledgehammer, busting it open. The group rushed into the room, Maxwell switching on the light. Pugh, whose job was to film the assault using DeDolph's cell phone, got cold feet. Maxwell would later testify that the British citizen, who was in the back of the stack, became sick when it occurred to him that the assault would take place. He dropped DeDolph's phone and left the embassy compound. He wanted no part of what he understood would come next.

Melgar, startled awake, jumped up on his bed. "It's you guys," he said, realizing they were there to assault him. "Let's go, fuckers."

DeDolph, Matthews, Madera-Rodriguez, and Maxwell lifted a mosquito net around Melgar's bed to get to him. DeDolph grabbed Melgar around the neck while Matthews restrained his arms and the Marines helped get Melgar prone on the bed. Matthews pulled out the duct tape and began taping Melgar's legs. He used a whole roll, but the duct tape wasn't sticking correctly, so he started a second roll, which worked.

DeDolph choked Melgar out quickly, and Melgar slumped into DeDolph's arms, unconscious. As Matthews started to restrain Melgar's arms again, Melgar came to, his face on his bed. Matthews shouted at DeDolph to choke him out again. DeDolph applied a second choke hold around Melgar's neck. DeDolph, using a blood choke, a standard MMA move, pressed his forearm against Melgar's neck and throat and held it there for as long as twenty seconds. Melgar went unconscious a second time.

On the other side of the room, Big Man removed his shirt, preparing to "molest" Melgar, as Maxwell would later testify. Then, as Matthews restarted his effort to bind Melgar's arms, he noticed Melgar's body was limp and "non-responsive." Matthews ordered DeDolph to get off Melgar, and they both turned the staff sergeant over onto his back. Melgar wasn't breathing and had no pulse. The SEALs panicked and started trying to resuscitate Melgar as he lay on his bed. DeDolph and Matthews soon realized that their compressions to restart his heart were ineffective because Melgar was on a mattress. They lifted Melgar from the bed and placed him on the floor to continue their efforts, but nothing worked. Matthews began CPR. "His chest rose and fell from my rescue breaths, and during one of the breaths, I saw red-tinted spittle come out of his mouth and hit me in the face," Matthews later told investigators.[1]

The SEALs sent Maxwell, the least senior among the group, to the Marine quarters to get a defibrillator. DeDolph, the medic, had gone to get a medical kit elsewhere in the apartment. By the time Maxwell returned to Melgar's room, desperation had set in. DeDolph and Matthews were kneeling next to Melgar's body, conducting a cricothyrotomy. The procedure requires an emergency incision in the front of the throat, above the thyroid, followed by placing a tube in the throat to let in air. Maxwell would later testify that although it was part of the emergency battlefield lifesaving tool kit, he considered the technique odd because DeDolph had strangled Melgar; he hadn't put anything down Melgar's throat. The cricothyrotomy assumes that there is a blockage in the airway in the neck.

After roughly an hour of trying to revive Melgar, DeDolph and Matthews accepted that he was dead. The sun was now coming up. DeDolph and Matthews stood over Melgar's lifeless body, which was still warm. The two Team 6 SEALs—who combined represented a US taxpayer investment of more than $10 million in training, equipment, and support as the most elite special operators the military can produce—used their training to cover up their crime. DeDolph turned to the two Marines and the two Malian security guards and said, "You were never here. We'll take care of it." The SEALs reasoned that Melgar's death was a tragic accident, a well-intentioned joke gone bad.

DeDolph and Matthews dismissed the others and began making calls to the embassy security officer and then to an emergency clinic. Eventually, they took Melgar to the clinic, where a nurse pronounced Melgar dead. The two SEALs arrived at the clinic with blood on their hands. Matthews was shirtless and DeDolph paced, "in a state of shock, repeating himself and not lucid," an embassy official would later tell investigators. The SEALs initially reported that Melgar had been drinking alcohol and that at some time after a late-night wrestling match, the two SEALs found the Green Beret in his bedroom in medical distress. It was then, DeDolph reported, that they'd started lifesaving measures.

When the two Team 6 operators returned to the embassy compound, they met with the two Marines and began a cover-up. Maxwell informed DeDolph that he'd taken his cell phone, which had some video of the attack, burned the SIM card, and tossed the phone in the Niger River. He and Madera-Rodriguez had also cleaned Melgar's room, removing debris from the destroyed mosquito netting and disposing of the duct tape. Over hours, the four servicemen settled on a story in which Melgar was drunk and died while wrestling with DeDolph. They printed out timelines for their alibis and coordinated and rehearsed them so that they matched but did not "line up perfectly," Maxwell would later testify. The cover story "seemed like it covered all the bases," Maxwell said. Next, the four created a list of possible witnesses from their evening out in Bamako. They debated how likely each potential witness would be to rat out the assault plan. The SEALs were ordered to return to Virginia Beach, and Maxwell and Madera-Rodriguez agreed that they would "keep tabs" on the potential witnesses.

Finally, Maxwell went to Pugh's quarters and woke him up. "Logan's dead," Maxwell said.

Maxwell testified that Pugh agreed to stick to the cover story.

Army Brig. Gen. Donald Bolduc, a longtime Special Forces officer and Army Ranger with two decades in the special operations community, received the notification June 5 that one of his men had died. When an aide described a late-night grappling session and convulsions, the general asked his aide to repeat the details. "I knew instantly it was bullshit," Bolduc recalled. Bolduc's aide asked the general why he was skeptical. "There was no fucking way these guys were wrestling at five a.m. and then found him dead." Bolduc directed his aide to treat Melgar's bedroom as a crime scene to preserve potential evidence.

As Melgar's teammates rehearsed their lies, Michelle Melgar sat in her Fort Bragg home, worried. She'd texted Logan first thing after waking up that morning, as usual, "Good morning, handsome."[2] When she did not receive a response to follow-up messages, she began to worry. Logan was conscientious about responding to her texts, even while on deployment, and it was Sunday, typically a day off at the embassy. Michelle had not heard from Logan for several hours when her doorbell rang. As she went to get the door, checking her phone one last time, she prayed it was her son, who often forgot his keys. Instead, two soldiers and a military chaplain in dress uniform were on her porch and delivered the news. Her husband, Staff Sgt. Logan Melgar, was dead. Before she could ask, the soldiers told her Logan was found sick and convulsive in his bed by his teammates and ultimately died.

"No, you're lying to me," Michelle told the soldiers, she would later say. Michelle pushed one of the soldiers through her front yard, up against a pine tree. "I talked to Logan three hours before you're telling me this happened. You're lying to me. He wasn't sick. You're fucking lying to me," she said. "Stop fucking lying to me. Those little fuckers did this to him."

The chaplain instructed the soldiers to stop reading the pronouncement and asked Michelle who the "little fuckers" were. She told him that her husband had problems with his SEAL roommates and that Logan had been sober and in perfect health when he'd said good night. If he died, his roommates had done something. Initially, officers at Fort Bragg did not believe Michelle Melgar's claims. She told her boys that the military's story was false. "I didn't lie to them," she said later. "I told them, 'Your dad didn't die sick. The people in his house killed him.'"[3]

Logan Melgar's body was laid to rest on November 20 in Arlington National Cemetery. For three months, Michelle Melgar struggled to get the Army to believe that her husband had been murdered in his US embassy-compound bedroom. She felt very alone, she would later say, and had frequent nightmares. Despite Gen. Bolduc's suspicions and Michelle's steadfast belief, investigators from the Army criminal investigation division had uncovered no evidence to contradict DeDolph and Matthews's story. Melgar's bedroom was photographed, and evidence had been collected and given an initial visual inspection by investigators, but nothing stood out. They maintained that Logan had spent the evening of his death drinking heavily and roughhousing with his teammates before retiring to his room, where he died from unknown causes. The Army would not classify Melgar's death as killed in action, and thus, Melgar was not initially allowed any of the burial or death benefits that come with the designation. His widow felt a second "betrayal" from the Army's decision. "What do you do for the service member killed by our own people?" she'd later say about her predicament at the time.

Meanwhile, DeDolph and Matthews reported back to Dam Neck. Although they were not suspected in Melgar's death, Team 6 prohibited them from deploying until they were cleared of any wrongdoing. DeDolph and Matthews remained part of Silver Squadron and were allowed to participate in training with their teammates. While still un-suspected, the SEALs stayed in touch with the two Marines, maintaining their cover-up.

IN THE YEARS SINCE 9/11, TEAM 6 HAD BEEN ABLE TO REMAIN UN-punished for battlefield transgressions and misconduct. The victims of their excessive violence were most frequently foreigners who met the definition of an enemy combatant. They were, for the American public, unnamed foreign "bad guys." But Melgar was a fellow American, a member of the larger special operations community. The SEALs would not find the same disinterest in their misconduct as they might have had it occurred in an Afghan village.

In September 2017, a medical examiner released an autopsy report to the Army. Logan Melgar's death was classified as a homicide, the result of asphyxiation. Logan Melgar was strangled to death. A separate toxicology report found no alcohol in Melgar's bloodstream when he died—just as Michelle had told the Army in the days after her husband was killed. The military now had a homicide investigation to conduct.

DeDolph and Matthews had become persons of interest in the case. The Army's criminal investigators turned the case over to the Naval Criminal Investigative Service, the NCIS. Based on Michelle Melgar's assertions that her husband had several conflicts with DeDolph and others on the task force, investigators began looking into Melgar's relationships with them. Interviews with two of Melgar's superiors in the 3rd Special Forces Group revealed that Melgar told his companions that the Team 6 operators, including DeDolph, were stealing cash from a task force informant fund. In addition, DeDolph and several other of Melgar's roommates were hiring prostitutes and bringing them to their shared embassy-compound quarters for sex. Melgar had confronted DeDolph over the alleged theft, and according to Michelle, the two had had at least one physical altercation in their quarters. In some of his calls to Michelle, Logan told her that the SEALs and another Green Beret had been pressuring Melgar to participate in something he would only describe as unacceptable. When

Michelle asked what they were pressuring him to do, Logan would only say that he would tell her when he had redeployed home, and he could handle the problem until then. In the weeks leading up to her husband's death, Michelle Melgar told investigators, the conflict and tension between Melgar and DeDolph and others had increased.

In Virginia Beach, DeDolph and Matthews told a different story. When confronted about stealing operational funds and soliciting prostitutes, the two SEALs told Team 6 and investigators that Melgar stole and was bringing sex workers back to their quarters, not them. Both continued to insist that Melgar had been drinking the night he died and that they'd found him unconscious in his room, despite the autopsy results, which showed the SEALs were lying to investigators. The SEALs' counteraccusations were more understandable when seen as a result of their training. Team 6 operators take a specialized course called Survival, Evasion, Resistance, Escape, or SERE training. While many branches of the special operations community receive SERE training, Tier 1 operators get a more classified, brutal training course to inoculate them in the event of arrest or capture by an adversary. Among the skills is counteraccusations. As they had when Melgar first died, DeDolph and Matthews were confronted with a choice between the truth and the cover-up. Again, two of the most highly trained operators in the US military chose the dishonorable course of action. Having killed Melgar and been confronted with his accusations that they had committed other criminal acts while in Mali, they smeared Melgar. Throughout the initial investigation, the SEALs communicated with Madera-Rodriguez, in an effort to coordinate their timelines and let the others know what they'd told investigators.

However, NCIS investigators got a break when they reexamined the contents of what was found in Melgar's room in the hours after his death. Underneath the bed, they found a piece of duct tape with bloodstains, a circumstance that did not fit the SEALs' description of what happened in Melgar's room. Witness statements also described DeDolph and Matthews leaving the club with Madera-Rodriguez and Maxwell, suggesting to investigators that others were involved.

For more than a year, NCIS investigated Melgar's death as a homicide. During that time, both DeDolph and Matthews remained at Team 6 on administrative leave. DeDolph was even promoted to chief petty officer. "It is another failure of leadership," Bolduc told a reporter at the time. "I mean senior leadership. It's unfortunate. He should have never been promoted. The investigation was started right away. They whisked them out of [Mali] as fast as they could." Bolduc continued, "I'm disappointed. But not surprised. It's utter bullshit."[4]

The Navy audited Team 6 and began digging into Melgar's claims about the SEALs stealing from the informant fund in Mali. Meanwhile, Michelle Melgar and her two sons waited for some sign of progress in the case. The boys, Michelle Melgar would later say, were distraught and angry and began expressing a hatred for Navy SEALs. The broader special forces community was agitated at the counteraccusations and smears DeDolph and Matthews hurled at Melgar. "These guys were smearing Melgar, which was adding insult to injury for Mrs. Melgar and her family," Gen. Bolduc later said. "It was disgusting." Michelle Melgar would later tell a military court, "Nobody was taking me seriously. It was a very isolating place to be. A very lonely place to be."

FINALLY, IN NOVEMBER 2018, THE NAVY CHARGED CHIEF PETTY Officer Tony DeDolph, Chief Petty Officer Adam Matthews, Gunnery Sgt. Mario Madera-Rodriguez, and Staff Sgt. Kevin Maxwell with a range of criminal acts, from felony murder and conspiracy to obstructing justice and hazing. DeDolph, having placed a choke hold on Melgar, received the most severe charges, including one for obstruction of justice for conducting a cricothyrotomy to "hide evidence of the injuries inflicted" on Melgar's throat. DeDolph and the three others faced life in prison for Melgar's death.

The announcement that four elite special operators, including two from Team 6, were charged with killing a Green Beret and trying to cover it up was shocking. For a unit used to media coverage about its battlefield accomplishments, the Melgar case was unwelcome as much for its tarnishing of the Team 6 brand as for the alleged acts themselves. The Melgar case made both morning and evening news broadcasts.

The most disciplined class of warriors—not just Team 6 and the Navy SEALs as a whole, but the larger special operations community—seemed to be showing signs of an internal crisis, the effects of two decades of violence and war. The case also shined a spotlight on just how broken the SEALs were by 2017. Matthews, for instance, was a typical mid-career SEAL. By the time he was charged, he had served fifteen years in the Navy, with eight combat deployments. His lawyers would later submit medical records showing a typical combination of physical and psychological afflictions: post-traumatic stress disorder, traumatic brain injury, spinal compression, a sleep disorder, and hearing loss. By any measure, Matthews was disabled, and yet, had he not been involved in Melgar's death, he would have been returned to the battlefield for potentially another decade. The SEAL leadership pushed hundreds of men like Matthews past their limit. The fallout in Iraq and Afghanistan was unparalleled violence, often against civilians. Now the violence was against their own. Beneath the lurid details of strangulation lurked a more disturbing question: If America's best operators were capable of killing a fellow serviceman and covering it up, what were they capable of on the battlefield?

CHAPTER 17

A "REAL TEAM GUY"

May 3, 2017—Mosul, Iraq

It was a grisly sight. The limp body of a young, barely conscious ISIS fighter covered in blood and dust was flung over the hood of a Humvee like a hunting kill as the vehicle rumbled down the road toward a compound outside Mosul, Iraq.

The men of SEAL Team 7, Alpha platoon, waited for him there. Minutes earlier, reports of the man's capture had played out over the radio. The SEALs watched the air strike and assault from a remove, more than a quarter mile away. An Apache helicopter fired two missiles into a two-story concrete building where a handful of ISIS holdouts were resisting the Iraqi Army's advance into the city, which had fallen to ISIS control months earlier. The fighter had been discovered in the rubble of the targeted building—the lone survivor. The Iraqis shot him in the leg but decided against killing him. Or leaving him there to die.

The most senior enlisted man among the SEALs was Chief Petty Officer Edward R. Gallagher. A short, chiseled, square-jawed thirty-eight-year-old father of three from Fort Wayne, Indiana, Gallagher didn't command the platoon. That role belonged to Lt. Jake Portier. But as a veteran of eight deployments and a twice-decorated Bronze Star recipient, including a "V" for valor, he outranked his teammates in combat experience. He'd served as a sniper, a door breacher, and, in his earliest deployment following the 2003 invasion of Iraq, a medic. And that morning, as the Iraqi Army Humvee approached the compound, the ISIS fighter desperately needed medical attention.

Gallagher hopped in a vehicle, racing to meet the Iraqis. On his radio he called ahead to his men.

"No one touch him," Gallagher said. "He's mine."[1]

By the time Gallagher pulled into the walled compound, the fighter had been tossed onto the ground. A crowd of SEALs and Iraqi soldiers stood above the man, gawking. He looked to be a teenager; he was rail-thin, almost malnourished, with no facial hair. His calf bled from a gun-shot wound and he appeared to have internal injuries—most likely from the blast and concussion of the Hellfire missiles that leveled the building where he'd been sheltered. If he'd had a weapon, it had been left on the battlefield. He lay there, unarmed, clinging to life. Gallagher made his way through the crowd and knelt beside the ISIS fighter.

For the SEALs watching, this was their first up-close look at the en-emy. Most of the new teammates were a generation younger than Chief Gallagher—SEALs who'd been small children on 9/11, who'd grown up during the Forever War. For several of them, this was their first time in combat. Unlike SEALs on prior deployments, these SEALs in Mosul were consigned to the fringes, directing air strikes and launching mortars a mile from their target. Wary of getting into another ground war in Iraq, the Pentagon called the SEALs' task against ISIS an advise-and-assist mission, where they helped support Iraqi government forces but would not engage the enemy directly. So far on the deployment, Gallagher had chafed at the restrictions.

The crowd thinned out as Gallagher began cutting open the fighter's pants, searching for more injuries. Two medics joined him to assist. It looked like the fighter would survive, the Americans assessed. His injuries were significant—including "blast lung" from the air strike—but not necessarily fatal if he got proper care. It seemed a foregone conclusion that the Iraqis wouldn't treat him—if anything he'd likely be tortured and left to die. Already in the first two months of the deployment, the SEALs had heard and seen evidence of Iraqi government soldiers torturing and executing ISIS captives. The SEALs from Alpha platoon had seen just how grim the prospects were for any ISIS fighter captured by the Iraqis fighting to free Mosul.

Gallagher made an incision in the young Iraqi's throat to create an airway—a cricothyrotomy. But Gallagher, who hadn't worked as a combat medic in years, botched it. One of the two other medics stepped in to help. Gallagher's teammate, a twenty-nine-year-old SEAL medic named T. C. Byrne, inserted a chest tube and stabilized the patient. The failed "cric," as the SEALs referred to the procedure, had caused the prisoner a lot of pain. Byrne injected the young fighter with ketamine to ease his suffering and knock him out. He was now stabilized and limp. Byrne stepped away, leaving Gallagher with another medic, Corey Scott, and the platoon's youngest SEAL, Ivan Villanueva, who had come over to help.

As Scott continued treatment, another teammate, the platoon's lead petty officer, Craig Miller, walked toward the group. Suddenly, he saw Gallagher pull a three-inch hunting knife from a sleeve on his back and plunge it into the right side of the prisoner's neck. Miller kept walking. Scott and Villanueva, each on one side of the captive, looked on, frozen and silent. Then Gallagher pulled the knife out and stabbed the prisoner again. This time, when Gallagher removed his knife, a rush of blood came out of the wound and pooled into the dirt beneath. Gallagher then stood up and walked away. Villanueva did the same. Only Scott remained by the man's side as he bled to death.[2]

A few moments later, Gallagher returned to the body, accompanied now by Lt. Portier, the platoon's officer in charge. Technically, Portier was Gallagher's superior. But Gallagher had been Portier's BUD/S instructor years earlier and Portier had no battlefield experience. Portier rarely, if ever, contradicted Gallagher; in some ways, their dynamic hadn't changed from their instructor-student days. Portier then called over several other members of Alpha platoon. Rather than collect evidence at a crime scene, Portier had another idea. Gallagher was up for reenlistment, the formal event when a service member commits to additional years of military service. Portier decided this was the right moment to lead the ceremony. Gallagher recited the oath of enlistment, his right hand held up, the dead Iraqi captive at his feet. Next, Portier wanted a photo taken, to memorialize the moment. Gallagher took a knee next to his victim. And before the shot was snapped, the chief petty officer grabbed the dead man by the hair and pulled his head from the dirt.

Later, Gallagher would share the photo with a SEAL back in the United States.

"Good story behind this," Gallagher texted. "I got him with my hunting knife."

THE SEALs WHO'D WITNESSED THE MAY 2017 STABBING REPORTED Gallagher to their chain of command. In fact, within an hour of the stabbing, Lead Petty Officer Miller had reported the incident to Lt. Portier. But nothing happened. In fact, several of Gallagher's men would claim, the stabbing was the beginning of a horrific, monthslong deployment during which they watched their platoon chief ingest a cocktail of steroids, opioids, and uppers and commit additional war crimes. Gallagher's boss, Master Chief Petty Officer Brian Alazzawi, warned the Alpha platoon crew that he was a popular SEAL, and that if they formally accused him of war crimes, the "frag radius" (the blast area) would be huge. Their troop commander, Lt. Cdr. Robert Breisch, told them they'd lose their Tridents for ratting out their chief.[3]

Still, one by one, in May 2018, SEALs from Alpha platoon sat down in a windowless San Diego conference room and unburdened themselves to federal agents.

"The guy's freakin' evil, man," Craig Miller, one of the witnesses to the stabbing, told NCIS agents. Miller said he witnessed the stabbing as he walked through the Mosul compound courtyard. "I looked down and I see this person laying there and he had, like, bandages on his leg, or whatever, and I see Eddie laying over him with a knife, sticking it into his neck." After walking away, Miller told the NCIS agents, he returned to the scene, where he found Lt. Portier conducting Gallagher's reenlistment ceremony. "And I was just thinking like this is the most disgraceful thing I've ever seen in my life."

Miller had set the formal investigation off a week earlier, when he insisted that Lt. Cdr. Breisch notify the commanding officer of Team 7, and the Naval Special Warfare Command, about what had happened in Mosul. According to the book *Alpha* by journalist David Philipps, Miller had to stand over Breisch's shoulder, dictating the allegations and ensuring that his troop commander sent the email. It took several weeks before NCIS began inviting the SEALs to their San Diego office, but it wasn't the first time Gallagher's wartime conduct had led to an investigation.

Six years earlier, a group of students from BUD/S class 292 sat in a classroom on San Clemente, the small mountainous island off the coast of Southern California. These SEAL students were in Third Phase, receiving weapons and explosives training. Soon they'd graduate BUD/S and pin their Tridents on. That day in 2012, one of the explosives instructors tried to explain to his frogmen-to-be what it truly meant to be a SEAL. He told the class about an incident that occurred on one of his previous deployments to Afghanistan. His team of SEAL snipers had been hunting for a senior Taliban target. Each time the SEALs tracked the Afghan, he kept himself surrounded by women and children. The SEALs knew the Taliban target was using his female family members as human shields. The Taliban understood the American rules of engagement. With women and children within striking range, American forces were unlikely to launch an attack. Finally, the SEALs had an opportunity to set up for a sniper shot on the target. A young sniper was put on the rifle and cleared to kill the man, but there was a problem: the target was cradling a small girl at his chest. The young SEAL sniper told his teammates he couldn't take the shot. "He was a pussy," the instructor told the class. "Thankfully," the instructor said, "we had a real Team guy with us that day." Another sniper got on the rifle and fired a single shot, killing both the girl and the Taliban target.

The story disturbed the students. Later, they gathered among themselves to talk it over. Someone in the group asked whether any of them could take the shot, if they had what it took to be a "real Team guy." The consensus was no. One student in class 292 said the story so troubled him that he began to wonder whether he had gotten into the wrong line of work. When the class returned to Coronado, they passed the troubling story on to guys who'd just graduated from class 287. Class 287 revealed that they, too, had heard the story, and that the "real Team guy" had identified himself. He was one of their BUD/S instructors, Eddie Gallagher.

When one of the students from class 287 was assigned to Alpha platoon at Team 7, Gallagher was the new chief. Now Gallagher told his men the shooting story again. Gallagher seemed to relish describing the incident. He told them he'd shot the little girl through the head to get to the Taliban commander, saying, "Sometimes you have to break a few eggs to make an omelet."[4]

(A lawyer for Gallagher later confirmed the incident but said the child's death was unintentional. Gallagher tried to hit the Taliban commander in the head, his lawyer said, but the shot was low, hitting the child and the militant holding her. Gallagher's lawyer later told the *San Diego Tribune* that his client "felt remorse" for the child's death, but the young men at BUD/S heard otherwise.[5])

As the investigation in San Diego continued, Corey Scott, one of the two other medics at the scene, told investigators that he was "a foot" from Gallagher when the chief stuck his knife into the prisoner. Scott explained that everything with the Iraqi was "under control" but that "all of a sudden Eddie just starts stabbin' the dude." Scott was at the captive's head, he told the agents. Gallagher, Scott recalled, said nothing during the initial stabbing or after. "He just pulled out his knife and started stabbing him." Gallagher stabbed the prisoner "probably two or three times," Scott said. He told the agents he froze. "I kind of looked around. I was like 'Who else is seeing this?' And then, like, I kind of stayed at the dude's head and—like for a few minutes until he died."

Ivan Villanueva, whom Gallagher used as a gopher to obtain the opioid painkiller tramadol, confirmed to NCIS that he saw Gallagher stab the prisoner.

Then four of Alpha's snipers told investigators that Gallagher shot multiple unarmed civilians in Mosul. It had gotten so bad, they said, that they began firing warning shots at civilians in Mosul to scare them off and protect them from their chief. One teammate would later say in a text, "I shot more warning shots to save civilians from Eddie than I ever did at ISIS."[6] Special Operator 1st Class Joshua Vriens, one of the snipers, accused Gallagher of shooting a teenage girl. "The guy was toxic," he told investigators. Another sniper, Dylan Dille, described seeing an older man walking near a river get hit with a sniper round.

Scott, too, told the investigators that Gallagher was an indiscriminate sniper. "You could tell he was perfectly O.K. with killing anybody that was moving." Gallagher, Scott claimed, shot an old man in the back and told the medic it was legal because the man "could've been going to get a gun." Gallagher, his teammates said, would then brag that he had more sniper kills than Chris Kyle. And like Kyle, Gallagher was both inventing some and using unarmed civilians to inflate his count. At one sniper hide site, Gallagher's teammates mocked their chief with graffiti: "Eddie G puts the laughter in manslaughter."[7]

In all, at least six SEALs from Alpha platoon risked their careers to allege criminal acts by Gallagher to investigators. In doing so, they violated a sacred code of the SEAL brotherhood: loyalty. It was an act of courage so foreign in the Teams that, from their platoon commander up to their troop senior chief and troop commander, the SEALs of Alpha platoon were repeatedly ignored and rebuffed as the group tried to turn Gallagher in.

Miller, Scott, Dille, and the others did not initially want to have Gallagher investigated by NCIS. They wanted him removed from a leadership position, quietly sent to a billet where he'd no longer have influence over other SEALs. They wanted to do to Gallagher what leaders of Team 6 had done in 2010 to Britt Slabinski: banish him. Instead, Gallagher's superiors protected him, and in doing so failed the SEALs of Alpha platoon.

In June, after the investigation was completed, NCIS agents detained Gallagher and raided his San Diego home and his Team 7 cage. Investigators found the alleged murder weapon, steroids, and, after obtaining his cell phone, text messages with the trophy photos boasting about knifing the ISIS prisoner. Five months after the Alpha platoon SEALs first gave evidence against their platoon chief, in September 2018, Gallagher was charged with murder, attempted murder, obstruction of justice, and posing with a dead body, among other charges. Prosecutors also charged Lt. Portier with failure to report a crime and obstruction.

Nancy Sherman, a Georgetown professor and military ethics expert who has advised senior Pentagon officials on the subject, suggested that the effects of two decades of war since 9/11 have contributed to moral decay in units like the SEALs. Sherman said that these small, secretive units are prone to ethical lapses because they have their own internal rules and norms. "They are internally regulated, taught that the wall of silence is honorable," Sherman said. "They are held in great regard. Their problematic notion of honor has to be balanced against the fact that they are good at what they do."

Allegations of war crimes, drug use, and retaliation against SEAL whistleblowers have increased, Sherman told me, in part because they have experienced an unprecedented amount of battlefield exposure. "Unchecked revenge impulses, sublevel trauma, leadership lapses. Layer with twenty years of war, older [operators], brain injuries—it's cumulative. It makes for a bad club. The effect is it undermines a democracy."[8]

"Everyone knows there's a problem in the SEALs," Sherman said. "But it is unclear how to rein them in."

On paper, the prosecution had a strong case against Gallagher. There were the three eyewitnesses to the stabbing, plus supporting testimony from several others, including one SEAL who alleged that Gallagher described the stabbing to him hours later, in Lt. Portier's presence. But if prosecutors were confident in their case against Gallagher, they did not understand just how powerful a symbol of heroism the Navy SEALs had become for much of the American public. That is, the prosecutors did not recognize that their biggest challenge would not be faced in a military court, but outside it.

"THIS IS NOT WHO EDDIE IS," ANDREA GALLAGHER TOLD THE *NEW York Times* after her husband was charged. "He is a lifesaver. He is that guy who runs into the burning building when other people are running out."[9]

Andrea Gallagher was a marketing professional, and she quickly seized the opportunity to defend her husband in the media and change the narrative. She had at her disposal the Navy SEAL brand and the backing of former military and law enforcement in the conservative media echo chamber.

While Gallagher sat in confinement, Andrea went on Fox News to decry the Navy's treatment of her husband and declare his innocence. Gallagher was not only innocent of the charges against him, she said; he was also a victim. The accusations were the result of a millennial mob who hated her husband because he was a tough boss. Gallagher would later say that his teammates had made up the story of a stabbing because they were "pussies" and "cowards." The accusations were part of a "millennial mutiny," a conspiracy against him, Gallagher said later.[10] When the Navy put Gallagher in a San Diego brig because they had evidence he sought retribution against his accusers, Andrea told Fox News that her husband suffered "human rights violations" and that investigators were withholding exculpatory evidence.

Andrea Gallagher's defense of her husband became a social media phenomenon with a legal fundraising campaign called "Free Eddie." She and some of her husband's former teammates sold T-shirts and had created a trending Twitter hashtag, #FreeEddie. Between the Fox News coverage and Twitter, Gallagher's case attracted the most influential Twitter user at the time: President Donald Trump. Gallagher's case fit squarely into Trump's worldview. When Trump ran for office in 2016, he told Fox News that the US had to "take out" the families of ISIS, a violation of international law.[11] In office, Trump saw a political opportunity in

Gallagher's case, to rail against the political correctness of the prosecution while draping himself in the heroics of the nation's war fighters, especially the Navy SEALs.

After watching Fox News promote Gallagher's case for months, Trump intervened, tweeting, "In honor of his past service to our Country, Navy Seal #EddieGallagher will soon be moved to less restrictive confinement while he awaits his day in court!"[12]

The case also attracted Make America Great Again supporters. Bernard Kerik, the former New York City police commissioner and a convicted felon, became an advisor to Andrea and Eddie Gallagher. Kerik helped Gallagher attract a new legal team, which included Marc Mukasey, an attorney for the Trump Organization. Representative Duncan Hunter, a Republican from Southern California and a former Marine who served on the House Armed Services Committee, was one of several conservative lawmakers who joined the Free Eddie movement. To his supporters, Gallagher was the victim of politicians who were "second-guessing our heroes." Gallagher had become a conservative cause, a new front in America's culture wars. "Our boys did their job," one Fox News host wrote, "it's time for us to have their back."[13]

Two dramatically different portraits of the accused were presented at Gallagher's court-martial in July 2019. Prosecutors portrayed Gallagher as a sociopathic murderer. To Gallagher's defense, he was a hero and a victim, unjustly accused by soft kids who didn't like to get their hands dirty in war.

The prosecution had eyewitnesses to the stabbing, a murder weapon, and text messages that seemed like confessions of the crime. But their case had several flaws. While they had witnesses to the stabbing and some photos after the prisoner was dead, they had no forensic evidence. Prosecutors had no body and no medical examination of cause of death. Prosecutors never even identified the dead prisoner, so their victim had no name. (He was later identified in *Alpha* as Moataz Mohamed Abdullah.) Then some of the SEALs who had spoken willingly to NCIS investigators refused to testify, including one of the three original witnesses to the stabbing, Ivan Villanueva. And for each of the alleged shootings of unarmed civilians, prosecutors had a problem common in war crimes cases that take place years after an alleged event: no physical evidence. Adding to the prosecution's challenges was that the lead prosecutor had been removed from the case just before the court-martial began, pending an investigation for misconduct.

In addition to Craig Miller's testimony about Gallagher stabbing the prisoner, the prosecution called three other witnesses to address additional incidents of alleged war crimes. Dylan Dille testified that he heard Gallagher fire his weapon and then immediately witnessed an older man collapse, but acknowledged that he did not see Gallagher pull the trigger. Two other witnesses testified that they saw unarmed civilians whom they believed Gallagher had shot. Ultimately, everything they witnessed was through a sniper's optical scope, and while it allowed them to see great distances, it was a lot like looking through a straw. None of the Alpha platoon SEALs saw what happened after the civilians dropped or were pulled to safety. The prosecution's case hinged on witnesses, and as the court-martial progressed, it became clear that the prosecutors had done a poor job of preparing them for taking the stand.

Meanwhile, Gallagher's attorney, Tim Parlatore, followed the path Andrea Gallagher had blazed in the press. This was a mutiny, Parlatore told the jury, not a murder case. Parlatore portrayed each of the witnesses as an embittered SEAL who was angry with Gallagher for holding them to a high standard on deployment. Parlatore repeatedly pointed out that there was no physical evidence to implicate his client. He also used the Alpha platoon SEALs' text messages to each other as evidence that they had conspired to take down their chief with false accusations in the hope of sinking Gallagher's career. Parlatore called witnesses who testified that they never saw Gallagher stab the prisoner, nor did they see any evidence of a knife wound or blood in the courtyard that day.

Gallagher would later say that one of the biggest moments of the trial for him, when he could sense that he was going to win, arose from testimony that had nothing to do with the case itself. When Gallagher's lawyers got the text messages between Dille, Miller, Scott, Vriens, Dalton Tolbert, and others in the platoon, Gallagher found one in particular that he asked his lawyers to draw out in testimony. When Josh Vriens,

one of the snipers who accused Gallagher of shooting a civilian, testified, Parlatore asked him about a text he had sent in which Vriens called
Marcus Luttrell a "coward and a liar." Vriens admitted that he did write
that text and he did believe that. For Gallagher, Vriens's view of Luttrell
revealed who the young SEAL sniper really was: a traitor to the Brotherhood. Vriens had said the quiet part out loud. While many SEALs viewed
Luttrell and his story similarly, it was verboten to bad-mouth him. "You
can't malign Marcus," an active-duty SEAL and one of Gallagher's former
teammates told me. "He's a made man."

"I was glad that it was put out there," Gallagher would say later about
Vriens's testimony, "because Marcus Luttrell is not a coward and a liar.
He's a freaking hero and it just showed the attitude of these kids....Josh
Vriens was probably in eighth grade when Red Wings went down and
wasn't in the Teams, but here he is talking trash about the one survivor....
He's just a pompous little prick. I was glad that the jury could see that...
that was a big moment for me...just so they could see the entitled attitude
and just like how immature these guys were."[14]

There were other problems for the prosecution. Gallagher was popular
in the Teams, and had strong support among former SEALs, especially
on the West Coast. His supporters took to Facebook to call out Gallagher's accusers as traitors—not real Team guys. The pressure on the Alpha platoon SEALs who were ratting out their boss was immense. Some
witnesses sought immunity in exchange for their testimony. When prosecutors balked, they refused to testify against Gallagher. Ivan Villanueva,
for example, had backed away from his previous statements to NCIS. He
lawyered up and refused to cooperate. That left Corey Scott, the medic
who told NCIS agents he saw Gallagher silently stab the prisoner at least
twice, as the only other witness who could corroborate Miller's testimony
of the stabbing. The prosecutors agreed to give him full immunity for his
testimony.

On the stand, he told the jury he saw Gallagher stab the prisoner in
the neck, and that afterward, Gallagher walked away. Scott said he stayed
with the prisoner until he "asphyxiated." Then, under cross-examination,

Tim Parlatore asked Scott why he used the word *asphyxiation*, meaning death by oxygen deprivation. Scott testified that asphyxiation was the prisoner's cause of death, and that he knew that because *he* was the person who asphyxiated the Iraqi captive, not Gallagher.

Scott testified that he was the person who killed the ISIS fighter by covering a breathing tube that was inserted in the captive's chest. Scott viewed this as mercy killing. "I knew he was going to die anyway and wanted to save him from waking up to whatever would have happened to him" at the hands of the Iraqi government forces.[15] In six previous interviews with prosecutors, Scott hadn't said a word about it. The prosecutor went after Scott for changing his testimony. "You can stand up there, and you can lie about how you killed the ISIS prisoner, so Chief Gallagher does not have to go to jail," the prosecutor said.[16] Scott denied that he was lying but acknowledged that he felt bad for Gallagher.

"He's got a wife and family," Scott replied. "I don't think he should spend the rest of his life in prison."

Scott's testimony shattered the prosecution's case.

On July 2, the jury deliberated for eight hours before returning not-guilty verdicts for all the serious charges, including murder, attempted murder, and obstruction. The jury did convict Gallagher of posing with the corpse for a photo, a minor, if grotesque, offense. Gallagher's rank was reduced one grade to petty officer first class and he was sentenced to time served. His acquittal for war crimes validated his status as hero and victim.

After the verdict, Trump tweeted, "Congratulations to Navy Seal Eddie Gallagher, his wonderful wife Andrea, and his entire family. You have been through much together. Glad I could help!" Later, Trump restored Gallagher's reduced rank. Another famous SEAL, Rob O'Neill, lent his credibility to the debate in support of Gallagher. "He's a great guy," O'Neill told the *Washington Times*. "He's a poster image of what a SEAL should be. I'd go to war with him tomorrow."[17]

At Naval Special Warfare, Gallagher's acquittal was not the end of the controversy, nor an adequate resolution. At the time, Rear Adm. Collin Green was leading the SEAL command. He and his senior enlisted advisor, Cmd. Master Chief William King, had dug into Gallagher's career when the case first surfaced. They didn't see a hero, or even an exemplary operator. Gallagher's record showed that he was in fact a "bad SEAL," Green and King told a confidant.[18] With a conviction for posing with the dead body, the two SEAL leaders saw one last chance at ensuring Gallagher faced some measure of justice for his actions.

Days before Gallagher was set to retire from the Navy, the SEAL command initiated a standard conduct review board. A group of senior enlisted SEALs—Gallagher's peers—would judge the chief. If they found his conduct, as convicted by the court-martial, to be unworthy of a SEAL, the board would revoke Gallagher's Trident. It was symbolic but otherwise had no consequence for his pension or record. But when President Trump learned of it, he stopped the review board. The secretary of the Navy, Richard Spencer, ultimately resigned.

The Gallagher case, in the end, had done nothing but deliver bad press for Naval Special Warfare. And the fallout still had not cut through to the most alarming problem. Gallagher's killing of the young girl in Afghanistan was bad enough, but the exploitation of the story and its use as a teaching tool at BUD/S compounded the offense by offering it as an example of honorable conduct for a future generation of SEALs. Gallagher's actions had screamed for intervention and responsible leadership. Instead, he was promoted to chief and given a platoon. If Gallagher could spend two decades in the Navy, rising to a position of authority, who else in the SEAL ranks with similar conduct could rise? Green and King knew that Gallagher's case marked a failure for the SEAL command. After the aborted review board effort, Adm. Green stepped down as commanding officer and asked for a transfer.

In January 2020, Eddie Gallagher retired as a Navy chief after twenty years of service, with full benefits and his Trident. To honor his retirement, Rep. Duncan Hunter read a tribute to Gallagher on the floor of the House of Representatives, to be entered into the *Congressional Record*. Gallagher was "one of the greatest warriors our Country has ever known," Hunter said.[19] "Instead of receiving a hero's welcome" when Gallagher returned from his 2017 Mosul deployment, "he became the target of a tyrannical witch-hunt." Despite his ordeal, Hunter continued, Gallagher "has decided to live free of anger and has forgiven the individuals who wronged him."

When faced with the prospect of civilian life, Gallagher followed the footsteps of so many SEALs before him: he wrote a book.

CHAPTER 18

"YOU WOULD LOVE THEM"

January 23, 2019—Las Vegas, Nevada

Adam Matthews was dressed as Rambo inside the University of Nevada, Las Vegas, sports complex a mile off the Vegas Strip. Despite having just been charged with felony murder, involuntary manslaughter, conspiracy, and obstruction of justice, among other charges, and with a trial most certainly looming on the horizon, he appeared to be having fun at the SHOT Show's annual Crye Precision party. The party was legendary for those at Team 6 who attended the expo. Crye made most of the tactical clothing that operators wore, as well as kneepads. Each year, the Crye invite is considered the hardest to get; the event is where vendors and gun industry employees can party with operators from Dam Neck and Fort Bragg. Because the expo attendees are almost exclusively men, Crye pays women from a popular Las Vegas strip club to join the party and mingle with men in long beards and arm-sleeve tattoos.

That year, the theme was a 1980s high school reunion, and the Crye organizers had transformed a basketball court to look like a high-school-gymnasium-turned-reunion. Costumes were required for attendance. As Matthews made his way through strippers and industry insiders, he spotted a petite woman with blond hair. Matthews asked the woman if she was lost. He introduced himself as Mike. The woman introduced herself as Michelle. The two flirted and danced. As the evening wore on, Michelle finally asked Mike which service he was in. Mike told her he was in the Navy: "I paint numbers on ships for a living."

She knew from his appearance and given the setting that Mike was likely a SEAL. Michelle knew he was lying and pressed him. Matthews asked her how she knew he was a SEAL. "Because only a SEAL would say some douchebag shit like that," Michelle Melgar replied. Mike eventually acknowledged he was a SEAL. Michelle asked, "Which team?"

"Does it matter?" Mike replied. "Why do you need to know?"

"I just do. I just need to know," Melgar said. She told him she thought he was from Team 6. She would later say that his face got pale. Melgar told Mike that it was unfortunate he was from Dam Neck.

"Why?" Mike asked.

"Because two of your dudes killed my husband," Michelle said.

"They're my best friends," Matthews, pretending to be Mike, said to Logan Melgar's widow. "They're not bad guys. If you were to sit down with them, you would love them," he told her.

"No, loving is going a bit far," Michelle said. "I can forgive."

"Bad choice of words," he said. "The situation has ruined their lives."

"At least they have a life," she replied. Melgar gave Mike—Matthews—a hug and told him that they should speak to each other. "It was very nice to meet you," she said.

"I'm so sorry for what happened to your husband," he said. "And if I could change it, I would."

Melgar left the party. She told her friends, as well as some of Logan's Green Beret teammates, that she had unknowingly spent time with a Dam Neck SEAL at the party.

The next day, Matthews, still as Mike, texted Melgar, "What's your living situation?"

"I have a room," Melgar replied.

"Can I come nap? Im [*sic*] dying," Matthews asked.

Melgar became uncomfortable. She told one of Logan's former team-mates, who offered to help.

"This is a friend of Mrs. Melgar," the Green Beret wrote. "Read carefully and heed this message. You will lose her number and will not contact her again. You're [*sic*] sentiment may be from a place of loyalty; however, in this situation it is completely inappropriate and unbecoming of a member of our community. This is a black mark in the SEAL community and your efforts are keeping the wound open. Do not contact her again. Actions have consequences."

But Matthews, still hiding his identity, did contact her again. He asked to meet her and "sit down somewhere private." He apologized to her, saying it was an "unbelievable coincidence" but that "I only wanted to talk to you."

Melgar reported the contact to Navy prosecutors after she identified Matthews from a photo they provided. She would come to believe that Matthews did not know who she was when they bumped into each other at the party. Still, she started carrying a handgun afterward. The NCIS opened an investigation into Matthews but did not bring charges. But the encounter did seem to unnerve Matthews.

A month after the run-in, Matthews agreed to a proffer session with prosecutors. He decided to plead guilty and testify against his coconspirators in exchange for reduced charges. Matthews told prosecutors that he and DeDolph, Maxwell, and Madera-Rodriguez intended to haze Melgar as part of a joke gone wrong. Matthews said that DeDolph choked Melgar out twice, and after the second time, Melgar became unresponsive. He acknowledged that the four servicemen concocted a cover story to conceal how Melgar had died. But Matthews withheld any mention of the British civilian who got cold feet, or Big Man and the second Malian guard who were in the room preparing for a sexual assault. The prosecutor, Lt. Cdr. Benjamin Garcia, offered Matthews a year in prison if he pleaded guilty to obstruction, conspiracy to commit assault, hazing, and unlawful entry.

Later, prosecutors informed Staff Sgt. Maxwell that Matthews had flipped. Not knowing what Matthews provided to prosecutors, Maxwell told a more fulsome story. He disclosed that there had been three more individuals present in Melgar's room and that among the plans was a sexual assault. Maxwell also laid out the extent of the conspiracy to cover up Melgar's death. Confronted by prosecutors, Matthews admitted that he'd withheld details during his first proffer session.

On May 15, 2019, Matthews formally pleaded guilty to the four lesser charges. Matthews told the court that he could not "describe how sorry I am for the death of Staff Sgt. Melgar." "I've carried the weight of Staff Sgt. Melgar's death every minute of every day since that night in Mali," Matthews said.[1]

Chris Reismeier, Matthews's attorney, told the court that although his client was guilty of a "stream of bad decision making," the SEAL operator's service counted as well. "Adam Matthews is a hero, too, and he should be treated as such."[2] One of Reismeier's concerns in his client's sentencing was whether he would receive a bad conduct discharge, which would preclude him from having access to Veterans Affairs benefits. Matthews, his lawyer told the court, did eight deployments as a SEAL. The toll on Matthews's physical and mental health from years of battlefield exposure was real and significant.

Then Michelle Melgar spoke. Stepping up to a small podium in the low-ceilinged courtroom, she shuffled some papers before taking a breath.

"This is just another thing I never thought I'd have to do, in addition to a thousand others, all caused by this situation. I don't know where to begin. I've waited so long for this moment, and here I am not even knowing what to say," Melgar told the court. "I love my husband," she said, before taking a moment to compose herself. "I miss him so much each and every day. He is my soulmate....So often we would talk about how lucky we were to find such a perfect love, to find what so many others would never have, feel, or know....Logan wasn't perfect, but he was perfect for me." Melgar began crying. "The pain, at times, has been so overwhelming," she said, trying to pull herself together and continue. "[I]t literally takes my breath right out of me....Like it's suffocating me—the irony of that isn't lost on me."[3]

Melgar described all that she and her two sons lost when her husband died, and told the court that he deserved for the truth of what happened to him to be made public. Then she addressed Matthews directly. "Thank you for finally coming forward with some of the truths that led to Logan's death; all I've wanted was the truth about what went on in his room that night....While you single-handedly have caused me a lot of pain, confusion, and sadness—I forgive you." Melgar told Matthews that she was sad for Matthews's family, for losing him to prison, and that she was sad that his "reckless choices" cost him his career and Logan's life. "You finally coming forward was the beginning of the end of this mess, and for that, I am grateful...."

"I know that no amount of prison time will bring my husband back to me," Melgar continued. "Therefore, I care not how much time you do or do not sit in a cell. The important thing to me is that you are no longer in a position to ever do this to another service member, and that you are no longer wearing the Trident that so many others wear honorably and with pride."[4]

Matthews was sentenced to a year in a naval brig and a dishonorable discharge for bad conduct. A few weeks later, a military judge sentenced Maxwell to four years in prison.

On a warm, rainy day in early August 2019, DeDolph and Madera-Rodriguez appeared inside a drab, two-story military courthouse at the Norfolk, Virginia, naval base. The Norfolk courthouse halls were narrow, cramped, and covered in dirty carpet and conveyed all the charm of a run-down police station. Inside, the courtroom itself was cramped, with a low dropped ceiling, fluorescent lighting, and cheap, closed blinds covering a single window. DeDolph, wearing a khaki dress uniform with black-rimmed glasses, looked slight—almost meek—more like a high school student than a lethal special operator as he sat between his lawyers. He and Madera-Rodriguez were there for an Article 32, a procedural hearing akin to a grand jury in a civilian criminal court. The prosecution would present evidence that it claimed demonstrated DeDolph and his codefendant's guilt. If the military judge found sufficient preliminary evidence, the defendants would face a court-martial.

The courtroom's gallery was small, filled with a few rows of wooden pews. Michelle Melgar sat holding her husband's treasured green beret in the first row. On each side of her were special forces soldiers who would accompany her during the court proceeding in Norfolk. In the next row, Nitza Melgar, Logan's mother, was joined by her sister, Delia. Thin and petite, Ms. Melgar had short, graying hair and wore a delicate gold chain with a cross around her neck. In the last two rows, a smattering of reporters had their notebooks and pens out, ready to take notes. No one from Team 6 or any of DeDolph's friends or family appeared in the courtroom. The veteran assaulter rarely, if ever, looked back at the gallery, instead staring forward at the judge and occasionally to his left at Lt. Cdr. Garcia and his prosecution team.

Nitza Melgar sat motionless and silent as Garcia read off the first five charges against DeDolph to begin the proceedings. Then he got to the sixth charge for obstruction of justice. "In that Special Warfare Operator Chief Tony DeDolph, on or about June 4, 2017, at or near Bamako, Mali, wrongfully endeavored to impede an investigation into the assault and death of Staff Sergeant Logan Melgar when he purposefully did conduct a cricothyrotomy upon SSG Melgar's body to hide evidence of the injuries inflicted to SSG Melgar's trachea." Melgar's mother exhaled deeply, her torso sinking into itself against the wooden pew. Nitza Melgar had spent thirty years in the Air Force as a registered nurse. The forensic description of what DeDolph and Matthews had done to her youngest child seemed to deprive her of oxygen. Each time throughout the hearing that Garcia or the witness described the emergency incision on her son's throat she would sink again, as if someone had pressed out all the air from her body. And each time, Delia reached out to rub her sister's shoulder and press her sister's hand with her own.

Matthews and Maxwell each testified over a phone line from their respective military prisons. They told much of the same stories that had come in their sentencing hearings a few months earlier. Maxwell testified that although the hazing started as a joke, it became less funny as the night wore on. "The intent wasn't very clear," Maxwell said. It was a "fun thing" to do to Melgar, and it "started as a joke" so that "we'd have something to hold over his head."[5]

Eventually, Maxwell said, DeDolph and his teammates introduced the idea of having Melgar's pants removed and the Malian guard sexually assaulting Melgar while he lay unconscious on his bedroom floor. Later, attorneys for DeDolph and Madera-Rodriguez asked Matthews if the plan included a sexual assault. Matthews denied that, testifying that their goal was to film Big Man so that it would only appear to Melgar that he had been sexually assaulted in the video. The Malian guards were there, Matthews testified, to "threaten sexual acts" while Melgar was tied up. Throughout his testimony, Matthews described the night's events without emotion, often using the language of minimization. The hazing, Matthews said, was "professional remediation." As the plan evolved and became less humorous, it "took more of an operational tone," he said. After the hazing, Matthews said the plan was to "debrief Melgar about his poor performance." When questioned about his efforts to hit on Mrs. Melgar and conceal his identity while describing himself and DeDolph, Matthews acknowledged that he had met her but described the encounter as "unplanned discussions." He denied that he intentionally sought out Michelle Melgar but admitted that he concealed his identity to her after he learned who she was, saying that his chance encounter was part of some higher calling guiding the two to meet. "Her husband had died," Matthews said, "and I felt that there was a purpose to the meeting."[6]

During Matthews's testimony, defense attorneys were able to cast doubt on the charge that Melgar's death was a premeditated murder, as charged. Matthews testified that he instructed DeDolph to seek Melgar's direct superior, Army Special Forces staff sgt. Jamie Morris. Matthews recounted that when they returned from the nightclub, DeDolph woke Morris, who quickly gave his approval for the hazing, and then went back to sleep. The defense also successfully challenged the charge that the cricothyrotomy was conducted to cover up how DeDolph killed Melgar. Although Maxwell testified that he found it strange since there had been no blockage of Melgar's throat, the prosecution had no witnesses or experts to support the charge.

During closing arguments, Madera-Rodriguez's lawyer, Colby Vokey, sought to minimize the events surrounding Melgar's death, saying, "The U.S. government is trying to make a mountain out of a molehill." Phil Stackhouse, DeDolph's lawyer, argued that while Melgar's death was "a horrible, tragic accident," it was only "joking around." Stackhouse conceded that his client had engaged in a cover-up but portrayed DeDolph and Matthews as doing so in an effort to take "responsibility" and protect Maxwell and Madera-Rodriguez. Stackhouse distilled the SEALs' culpability in a conspiracy to obstruct justice and cover up the killing of Melgar as, essentially, a noble act of taking the fall for others who committed the crime. Stackhouse had unknowingly introduced the notion that the Team 6 code—lying to protect a teammate—was an honorable course of action. Whether he meant to or not, DeDolph's attorney had harkened back to the ethos that Cdr. Dick Marcinko had purposefully built into his elite military unit.

The conduct that led to Melgar's death represented the lowest form of behavior during deployment. Melgar was troubled by his teammates soliciting prostitutes, but what drew his ire was that by bringing them back to the embassy compound, DeDolph and others were risking their security. The tension with his teammates grew less from his discovery that they were pocketing money than from the fact that he had refused their offer to bring him in on the theft. But if Melgar's death was a tragic accident, a prank gone wrong, as the SEALs would later claim, then how they conducted themselves afterward also indicted their pathology. At each turn, from the moment Melgar died until they faced court-martial, DeDolph and Matthews, in particular, refused to take responsibility for their conduct. Somehow, neither their training nor their elite military experience provided them with a road map for doing the right thing.

And yet, inside Team 6, there was no introspection. As they had time and again since the days of Marcinko, the leadership sought to downplay any misconduct as aberrant and isolated. DeDolph and Matthews weren't reflective of the command and ethos, SEAL leaders told the Pentagon, civilians, Congress, the media, or anyone else who inquired. The Team 6 command turned their collective back on DeDolph and Matthews, refusing to talk about the case, even internally. The command's leadership wanted to move on, effectively erasing any sign that the two had served in the unit.

"The misbehavior comes in waves, and please, believe me, I'm not being partisan when I say this, the SEALs have a tough time with it," Gen. Bolduc told a reporter. "It always happens in warfare. You always have some of those guys who [are] waiting all their life to show that they're a psychopath or they're trying to impress one another—it's juvenile that they're trying to show how tough they are in a perverted manner."[7]

IN MID-JANUARY 2021, DEDOLPH'S COURT-MARTIAL FINALLY ARrived. The coronavirus pandemic in 2020 and pretrial motions kept delaying the case. The testimony in Maxwell's and Matthews's courts-martial and sentencing made it unlikely that prosecutors could get a conviction for the felony murder charge or manslaughter, the two most serious charges. But it was also clear DeDolph had been most culpable, having led the planning and then asphyxiating Melgar with a choke hold. DeDolph's lawyers successfully argued to suppress Maxwell's testimony about sexually assaulting Melgar as part of the plan. After nearly four years of cover-up, DeDolph agreed to take responsibility for Melgar's death. He decided to plead to involuntary manslaughter, obstruction of justice, hazing, and conspiracy to commit assault. Lt. Cdr. Garcia dropped the murder charges and recommended a reduction from the potential twenty-two-year prison sentence DeDolph faced if convicted by a jury.

DeDolph's lawyer, Phil Stackhouse, submitted character statements from nearly seventy people attesting to his client's courage and heroism on the battlefield. DeDolph was sentenced to ten years in prison, a reduction in rank and pay, and a bad-conduct discharge. He also had to agree never to write a book or otherwise attempt to profit from his story. The requirement was a direct response to the SEALs profiting off their service.

"On multiple occasions," Stackhouse later told the Associated Press, "his actions and heroism and that of three or four other guys with him are going to have a lasting impact on our country. And nobody is going to know what he did."[8]

Stackhouse called one of DeDolph's superiors as a character witness. The retired Team 6 master chief was a legendary operator at the command. He'd served in nearly all the Forever Wars, with at least a dozen combat deployments. He was there to portray DeDolph as a member of Dam Neck's elite tribe. He would testify that DeDolph had been chosen to be part of a small team of SEALs to conduct a sensitive mission. But neither Stackhouse nor his client, the prosecution, or the judge knew that the revered operator had his own troubled past. A few years earlier, the master chief had sent an unsolicited picture of his penis via text message to a Virginia Beach high school student. In the photo, he'd cropped out his face, but his military badge was visible on his pants in the image. The parents of the girl alerted the command and threatened to press charges. For reasons that are unknown, they did not. But the leadership at the command forced the master chief to retire. Having the master chief as DeDolph's character witness recalled what Marcinko had discovered years after he'd retired and served time in prison: having intentionally avoided comprehensive psychological reviews of his selections for Team 6 during its creation, he'd built the command in his own image. "If I was fucked up," Marcinko told me, "then we were all fucked up."[9]

DAM NECK DIDN'T REACT TO DEDOLPH'S CONVICTION AND SENtencing. In the nearly four years since Melgar's death, Team 6 conducted no public reckoning over the case. One retired SEAL leader said the goal was to throw DeDolph and Matthews to the wolves, disown them, and then pretend they'd never been members of their tribe. No one wanted Team 6's culture to be laid bare inside the Norfolk base courtroom. Protect the brand, ignore any dishonor, don't look back, and move on—this was the unmistakable internal message inside the Team 6 community. No one would say that Melgar died because the Team 6 screening failed. DeDolph and Matthews were aberrations, a tiny fraction of the great SEALs who made up the command. Dam Neck is indeed filled with good, moral, courageous SEALs. But it is also true that what qualified DeDolph and Matthews for membership at Dam Neck is what cost Staff Sgt. Logan Melgar his life.

During Staff Sgt. Maxwell's sentencing, Marine Col. Glen Hines, the judge in Maxwell's case, asked what no one else would. As he sifted through the evidence in preparation for sentencing, Col. Hines said that a question began to form in his mind. "If I don't make a few comments about the facts and evidence in this case, I would be derelict in my duty as a military judge." He called it the "How Question." He wasn't asking about the factual "how," he said, "but the overarching question of how something like this can happen in the year 2017." Hines admitted he had no familiarity with the special operations community. The next question, he said, was "Where are the officers? Where were they? Where are any civilians [with] sufficient authority to exert some sort of supervision over our service members who are deployed to a place like Mali?

"The bottom line is that this court-martial is ill-equipped nor is it the appropriate vehicle to answer these questions, but there are entities in the Department of Defense and the United States government who are equipped to investigate these overarching questions and to answer for us: How does this happen in today's age?

"And frankly, the question needs to be answered, because if we don't get to the bottom of it, this is going to happen again at some point in the future."[10]

EPILOGUE

THERE IS NO MOMENT MORE SOLEMN IN THE LIFE OF A SEAL than when he receives his Trident. The American eagle, with its tripartite symbol, which combines an anchor, flintlock pistol, and trident, is pinned to the chest of each graduate of BUD/S. It is worn only by those who have demonstrated the capability to survive their training and operate at the highest level amid the most arduous conditions. Few designations are more coveted within the US military. And few, if any, command as much respect.

But the Trident embodies a contradiction central to the SEALs: we ask these men to do terrible things and do so with the utmost honor. Like so many tasks assigned to the SEALs, this may seem, to outside observers, to be impossible. But it is not. It requires exceptional men capable of exceptional courage—physical and moral. And many of the men I spoke to for this book have demonstrated that. Unfortunately, the Teams haven't fulfilled this ideal. Instead, too many SEALs have taken an easier path, navigating this contradiction through lies, cover-ups, and silence. The command has enabled this—through willful blindness of misdeeds and the use of misdirection through promotions and medals even for those whose conduct has been questioned by many of their peers.

The SEALs are not alone in this active denial. The American public launders this uncomfortable truth through the hero myth of the SEAL. This is perpetuated—and commodified—by the media, publishing, and Hollywood. We celebrate the SEALs' acts of bravery and bask in their victories, but we fail to show the courage to confront the truth—and what it means for our nation each time that emblem is awarded to a new SEAL.

For all the bravery of the Navy SEALs, there has been a consistent lack of moral courage when it comes to facing the truth. In the days and weeks after 9/11, the George W. Bush administration wrote a blank check for a military action that continues twenty years later. In August 2021, President Joseph Biden withdrew the last US troops from Afghanistan, formally ending the war there twenty years after it began. But withdrawing the troops did not end American conflict abroad. Even as the Biden administration withdrew forces from Afghanistan, it made clear that it would shift some of those same resources to nearby countries so that the US military could conduct "over the horizon" counterterrorism operations. "Our troops are not coming home," Rep. Tom Malinowski, Democrat of New Jersey, said at a congressional hearing shortly after the Afghanistan withdrawal. "We need to be honest about that. They are merely moving to other bases in the same region to conduct the same counterterrorism missions, including Afghanistan." The Afghanistan War represents only part of the endless War on Terror. The political decision by the Bush administration to invade Iraq, topple Saddam Hussein's regime, and occupy the country, for example, may represent America's single worst foreign policy decision in its history. Each conflict generates the next. American forces will remain in Syria, Somalia, Mali, Burkina Faso, Niger, Yemen, and the Philippines, where they will potentially be used to conduct lethal operations. The collective toll is not yet over. And yet we have already begun to see the costs of these conflicts.

The American government has portrayed these men as our mightiest warriors. The public has viewed them as the most heroic and brave. But the SEALs themselves, who have been promoted as the best of what the American military has to offer, are aware that they also are casualties of the conflict. Some of their wounds occurred when bullets and bombs hit their bodies on battlefields. Many more lay deeper, developing night after night, deployment after deployment, year after year, when they were sent to kill those deemed America's enemy. The psychological and physical tolls are significant. Nearly every operator who served in these wars exits the military with varying levels of measurable disability. Some have hearing loss, brain injuries, scars, arthritis in their knees, backs, joints; all aged decades due to their service. But many more carry a kind of collective moral injury, a burden that all Americans must share.

Even those who have exploited their service for wealth and celebrity are conscious of these moral injuries. In 2014, after Robert O'Neill separated from the Navy and began a new public speaking career, the former Red Squadron team leader expressed concern for how his men would fare after they finished their service. "All of these guys have killed more people than any criminal in American history," O'Neill said. "I worry about how they are going to handle getting out."

No American servicemen have ever conducted as much war, in such a personal way, as those from SEAL Team 6 and the rest of the forces that make up special operations. There is no precedent in our history, and so we are collectively embarking on a journey where the destination is not clear. And what indications we have so far are not promising.

For the better part of the past five years, when the first SEAL scandals became public—drug abuse, war crime allegations, excessive battlefield drinking, sexual assault, and gun smuggling, to name just a few—the refrain from the Naval Special Warfare community was that they didn't have a problem. Navy SEAL commanders said each case was isolated and didn't reflect a trend or some kind of larger cultural problem. When Matt Bissonnette and Rob O'Neill revealed accounts of the bin Laden raid, the official NSW response was a stern letter to active-duty SEALs that implicitly chided post-service profiteering but did nothing to rebut any lies. When Chris Kyle published *American Sniper*, with misleading, inaccurate, and outright false accounts of his career and service, the response was the same. Even when SEALs violated their own "quiet professional" ethos, the mafia-like culture in the Teams that Marcinko exploited in establishing Team 6 only exacerbated a growing problem. And as in any war, providing oversight, not to mention criticism, of an elite band of warriors—national heroes—is not just unpopular but political suicide.

After Eddie Gallagher was acquitted of the most severe charges in 2019, the commander of Naval Special Warfare, Rear Adm. Collin Green, wrote to his force, saying the SEALs had a "problem." That was the first sincere admission on record, and represented a break, timid as it was, from a decades-long refusal to acknowledge any wrongdoing. While Eddie Gallagher did not represent most Navy SEALs, the SEAL ranks were filled with others like him. It was the same phenomenon that had played out forty years earlier, when SEALs had in their ranks many Eddie Leasures, a consequence of the Vietnam War. Ens. Penney was one casualty. The SEALs were fewer then, their influence in the military and American culture less pervasive. From Fast Eddie Leasure to Fast Eddie Gallagher, SEAL culture had suffered from combat exposure. But by 2020, the effect and consequences threatened the public myth of SEAL integrity and invincibility.

How, then, do we weigh the SEALs' public image against the corrupt and violent acts carried out—and covered up—by SEAL operators and leaders? How do we make sense of men like Marcus Luttrell, Chris Kyle, Matthew Bissonnette, Robert O'Neill, and Britt Slabinski? As much as any member of Team 6, Slabinski typifies the unit's post-9/11 years. Slabinski is a casualty of our Forever Wars and of glaring leadership failures, and emblematic of complete resistance to accountability or reform. The enlisted SEALs of Team 6 committed transgressions and, when potentially exposed, went to great lengths to cover up their conduct. But there is oversight built into the structure of the special forces—and the military more broadly. The enlisted answer to the officers, the officers answer to civilians, civilians answer to Congress, and Congress answers to American citizens. It is with ordinary American citizens, then, that the responsibility ultimately rests.

There have been very few reform efforts, if any, and the ones that may have happened have not been made public, a surprising outcome given all the books about leadership and character written by the SEALs themselves. Given my decade of reporting on the SEALs, I know just how entrenched the problems are. But I also know that change is possible, and what it might look like. The culture and code of silence and deceit can be eradicated, but it requires, ultimately, that the SEALs face what they already know to be true about what has occurred in Afghanistan, Iraq, Somalia, Yemen, and beyond, and admit they betrayed their duty to their country.

One place to look for an accountability blueprint for addressing the SEALs' transgressive code is in Australia. In November 2020, the Australian Defence Force released an inspector general's report on alleged war crimes committed by Australia's special forces in Afghanistan over eleven years, ending in 2016. The report detailed allegations of thirty-nine unlawful killings as well as incidents of prisoner abuse. In most of the unjustified killings, the Afghan victim was unarmed, and the majority of the victims were in Australian custody when they were killed. Nineteen Australian commandos were identified as being directly involved or complicit in war crimes. The report traced a culture of impunity, violations of the laws of war, and cover-ups. All the incidents involved the Special Air Service Regiment (SASR), the Australian equivalent of Team 6, or a sister special operations unit. The author, Maj. Gen. Paul Brereton, described one alleged war crime, which was redacted in the public version, as "possibly the most disgraceful episode in Australia's military history."[1] The report was thorough and largely accepted as accurate by the military brass as well as by the public.

The origins of the inquiry came from a study conducted by a civilian sociologist, Dr. Samantha Crompvoets, who surveyed the special forces community for the head of the command, Maj. Gen. Jeff Sengelman. Dr. Crompvoets looked at the sociology and cultural traits of special forces, conducting dozens of interviews with current and retired soldiers. In her study, the soldiers began to casually disclose witnessing or participating in war crimes, including murder and torture of detainees. After completing and submitting her report, Dr. Crompvoets shared what she heard in her interviews with Sengelman, who was by then serving as the Australian Army chief of staff. She understood that what she heard likely reflected just a small part of the problem. The inspector general report released in 2020 was the result of Dr. Crompvoets's recommendation. And while the media covered the report extensively, neither Australian politicians nor the public have called for any wholesale reforms.

Overall, the Australian report placed the responsibility on the enlisted soldiers at the tactical and battlefield level in the 2nd Commando Regiment, the Australian equivalent of Army Rangers. But the assessment of officers in SASR was different. Recognizing that officers in the premier commando unit are too well trained not to understand how the unit's ethos could end up creating a culture for war crimes, the report was more damning of the SASR commanding officers. The officers, the report said, "bear significant responsibility for contributing to the environment in which war crimes were committed, most notably those who embraced or fostered the 'warrior culture' and empowered, or did not restrain, the clique of noncommissioned officers who propagated it. That responsibility is to some extent shared by those who, in misconceived loyalty to their Regiment, or their mates, have now been prepared to 'call out' criminal conduct or, even to this day, decline to accept that it occurred in the face of incontrovertible evidence, or seek to offer obscure and unconvincing justifications and mitigations for it."[2]

The report recommended that the nineteen commandos identified in the investigation, all of whom appear to be enlisted, be referred for possible criminal prosecution for murder.[3] In the fallout, thirteen of the soldiers were issued notices that they were likely to be discharged. The report also recommended that the military revoke a meritorious unit award that had been given at the conclusion of several of the deployments.

The report—and the fact that it was made public—was significant. News reports about some of the alleged war crimes in the report also helped the public understand how broken their elite military commandos' moral compasses had become. One video of an operation in Afghanistan showed an Australian soldier executing an unarmed and compliant Afghan man for no reason other than to kill. As shown in the video taken by a teammate on the mission, the shooting was an unambiguous murder.

There were few in Australia who defended the incident, but that didn't remain true when the inspector general's report made recommendations for accountability. One was that that unit be stripped of any collective military awards they'd received from any deployment during which war crimes were committed. The report did not suggest that the majority of commandos who did not behave illegally or dishonorably deserved to be punished along with those who did, but rather that the military could not in good conscience issue a unit award for meritorious conduct when part of the unit had committed war crimes. Don't punish the group for a few bad apples, the military and its public supporters argued in response. And in 2021, the Australian Defence Force rejected the recommendation.

If replicated by the US Department of Defense, and actually carried out, a similar process would mean an independent investigation into Naval Special Warfare and SEAL Team 6, perhaps reporting the findings to congressional committees that oversee the military. Investigators would likely have to offer immunity in order to induce SEAL cooperation, and the investigation could serve as an informal truth-and-reconciliation commission for SEAL crimes. A final report would need to make substantial recommendations to both the Defense Department and Congress about potential consequences of the findings as well as reforms. What is certain is that without Congress's involvement, either through oversight or administering the investigation itself, there will be no chance of reform.

To date, the US military has not chosen to follow the Australian example. In the fallout of the SEAL scandals, which were frequently and widely covered by the US media, Congress required the Special Operations Command to conduct ethics training, accountability, and culture reviews in 2018 and 2019. In 2020, SOCOM determined that the recommendations from the previous studies had not been incorporated. That report, too, found that ethics were no problem in their units, including the Navy SEALs.

Days after President Joseph Biden's inauguration, the Defense Department's inspector general announced in an internal department memo that it would conduct a review regarding how the Special Operations Command had implemented the department's laws of war regulations and whether possible war crimes were reported or investigated as required. The independent review will cover both special operations forces, such as the Navy SEALs and Army Green Berets, but also the geographic command that oversees where most special operations have conducted their operations since 9/11.

The SEALs have struggled to maintain their image, especially after the Eddie Gallagher and Logan Melgar cases. When Adm. Green stepped down as the Naval Special Warfare commander, the Navy sought to replace him with an admiral who would clean up the Teams, a mandate from both the Navy's civilian leadership and Congress. The Navy, unfortunately, still faced a fundamental problem. How could the SEALs correct their course, fix their ethical corruption, if three of the most senior SEAL admirals were themselves party to or responsible for so many of the past twenty years' misconduct? By the time of this writing, that was the position of the Navy SEALs.

On September 11, 2020, Rear Adm. H. Wyman Howard III was sworn in as the new commanding officer for the three thousand Navy SEALs. In the years since he'd led Team 6 as a captain, Howard had served in the Pentagon, JSOC, and then a tour as the commanding officer of the Special Operations Command Central. With a mandate to rehabilitate the SEALs, the two-star admiral who had once shown off a bloodied hatchet after an operation and advised his peers to "protect the brand" had been given the task of holding the SEALs accountable. It was unclear how committed Howard would be to reforming the force's culture. A few months after he took over in Coronado, after Joseph Biden won the 2020 presidential election, Adm. Howard set his sights on a different job. During the transition, Michèle Flournoy, the former undersecretary of defense for policy in the Obama administration, became Biden's leading candidate for defense secretary. Flournoy agreed to make Howard her military assistant, a position that would ensure he would earn a third star.

The move evaporated when Biden nominated Gen. Lloyd J. Austin III instead.

Howard remains at the helm of the SEALs; in his first seven months as commander, he cut the number of SEAL platoons while expanding the number of SEALs in each platoon. The administrative move is meant to reduce the overall number of Navy SEALs, in the hope that by reducing quantity, he can increase the quality of SEALs in the service.

Given the promotions and career achievements of the SEAL leaders who've failed to check the excessive violence, there is significant doubt about whether anything will change in the Teams without significant pressure from Congress.

In March 2021, the Navy issued Adm. Peter Vasely his second star. The former Blue Squadron commander, who witnessed one of his men trying to behead an enemy casualty in Afghanistan, was also assigned to lead the Special Operations Command task force in Afghanistan. In August 2021, Rear Adm. Vasely led US forces as they conducted their final withdrawal from Afghanistan.

As a three-star, Vice Adm. Timothy Szymanski was the highest-ranking Navy SEAL in the spring of 2021. Szymanski serves as the deputy commander of the Special Operations Command, a powerful position that could help him earn a fourth star. Neither Howard, Vasely, nor Szymanski answered questions or commented on details related to the events in this book.

THERE IS REASON TO BE HOPEFUL, HOWEVER, ABOUT BRINGING AN end to the SEAL code of silence and corruption. One distinctive and seemingly incompatible Team 6 characteristic is that in their team dynamic, the SEALs withhold virtually nothing among themselves. Their team room is their ultimate safe space, a place where honesty is not only consistent but prevalent. It is from these SEALs that I gathered this account. In their reality, the reporting in the preceding pages includes some of the worst-kept secrets among the Navy SEALs and Team 6. These SEALs spoke because they were frustrated, disheartened, and disillusioned with Naval Special Warfare. These accounts, in a sense, are theirs: the reality of what they did, saw, and knew while dedicating themselves to uphold American values and protect the Constitution. They represent the most patriotic among their peers precisely because they seek accountability and reform in their community.

Some will decry public accountability as a form of second-guessing our warriors, but nothing could be further from the truth. Democracy and freedom are founded on an informed public, on vigorous public debate, and on the accountability of our government institutions, which serve the nation. This is true whether it is the president who lies for political gain, or an enlisted SEAL who lies for financial profit. If the American public truly cares about the fate of the men who have shouldered too much of our national burden—knowing what they did, what they went through, and how they continue to pay for their service—then it is critical that citizens demand accountability. Americans who celebrate the heroics of SEAL Team 6 must also understand the costs of their exploits.

Only then will the military have the mandate to fix the SEALs and create a unit that is as righteous and honorable as it is effective.

ACKNOWLEDGMENTS

An investigative reporter is only as good as their sources, and I hope to repay the time and energy my sources provided to me. It is impossible to name or even describe those who have helped on a book of this kind, so I can only say thank you to them. You have done a great service with your courage and efforts to address a grave problem in the military. There is honor in anonymity.

This book grew out of a fourteen-thousand-word article for *The Intercept*. It is not hyperbolic to say that, at the time, *The Intercept* was one of the few news organizations that would devote the time and resources to such a project. I am grateful to Betsy Reed, *The Intercept*'s editor in chief; Roger Hodge, who, as my editor, worked with me from its inception and made it better than I could have imagined; Jeremy Scahill, my friend and colleague, who convinced me to join *The Intercept* and then worked to make the story better; John Thomason, who fact-checked the story; and Lynn Oberlander, then *The Intercept*'s general counsel. *The Intercept* is a vital news organization, and I am lucky to work there. Please consider becoming a donor.

I also want to thank previous editors and friends who have either directly or indirectly helped or encouraged my pursuit of this story and others like it. They are Richard Esposito, Mark Schone, Sharon Weinberger, Vanessa Gezari, Dan Schilling, Jim Risen, and Seymour Hersh, in no particular order.

This book would not have been possible without Alessandra Bastagli, who first acquired it for what was then called Nation Books. I am forever grateful for her taking a chance on a new author. Katy O'Donnell edited this book with diligence, grace, and a sharp eye for all my flaws as a writer and reporter. She was patient with a slow author, and always encouraging, which lifted me when lifting was what I needed. I hope we work together in the future. Hillary Brenhouse joined Bold Type Books as I was finishing my draft but has been nothing but a supportive and enthusiastic editorial director. Bold Type is in good hands. Clive Priddle, my publisher, has supported this book, and me, for reasons I still do not understand. I am grateful nonetheless. The Hachette team was fantastic: Julie Ford provided excellent insight and legal advice; Yemile Bucay and Sara Krolewski, who fact-checked the book, did a great job; Melissa Veronesi, Susan Van-Hecke, and the Hachette production team have been great. They have my gratitude for managing the publishing with great skill and patience.

I am glad that I have Eric Lupfer as a literary agent. He is a sharp mind, a skilled editor, and, to my great fortune, capable of fixing problems ranging from publishing complications to framing a book. Doing so as well as he does is a difficult feat, but he does it with confidence, affability, and talent.

All four of my parents—Sheila McMackin, Steve Cole, Patricia Stahl, and Dr. Steven Fox—deserve both thanks and acknowledgment for forty-plus years of encouragement, support, love, and, most important, a passion for learning and inquisition. I was a reporter well before I understood, and my parents (and theirs) are the reason. Neither this book nor my career would have been possible without the support of my entire family, which came to include Ellen and Scott Hand. I am fortunate to call them my mother- and father-in-law. They generously made their home available for me to use as a space in which to write this book. In normal times, that is kind. During a pandemic, it is a godsend and gift, which I can never fully repay.

Every writer and journalist has one friend on whom they rely for all things big and small, and without whom a book cannot be written or sanity preserved. For me, that friend is Johnny Dwyer. Johnny helped with this book from inception until the very end. He made this book immeasurably better, and if it is any good at all, it is because of his contribution. He is a phenomenal writer and reporter in his own right, an author of two incredible works of journalism. He is a wonderful human being. That is a rare combination of qualities, and I am lucky that he is such a good friend.

While I am proud of this work, it did come at a great cost to those I love most. My children, Jackson, June, Clara, and my wife, Lizzie, were left to navigate many weeks with little or no sign of me, a burden that has consequences. I am grateful that despite my absence, they all still love me and support my work. This is not a book for them now, but I hope my children will read it when they grow up to understand what their father was trying to accomplish. I hope then that they will be proud. Lizzie, my wife of thirteen years, sacrificed the most. She had to carry the most weight, shouldering an unfair burden while I wrote. She held our family together during a pandemic, and no work of journalism measures up to that accomplishment. It is to her, the love of my life, that I dedicate this book. Without her, it would not have been possible. Thank you.

NOTES

PROLOGUE

1. "Pres. Donald Trump Presents the Medal of Honor," ABC News, video streamed live on May 24, 2018, https://youtu.be/whZygwtSL6M.

2. "Master Chief Special Warfare Operator (SEAL) Britt K. Slabinski," US Navy, www.navy.mil/MEDAL-OF-HONOR-RECIPIENT-BRITT-K-SLABINSKI/.

CHAPTER I

1. James R. Stockman, *Marines in World War II: Historical Monograph: The Battle for Tarawa* (Pickle Partners, [1947] 2013), 57, www.scribd.com/read/259892797/Marines-In-World-War-II-The-Battle-For-Tarawa-Illustrated-Edition#__search-menu_109709.

2. Francis D. Fane and Don Moore, *Naked Warriors: The Story of the U.S. Navy Frogmen* (New York: St. Martin's Paperbacks, 1996), 8.

3. Fane and Moore, 8.

4. "SEAL History: Origins of Naval Special Warfare—WWII," Navy SEAL Museum, www.navysealmuseum.org/about-navy-seals/seal-history-the-naval-special-warfare-storyseal-history-the-naval-special-warfare-story/seal-history-origins-of-naval-special-warfare-wwii.

5. Elizabeth K. Bush, *America's First Frogman: The Draper Kauffman Story* (Annapolis, MD: Naval Institute Press, 2004), 87.

6. Fane and Moore, *Naked Warriors*, 87.

7. In a tradition of two fleets for two oceans, the Navy assigned the NCDU to the European theater of the war, while the UDTs were sent to the Pacific. After the war, Naval Special Warfare would combine the two into UDT.

8. Orr Kelly, *Brave Men, Dark Waters: The Untold Story of the Navy SEALs* (New York: Open Road, 2014), 27.

9. Fane and Moore, *Naked Warriors*, 95.

10. Roy Boehm and Charles W. Sasser, *First SEAL* (New York: Atria, 1997), 79.

11. Boehm and Sasser, *First SEAL*, 76.

12. Kelly, *Brave Men, Dark Waters*, 23.

13. William H. Hamilton Jr. and Charles W. Sasser, *Night Fighter: An Insider's Story of Special Ops from Korea to SEAL Team 6* (New York: Arcade, 2016), loc. 544, Kindle; Fane and Moore, 8.

14. Boehm and Sasser, *First SEAL*, loc. 101.

15. Hamilton and Sasser, *Night Fighter*, loc. 162.

16. Hamilton and Sasser, loc. 161.

17. "President Kennedy's Special Message to the Congress on Urgent National Needs, May 25, 1961," John F. Kennedy Presidential Library and Museum, www .jfklibrary.org/archives/other-resources/john-f-kennedy-speeches/united-states -congress-special-message-19610525.

Later, JFK would describe this new warfare for which he wanted a new breed of soldier: "This is another type of war, new in its intensity, ancient in its origin—war by guerrillas, subversives, insurgents, assassins, war by ambush instead of by combat; by infiltration, instead of aggression, seeking victory by eroding and exhausting the enemy instead of engaging him. It is a form of warfare uniquely adapted to what has been strangely called 'wars of liberation,' to undermine the efforts of new and poor countries to maintain the freedom that they have finally achieved. It preys on economic unrest and ethnic conflicts. It requires in those situations where we must counter it, and these are the kinds of challenges that will be before us in the next decade if freedom is to be saved, a whole new kind of strategy, a wholly different kind of force, and therefore a new and wholly different kind of military training." "June 6, 1962: Remarks at West Point," Presidential Speeches, Miller Center, University of Virginia, https://millercenter.org /the-presidency/presidential-speeches/june-6-1962-remarks-west-point.

18. Hamilton and Sasser, *Night Fighter*, loc. 1849.

19. Craig Whitney, "Navy's 'Seals,' Super-Secret Commandos, Are Quitting Vietnam," *New York Times*, November 29, 1971.

20. Kelly, *Brave Men, Dark Waters*, 146.

21. Robert A. Gormly, *Combat Swimmer: Memoirs of a Navy SEAL* (New York: Onyx, 1999), 153.

CHAPTER 2

1. Rebecca Grant, "The Crucible of Vietnam," *Air Force*, February 2013, www .airforcemag.com/PDF/MagazineArchive/Documents/2013/February%202013 /0213vietnam.pdf.

2. Author interview with Rebecca Penney.

3. Author interview with BUD/S classmate of Ens. Penney and former member of UDT-21.

4. Author interview with retired SEAL officer.

5. Author interview with a second BUD/S classmate of Penney.

6. Author interview with a third BUD/S classmate of Penney.

7. John Carl Roat, *Class-29: The Making of U.S. Navy SEALs* (New York: Random House, 2008), 53.

8. Author interview with Richard Marcinko.

9. Author interview with Richard Marcinko.

10. According to interviews with a half-dozen members of UDT-21.

11. Leasure's hazing of Ens. Penney, who was ultimately the victim of a sexual assault, was confirmed by several former UDT-21 operators, in addition to a close teammate of Leasure at the time.

12. Email to the author from Maura Beard, September 2019.

CHAPTER 3

1. William G. Boykin with Lynn Vincent, *Never Surrender: A Soldier's Journey to the Crossroads of Faith and Freedom* (New York: FaithWords, 2008), 120.

2. Boykin with Vincent, 110.

3. Richard Marcinko with John Weisman, *Rogue Warrior* (New York: Pocket, 1992).

4. Marcinko with Weisman, 33–37.

5. Timothy L. Bosiljevac, "The Teams in 'Nam: U.S. Navy UDT/SEAL Operations of the Vietnam War" (master's thesis, Emporia State University, 1987), 20.

6. Marcinko with Weisman, *Rogue Warrior*.

7. William H. Hamilton Jr. and Charles W. Sasser, *Night Fighter: An Insider's Story of Special Ops from Korea to SEAL Team 6* (New York: Arcade, 2016), loc. 344, Kindle.

8. Marcinko with Weisman, *Rogue Warrior*, 234.

9. Marcinko with Weisman, 205.

10. Author interview with Richard Marcinko.

11. Author interview with Dr. Michael Whitley, 2020.

12. Author interview with Richard Marcinko.

13. Orr Kelly, *Brave Men, Dark Waters: The Untold Story of the Navy SEALs* (New York: Open Road, 2014), 214.

14. Interview with the author.

15. Email with the author.

16. William H. McRaven, *Sea Stories: My Life in Special Operations* (New York: Grand Central, 2019), 127.

17. Marcinko with Weisman, *Rogue Warrior*, 321.

18. Robert A. Gormly, *Combat Swimmer: Memoirs of a Navy SEAL* (New York: Onyx, 1999), 174.

19. Gormly, 176.

20. Gormly, 176.

CHAPTER 4

1. Author interview with SEAL Team 6 operator.

2. Richard Marcinko with John Weisman, *Rogue Warrior* (New York: Pocket, 1992), 332.

3. For much of the Sheridan account, I relied on the reporting in both *Soldier of Fortune* magazine and the *Los Angeles Times*.

4. Dale Andrade, "SEALS' Top Secret II," *Soldier of Fortune*, June 1995.

5. Martha L. Willman, "Navy Weapons Base Guard, Wife Recall 30 Hours of Terror," *Los Angeles Times*, March 28, 1987.

6. Dale Andrade, "SEALS' Top Secret III," *Soldier of Fortune*, July 1995.

7. Author interview with Ralph Blincoe, 2019.

8. Author interview with anonymous Navy investigator.

9. Robert A. Gormly, *Combat Swimmer: Memoirs of a Navy SEAL* (New York: Onyx, 1999), 233.

10. Author interview with Bailey.

11. *POG*, pronounced "pogue," is derisive military slang for Person Other than a Grunt, and means nonfighting military personnel, usually assigned to a rear-element or safe headquarters position.

CHAPTER 5

1. Mark Owen [Matthew Bissonnette] with Kevin Maurer, *No Hero: The Evolution of a Navy SEAL* (New York: Dutton, 2014).

2. Author interview with a retired SEAL Team 6 officer.

3. Dick Couch, *A Tactical Ethic: Moral Conduct in the Insurgent Battlespace* (Annapolis, MD: Naval Institute Press), 91.

4. According to Dieter's wife and a longtime SEAL Team 6 operator who heard it from Dieter the next day.

5. Author interview with Dieter, 2020.

6. United Nations International Criminal Tribunal for the Former Yugoslavia, "Jelisic Case: Goran Jelisic Acquitted of Genocide and Found Guilty of Crimes Against Humanity and Violations of Laws or Customs of War," press release, October 19, 1999, www.icty.org/en/press/jelisic-case-goran-jelisic-acquitted-genocide-and-found-guilty-crimes-against-humanity-and; "The Tribunal Remembers: Brčko—May 1992," International Criminal Tribunal for the Former Yugoslavia (ICTY), video, May 9, 2016, https://youtu.be/Baa_IQBk-gc.

CHAPTER 6

1. Donald H. Rumsfeld, "A New Kind of War," *New York Times*, September 27, 2001.

2. *Fiscal Year 2001 Department of Defense Overview*, US Department of Defense, Office of the Under Secretary of Defense (Comptroller), https://comptroller.defense.gov/Portals/45/documents/cfs/fy2001/04_Overview-Agency-Wide-FY2001.pdf.

3. Rowan Scarborough, *Rumsfeld's War: The Untold Story of America's Anti-Terrorist Commander* (Washington, DC: Regnery, 2004), loc. 330, Kindle.

4. Dan Schilling and Lori Chapman Longfritz, *Alone at Dawn: Medal of Honor Recipient John Chapman and the Untold Story of the World's Deadliest Special Operations Force* (New York: Grand Central, 2019).

5. This command dynamic is addressed at length in three books about Operation Anaconda: Schilling and Longfritz, *Alone at Dawn*; Sean Naylor, *Not a Good Day to Die: Chaos and Courage in the Mountains of Afghanistan* (New York: Berkley, 2005); and Malcolm MacPherson, *Roberts Ridge: A Story of Courage and Sacrifice on Takur Ghar Mountain, Afghanistan* (New York: Delacorte, 2005).

6. The existence of Kernan and Szymanski's request to Mako 31, and the team's response, including the text of their message, is found in Schilling and Longfritz, *Alone at Dawn*, 195–196.

7. Schilling and Longfritz, 196.

8. Slabinski interview with Malcolm MacPherson obtained by the author.

9. Slabinski interview with Malcolm MacPherson obtained by the author.

10. Slabinski interview with Malcolm MacPherson obtained by the author.

11. According to audio and video footage from AC-130 obtained by the author.

12. According to Jay Hill's sworn witness statement obtained by the author.

13. Chapman's autopsy obtained by the author, and Schilling and Longfritz, *Alone at Dawn*, 260.

14. According to a special operator who witnessed the remarks.

CHAPTER 7

1. According to a retired SEAL, a special operations veteran, and a senior enlisted Air Force source.

2. According to multiple Red Team members who served with Hyder.

3. Unpublished interview of Slabinski by Malcolm MacPherson obtained by the author.

4. According to a witness.

CHAPTER 8

1. "'Lone Survivor' SEAL Recounts Deadly Battle," *CBS This Morning*, video, December 9, 2013, https://youtu.be/FTuf5PRnbFg.

CHAPTER 9

1. Stanley McChrystal, *My Share of the Task: A Memoir* (New York: Portfolio, 2013), 92.

2. The origin of the Winkler tomahawks into Delta comes from the author's interviews with a Delta C Squadron member and several members of SEAL Team 6.

3. According to a former C Squadron operator and a former member of SEAL Team 6.

4. According to multiple former Team 6 SEALs.

5. According to two former SEAL Team 6 leaders briefed on the incident.

6. *Anderson Cooper 360°*, April 17, 2006.

7. According to two senior SEAL Team 6 leaders at the time.

8. Dick Couch, *The Sheriff of Ramadi: Navy SEALs and the Winning of al-Anbar* (Annapolis, MD: Naval Institute Press, 2008), 123.

9. When Foreman denied the account his former superiors provided me, he was an employee of Matbok, a military equipment manufacturer. Their products, which Foreman helps design, have been purchased by the Navy SEALs and the Special Operations Command.

CHAPTER 10

1. George Robert Elford, *Devil's Guard* (New York: Dell, 1971), 108–109.

2. Justin K. Sheffield, *Mob VI: A SEAL Team Six Operator's Battles in the Fight for Good over Evil* (Conroe, TX: Defiance, 2020), 69.

3. According to three retired SEAL Team 6 leaders.

4. According to a former SEAL with direct knowledge and confirmed by a second Team 6 leader.

5. According to a former SEAL leader.

6. According to three retired SEAL Team 6 leaders.

7. According to three former SEAL Team 6 leaders.

8. According to a summary of the subsequent NCIS investigation.

9. According to a retired SEAL Team 6 leader.

10. According to two retired SEAL Team 6 leaders.

11. According to two retired SEAL Team 6 leaders.

12. According to a summary of an NCIS document provided by a Navy official.

13. According to three former SEAL Team 6 leaders with knowledge of the subsequent 2010 inquiries.

14. Sheffield, *Mob VI*, 139.

15. Mike Ritland and Eddie Penney, "Eddie Penney," February 1, 2019, *Mike Drop*, podcast, https://youtu.be/7yByshNvc4E, 66:16.

16. Ritland and Penney, 00:49.

17. Motoko Rich, "He Lived to Tell the Tale (and Write a Best Seller)," *New York Times*, August 9, 2007.

18. Marcus Luttrell with Patrick Robinson, *Lone Survivor: The Eyewitness Account of Operation Redwing and the Lost Heroes of SEAL Team 10* (New York: Little, Brown, 2007), 166–168.

19. Luttrell with Robinson, 176.

20. Luttrell with Robinson, 209.

21. Luttrell with Robinson, 227.

22. Luttrell with Robinson, 219.

23. James Gordon Meek, "Afghanistan Reports Posted on WikiLeaks Include Details of L.I. Navy SEAL Michael Murphy's Death," *New York Daily News*, July 27, 2011.

24. "Lieutenant Michael P. Murphy (SEAL)," US Navy, www.navy.mil /MEDAL-OF-HONOR-RECIPIENT-MICHAEL-P-MURPHY/.

25. According to several former senior SEAL Team 6 leaders.

26. According to a former SEAL Team 6 leader.

27. According to three people with direct knowledge.

28. According to two retired SEAL Team 6 leaders.

29. According to a retired SEAL Team 6 leader with direct knowledge.

30. The former senior enlisted leader's efforts were confirmed by a second SEAL Team 6 leader.

CHAPTER 11

1. According to a SEAL Team 6 operator who took part in the rescue.

2. According to multiple SEAL Team 6 sources.

3. Adam Goldman, "3 Shots, 3 Kills? SEALs Rescue in 2009 Not So Tidy," Associated Press, October 11, 2013.

4. All quotes in the Norgrove section come from witness testimony released as part of a CENTCOM investigation into the operation. The investigation was subsequently released by the Department of Defense, with redactions. Although all the SEALs' names are redacted, the documents refer to their position or rank; with the author's sources, each individual quoted was able to be identified.

5. Sean Naylor, *Not a Good Day to Die: Chaos and Courage in the Mountains of Afghanistan* (New York: Berkley, 2005), 372.

6. According to two retired SEAL Team 6 officers.

7. According to two retired SEAL Team 6 officers.

8. Gen. Joseph Votel, "Investigation Findings and Recommendations," November 9, 2010, Encl. B, p. 18.

9. According to the three SEAL Team 6 veterans, including two who were present for the mast.

10. According to multiple SEAL Team 6 sources.

11. Matthew Cole, "The Crimes of SEAL Team 6," *The Intercept*, January 10, 2017, https://theintercept.com/2017/01/10/the-crimes-of-seal-team-6/.

12. Mark Mazzetti, Nicholas Kulich, Christopher Drew, Serge F. Kovalevski, Sean D. Naylor, and John Ismay, "SEAL Team 6: A Secret History of Quiet Killings and Blurred Lines," *New York Times*, June 6, 2015, www.nytimes.com/2015/06/07 /world/asia/the-secret-history-of-seal-team-6.html.

13. According to a SEAL Team 6 leader.

14. Mazzetti et al., "SEAL Team 6."

15. Cole, "The Crimes of SEAL Team 6."

16. According to three Team 6 sources, including one who took part in the mission.

17. According to several former members of SEAL Team 6, including one with direct knowledge.

18. Mazzetti et al., "SEAL Team 6."

CHAPTER 12

1. According to multiple SEAL Team 6 sources.
2. According to a Team 6 operator and special operations source.
3. According to a Team 6 operator and special operations source.
4. According to three Team 6 SEALs and a special operations source.
5. According to three Team 6 SEALs and a special operations source.
6. According to three Team 6 SEALs and a special operations source.
7. According to two former SEAL Team 6 operators and a special operations source.
8. According to a Team 6 operator and special operations source.
9. According to a Team 6 SEAL who was present.

CHAPTER 13

1. Much of this account, and all the quotations, come from depositions of Matthew Bissonnette, Elyse Cheney, Ben Sevier, and Robert Luskin in Bissonnette's malpractice lawsuit against attorney Kevin Podlaski.
2. Bissonnette deposition, November 16, 2016.
3. Sevier deposition, January 6, 2017.
4. Chris Kyle with Scott McEwen and Jim DeFelice, *American Sniper: The Autobiography of the Most Lethal Sniper in U.S. Military History* (New York: HarperCollins, 2013), 4.
5. Kyle with McEwen and DeFelice, 86.
6. Kyle with McEwen and DeFelice, 4.
7. Kyle with McEwen and DeFelice, 5.
8. James Hatch and Christian D'Andrea, *Touching the Dragon: And Other Techniques for Surviving Life's Wars* (New York: Knopf, 2018), 323.
9. Hatch and D'Andrea, 86.
10. Kyle with McEwen and DeFelice, *American Sniper*, 244.
11. Kyle with McEwen and DeFelice, 298.
12. Email between Kyle and Willink obtained by the author.
13. *CBS This Morning*, February 8, 2012.
14. Rebecca Keegan, "'Act of Valor' Must Balance Publicity, Secrecy with Navy SEALs," *Los Angeles Times*, February 12, 2012, www.latimes.com/entertainment/la-xpm-2012-feb-12-la-ca-act-of-valor-20120212-story.html.
15. Daniel Klaidman, "For Navy SEALs, the Biggest Threat May Be Hollywood," *Newsweek*, November 5, 2012.
16. Julie Bosman, "A Wave of Military Memoirs with You-Are-There Appeal," *New York Times*, March 19, 2012, www.nytimes.com/2012/03/19/books/new-military-memoirs-find-an-audience.html.
17. Bosman, "A Wave of Military Memoirs."
18. "SEAL's First-Hand Account of Bin Laden Killing," *60 Minutes*, September 24, 2012, www.cbsnews.com/news/seals-first-hand-account-of-bin-laden-killing/.
19. Witness interview with the author.

20. "TSNN Top 250 Dashboard," Trade Show News Network, www.tsnn.com /index.php/tsnn-top-250-dashboard.

21. According to a former senior member of SEAL Team 6 with direct knowledge of Rose's allegations.

22. *Bissonnette v. Podlaski*, Case No. 1:15-cv-00334-SLC (Northern District of Indiana, Fort Wayne Division, June 5, 2018).

23. According to a retired Navy SEAL officer.

CHAPTER 14

1. "Vice President Joe Biden's Remarks at the 2012 Democratic National Convention—Full Speech," Obama for America, https://youtu.be/rszJuCDqxEw, 23:22.

2. Maureen Dowd, "Who's Tough Enough?," *New York Times*, January 31, 2012, www.nytimes.com/2012/02/01/opinion/dowd-whos-tough-enough.html.

3. Phil Bronstein, "The Man Who Killed Osama bin Laden…Is Screwed," *Esquire*, February 11, 2013, www.esquire.com/news-politics/a26351/man-who-shot -osama-bin-laden-0313/.

4. "Survivor," *60 Minutes*, December 8, 2013.

5. Jose A. Del Real, "Sorrow and Scrutiny After a Teenager's Death at Football Practice," *New York Times*, August 18, 2017, www.nytimes.com/2017/08/18 /nyregion/joshua-mileto-funeral-long-island.html.

6. Forrest S. Crowell, "Navy SEALs Gone Wild: Publicity, Fame, and the Loss of the Quiet Professional" (master's thesis, Naval Postgraduate School, 2015), v, https://calhoun.nps.edu/handle/10945/47927.

7. Crowell, 2.

8. Crowell, 52.

9. According to two retired SEAL Team 6 leaders.

CHAPTER 15

1. Sean D. Naylor and Christopher Drew, "SEAL Team 6 and a Man Left for Dead: A Grainy Picture of Valor," *New York Times*, August 27, 2016, www .nytimes.com/2016/08/28/world/asia/seal-team-6-afghanistan-man-left-for-dead .html. This chapter is the result of a combination of sources, some on the record, some not, as well as primary source documents, including audio and video.

2. Unpublished audio interview of Slabinski obtained by the author.

3. According to two retired special operations personnel and confirmed by documents obtained by the author.

4. According to 2019 email Hartwell wrote obtained by the author.

5. According to two senior special operations personnel with knowledge of the September 2016 meeting.

6. According to a former senior enlisted special operator who discussed the Szymanski confrontation with Webb shortly after it occurred, and confirmed by a retired special operations officer.

7. Author interview with SEAL Team 6 officer.

8. Author interview with retired SEAL Team 6 leader.

9. Sean D. Naylor, "The Navy SEALs Allegedly Left Behind a Man in Afghanistan. Did They Also Try to Block His Medal of Honor?," *Newsweek*, May 7, 2018, www.newsweek.com/2018/05/18/navy-seals-seal-team-6-left-behind-die-operation-anaconda-slabinski-chapman-912343.html.

10. Slabinski statement for Chapman Service Cross package, September 9, 2002, obtained by the author.

11. Interview with the author.

12. According to a senior Pentagon official and retired special operations source.

13. According to notes of Dunford's statements provided by a source.

14. Interview with the author.

15. Interview with the author.

CHAPTER 16

1. Dan Lamothe and Brad Wolverton, "Sex, Alcohol and Violence Collide in Murder Case Ensnaring SEALs and Marines," *Washington Post*, April 16, 2019, www.washingtonpost.com/world/national-security/sex-alcohol-and-violence-collided-in-murder-case-ensnaring-seals-and-marines/2019/04/16/201404d4-57dd-11e9-8ef3-fbd41a2ce4d5_story.html.

2. Kevin Maurer, "Slain Green Beret Widow Speaks: 'I Knew They Were Lying,'" *Daily Beast*, June 25, 2019, www.thedailybeast.com/green-beret-logan-melgars-widow-speaks-about-mali-case-i-knew-they-were-lying.

3. "Mrs. Melgar," July 3, 2019, episode 48, *SOF Bad Monkey*, podcast.

4. Kevin Maurer, "Navy SEAL Promoted After Choking Green Beret to Death," *Daily Beast*, January 28, 2020, www.thedailybeast.com/navy-seal-tony-dedolph-was-promoted-after-choking-green-beret-logan-melgar-to-death.

CHAPTER 17

1. Special Warfare Operator 1st Class Dylan Dille's testimony during the Gallagher court-martial, June 19, 2019.

2. For this account, I relied on a combination of news sources. One journalist's reporting led the coverage, Dave Philipps of the *New York Times*. In reconstructing parts of this account, I also relied on his excellent book, *Alpha: Eddie Gallagher and the War for the Soul of the Navy SEALs* (New York: Crown, 2021). I also interviewed two of Gallagher's SEAL teammates who served with him at Team 7 in 2017, both of whom also had Gallagher as their BUD/S instructor years earlier. These SEALs confirmed many of the details that had been widely reported both before and after Gallagher's court-martial, including what they told NCIS investigators. The quotes all derive from NCIS files of the investigation that I did not have direct access to. In those cases, I again relied on Philipps's *Alpha*, which I recommend for any reader who is interested in learning more about the 2017 Mosul deployment and the Gallagher case.

3. Dave Philipps, "Navy SEALs Were Warned Against Reporting Their Chief for War Crimes," *New York Times*, April 23, 2019, www.nytimes.com/2019/04/23/us/navy-seals-crimes-of-war.html.

4. According to an Alpha platoon SEAL who witnessed the remarks; Matthew Cole, "Donald Trump Keeps Navy SEALs Above the Law," *The Intercept*, December 5, 2019, https://theintercept.com/2019/12/05/donald-trump-eddie-gallagher-navy-seals/.

5. Andrew Dyer, "Gallagher's Defense Attorney Questions Why Navy Is Investigating His Client for 9-Year-Old Allegation," *San Diego Union-Tribune*, April 23, 2019.

6. Julie Watson and Brian Melley, "Fellow SEALs Say Chief Shot Girls and Old Man in Iraq," Associated Press, June 21, 2019.

7. Philipps, *Alpha*, 57.

8. Interview with the author.

9. Dave Philipps, "Decorated Navy SEAL Is Accused of War Crimes in Iraq," *New York Times*, November 15, 2018, www.nytimes.com/2018/11/15/us/navy-seal-edward-gallagher-isis.html.

10. Aaron Singerman and Eddie Gallagher, "The Story of Navy SEAL Chief Eddie Gallagher: In His Own Words," January 21, 2021, *REDCON1*, podcast, https://youtu.be/tVTHOgFZB0A.

11. Carrie Dann, "Trump on ISIS Terrorists: 'You Have to Take Out Their Families,'" NBC News, December 2, 2015, www.nbcnews.com/politics/2016-election/trump-isis-terrorists-you-have-take-out-their-families-n472711.

12. Eli Watkins and Ryan Browne, "Trump: Navy SEAL Charged with Murder Moving to 'Less Restrictive Confinement,'" CNN, March 30, 2019, www.cnn.com/2019/03/30/politics/donald-trump-eddie-gallagher/index.html.

13. Pete Hegseth, "I'm with the Warfighters—Count Me Out of Second-Guessing Our Heroes," Fox News, May 23, 2019, www.foxnews.com/opinion/pete-hegseth-im-with-the-american-warfighters.

14. Singerman and Gallagher, "The Story of Navy SEAL Chief Eddie Gallagher."

15. Dave Philipps, "Navy SEAL War Crimes Witness Says He Was the Killer," *New York Times*, June 20, 2019, www.nytimes.com/2019/06/20/us/navy-seal-edward-gallagher-corey-scott.html.

16. Philipps, "Navy SEAL War Crimes Witness."

17. Mike Glenn, "Robert O'Neill Backs Donald Trump, Edward Gallagher in Navy SEAL Dispute," *Washington Times*, November 25, 2019, www.washingtontimes.com/news/2019/nov/25/robert-oneill-backs-trump-edward-gallagher-navy-se/.

18. According to a retired SEAL leader who discussed the Gallagher case with them.

19. "In Recognition of SOC (SEAL) Edward Gallagher USN," *Congressional Record*, January 7, 2020, www.congress.gov/116/crec/2020/01/07/modified/CREC-2020-01-07-pt1-PgE3-4.htm.

CHAPTER 18

1. Ben Finley, "Navy SEAL Gets Year in Brig for Hazing Death of Green Beret," Associated Press, May 16, 2019, https://apnews.com/article/us-army-us-news-norfolk-us-navy-seals-virginia-a5749278547d49b49968f65064106b36.

2. Dan Lamothe, "Navy SEAL Pleads Guilty in Hazing Death of Special Forces Soldier in Mali," *Washington Post*, May 16, 2019, www.washingtonpost.com/world/national-security/navy-seal-pleads-guilty-in-hazing-death-of-special-forces-soldier-in-mali/2019/05/16/9482ad52-77f9-11e9-b3f5-5673edf2d127_story.html.

3. Dan Lamothe (@DanLamothe), "The widow of Logan Melgar gave a lengthy statement last month as a Navy SEAL pleaded guilty in her husband's death in Mali. A Marine Raider is expected to plead guilty tomorrow. Here is what Michelle Melgar had to say, and my latest story about the case. https://www.washingtonpost.com/national-security/2019/06/05/troops-charged-green-berets-death-mali-planned-record-him-being-sexually-assaulted-marine-says/," Twitter, June 5, 2019, 4:05 p.m., https://twitter.com/DanLamothe/status/1136363558441234434/photo/4.

4. Dan Lamothe (@DanLamothe), "The widow of Logan Melgar."

5. Kevin Maxwell testimony, Article 32 hearing for DeDolph and Madera-Rodriguez, July 2019.

6. Adam Matthews testimony, Article 32 hearing for DeDolph and Madera-Rodriguez, July 2019.

7. Stavros Atlamazoglou, "Murder in Mali: The Trials of a Navy SEAL and Marine Raider Get Postponed," *SOFREP*, March 19, 2020, https://sofrep.com/news/murder-in-mali-the-trials-of-a-navy-seal-and-marine-raider-get-postponed/.

8. Ben Finley, "Navy SEAL Gets 10 Years for His Role in Green Beret's Death," Associated Press, January 25, 2021.

9. Author interview with Marcinko.

10. Audio recording of Maxwell sentencing hearing obtained by the author.

EPILOGUE

1. *Inspector-General of the Australian Defence Force Afghanistan Inquiry: Part 1—The Inquiry, Part 3—Operational, Organisation, and Cultural Issues*, Commonwealth of Australia, November 6, 2020, https://afghanistaninquiry.defence.gov.au/.

2. *Inspector-General of the Australian Defence Force Afghanistan Inquiry*, 33.

3. *Inspector-General of the Australian Defence Force Afghanistan Inquiry*, 40. Details about the individual commandos are redacted in the report released to the public.

INDEX

ABC News, 235
Academi, 219
accountability, command without
  beheadings, 165
  expansion and, 144, 149
  exposed, 195
  leaving man behind, 8
  mutilations and war crimes, 164–165,
    166, 173
  Norgrove cover-up, 198–199
  with oversight reduced, 61, 62, 68,
    144, 157, 173, 248, 316
  reform, 247, 312–316, 318
  sexual assault cover-up, 37–38
  truth and honor disregarded, 8, 9
  for war crimes, 153, 173–177
Act of Valor (film), 227–228
Adam, Jean, 202–204
Adam, Scott, 202–204
admiral's mast, 67, 198
Afghanistan, 150, 162, 165
  Bagram, 104–110
  CIA in, 100–102, 104, 106, 126, 141,
    173–175, 254
  civilians killed in, 176
  Green Berets in, 100–102, 137
  Kunar Province, 136–141, 146,
    167–171, 184–202, 243–245, 292
  Northern Alliance, 100–101, 105
  Operation Anaconda, 106–108, 254
  Operation ANSTRUTHER,
    184–202
  Operation Enduring Freedom,
    100–101, 166, 177–178
  Operation Pantera, 200, 201
  Operation Red Wings, 136–141, 146,
    167–171, 185, 243, 244–245, 292
  Shah-e-Kot, 105–108, 111, 121, 129,
    254
  Task Force 11 in, 100–102, 104–110,
    121–124, 128
  training for, 102–103
  withdrawal, 310
  See also Takur Ghar, Afghanistan
AFSOC (Air Force Special Operations
  Command), 251, 257
after-action review, 170–171
aggression
  controlled, 78, 83, 86
  increased, 150–151

Air Force, US
　Operation Urgent Fury and, 59–60
　720th Special Tactics Squadron, 254
　SOC, 251, 257
　24th Special Tactics Squadron, 103,
　　115, 254
Air Force Cross, 131, 255, 257, 260
Air Force Special Operations Command
　(AFSOC), 251, 257
Airborne School, US Army, 32
Alazzawi, Brian, 284
alcohol. *See* drinking
Alligator landing craft, 15–16
Alpha (Philipps), 285
Alpha platoon, SEAL Team 7, 281–288,
　291
American Sniper (film), 245
American Sniper (Kyle, C.)
　falsehoods in, 221–226, 228, 311–312
　on observation mission, 223
　Willink on facts of, 224–225, 226
amorality
　government-sanctioned acts, 49, 309
　operators, 49–50, 68
　Red Cell, 63, 66–67
　See also mutilation, bodies
anchor, Trident and, 309
Anderson, Marc, 117
Andrade, Dale, 76
Andrews, Greg, 188–194, 197–199
Anheuser-Busch logo, 24
Apache helicopters, 281
AQI (al Qaeda in Iraq), 154
AQIM (al Qaeda in the Islamic
　Maghreb), 269
Army, US
　Airborne School, 32
　Green Berets, 100–102, 137, 271–275,
　　298–299, 316
　Medal of Honor and, 3
　101st Airborne, 106
　160th SOAR, 106, 117, 137–138,
　　184–185, 187–188, 191, 195–196,
　　207, 209, 210, 211, 213

Operation Urgent Fury and, 59–60
Rangers, 8, 40, 60, 92, 111, 116–117,
　193–194, 275
10th Mountain Division, 106
3rd Special Forces Group, 268, 270,
　277
See also Delta Force, US Army
Article 32, 301–302
Associated Press (news agency), 306
athletes, 39, 46, 133
attrition rate, BUD/S training program,
　30, 31–32
Austin, Lloyd J., III, 317
Australia, war crimes, 313–315
Australian Defence Force, 313, 315
authorities
　emergency assault, 181, 202
　Title 50, 173
autopsies
　Chapman, John "Chappy," 256
　Melgar, Logan Joshua, 277, 278
Axelson, Matthew, 137, 138, 170

Babin, Leif, 225
Bagram, Afghanistan, 104–110
Bailey, Larry, 72–76
Bainbridge, USS, 181, 182, 184
banishment, 247, 263, 287
Basir, Mullah (Maulawi) Abdul, 186–187
battlefield. *See* combat
Bay of Pigs (1961), 23
Beckwith, Charlie, 41–42
beheadings, 7, 127, 163–166, 177,
　200–201, 215, 247, 258, 263, 318
Benny Boys, 34, 35
Biden, Joseph, 237–238, 310, 316, 317
Big Man (security guard), 272, 273, 299
The Big Mish, 208
bin Laden, Osama, 6, 99, 100, 168
　canoeing of, 212–213
　drone video and, 121, 129
　hat of, 220
　hunt for, 101–102, 104–105, 107,
　　121–123, 129, 134, 208

operators lying about killing, 241–244
Red with killing of, 212, 213, 214, 230, 241, 242, 243–244
bin Laden raid
  book deals, 217, 218, 219–221, 226, 229–230
  CIA and, 208, 209, 210, 230
  commodification of, 230
  corpse identified, 213
  corpse shootings, 212–213, 214, 230, 241
  details leaked, 240, 311
  with kill orders, 210–211
  politics and, 238, 239, 247–248
  Red Squad, 207–214, 241, 311
  rivalry over, 241–243
Bissonnette, Matthew, 133–134, 136, 145, 146–149, 311, 312
  banishment and Rock of Shame, 247
  book deal, 217, 218, 219–221, 226, 229–230
  corpse of bin Laden shot by, 213, 230
  with hat of bin Laden, 220
  investigations into, 231, 233–234, 245
  as leader, 208–209, 218, 233
  lying and taking credit from teammates, 213–214, 230–231, 243
  O'Neill and, 240–241
  as Owen, Mark, 230, 232–233, 234, 240, 245
  profiteering by, 234–235
  self-promotion, 209, 210, 211–214, 228–230, 245–246
Blaber, Peter, 107, 108
Black Hawk helicopters
  bin Laden raid, 207, 209, 210, 211, 213
  Mogadishu, 6, 92, 93, 100
Black Squadron, SEAL Team 6, 144
blast lung, 283
"bleed out" videos, 135
Blincoe, Ralph, 68
Blue Squadron, SEAL Team 6, 153, 162, 167

beheadings, 163–166, 200–201, 215, 263, 318
  ears collected by, 215
  with skinnings, 163
Blue Team, SEAL Team 6, 48, 51, 52–54, 87–88, 91, 124
bodies. *See* mutilation, bodies
Boehm, Roy, 20
Bolduc, Donald, 275, 276, 279, 305
books
  deals, 217, 218, 219–221, 226, 229–230
  tours, 167–168, 170
Bosnia, war crimes, 93–94
Boxer, USS, 180
brain injuries, 280, 288, 311
Brave Men, Dark Waters (Orr), 49
Breisch, Robert, 284, 285
Brennan, John O., 210–211
Brereton, Paul, 313
bribery, 70, 235
Brown, Robert, 75, 76
brutality, violence and, 8, 25, 127–128, 135, 149–150, 158, 161–162, 173
BUD/S training program, 84
  attrition rate, 30, 31–32
  class 292, 285–286
  with CQD, 136
  graduates, 2, 33, 52, 87, 124, 145, 155, 270
  Hell Week, 30, 31–32
  high school students replicating, 246
  rigors of, 28–31
  Trident and, 309
  videos, 91
Budweiser, 24
  See also Trident
Burns, Matt, 193, 194
Bush, George W.
  administration, 99, 103, 150–151, 167, 245, 310
  Kerry and, 239
  Operation Enduring Freedom, 100–101, 177–178
Byrne, T. C., 279

CAG (Combat Applications Group), 93
  See also Delta Force, US Army
Calland, Albert, 145
callouts, 146, 176
Camp, Joe, 75
canoeing, 172, 174, 176, 212–213, 215
captain's mast, 56, 61, 263
Caracci, Christopher, 91
Carter, Ash, 255, 262
Carter, Jimmy, 40, 41, 44, 59, 60
cash
  fund theft, 269–270, 277, 279
  missing ransom, 184
Castro, Fidel, 59
CB (cockbreath), 65, 72
CCTs. *See* combat controllers
celebrity status, cultivation of, 246
Central Intelligence Agency (CIA)
  in Afghanistan, 100–102, 104, 106,
    126, 141, 173–175, 254
  bin Laden raid and, 208, 209, 210, 230
  Jelisić and, 94
  in Mali, 269
  Omega program, 173
  Operation Red Wings, 141
  operators as contractors for, 219
  Phoenix Program, 26, 33
  Special Activities Division, 100–102,
    104, 135, 173–174
Chapman, Brianna, 118, 265
Chapman, John "Chappy"
  abandoned and left behind, 6, 7–8,
    113–115, 117, 119, 252–257, 260,
    262, 264
  Air Force Cross, 131, 255, 257, 260
  autopsy, 256
  as CCT, 5, 7–8, 98, 103, 112–113,
    115, 119, 254, 257
  family, 118, 131, 260, 264–265
  fighting alone, waiting for backup,
    115–116, 118, 131, 251, 254–257,
    259, 261, 265
  Medal of Honor, 251, 254, 255,
    256–262, 264–265

Redbeard video and, 259
  with Roberts rescue attempt, 112–115
  at Takur Ghar, 5–8, 98, 109–110,
    112–119, 130–131, 251–261,
    264–265
Chapman, Madison, 118, 265
Chapman, Valerie, 118, 265
character, of operators, 86–87, 92
Charlie Platoon, SEAL Team 6, 154,
  155–156, 158
Cheney, Elyse, 217, 219, 220
Chief Consulting LLC, 231, 233
children
  as human shields, 285
  killing of, 128, 157, 159, 162, 173, 286
  left unharmed, 161, 175–176, 225–226
Chinooks. *See* helicopters
CIA. *See* Central Intelligence Agency
Civil War, US, 2–3
civilians
  deaths with command failure,
    122–123, 128
  killing of, 123, 126, 157–160, 162,
    173, 176, 285–287, 291–292, 294
  safety with callouts, 146
  violence against, 280
Clinton, Bill, 93, 94, 238, 239
Close Quarters Defense (CQD), 84–89,
  91–92, 102, 103, 135–136
cockbreath (CB), 65, 72
Cold War, 22, 23
combat
  CQD, 84–89, 91–92, 102, 103, 135–136
  under duress, 139–140
  ethics, 83–84, 86–87, 92, 127, 136,
    152, 199
  misconduct, 149, 174
  rules of engagement, 65, 75, 126, 146,
    156–159, 172–173, 176, 222, 285
Combat Applications Group (CAG), 93
  See also Delta Force, US Army
combat controllers (CCTs)
  call sign, 7, 115
  responsibilities, 103, 106

Takur Ghar and, 5, 7–8, 98, 103, 108,
    112–113, 115, 119, 254, 257
command
    AFSOC, 251, 257
    after-action review bypassed and
        failure of, 170–171
    Blue Squadron and failure of,
        163–166
    chain of, 41, 48, 54–55, 104, 106–108,
        127, 183, 223, 262, 270, 284
    civilian deaths and failure of,
        122–123, 128
    DeDolph promotion and failure of,
        279
    in denial and without moral courage,
        150, 198, 310, 311–312
    ethics of, 85–89, 170–171
    expansion with inexperienced, 144
    failure to report wrong doings to, 160,
        164
    Gallagher, Edward R., and failure of,
        294
    Gallagher, Edward R., protected by,
        287
    Gray Team without training and
        failure of, 124–125, 128, 144,
        162–163
    integrity upended, 53–56, 89, 309–310
    Naval Special Warfare Command,
        223–224
    with Objective Bull review, 128
    Operation Red Wings and failure of,
        140–141
    Quest rescue mission and failure of,
        202–203
    reporting wrong doings to, 284–287
    SOCAFRICA, 269
    SOCOM, 99–100, 315
    Takur Ghar and failure of, 109–111,
        171
    tomahawks and, 153
    war crimes, 150, 153
    See also accountability, command
        without

Commons, Matthew, 117
Communism, 22, 23
conspiracy, 70, 71, 279, 297, 299, 300,
    304, 305
Constellis, 219
Constitution, US, 199
consulting work salary, 235
Cooper, Anderson, 139, 244
Cooper, Bradley, 245
Cooper, David, 154, 155, 157, 158, 234
corrupt culture, 8–9
Couch, Dick, 87, 159
Coulter, Tom, 34, 36, 37–38, 54, 56–57
counteraccusations, 278
court-martial, 47, 56, 67, 290–291, 294,
    302, 304–305, 307
cover-ups, 11, 63
    death of Melgar, Logan Joshua,
        274–276, 278–280, 299–300, 302,
        303, 304, 305
    death of Norgrove, 192–199
    Marcinko and Mercedes accident,
        55–57
    sexual assault, 36–38
    of Takur Ghar with Medal of Honor,
        4, 9, 251, 253–255, 259, 264–265
cowards, 168
CQD (Close Quarters Defense), 84–89,
    91–92, 102, 103, 135–136
cricothyrotomy, 273–274, 279, 283,
    303–304
criminal charges, 279–280, 288–293, 312
criminals, 24, 46, 61, 204
Crompvoets, Samantha, 313–314
Crose, Bradley, 117
Crowell, Forrest, 246–247
Crye Precision, 297–298
Cuba, 23, 59
Cucci, Frank, 91
culture, SEALs, 28–29, 235
    corrupt, 8–9
    drinking, 33, 34–35, 37, 46, 52, 55, 66,
        67, 93, 240, 271–272
    of exploiting weakness, 36, 38

culture, SEALs (*continued*)
   hazing, 34–38
   mafia-like, 174–175, 312
   Vietnam and, 25
   See also accountability, command
     without
Cummings, Clark, 94
Cunningham, Jason, 117
Cuomo, Chris, 235

DAI (Development Alternatives
   Incorporated), 185
Dailey, Frank, 254–255
Daily News (newspaper), 169
Day-Lewis, Daniel, 147
De Niro, Robert, 219
DeDolph, Tony, 270–274, 276–279, 299,
   301–307
DeFelice, Jim, 225
Delta Force (1st Special Forces
   Operational Detachment–Delta),
   US Army
   bin Laden and, 101, 104
   Black Hawk Down incident, 6, 92,
     93, 100
   as CAG, 93
   CCTs and, 103
   culture, 147
   fighting-style tournament, 91
   Fort Bragg, 51
   Iraq War, 146–148
   Operation Anaconda, 106–108
   Operation Eagle Claw, 40–42
   selection process, 147
   SHOT Show and, 232
   special operations, 44–45, 50, 51,
     91–93, 100–101, 103–104, 106–107,
     124, 146–149, 154, 156
   Task Force 11, 100–102, 104, 106–108
   Task Force Green, 92
   Tier 1 role, 44, 45, 50
   tomahawks and, 147–148, 149
   training, 124
   war crimes, 148

Delta Platoon, SEAL Team 6, 154,
   155–156
Department of Defense, US, 11, 223,
   307, 315
Desert One. *See* Operation Eagle Claw
Development Alternatives Incorporated
   (DAI), 185
DEVGRU (Naval Special Warfare
   Development Group). *See* Seal
   Team 6
Devil's Guard (Elford), 161–162, 163
Dieter, Duane, 170
   with CQD, 84–89, 91–92, 102, 103,
     135–136
   ethics of, 89–92, 144
   SEAL Team 6 training with, 77–92,
     94, 102–103
Dietz, Danny, 137, 138
Dille, Dylan, 287, 291
dip test, 61
direct action raids, 25, 155
"don't ask, don't tell," with hazing, 35, 38
Dowd, Maureen, 238
drinking, culture, 33, 34–35, 37, 46, 52,
   55, 66, 67, 93, 240, 271–272
drones. *See* videos, drone
drownings, 60–61
Drug Enforcement Agency, 82
drug use, 284, 288
   See also drinking, culture
Dunford, Joseph, 260–261, 262, 263, 264
Dutton, 217, 220–221, 229–230

eagles
   Operation Eagle Claw, 39–44, 99
   Trident and, 24, 309
ear collection, 215
Eastwood, Clint, 245
18 X-Ray program, 268
Electronic Arts, 229
Element Group, 231–232, 233
Elford, George Robert, 161–162, 163
Elizabeth II (Queen of England), 192,
   194, 199

embassy, US, 39–44, 99, 269
emergency assault authority, 181, 202
Espionage Act, 245
Esquire (magazine), 241–243
ethics
    combat, 83–84, 86–87, 92, 127, 136,
        152, 199
    of command, 85–89, 170–171
    of Dieter, 89–92, 144
    publicity and, 91
ethos
    quiet professional, 10, 140, 208,
        211–214, 215, 243–244, 246, 312
    SEAL Team 6, 10
    violations and reform, 247
    See also mafia ethos

F-105 aircraft, 28
Facebook, 292
Fannies, hazing at (gay bar), 34, 37
Farias, Arturo, 65, 66
fatal funnel, 196
FBI, 184
fight song, frogmen, 21
Fighting Lions, 51
fighting-style tournament, Delta Force,
    91
Filkins, Dexter, 10
films, Hollywood, 21, 43, 147, 169, 183,
    227–228, 241, 244, 245, 310
Firearm Industry Trade Association,
    232–233
1st Special Forces Operational
    Detachment–Delta. *See* Delta Force
flintlock pistol, Trident and, 24, 309
Flournoy, Michèle, 316
FNG (Fucking New Guy), 32, 33
"follow your shot," assault training, 212
Ford, Gerald, 1
Foreman, James, 153–160, 223
Forever Wars, 10, 72, 134, 178, 269, 282,
    306, 312
Fort Bragg, North Carolina, 51, 93, 267,
    268, 275, 276, 297

Fox News, 243, 289–290
fraud, 53, 68–71
Freedom of Information Act, 37
frogmen, 2, 10
    with autonomy, 22, 23
    culture, 33
    elite operator, 20, 23–24
    fight song, 21
    first generation of, 31
    hazing, 34–38
    Hell Week for, 18
    in Korean War, 22
    Marcinko, 43, 47, 56
    at Naval Amphibious Base Little
        Creek, 27
    Trident, 32
    UDTs, 18–24, 27–29, 32–37, 43, 46,
        69, 155
    in Vietnam War, 23, 28
    after World War II, 21
    in World War II, 18–29, 43
    See also SEALs, US Navy
The Frogmen (film), 21, 43
Fucking New Guy (FNG), 32, 33
Fussell, John, 188, 190–191, 195–197

Gaddafi, Muammar, 208
Gallagher, Andrea, 289–290, 293
Gallagher, Edward R., 316
    acquittal, 312
    civilians killed by, 285–287, 291–292,
        294
    command protecting, 287
    with ISIS fighter, 281–284, 286–287
    with murder charges and acquittal,
        288–293
    punishment for, 293
    with review board, 294
    supporters, 292, 293, 294–295
    Trump and, 289–290, 293–294
    war crimes and, 283–285
Garcia, Benjamin, 299, 302, 305
Geneva Conventions, 152, 167
Gilbert Islands, 16

global brand, SEAL Team 6 as,
    215–216, 220, 228, 246
Gold Squadron, SEAL Team 6, 153–154,
    160, 166, 173–174, 202–204, 223
Gold Team, SEAL Team 6, 48, 51, 94,
    103, 124
Gormly, Robert, 55–57, 70–71
Grabowsky, Ted, 25–26
Gray Team, SEAL Team 6, 124–128,
    144, 162–163
Green, Collin, 293–294, 312
Green Berets, US Army, 298–299, 316
    murder of, 271–275
    Operation Red Wings, 137
    with Task Force 11, 100–102
    See also Melgar, Logan Joshua
Green Team, SEAL Team 6, 57, 78, 79,
    84–86, 91, 102–103, 131, 136
    command failure with Gray Team
        bypassing, 124–125, 128, 144,
        162–163
    graduates, 133–134
    nepotism with screening process,
        145–146
Grenada, 59–60, 63, 68
guerilla forces, counter, 22–23, 25
Gul, Amin, 187
Gulab, Mohammed, 138–139, 140

Hagenbeck, Franklin, 106
Hamilton, William H., Jr., 23–24, 25,
    43, 45, 61, 62, 67
Hanks, Tom, 183
Hartwell, George, 256
Hatch, James, 136–137, 138, 139, 141,
    143, 222–223
hatchets. See tomahawks
Hayward, Thomas, 45
hazing
    as professional remediation, 272, 303
    sexual assault and, 34–38, 272, 273,
        299, 303, 305
    tape job, 271–272

HBO, 229, 245
Heat (film), 127
Heath, Monty, 123, 127
helicopters
    Apache, 281
    Black Hawk, 6, 92, 93, 100, 207, 209,
        210, 211, 213
    Chinook, 5, 8, 97–98, 109–111,
        116, 121–122, 129–130, 136–138,
        184–185, 187, 254–255
    crashes, 4, 98, 110, 116, 117, 136, 207,
        211, 218, 229
    Kunar Province, 136–141
    Objective Wolverine, 129–130
    160th SOAR, 106, 117, 137–138,
        184–185, 187–188, 191, 195–196,
        207, 209, 210, 211, 213
    Operation Eagle Claw, 40–42
    RH-53, 40, 41
    at Takur Ghar, 97–98, 109, 110, 112,
        114, 116, 131, 141, 255
Hell Week, 18, 30, 31–32
heroism, 212
    acts of, 81, 131, 140
    myth of, 8, 263, 288–289, 310
Hill, Jason, 115
Hillier, Luke, 233
Hines, Glen, 307
Hitler, Adolf, 94
Holland, Kevin, 147–148
Hollywood films, 21, 43, 147, 169, 183,
    227–228, 241, 244, 245, 310
homicide
    of ISIS fighter, 284–286, 287,
        292–293
    punishment for, 279–280, 301, 305
    See also Melgar, Logan Joshua
hood drill (hooded box test), 79–80, 103,
    136
Hooser, Pete Van, 200
hostages
    with cash missing, 184
    execution of, 203

investigation into death of, 192–199
Maersk Alabama, Somali pirates and, 179–184, 202, 240
Norgrove mission, 184–202
Quest mission and Somali pirates, 202–203
US Embassy in Iran, 39–44, 99
hot wash, 191–192
Howard, Hugh Wyman, III, 150, 153, 231, 234, 235, 316–317
criticism of, 151–152
Green Team and, 145–146
stump muster and, 214–215
tomahawks and, 148, 149
human shields, Taliban with, 285
Hunter, Duncan, 290, 294–295
Hussein, Saddam, 150, 310
Hyder, Vic "Waingro," 111, 134
bodies mutilated by, 123–124, 125, 127, 128
civilians killed by, 123, 126
as Gray Team officer, 125–128, 163
Objective Bull and, 121–124, 128
sidelining of, 135
at Takur Ghar, 116–117

ice-cream cone, self-licking, 150
Instagram, 246
integrity, 197
command, 53–56, 89, 309–310
See also morals
International Criminal Tribunal, 94
investigations
beheading, 164–165
into Bissonnette, 231, 233–234, 245
death of Norgrove, 192–199
hazing and sexual assault, 37–38
homicide of ISIS fighter, 283, 284–288
homicide of Melgar, Logan Joshua, 276, 277–279
Red Cell and torture, 66–67
into regular SEAL units, 129

rigged, 165
SEAL Team 6, 67–71, 129
See also Naval Criminal Investigative Service
Iran, 39–44, 99
Iranian hostage crisis. *See* Operation Eagle Claw
Iraq, 150, 245, 281–295
Iraq War, 146–148, 149, 150, 153–160
ISIS fighter, 281–287, 292–293
Ives, Ben, 189, 191–194, 196–199

James, Deborah Lee, 256, 260
Jelisić, Goran, 93–94
Johnson, Jeh, 229–230
Joint Special Operations Command (JSOC), 269
birth of, 44, 72, 99
9/11 and, 99–100, 143
Norgrove rescue mission and, 186
Operation Gothic Serpent, 6, 92, 93, 100
Operation Just Cause, 92
Operation Urgent Fury, 59–60, 63, 68
with operational rules revised, 176
Takur Ghar and, 7, 255–256
US presidents and, 22–23, 44
Jolly Roger, 51
JSOC. *See* Joint Special Operations Command
Justice Department, US, 245

Karzai, Hamid, 175
Kauffman, Draper, 18–19, 30
Keener, Fred, 29
Keith, Thomas, 34–35
Kelly, Orr, 49
Keltner, Scott, 247
Kelz, Jim, 83–84
Kennedy, John F., 1, 22–24, 45
Kent, Dave, 94
Kerik, Bernard, 290

Kernan, Joseph, 104, 107–109, 110, 111–112, 171
  failure with Gray Team bypassing training, 124–125, 128, 144, 162–163
  Takur Ghar and, 258
Kerry, John, 239
khat, 182
kidnappings, 25, 64, 185–187, 225–226
  See also hostages
kill shots, 29, 123
  See also photographs
killers
  operators as, 24–26, 28, 49–50, 126–127, 157–160, 166, 193–194, 199, 311
  serial, 49–50, 126–127, 166
killing
  of bin Laden by Red, 212, 213, 214, 230, 241, 242, 243–244
  "bleed out" videos, 135
  of children, 128, 157, 159, 162, 173, 286
  of civilians, 123, 126, 157–160, 162, 173, 176, 285–287, 291–292, 294
  for fun, 174
  machines, 167
  mercy, 293
  operators lying about al Kuwaiti, 213, 230–231
  operators lying about bin Laden, 241–244
  orders for bin Laden, 210–211
  of Somali pirates, 182–183, 203
  thrill of, 166
kills
  counting, 159, 166, 177, 221–223
  knife, 26
  post-mission photographs of, 29, 123, 171–172, 174, 176, 190, 192, 193
King, Larry, 72
King, William, 194, 294
knife kills, 26
Korean War, frogmen in, 22

Kristensen, Erik, 137
Kunar Province, Afghanistan
  Norgrove rescue mission, 184–202
  Operation Red Wings, 136–141, 146, 167–171, 185, 243–245, 292
Kurilla, Erik, 192–194
al Kuwaiti, Abu Ahmed, 211, 213, 230–231
Kyle, Chris "the Legend," 312
  civilians killed by, 158, 159–160, 287
  death of, 236
  with false accounts of career, 221–226, 228, 311–312
  medal count, 224, 225
  PTSD and, 221, 226, 245
  self-promotion, 158–159, 221–223, 228
Kyle, Taya, 221

landing craft, 15–16, 33
The Last of the Mohicans (film), 147
Lauer, Matt, 167, 169
leadership. See command
Leasure, George Edward "Fast Eddie," 33–34, 35, 36, 37, 38, 312
leave no man behind, 8, 42, 251, 253
  See also Chapman, John
Lincoln, Abraham, 1, 3
lions, 51
London Bridge Trading, 233
Lone Survivor (film), 244
Lone Survivor (Luttrell), 221
  inaccuracies in, 167–168, 170, 228, 243
Longfritz, Lori Chapman, 260
Lowell, Abbe, 75
Luttrell, Marcus, 187, 221, 292, 312
  with Lone Survivor inaccuracies, 167–168, 170, 228, 243
  Operation Red Wings, 137, 138–140, 141, 169, 244–245
  self-promotion, 244
  Team Never Quit and, 244–245
Lynch, Jessica, 180
Lyons, James "Ace," 61

MacArthur, Douglas, 129
Macay, Phyllis, 202–204
MacDonald, Ken, 46
MacPherson, Malcolm, 110, 252, 253
Mad Turk (operator), 135
Madera-Rodriguez, Mario, 271–275, 278–279, 299, 301–304
Maersk Alabama hostage rescue, 179–184, 202, 240
mafia ethos, SEAL Team 6, 175, 200, 292, 312
  amorality and, 49–50
  Marcinko and, 47, 49, 52, 54, 57, 62, 69, 125, 174, 235
  secrets with, 52, 127
Maguire, Joseph, 32–33, 35, 36, 38, 155, 170–171, 228
Maguire, Kathy, 36, 38
Mako 30. *See* Red Team, SEAL Team 6
Mako 31, SEAL Team 6, 107–108, 110
Mali, al Qaeda in, 269
Malinowski, Tom, 310
Marcinko, Richard "Demo, Dick," 175, 304, 306, 312
  conspiracy and, 70, 71
  fraud and, 68–71
  as frogman, 43, 47, 56
  investigations, 67–71
  mafia ethos and, 47, 49, 52, 54, 57, 62, 69, 125, 174, 235
  Operation Eagle Claw and, 43–44
  Red Cell and, 61–71
  Rogue Warrior, 72–76, 220, 225, 235
  SEAL Team 6 and, 44–50, 52–57, 61–62, 67–71, 110, 118, 124–125, 145, 174, 235
  unprofessionalism and ousting of, 54–56, 67–69
  in Vietnam War, 43, 72–76
Marines, US, 154
  Operation Eagle Claw, 40, 42
  pilots, 40
  Raiders, 20, 271–272
  2nd Division, 15–16

Martin, Andy, 108
Mason, John, 68–70
Massoud, Ahmad Shah, 100
Matthews, Adam, 271–274, 276–280, 297–307
Mattis, James, 261, 264
Maxwell, Kevin, 271–275, 278–279, 299–305, 307
McChrystal, Stanley, 143, 150–151, 152, 162, 193
McRaven, Claude C., 52
McRaven, William, 52–54, 146, 175–176, 204, 226
  on *Act of Valor*, 227–228
  bin Laden raid and, 209–210
  Maersk Alabama hostage rescue and, 180–184
  Norgrove cover-up and, 198–199
  on publicity and social media, 227
  Quest rescue mission and, 202–203
  with six principles of operation, 209
Medal of Honor
  Chapman, John "Chappy," 251, 254, 255, 256–262, 264–265
  with cover-up at Takur Ghar, 4, 9, 251, 253–255, 259, 264–265
  legacy, 2–3
  for Operation Red Wings, 170
  Slabinski, 1–4, 9–10, 261, 262–264
  Takur Ghar and, 1–4, 9–10, 251–254, 264–265
Medal of Honor (video game), 229
media, 238, 293
  frogmen myth in, 20–21
  homicide cover-up in, 280
  lying and speaking to, 247
  Objective Bull in, 128
  Operation Red Wings in, 169
  personality and, 72
  Rumsfeld on War on Terror, 98–99
  SEAL culture in, 25, 235
  SEAL Team 6 in, 72–76, 200, 201, 228, 252
  social, 227, 233, 246, 289, 292

Melgar, Logan Joshua, 316
  autopsy, 277, 278
  cover-up, 274–276, 278–280,
    299–300, 302, 303, 304, 305
  criminal charges filed for death of,
    279–280
  death, 273–274, 302, 304, 306–307
  family, 267–270, 275–279, 298–302,
    303
  homicide investigation, 276, 277–279
  plot against and assault on, 271–273
  with SOCAFRICA in Mali, 269
Melgar, Michelle, 267–270, 275–279,
  298–303
Melgar, Nitza, 302
Mercedes Benz accident and cover-up,
  55–57
mercy killing, 293
MI6, 186
Miller, Craig, 283–285, 287, 291–292
Miller, Eric, 271
Minnesota Multiphasic Personality
  Inventory (MMPI), 46–47
MMA (mixed martial arts), 136, 149,
  155, 273
MMPI (Minnesota Multiphasic
  Personality Inventory), 46–47
MOB-6 (Mobility 6), SEAL Team 2,
  45, 57
Mogadishu, Somalia, 6, 92, 93, 100
Moore, Scott, 149, 163, 164, 165–166,
  180–183
moral courage, truth and lack of, 150,
  198, 310, 311–312
morals
  without, 49–50, 63, 66–68, 309
  collapse, 8
  decay, 288
  flexible, 123
  injury, 311
  integrity and, 53–56, 89, 197,
    309–310
  operators with, 50, 68, 85, 126–127,
    307, 309

Morganti, Brett, 113, 252
Morris, Jamie, 272, 303
Mosul, Iraq, 281–295
Mother Jones (magazine), 239
Mukasey, Marc, 290
Munich Olympics (1972), 39
murder
  charges against Gallagher, Edward R.,
    288–293
  of Green Beret, 271–275
  See also Melgar, Logan Joshua
Murphy, Michael, 137–138, 139, 170
Muse, Abduwali Abdukhadir, 179, 181,
  182
mutilation, bodies
  without accountability, 164–165, 166,
    173
  beheadings, 7, 127, 163–166, 177,
    200–201, 215, 247, 263, 317
  canoeing, 172, 174, 176, 212–213,
    215
  ear collection, 215
  by Hyder, 123–124, 125, 127, 128
  Iraq War, violence and retaliatory,
    148
  photographs, 29, 215
  reasons for, 166
  of Roberts, 7, 8, 9, 98, 117, 118, 127,
    134
  SEAL Team 6 on ethics of, 127
  skinning, 149, 163
  with tomahawks, 149
mutilations, retaliatory, 148
myth
  of frogmen in media, 20–21
  of heroism, 8, 263, 288–289, 310
  of SEAL Team 6, 9–10, 228, 244,
    310
  of Takur Ghar, 253–254
  See also cover-ups

National Geospatial-Intelligence
  Agency (NGA), 254, 255–256
National Security Agency (NSA), 100

Native American warrior self-image, 51–52, 127, 145–149, 152–153
Naval Academy, US, 8, 87, 104, 111, 125, 145, 162, 267
Naval Combat Demolition Unit (NCDU), 17–18, 19, 20
Naval Criminal Investigative Service (NCIS, Naval Investigative Service), 37–38, 67, 129, 164–165, 234
    homicide of ISIS fighter, 283, 284–288
    homicide of Melgar, Logan Josha, 277–279
Naval Investigative Service (NIS), 37–38, 67–71, 234
Naval Special Warfare, 19, 37, 45, 49, 104, 144, 168
Naval Special Warfare Command, 223–224
Naval Special Warfare Development Group (DEVGRU). See SEAL Team 6
Navy, US
    Operation Urgent Fury and, 59–60, 68
    Seabees, 17
    in World War II, 15–16
    See also SEALs, US Navy
Navy Cross, 2, 131, 167, 170, 258, 261
"Navy SEALs Gone Wild" (Crowell), 246
Nazis, 161
NCDU (Naval Combat Demolition Unit), 17–18, 19, 20
NCIS. See Naval Criminal Investigative Service
Neiderberger, Kenneth, 263
New York Times (newspaper), 167, 200, 201, 228, 238, 247, 252
    Rumsfeld in, 98–99
    on SEALs in Vietnam, 25
New York Times bestseller list, 167, 221
New Yorker (magazine), 220
Newsweek (magazine), 139, 228, 259
NGA (National Geospatial-Intelligence Agency), 254, 255–256

Nimitz, USS, 41–42
9/11, 10, 19, 100, 102, 134, 219, 245, 310
    Team 6 SEALs shortage after, 103
    War on Terror and, 8, 9, 98–99, 143, 150–151, 167, 177
NIS (Naval Investigative Service), 37–38, 67–71
No Easy Day (Owen), 230, 232–233, 234, 240, 245
nonjudicial punishments, 56, 61, 67, 198
Norgrove, Linda
    drone video and, 187, 189, 193–194
    investigation into death of, 192–199
    as MI6 agent, 186
    rescue mission, 184–202
Noriega, Manuel, 92
Northern Alliance, 100–101, 105
NSA (National Security Agency), 100
nuclear weapons, 22, 100

Obama, Barack, 177–178, 210, 255, 260
    Maersk Alabama mission and, 180, 181, 184, 202
    Norgrove mission and, 192, 194, 199
    politics and, 237–239, 247–248
    Quest mission and, 202
Objective Bull (Wedding Party bombing), 121–124, 128
Objective Wolverine, 129–130, 134
O'Connell, James, 145
Oliva, Tom, 188–189, 191–192, 194, 199
Olson, Eric T., 89–92, 93, 155
Omaha Beach, 19, 20
Omar, Mullah, 101, 105
Omega program, CIA, 173
omertà, 174
101st Airborne, US Army, 106
160th Special Operations Aviation Regiment (SOAR), US Army, 106, 117, 137–138
    bin Laden raid, 207, 209, 210, 211, 213
    Norgrove rescue mission, 184–185, 187–188, 191, 195–196

O'Neill, Robert, 138, 139, 143, 145, 149, 151, 264, 312
  with banishment and Rock of Shame, 247
  Bissonnette and, 240–241
  corpse of bin Laden shot by, 212–213, 214, 241
  Gallagher, Edward R., and, 293
  as Green Team graduate, 133–134, 136
  as leader, 208–209
  as leaker of bin Laden raid details, 240, 311
  lying about killing bin Laden, 241–244
  with Native American warrior self-image, 152–153
  self-promotion, 209, 210, 211–213, 214, 240–242
  as "The Shooter," in *Esquire* magazine, 241–243
  speaking engagements, 246
OP-06D (Red Cell), 61–71
Operation Anaconda (2002), 106–108, 254
  See also Takur Ghar, Afghanistan
Operation ANSTRUTHER (2010), 184–202
Operation Eagle Claw (Desert One) (1979), 39–44, 99
Operation Enduring Freedom (2001–2014), 100–101, 166, 177–178
Operation Gothic Serpent (1993), 6, 92, 93, 100
Operation Just Cause (December 1989–January 1990), 92
Operation Lightning Dawn (2009), 179–184, 202, 240
Operation Pantera (2008), 200, 201
Operation Red Wings (2005), 136–141, 146, 167–171, 185, 243–245, 292
Operation Tossed Salad (2017), 271–275, 299–300, 303, 305, 306

Operation Urgent Fury (1983), 59–60, 63, 68
operators, 20, 23, 34
  amoral, 49–50, 68
  athletes, 46, 133
  character of, 86–87, 92
  as CIA operators, 219
  with controlled aggression, 78, 83, 86
  criminals, 24, 46, 61, 204
  for Delta selection, 147
  elite caliber, 146, 309
  as killers, 24–26, 28, 49–50, 126–127, 157–160, 166, 193–194, 199, 311
  lying and taking credit from teammates, 213–214, 230–231, 241–244
  Mad Turk, 135
  moral, 50, 68, 85, 126–127, 307, 309
  9/11 and shortage of, 103
  as quiet professionals, 10, 140, 208, 211–214, 215, 243–244, 246, 312
  Red and bin Laden raid, 211–212, 213, 214, 241
  for SEAL Team 6 selection, 46–50, 57, 145, 196–197
  self-promotion, 158–159, 209, 210, 211–214, 221–223, 228–230, 240–242, 244–246
  sociopaths, 47, 49–50, 126–127, 166, 203, 290
  See also Tier 1 teams
The Operator (O'Neill), 243
ops computer, 171
oversight
  liabilities with excessive, 203
  reduced, 61, 62, 68, 144, 157, 173, 248, 315
Owen, Mark, 230, 232–233, 234, 240, 245
  See also Bissonnette, Matthew

Panama, 92
Parlatore, Tim, 291–293

passing the buck, 197

pathologies, 8, 46, 52, 184, 304

Pelley, Scott, 230

Penney, Ann, 36

Penney, Eddie, 166

Penney, Ralph Stanley, Jr., 39, 155, 171, 312
    BUD/S and, 28–32
    death and cover-up, 36–38
    hazing and, 34–38
    as leader, 32
    with UDT-21, 27–29, 32, 34–37

Penney, Ralph Stanley, Sr., 28–29, 36

Penney, Rebecca, 28, 37, 38

Pentagon
    Kennedy and, 22, 23
    with Kyle, Chris, kill claims, 221
    Operation Eagle Claw and, 41, 42–44

personality, 242
    force of, 33–34, 49, 72, 152
    group, 51–52, 127–128, 145–149, 152
    MMPI, 46–47

Petraeus, David, 150, 192, 194, 195

Philipps, David, 285

Phillips, Frank, 65, 66

Phillips, Richard, 179–184, 202

Phoenix Program, CIA and, 26, 33

photographs
    mutilated bodies, 29, 215
    of people killed during missions, 29, 123, 171–172, 174, 176, 190, 192, 193
    of slain ISIS fighter, 284

pirates, 47, 51, 64, 179–184, 202–203, 240

"Pogue Warrior" (Andrade), 76

politics
    bin Laden raid and, 238, 239, 247–248
    Navy SEALs and, 238–240, 246
    Obama and, 237–239

polygraph test, 184

Portier, Jake, 282, 283–284, 285, 288

post-traumatic stress disorder (PTSD), 221, 226, 245, 280

presidents, special operations and US, 22–23, 44, 51, 215

"President's Own," SEAL Team 6 as, 51, 215

prisoner
    abuse, 313
    training, 87

prisons, 24, 93–94, 302, 305

professional remediation, hazing as, 272, 303

profiteering, 234–235, 311

prostitutes, 270, 272, 277, 304

PRUs (provincial reconnaissance units), 26, 33

psychological evaluations, 46–47, 49, 57, 306

psychological trauma, 118, 128, 131, 175, 247, 280, 311

psychological warfare, 161, 175

psychologists, 46, 49, 84, 92, 203

psychology, SEALs, 8, 9, 49–50, 57, 84, 92, 203, 235

PTSD (post-traumatic stress disorder), 221, 226, 245, 280

publicity
    book tours, 167–168, 170
    celebrity status and, 246
    combat under duress and, 139–140
    criticism, 227
    fighting-style tournament, 91
    with hunt for bin Laden, 208
    with SEAL Team 6 as global brand, 215–216, 220, 228, 246
    self-promotion and, 209, 210, 221–223, 228–230, 241–246
    with training videos, 91

Pugh, Alan, 271–272, 275

punishments, 199
    banishment, 247, 263, 287
    for Gallagher, Edward R., 293
    for homicide, 279–280, 301, 305

punishments (*continued*)
  inconsequential, 165
  for leaking bin Laden raid details,
    240, 311
  nonjudicial, 56, 61, 67, 198
  prison sentences, 71
  removal from units, 135, 148, 172–173,
    201–202, 240, 247, 287
purpose, principles of operation, 209

al Qaeda
  Chapman, John "Chappy," attacked
    by, 115–116
  in Mali, 269
  with mutilation of Roberts, 7, 8, 9, 98,
    117, 118, 134
  Objective Wolverine, 129–130, 134
  Operation Anaconda and, 106–108
  with retaliatory mutilations, 148
  as threat, 5, 6, 99, 101, 105, 125, 128,
    140, 150
  See also Takur Ghar, Afghanistan
al Qaeda in Iraq (AQI), 154
al Qaeda in the Islamic Maghreb
  (AQIM), 269
Quest rescue mission, hostages,
  202–203
quiet professionals
  ethos, 10, 140, 208, 211–214, 215,
    243–244, 246, 312
  Red and bin Laden raid, 211–212,
    213, 214, 230, 241, 242, 243–244
  See also publicity

Raiders, US Marines, 20, 271–272
Ramadi, Iraq War (2006), 153–160
RAND military analyst, 26
Rangers, US Army, 8, 40, 60, 92, 111,
  116–117, 193–194, 275
Raser, Susan, 128–129
ratting out (snitching), 68, 69, 129, 284
Reagan, Ronald, 59–60, 100
recce troop, 103
recruitment videos, 227

Red (operator), bin Laden raid and,
  211–212, 213, 214, 230, 241, 242,
  243–244
Red Cell (OP-06D), 61–71
Red Squadron, SEAL Team 6, 145, 231,
  233
  bin Laden raid, 207–214, 241, 311
  in books, 167–168
  with cash missing, 184
  Iraq War, 150–153
  on Luttrell, 168
  Maersk Alabama hostage rescue,
    179–184, 202, 240
  with Native American warrior self-
    image, 152–153
  Red and bin Laden raid, 211–212,
    213, 214, 241, 242, 243–244
Red Team (Mako 30), SEAL Team 6,
  83–84, 93, 119, 131, 133, 143, 150,
  159, 188
  on ethics and mutilation of bodies,
    127
  Gray Team officers and, 125–128, 163
  Kunar Province, 136–141
  Mad Turk, 135
  with Native American warrior
    self-image, 51–52, 127, 145–149,
    152–153
  Objective Bull, 121–124, 128
  Objective Wolverine, 129–130, 134
  Operation Anaconda, 107
  Operation Red Wings, 136–141, 146,
    167–171, 185, 243–245, 292
  with Roberts rescue attempt,
    112–115, 116
  at Takur Ghar, 97–98, 103, 109–118,
    135, 259–260
  with Task Force 11, 102, 104–105, 121
  tomahawks and, 147, 148–149, 153,
    208, 234
  See also Takur Ghar, Afghanistan
Redbeard video, 259
Reismeier, Chris, 300
Reiter, Michael, 32

repetition, principles of operation, 209
retirement, 218–219
revenge, 223, 288
    for 9/11, 103
    for Roberts, 124, 127, 128, 130, 134
RH-53 helicopters, 40, 41
Richards, Thomas, 33
Riggle, Bob, 202–204
RJO Apparel, 246
Roberts, Neil C. "Fifi," 126, 215
    family, 118
    rescue attempt, 112–115, 116, 262
    revenge for, 124, 127, 128, 130, 134
    SAW rifle of, 130–131, 134
    at Takur Ghar, 5, 7, 8, 9, 97–98,
        110–115, 116, 117, 118, 130, 134,
        135, 262
Roberts Ridge. See Takur Ghar,
    Afghanistan
Roberts Ridge (MacPherson), 252, 253
Robinson, Patrick, 167
Rock of Shame, SEAL Team 6, 247
Rodgers, Fran, 77–78, 79, 86
Rogue Warrior (Marcinko), 220, 235
    falsehoods in, 72–76
    series, 225
Rolling Stone (magazine), 227
Romney, Mitt, 238
Roosevelt, Franklin D., 16
Rose, Steve, 233–234
Rowland, Jimmy, 37
rules of engagement, 65, 75, 126, 146,
    156–159, 172–173, 176, 222, 285
Rumsfeld, Donald, 98–100, 169
Ryan, Phil, 190, 192, 193, 194

sadism, 25, 135
salary
    consulting work, 235
    speaking engagements, 246
    Tier 1 teams, 218
SASR (Special Air Service Regiment),
    313–314
Saturday Evening Post (newspaper), 20

SAW rifle, of Roberts, 130–131, 134
scandals, 175, 261, 311, 315
Schamberger, Robert, 52–54, 60, 199
Scott, Corey, 279, 286, 287, 291,
    292–293
Scouts, 20
screenings, psychological, 46–47, 49, 57,
    306
SDVT-1 (SEAL Delivery Vehicle Team
    One), 140
SDVT-2 (SEAL Delivery Vehicle Team
    Two), 87
Seabees, US Navy, 17
Seal Beach naval weapons facility, 63–66
SEAL Delivery Vehicle Team One
    (SDVT-1), 140
SEAL Delivery Vehicle Team Two
    (SDVT-2), 87
SEAL Team 6 (Naval Special Warfare
    Development Group, DEVGRU),
    2, 225, 235
    bin Laden and, 104
    birth of, 44–50
    Black Squadron, 144
    Blue Squadron, 153, 162–167, 200–201,
        215, 263, 317
    Blue Team, 48, 51, 52–54, 87–88, 91,
        124
    CCTs and, 103
    chain of command, 104, 106–108
    Charlie Platoon, 154, 155–156, 158
    command failure at Takur Ghar,
        109–111, 171
    command integrity upended by,
        53–56, 89, 309–310
    Delta Platoon, 154, 155–156
    drownings, 60–61
    with erosion of standards, 124–125,
        128, 144, 145
    on ethics and mutilation of bodies,
        127
    ethos, 10
    expansion, 143–144, 149
    with fighting-style tournament, 91

SEAL Team 6 (Naval Special Warfare
  Development Group, DEVGRU)
  (*continued*)
  as global brand, 215–216, 220, 228, 246
  Gold Squadron, 153–154, 159–160,
    166, 173–174, 202–204, 223
  Gold Team, 48, 51, 94, 103, 124
  with government-sanctioned amoral
    acts, 49, 309
  Gray Team, 124–128, 144, 162–163
  Green Team, 57, 78, 79, 84–86,
    91, 102–103, 124–125, 128, 131,
    133–134, 136, 144–146, 162–163
  interviews with, 11
  investigations, 67–71, 129
  Mako 31, 107–108, 110
  Marcinko and, 44–50, 52–57, 61–62,
    67–71, 110, 118, 124–125, 145, 174,
    235
  in media, 72–76, 200, 201, 228, 252
  moral collapse, 8
  myth of, 9–10, 228, 244, 310
  NCDU and, 17–18
  9/11 and, 99
  with Objective Bull review, 128
  Operation Anaconda, 106–108
  Operation Just Cause, 92
  Operation Urgent Fury and, 60, 68
  with operational rules revised, 176
  with operator shortage after 9/11, 103
  as "President's Own," 51, 215
  professionalizing of, 56–57
  promotional videos of tactics, 229
  with rank outweighed by experience
    and knowledge, 110, 118
  Red Cell and, 61–71
  renaming of, 69
  Rock of Shame, 247
  selection process, 46–50, 57, 145,
    196–197
  SHOT Show and, 232–233, 297–299
  Silver Squadron, 184–199, 240,
    269–270, 276–277

Task Force Blue, 92
Tier 1 role, 5, 48–51, 62
training, 48–49, 57, 77–92, 94, 102–103
unit organization, 48–49, 51, 52
  See also mafia ethos, SEAL Team 6;
    Red Squadron, SEAL Team 6; Red
    Team, SEAL Team 6
SEAL Teams
  1, 24–26, 44, 45
  2, 33–34, 36, 44, 45, 54, 55, 72–76,
    92, 133
  3, 45, 153–160, 223
  4, 60, 92, 133
  5, 45, 133, 146, 217
  7, 227, 270, 281–288, 291
  8, 145
  10, 140, 167
SEALs, US Navy
  creation of, 23–25
  hazing, 34–38
  internal disciplinary process, 128–129
  operator types, 20, 23–24, 34, 46, 61,
    204
  politics and, 238–240, 246
  predecessors to, 20
  psychology, 8, 9, 49–50, 57, 84, 92,
    203, 235
  reputation in military, 25–26, 28
  Trident, 2, 24, 32, 309
  in Vietnam War, 29, 43, 46, 72–76
  See also culture, SEALs
2nd Division, US Marines, 15–16
secrets
  agreement violations, 229–230
  code of silence, 165, 168, 174, 288,
    290
  with mafia ethos, 52, 127
  Title 50 authority, 173
  Top Secret, 11
  war crimes, 148, 149
  See also cover-ups
security, principles of operation, 209
self-licking ice-cream cone, 150

self-promotion, operators, 158–159
  bin Laden raid, 209, 210, 211–213,
    214, 240
  publicity and, 209, 210, 221–223,
    228–230, 241–246
Sengelman, Jeff, 313–314
September 11. *See* 9/11
SERE (Survival, Evasion, Resistance,
    Escape) training, 278
serial killers, 49–50, 126–127, 166
720th Special Tactics Squadron, US Air
    Force, 254
Sevier, Ben, 217, 219–220
sexual assault, hazing and, 34–38, 272,
    273, 299, 303, 305
Shah, Ahmad, 137–139, 140, 167–168,
    170
Shah-e-Kot, Afghanistan, 105–108, 111,
    121, 129, 254
Sheehy, Sean, 94
Sheffield, Justin, 166
Sheridan, Margaret, 63–64, 65, 66
Sheridan, Ronald, 63–67
The Sheriff of Ramadi (Couch), 159
Sherman, Clay, 83, 84, 85
Sherman, Nancy, 288
"The Shooter," in *Esquire* magazine
    story, 241–243
  See also O'Neill, Robert
SHOT (Shooting, Hunting, Outdoor
    Trade) Show, 232–233, 297–299
silence
  code of, 165, 168, 174, 288, 290
  condoning through, 175
Silver Squadron, SEAL Team 6,
    184–199, 240, 269–270, 276–277
Simon and Schuster, 71, 75
simplicity, principles of operation, 209
60 Minutes (television news magazine),
    72, 139, 230
skinning the dead, 149, 163
Slabinski, Britt "Slab," 103, 107, 108, 312
  banishment of, 263, 287

beheadings, Blue Squadron and,
    162–165, 200–201, 263
  as leader, 102–103
  Medal of Honor and, 1–4, 9–10, 261,
    262–264
  myth of heroism and, 263
  Navy Cross, 2, 131, 258, 261
  Objective Wolverine, 129–130, 134
  removal of, 201–202
  speaking and lying to media, 247
  Takur Ghar and, 3–9, 97, 98,
    109–110, 112–118, 134, 141,
    251–254, 256–258, 260, 264–265
  with training lie, 102
Smallman, John, 165
Smethers, Richard, 174, 175
snitching (ratting out), 68, 69, 129, 284
SOAR. *See* 160th Special Operations
    Aviation Regiment, US Army
SOCAFRICA (Special Operations
    Command Africa), 269
social media, 227, 233, 246, 289, 292
sociopaths, 47, 49–50, 126–127, 166,
    203, 290
SOCOM (Special Operations
    Command), 99–100, 316
Soderberg, Kyle, 129
Soldier of Fortune (magazine), 67, 75
Somalia
  Mogadishu, 6, 92, 93, 100
  pirates with hostages, 179–184,
    202–203, 240
souvenirs/trophies, war, 68, 75, 215, 220
Soviet Union, 22, 59, 99, 140
Special Activities Division, CIA,
    100–102, 104, 135, 173–174
Special Air Service Regiment (SASR),
    313–314
special operations
  with autonomy, 22, 23, 25–26
  leave no man behind, 8
  principles of, 209
  with Tarawa Atoll lessons, 17

special operations (*continued*)
  Tier 1 teams, 5, 44, 48–51, 62, 103,
    183, 208, 218, 232, 278
  US presidents and, 22–23, 44, 51, 215
  See also Joint Special Operations
    Command
Special Operations Command
  (SOCOM), 99–100, 229, 315
Special Operations Command Africa
  (SOCAFRICA), 269
Special Operations Teams, 23
speed, principles of operation, 209
Spencer, Richard, 294
Spielberg, Steven, 229, 245
SS officer, 161
St. Martin's Press, 228
Stackhouse, Phil, 304, 305–306
standards, erosion of, 124–125, 128,
    144, 145
Sterett, USS, 202
stress, 253
  processing, 87
  PTSD, 221, 226, 245, 280
  shooting under, 103
stump muster, 214–215
suicide, after hazing, 36–37, 38
Sunni/Baathist insurgency, 150, 154, 158
surprise, principles of operation, 209
Survival, Evasion, Resistance, Escape
  (SERE) training, 278
Svitak, Philip, 117
Szymanski, Timothy, 87–89, 91, 104,
    107–109, 110, 111, 136, 317
  Blue Squadron and, 163–165
  with Chapman, John "Chappy," and
    Medal of Honor, 257–258
  Iraq War, 149
  with Slabinski, 201–202, 258

tactical gear manufacturers, 233–234
Takur Ghar, Afghanistan (Roberts
  Ridge)
  battle at, 3–9, 97–98, 112–115, 134

Chapman, John "Chappy," at, 5–8,
    98, 109–110, 112–119, 130–131,
    251–261, 264–265
  command failure, 109–111, 171
  drone video of, 7–8, 98, 114, 115, 251,
    253, 254, 255–257, 259, 261
  helicopters at, 97–98, 109, 110, 112,
    114, 116, 131, 141, 255
  JSOC and, 7, 255–256
  Medal of Honor and, 1–4, 9–10,
    251–254, 264–265
  Medal of Honor and cover-up at, 4, 9,
    251, 253–255, 259, 264–265
  myth of, 253–254
  Objective Wolverine and, 130
  Redbeard video, 259
  Roberts at, 5, 7, 8, 9, 97–98, 110–115,
    116, 117, 118, 130, 134, 135, 262
  Roberts rescue attempt, 112–115,
    116
  Slabinski at, 3–9, 97, 98, 109–110,
    112–118, 134, 141, 251–254,
    256–258, 260, 264–265
  at 3:20 a.m., roughly, 110–119
Taliban, 6, 101, 105, 140, 162
  with human shields, 285
  with Norgrove as hostage, 184–202
  Operation Anaconda and, 106–108
tape job, hazing, 271–272
Tarawa Atoll, 16, 17, 109
Task Force 11, in Afghanistan, 100–102,
    104–110, 121–124, 128
Task Force Blue, 92
Task Force Green, 92
Task Force White, 92
Task Unit Bruiser, SEAL Team 3,
    155–160, 223
TAT (Terrorist Action Team), 41
tattoos, 134, 152, 166, 297
TBI (traumatic brain injury), 280
Team Never Quit, 244–245
"Ten and Two" mission, 104
10th Mountain Division, US Army, 106

terrorism, 39
    Operation Enduring Freedom, 100–101, 166, 177–178
    psychology of, 46
    Red Cell and counter-, 61–71
    War on Terror, 8, 9, 98–99, 143, 150–151, 167, 177
    See also 9/11
Terrorist Action Team (TAT), 41
theft, cash fund, 269–270, 277, 279
"They Hit the Beach in Swim Trunks" (*Saturday Evening Post*), 20
3rd Special Forces Group, US Army, 268, 270, 277
Tier 1 teams, 5, 44–45, 48–51, 62, 103, 208
    autonomy of, 183
    with counteraccusations, 278
    salary, 218
    SHOT Show and, 232–233, 297–299
    See also Delta Force; frogmen; SEAL Team 6; 24th Special Tactics Squadron
Title 50 authority, 173
Toboz, Stephen "Turbo," 114, 117
Today Show (television news show), 167, 169
tomahawks (hatchets)
    Delta Force and, 147–148, 149
    Geneva Conventions, 152
    Red Team and, 147, 148–149, 153, 208, 234
Top Secret, 11
Tora Bora mountains, 101, 105, 121, 208
torture, 167, 314
    of ISIS captives, 283
    Red Cell with, 66–67
Touching the Dragon (Hatch), 139, 222–223
training
    for Afghanistan, 102–103
    bin Laden raid, 209–210

    for Bosnia mission, 94
    CQD, 84–89, 91–92, 102, 103, 135–136
    Delta Force, 124
    with ethics of combat, 86–87, 92, 136, 199
    ethics of command and, 85–89
    "follow your shot" with assault, 212
    Gray Team bypassing, 124–125, 128, 144, 162–163
    Green Team, 57, 78, 79, 84–86, 91, 102–103, 124–125, 128, 131, 133–134, 136, 144–146, 162–163
    hood drill, 79–80, 103, 136
    without operational purpose, 93
    SEAL Team 6, 48–49, 57, 77–92, 94, 102–103
    SERE, 278
    stress processing and prisoner, 87
    Taliban camps, 105
    video, 79
    See also BUD/S training program
trauma, psychological, 118, 128, 131, 175, 247, 280, 311
traumatic brain injury (TBI), 280
travel fraud, 53, 68–69
Travers, Peter, 227
Trebon, Gregory, 104, 106, 107–108, 109, 110, 121
Trident, Navy SEAL, 222, 284, 301, 309
    book tours and, 168
    BUD/S training program and, 2, 32
    Budweiser and, 24
    command, ethics and, 88
    politics and, 239–240
Triple Canopy, 219
trophies/souvenirs, war, 68, 75, 215, 220
Trump, Donald J., 260, 261
    Gallagher, Edward R., and, 289–290, 293–294
    Takur Ghar cover-up and, 1–4, 9, 264–265

truth
  counteraccusations and, 278
  denial of, 11
  disregarded, 8, 9
  with moral courage lacking, 150, 198,
    310
  See also cover-ups
24th Special Tactics Squadron, US Air
  Force, 103, 115, 254

UDTs. *See* Underwater Demolition
  Teams
Ullman, Roger, 180–181, 183
Underwater Demolition Teams (UDTs),
  18–24, 46, 69
  2, 155
  4, 43
  21, 27–29, 32–37
  See also frogmen
Uniform Code of Military Justice, 198
United States (US)
  amoral acts sanctioned by, 49, 309
  Civil War, 2–3
  Constitution, 199
  Department of Defense, 11, 223, 307,
    315
  embassy, 39–44, 99, 269
  Justice Department, 245
  Marines, 15–16, 20, 40, 42, 154,
    271–272
  Naval Academy, 8, 87, 104, 111, 125,
    145, 162, 267
  presidents and special operations,
    22–23, 44, 51, 215
  See also Air Force, US; Army, US;
    Navy, US
Utah Beach, 19, 20

Vasely, Peter, 201, 247, 317
  as beheading witness, 164, 165
  as Gray Team officer, 162–163
Vaught, James, 226–227
Veterans Affairs benefits, 300

Veterans for a Strong America (VSA),
  239
videos
  of attack on Melgar, Logan Joshua,
    274, 303
  "bleed out," 135
  BUD/S training program, 91
  CQD, 85–86, 88
  Kunar Province, 137
  Obama attack ad, 239
  promotional SEAL Team 6 tactics, 229
  recruitment, 227
  Red Cell, 65–67
  Redbeard, 259
  training, 79
  war crimes, 314–315
videos, drone
  bin Laden and, 121, 129
  Norgrove and, 187, 189, 193–194
  Objective Wolverine, 129–130
  Takur Ghar, 7–8, 98, 114, 115, 251,
    253, 254, 255–257, 259, 261
Vietnam War, 55, 99, 161–162
  frogmen in, 23, 28
  SEAL Team 1 in, 24–26
  SEAL Team 2 in, 33–34, 72–76
  SEALs in, 29, 43, 46
Villanueva, Ivan, 279, 290, 292
violence
  with aggression, 78, 83, 86, 150–151
  brutality and, 8, 25, 127–128, 135,
    149–150, 158, 161–162, 173
  excessive, 150, 172
  responses to, 135
  violence creating more, 175, 177
  with war crimes, 8
  See also civilians; mutilations, bodies
Vokey, Colby, 304
vortex ring state, 210
Votel, Joseph, 195, 197, 198
Vriens, Joshua, 287, 291–292
VSA (Veterans for a Strong America),
  239

Wahlberg, Mark, 244
Walker, Hunter, 239
war crimes
 without accountability, 153,
   173–177
 Australia, 313–315
 Bosnia, 93–94
 Gallagher, Edward R., and, 283–285
 Geneva Conventions, 152, 167
 Iraq War, 148, 149–150
 killing of civilians, 123, 126, 157–160,
   173, 176, 285–287, 291–292, 294
 trophies, 68, 75, 215, 220
 videos, 315
 violence with, 8
 See also mutilations, bodies
War on Terror, 8, 9, 98–99, 143,
   150–151, 167, 177
war souvenirs/trophies, 68, 75, 215,
   220
Washington Times (newspaper), 293
waterboarding, 66
weapons
 cache, 139

 fraud, 70–71
 See also tomahawks
Webb, Marshall "Brad," 257–258
Wedding Party bombing (Objective
   Bull), 121–124, 128
Whitley, Michael, 46–47
Widmark, Richard, 21
William Morrow, 221
Williams, Jeromy, 111
Willink, John "Jocko, Helmet Head,"
   154, 223
 on *American Sniper*, 224–225, 226
 Task Unit Bruiser and, 155–160
Winkler, Daniel, 147, 148, 152, 208, 234
Work, Robert, 261, 262, 264
World War II
 frogmen after, 21
 frogmen in, 18–29, 43
 US Marines in, 15–16
Wyman. *See* Howard, Hugh Wyman, III

al-Zawahiri, Ayman, 104
Zero Dark Thirty (film), 241
Zinke, Ryan, 239, 246

MATTHEW COLE is an investigative journalist at *The Intercept*. He has covered national security since 2005, reporting extensively on the CIA's post-9/11 transformation, on the conflicts in Afghanistan and Pakistan, and on US intelligence operations. He was previously an investigative producer for ABC and NBC News, and a freelance magazine reporter before that. He has won a Deadline Club Award and has received two Emmy nominations for his reporting. A graduate of Columbia University's Graduate School of Journalism, Cole lives in New York City with his family.